# Bed & Breakfast U.S.A.

## WEST AND MIDWEST 1996

B&Bs can be your home away from home! With hundreds of listings under $50 a night, this indispensable directory gives you the keys to America's best alternative to hotels and shows you why B&Bs are the *only* way to travel. For business or pleasure, this information-packed book is every traveler's constant companion.

◆

**"A valuable source of information."**

—*New York Times*

◆

PEGGY ACKERMAN and her husband, MICHAEL ACKERMAN, are co-directors of the national Tourist House Association, based in Greentown, Pennsylvania. Founded by Betty Rundback in 1976, the Association now has over 1,300 members, all carefully screened by the Association to ensure the best homestay experience for travelers.

# Bed & Breakfast U.S.A.

# West and Midwest 1996

PEGGY ACKERMAN

*Tourist House Association of America*

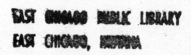
Ⓟ

A PLUME BOOK

MAI 350 0370r

PLUME
Published by the Penguin Group
Penguin Books USA Inc., 375 Hudson Street, New York, New York 10014, U.S.A.
Penguin Books Ltd, 27 Wrights Lane, London W8 5TZ, England
Penguin Books Australia Ltd, Ringwood, Victoria, Australia
Penguin Books Canada Ltd, 10 Alcorn Avenue, Toronto, Ontario, Canada
M4V 3B2
Penguin Books (N.Z.) Ltd, 182–190 Wairau Road, Auckland 10, New Zealand

Penguin Books Ltd, Registered Offices:
Harmondsworth, Middlesex, England

Published by Plume, an imprint of Dutton Signet,
a division of Penguin Books USA Inc.

First Printing, January, 1996

10 9 8 7 6 5 4 3 2 1

Permission to use photographs on the back cover is gratefully acknowledged to
Charlotte's Apple Blossom Inn, Plattsburg, Missouri *(top)*, and Ahlf House Bed
& Breakfast, Grants Pass, Oregon.

℗ REGISTERED TRADEMARK—MARCA REGISTRADA

LC card number: 86-649303

Printed in the United States of America

Set in Palatino and Optima
Designed by Stanley S. Drate/Folio Graphics Co. Inc.

If you want to be listed in future editions of this guide, DO NOT WRITE TO
PLUME OR PENGUIN. See page 315 for a membership application, or write to:
    Tourist House Association
    RD 1, Box 12A
    Greentown, PA 18426
Applications will be accepted until March 31, 1996.

The book you are holding is the result of one woman's hard work and big dreams. In 1974, my mother, Betty Revits Rundback, began thinking about how to celebrate the American Bicentennial in 1976. She decided to take her family of seven on a cross-country tour, but didn't like the idea of staying in motels night after night. She wanted her children to really see the country, and to get to know its people along the way. Remembering back to her own childhood, when the house down the road offered comfortable lodging and a bountiful breakfast to travelers, she set out to create a similar experience for us. She never expected to spend months at the New York Public Library doing it! But that's exactly what she did, going through every telephone directory in America to find listings of family-style guesthouses, contacting all the owners individually, and finally assembling them into a pamphlet in time for the Bicentennial. With the information Betty had gathered, she founded the Tourist House Association of America, which she ran enthusiastically and successfully until her death on July 4, 1990. My wife, Peggy, now continues her work of bringing together guests and hosts from around the world. We dedicate this book to her, in loving memory of her warmth, compassion, and spirit.

—Michael Ackerman

# Contents

**Reservation service organizations appear here in boldface type.**

Reservation service organizations appear here in boldface type.

Reservation service organizations appear here in boldface type.

**Reservation service organizations appear here in boldface type.**

**Reservation service organizations appear here in boldface type.**

**Reservation service organizations appear here in boldface type.**

**Reservation service organizations appear here in boldface type.**

**Reservation service organizations appear here in boldface type.**

Reservation service organizations appear here in boldface type.

Reservation service organizations appear here in boldface type.

Reservation service organizations appear here in boldface type.

Reservation service organizations appear here in boldface type.

Reservation service organizations appear here in boldface type.

# *Preface*

If you are familiar with earlier editions of *Bed & Breakfast U.S.A.*, you know that this book has always been a labor of love. It is personally gratifying to see how it has grown from the first sixteen-page edition, titled *Guide to Tourist Homes and Guest Houses*, which was published in 1975 and contained 40 individual listings. Twenty years later, the eighteenth revised edition listed 1,305 homes and 111 reservation agencies, giving travelers access to over 11,000 host homes. This spectacular success indicates how strongly the revived concept of the guest house has recaptured the fancy of both travelers and proprietors. In fact, the book has become so big that we've divided it into three separate books for 1996! We hope you like this new, easier-to-use format.

On the other hand, what was welcomed as a reasonably priced alternative to the plastic ambience of motel chains has, in some instances, lost its unique qualities. Our mailbox is crammed with letters from grand hotels, condominium rental agencies, campground compounds, and chic inns with nightly tariffs topping the $100 mark. All share a common theme—they all serve breakfast and they all want to be listed in *Bed & Breakfast U.S.A.* Who can blame them? Since 1976, over half a million people have bought this best-selling guide.

We also receive a substantial amount of mail from our readers and we have tailored our book to meet their needs. We have given a great deal of thought to what we feel a B&B should be and are again focusing on our original definition: an owner-occupied residence with breakfast included at a fair rate, where the visitor is made to feel more like a welcome guest than a paying customer.

Because of personal experience, and comments from our readers, *Bed & Breakfast U.S.A., West and Midwest* will go back to the basics. We will no longer accept bed & breakfasts over $85 (this does not include reservation services, suites, cottages, apartments, or qualified inns) or with rates exceeding $40 when there are five guests sharing one bath; or if they do not offer breakfast (when paying $35–$40, no one wants to go out to a restaurant for breakfast—no matter how close it may be, it's just not the same as breakfast "at home").

As a result of these new guidelines, we will regretfully have to delete a great number of listings that have been on our roster for years. This does not imply in any way that these B&Bs aren't nice; it simply means that, in our opinion, they do not fit the traditional

B&B experience. I'm sure we will be receiving hundreds of letters from irate members disputing our opinion and pointing out that rising operating expenses must be reflected in their charges. Newcomers to the business decry our stand and tell us of the high costs that must somehow be recouped. While we sympathize and fully understand their positions, we must, in all fairness, be firm.

This is not a project for which listings have been compiled just for the sake of putting a book together; bigger isn't necessarily better. *Bed & Breakfast U.S.A., West and Midwest* is a product of a membership organization whose credo is "Comfort, cleanliness, cordiality, and fairness of cost." We solicit and rely on the comments of our readers. For this purpose, we include a tear-out form on page 325. If we receive negative reports, that member is dropped from our roster. *Bed & Breakfast U.S.A., West and Midwest* is looking for B&Bs set up to accommodate disabled guests. See page 325 for more information. We genuinely appreciate comments from guests—negative if necessary, positive when warranted. We want to hear from you!

All of the B&Bs described in this book are members of the Tourist House Association of America, RD 1 Box 12A, Greentown, Pennsylvania 18426. THAA dues are $45 annually. We share ideas and experiences by way of our newsletter and sometimes arrange regional seminars and conferences. To order a list of B&Bs that joined after this edition went to press, use the form in the back of this book.

PEGGY ACKERMAN
Tourist House Association of America

*January 1996*

Even after careful editing and proofreading, errors occasionally occur. We regret any inconvenience to our readers and members.

# Acknowledgments

A special thanks to all the travel writers and reporters who have brought us to the attention of their audiences.

To my family, Mike Ackerman, Travis Kali, and Justin Ackerman, the three men in my life—thank you for all the encouragement and support you have shown; to Mary Kristyak Donnelly, a superb mother, grandmother, and best friend—I admire you so; to Bill Donnelly, dad and joke teller; to the grandmothers, Ann Revits and Helen Kristyak.

A final note of thanks to my editor, Leslie Jay, for her deeply appreciated assistance. Never too much, always a smile.

# 1

# *Introduction*

Bed and Breakfast is the popular lodging alternative to hotel high-rises and motel monotony. B&Bs are either private residences where the owners rent spare bedrooms to travelers, or small, family-operated inns offering a special kind of warm, personal hospitality. Whether large or small, B&Bs will make you feel more like a welcome guest than a paying customer.

The custom of opening one's home to travelers dates back to the earliest days of Colonial America. Hotels and inns were few and far between in those days, and wayfarers relied on the kindness of strangers to provide a bed for the night. Which is why, perhaps, there is hardly a Colonial-era home in the mid-Atlantic states that does not boast: "George Washington Slept Here!"

During the Depression, the tourist home provided an economic advantage to both the traveler and the host. Travelers always drove through the center of town; there were no superhighways to bypass local traffic. A house with a sign in the front yard reading "Tourists" or "Guests" indicated that a traveler could rent a room for the night and have a cup of coffee before leaving in the morning. The usual cost for this arrangement was $2. The money represented needed income for the proprietor as well as the opportunity to chat with an interesting visitor.

In the 1950s, the country guest house became a popular alternative to the costly hotels in resort areas. The host compensated for the lack of hotel amenities, such as private bathrooms, by providing comfortable bedrooms and bountiful breakfasts at a modest price. The visitors enjoyed the home-away-from-home atmosphere; the hosts were pleased to have paying houseguests.

The incredible growth in international travel that has occurred over the past 30 years has provided yet another stimulus. Millions of Americans now vacation annually in Europe, and travelers have become enchanted with the bed and breakfast concept so popular in England, Ireland, and other parts of the Continent. In fact, many well-traveled Americans are delighted to learn that we "finally" have B&Bs here. But, as you now know, they were always here—just a rose by another name.

Bed and breakfasts are for:

- **Parents of college kids:** Tuition is costly enough without the added expense of Parents' Weekends. Look for a B&B near campus.
- **Parents traveling with children:** A family living room, playroom, or backyard is preferable to the confines of a motel room.
- **"Parents" of pets:** Many proprietors will allow your well-behaved darling to come, too. This can cut down on the expense and trauma of kenneling Fido.
- **Business travelers:** Being "on the road" can be lonely and expensive. It's so nice, after a day's work, to return to a home-away-from-home.
- **Women traveling alone:** Friendship and conversation are the natural ingredients of a guest house.
- **Skiers:** Lift prices are lofty, so it helps to save some money on lodging. Many mountain homes include home-cooked meals in your room rate.
- **Students:** A visit with a family is a pleasant alternative to camping or the local "Y."
- **Visitors from abroad:** Cultural exchanges are often enhanced by a host who can speak your language.
- **Carless travelers:** If you plan to leave the auto at home, it's nice to know that many B&Bs are convenient to public transportation. Hosts will often arrange to meet your bus, plane, or train for a nominal fee.
- **Schoolteachers and retired persons:** Exploring out-of-the-way places is fun and will save you money.
- **History buffs:** Many B&Bs are located in areas important to our country's past. A number have the distinction of being listed on the National Register of Historic Places.
- **Sports fans:** Tickets to championship games are expensive. A stay at a B&B helps to defray the cost of attending out-of-town events.
- **Antique collectors:** Many hosts have lovely personal collections, and nearby towns are filled with undiscovered antique shops.
- **House hunters:** It's a practical way of trying out a neighborhood.
- **Relocating corporate executives:** It's more comfortable to stay in a real home while you look for a permanent residence. Hosts will often give more practical advice than professional realtors.
- **Relatives of hospitalized patients:** Many B&Bs are located near major hospitals. Hosts will offer tea and sympathy when visiting hours are over.
- **Convention and seminar attendees:** Staying at a nearby B&B is less expensive than checking into a hotel.

And everyone else who has had it up to here with plastic motel monotony!

## What It Is Like to Be a Guest in a B&B

The B&B descriptions provided in this book will help you choose the places that have the greatest appeal to you. A firsthand insight into local culture awaits you; imagine the advantage of arriving in New York City or San Francisco and having an insider to help you sidestep the tourist traps and direct you to that special restaurant or discount store. Or explore the countryside, where fresh air and home-cooked meals beckon. Your choice is as wide as the U.S.A.

Each bed and breakfast listed offers personal contact, a real advantage in unfamiliar environments. You may not have a phone in your room or a TV on the dresser. You may even have to pad down the hall in robe and slippers to take a shower, but you'll discover that little things count.

- In Williamsburg, Virginia, a visitor from Germany opted to stay at a B&B to help improve her conversational English. When the hostess saw that she was having difficulty understanding directions, she personally escorted her on a tour of Old Williamsburg.
- In Pennsylvania, the guests mistakenly arrived a week prior to their stated reservation date and the B&B was full. The hostess made a call to a neighbor who accommodated the couple. (By the way, the neighbor has now become a B&B host!)
- In New York City, a guest was an Emmy Award nominee and arrived with his tuxedo in need of pressing. The hostess pressed it; when he claimed his award over nationwide TV, he looked well groomed!

Expect the unexpected, such as a pot of brewed coffee upon your arrival, or fresh flowers on a nightstand. At the very least, count on our required standard of cleanliness and comfort. Although we haven't personally visited all of the places listed, they have all been highly recommended by chambers of commerce or former guests. We have either spoken to or corresponded with all of the proprietors; they are a friendly group of people who enjoy having visitors. They will do all in their power to make your stay memorable.

Our goal is to enable the traveler to crisscross the country and stay only at B&Bs along the way. To achieve this, your help is vital. Please take a moment to write us of your experiences; we will follow up on every suggestion. Your comments will serve as the yardstick by which we can measure the quality of our accommodations. For your convenience, an evaluation form is included at the back of this book.

## Cost of Accommodations

Bed and breakfast, in the purest sense, is a private home, often referred to as a "homestay," where the owners rent their spare bedrooms to travelers. These are the backbone of this book.

However, American ingenuity has enhanced this simple idea to include more spectacular homes, mansions, small inns, and intimate hotels. With few exceptions, the proprietor is the host and lives on the premises.

There is a distinction between B&B homestays and B&B inns. Inns are generally defined as a business and depend upon revenue from guests to pay expenses. They usually have six or more guest rooms, and may have a restaurant that is open to the public. The tariff at inns is usually higher than at a homestay because the owners must pay the mortgage, running expenses, and staff, whether or not guests come.

Whether plain or fancy, all B&Bs are based on the concept that people are tired of the plastic monotony of motels and are disappointed that even the so-called budget motels can be quite expensive. Travelers crave the personal touch, and they sincerely enjoy "visiting" rather than just "staying."

Prices vary accordingly. There are places listed in this book where lovely lodging may be had for as low as $40 a night, and others that feature an overnight stay with a gourmet breakfast in a canopied bed for $95. Whatever the price, if you see the sign ✪ , it means that the B&B has guaranteed its rates through 1996 to holders of this book, so be sure to mention it when you call or write! (If there is a change in ownership, the guarantee may not apply. Please notify us in writing if any host fails to honor the guaranteed rate.)

Accommodations vary in price depending upon the locale and the season. Peak season usually refers to the availability of skiing in winter and water sports in summer; in the Sunbelt states, winter months are usually the peak season. Some B&Bs require a two-night weekend minimum during peak periods, and three nights on holiday weekends. Off-season rate schedules are usually reduced. Resorts and major cities are generally more expensive than out-of-the-way places. However, B&Bs are always less expensive than hotels and motels of equivalent caliber in the same area. A weekly rate is usually less expensive than a daily rate. Special reductions are sometimes given to families (occupying two rooms) or senior citizens. Whenever reduced rates are available, you will find this noted in the individual listings.

## Meals

**Breakfast:** *Continental* refers to fruit or juice, rolls, and a hot beverage. Many hosts pride themselves on home-baked breads, homemade preserves, as well as imported teas and cakes, so their Continental breakfast may be quite deluxe. Several hosts have regular jobs outside the home, so you may have to adjust your schedule to theirs. A "full" breakfast includes fruit, cereal and/or eggs, breakfast meats, breads, and a hot beverage. The table is set family-style and is often the highlight of a B&B's hospitality. Either a Continental breakfast or full breakfast is included in the room rate unless otherwise specified.

**Other Meals:** If listed as "available," you can be assured that the host takes pride in his or her cooking skills. The prices for lunch or dinner are usually reasonable but are not included in the quoted room rate unless clearly specified as "included."

## Making Reservations

- Reservations are a MUST or you may risk missing out on the accommodations of your choice. Reserve *early* and confirm with a deposit equal to one night's stay. If you call to inquire about reservations, please remember the difference in time zones. When dialing outside of your area, remember to dial the digit "1" before the area code.
- Many individual B&Bs now accept charge cards. This information is indicated in the listings by the symbols MC for Master-Card, AMEX for American Express, etc. A few have a surcharge for this service, so inquire as to the policy.
- Cash or traveler's checks are the accepted method of paying for your stay. Be sure to inquire whether or not tax is included in the rates quoted so that you will know exactly how much your lodging will cost.

- Rates are based on single or double occupancy of a room as quoted. Expect that an extra person(s) in the room will be charged a small additional fee. Inquire when making your reservation what the charge will be.
- If a listing indicates that children or pets are welcome, it is expected that they will be well behaved. All of our hosts take pride in their homes and it would be unfair to subject them to circumstances in which their possessions might be abused or the other houseguests disturbed by an unruly child or animal.
- Please note that many hosts have their own resident pets. If you are allergic or don't care to be around animals, inquire before making a reservation.
- In homes where smoking is permitted, do check to see if it is restricted in any of the rooms. Most hosts object to cigars.
- Where listings indicate that social drinking is permitted, it usually refers to your bringing your own beverages. Most hosts will provide ice; many will allow you to chill mixers in the refrigerator, and others offer complimentary wine and snacks. A few B&B inns have licenses to sell liquor. Any drinking should not be excessive.
- If Yes is indicated in the listings for airport/station pickup, it means that the host will meet your plane, bus, or train for a fee.
- Feel free to request brochures and local maps so that you can better plan for your visit.
- Do try to fit in with the host's house rules. You are on vacation; he or she isn't!
- A reservation form is included at the back of this book for your convenience; just tear it out and send it in to the B&B of your choice.

## Cancellations

Cancellation policies vary from one B&B to another, so be sure to read the fine print on the reservation form. Many require a 15-day notice to refund the entire deposit, after which they will refund only if the room is rebooked. When a refund is due, most keep a processing fee and return the balance. A few keep the deposit and apply it to a future stay.

While these policies may seem harsh, please keep in mind that B&Bs are not hotels, which commonly overbook and where no-show guests can easily be replaced. Your host may have turned down a prospective guest, and may have bought special breakfast food in anticipation of your visit and should not be penalized. If you feel you've been unfairly treated in a cancellation situation, please do let us know.

## B&B Reservation Services

There are many host families who prefer not to be individually listed in a book, and would rather have their houseguests referred by a coordinating agency. The organizations listed in this book are all members of the Tourist House Association. They all share our standards regarding the suitability of the host home as to cordiality, cleanliness, and comfort.

The majority do a marvelous job of matching host and guest according to age, interests, language, and any special requirements. To get the best match, it is practical to give them as much time as possible to find the host home best tailored to your needs.

Many have prepared descriptive pamphlets describing the homes on their rosters, the areas in which the homes are located, and information regarding special things to see and do. *Send a self-addressed, stamped, business-size envelope to receive a descriptive directory by return mail along with a reservation form for you to complete.* When returning the form, you will be asked to select the home or homes listed in the brochure that most appeal to you. (The homes are usually given a code number for reference.) The required deposit should accompany your reservation. Upon receipt, the coordinator will make the reservation and advise you of the name, address, telephone number, and travel instructions for your host.

A few agencies prepare a descriptive directory and *include* the host's name, address, and telephone number so that you can contact the host and make your arrangements directly. They charge anywhere from $2 to $11 for the directory.

Several agencies are *membership* organizations, charging guests an annual fee ranging from $5 to $25 per person. Their descriptive directories are free to members and a few of them maintain toll-free telephone numbers for reservations.

Most reservation services have a specific geographic focus. The coordinators are experts in the areas they represent. They can often make arrangements for car rentals, theater tickets, and touring suggestions, and offer information in planning a trip best suited to your interests.

Most work on a commission basis with the host, and that fee is included in the room rates quoted in each listing. Some make a surcharge for a one-night stay; others require a two- or three-night minimum stay for holiday periods or special events. Some will accept a credit card for the reservation, but the balance due must be paid to the host in cash or traveler's checks.

All of their host homes offer a Continental breakfast, and some may include a full breakfast.

Many reservation services in the larger cities have, in addition to the traditional B&Bs, a selection of apartments, condominiums, and houses *without hosts in residence*. This may be appealing to those travelers anticipating an extended stay in a particular area.

Statewide services are listed first in the section for each state. City or regionally based organizations are listed first under the heading for that area. For a complete description of their services, look them up under the city and state where they're based.

NOTE: When calling, do so during normal business hours (for that time zone), unless otherwise stated. Collect calls are not accepted.

# 2

# *How to Start Your Own B&B*

## What It's Like to Be a Host

Hosts are people who like the idea of accommodating travelers and sharing their home and the special features of their area with them. They are people who have houses too large for their personal needs and like the idea of supplementing their income by having people visit. For many, it's a marvelous way of meeting rising utility and maintenance costs. For young families, it is a way of buying and keeping that otherwise-too-large house, as well as a way of furnishing it, since many of the furnishings may be tax deductible. Another advantage is that many state and local governments have recognized the service that some host families perform. In browsing through this book you will note that some homes are listed on the National Historic Register. Some state governments allow owners of landmark and historical houses a special tax advantage if they are used for any business purpose. Check with the Historical Preservation Society in your state for details.

If you have bedrooms to spare, if you sincerely like having overnight guests, if your home is clean and comfortable, this is an opportunity to consider. It is a unique business because *you* set the time of the visit and the length of stay. (Guest houses are not boarding homes.) You invite the guests at *your* convenience, and the extras, such as meals, are entirely up to you. You can provide a cup of coffee, complete meals, or just a room and shared bath. Remember that your income may be erratic and should not be depended upon to pay for monthly bills. However, it can afford you some luxuries.

Although the majority of hosts are women, many couples are finding pleasure in this joint venture. The general profile of a typical host is a friendly, outgoing, flexible person who is proud of his or her home and hometown. The following information and suggestions represent a guideline to consider in deciding whether becoming a B&B host is really for you.

There are no set rules for the location, type, or style of a B&B. Apartments, condos, farmhouses, town houses, beach houses, vacation cottages, houseboats, mansions, as well as the traditional one-family dwelling are all appropriate. The important thing is for the host to be on the premises. The setting may be urban, rural, or suburban, near public transportation or in the hinterlands. Location is only important if you want to have guests every night. Areas where tourism is popular, such as resort areas or major cities, are often busier than out-of-the-way places. However, if a steady stream of visitors is not that important or even desirable, it doesn't matter where you are. People will contact you if your rates are reasonable and if there is something to see and do in your area, or if it is near a major transportation route.

## *Setting Rates*

Consider carefully four key factors in setting your rates: location, private versus shared bath, type of breakfast, and your home itself.

**Location:** If you reside in a traditional resort or well-touristed area, near a major university or medical center, or in an urban hub or gateway city, your rates should be at least 40 percent lower than those of the area's major motels or hotels. If you live in an out-of-the-way location, your rates must be extremely reasonable. If your area has a "season"—snow sports in winter, water sports in summer—offer off-season rates when these attractions are not available. Reading through this book will help you to see what the going rate is in a situation similar to yours.

**The Bath:** You are entitled to charge more for a room with private bath. If the occupants of two rooms share one bath, the rate should be less. If more than five people must share one bathroom, you may have complaints, unless your rates are truly inexpensive.

**The Breakfast:** Figure the approximate cost of your ingredients, plus something for your time. Allow about $2 to $3 for a Continental breakfast, $4 to $5 for a full American breakfast, and then *include* it in the rate.

**Your Home:** Plan on charging a fair and reasonable rate for a typical B&B home, one that is warm and inviting, clean and comfortable. If your home is exceptionally luxurious, with king-size beds, Jacuzzi baths, tennis courts, or hot tubs, you will find guests who are willing to pay a premium. If your home is over 75 years old, well restored, with lots of antiques, you may also be able to charge a higher rate.

## The Three Bs—Bed, Breakfast, and Bath

**The Bedroom:** The ideal situation for a prospective host is the possession of a house too large for current needs. The children may be away at college most of the year or may have left permanently, leaving behind their bedrooms and, in some cases, an extra bath. Refurbishing these rooms does not mean refurnishing; an extraordinary investment need not be contemplated for receiving guests. Take a long, hard look at the room. With a little imagination and a little monetary outlay, could it be changed into a bedroom *you'd* be pleased to spend the night in? Check it out *before* you go any further. Are the beds comfortable? Is the carpet clean? Are the walls attractive? Do the curtains or shades need attention? Are there sturdy hangers in the closet? Would emptying the closet and bureau be an impossible task? Is there a good light to read by? A writing table and comfortable chair? Peek under the bed to see if there are dust balls or old magazines tucked away. While relatives and friends would "understand" if things weren't perfect, a paying guest is entitled to cleanliness and comfort.

Equip the guest bureau or dresser with a good mirror, and provide a comfortable chair and good reading light. The clothes closet should be free from your family's clothing and storage items, and stocked with firm, plastic hangers, a few skirt hangers, and some hooks. Sachets hung on the rod will chase musty odors. Provide room-darkening shades or blinds on the windows. And, if your house is located on a busy street, it is wise to have your guest bedrooms in the rear. Paying guests are entitled to a good night's rest! If your tap water is not tasty, it is thoughtful to supply bottled water.

If the idea of sprucing up the room has you overwhelmed, forget the idea and continue to be a guest rather than a host! If, however, a little "spit and polish," replacement of lumpy mattresses, sagging springs, and freshening the room in general presents no problem, continue!

Mattresses should be firm, covered with a mattress pad, attractive linens, and bedspread. Although seconds are OK, good-quality linens are a wise investment, since cheap sheets tend to pill. Offer a selection of pillows of various firmnesses—a choice of down or fiberfill is the ultimate in consideration! Twin beds are often preferred, since many people do not wish to share a bed. Sofa beds are really not comfortable and should be avoided. Is there a bedside lamp and night table on each side of the bed? Bulbs should be at least 75 watts for comfortable reading. A luggage rack is convenient for guests and keeps the bedspread clean. Provide a varied assortment of books, current magazines in a rack, a local newspaper, and some information on what's doing in your town along with a map. If yours is a shared-bath accommodation, do provide a well-lit mirror and convenient electric outlet for makeup and shaving purposes. It will take the pressure off the bathroom! A fresh thermos of ice water and drinking glasses placed on an attractive dresser tray is always appreciated. Put it in the room while the guest is out to dinner, right next to the dish of hard candy or fruit. A fancy candlestick is a pretty accessory and a useful object in case of a power failure. Dresser drawers should be clean and lined with fresh paper. A sachet, flashlight, and a pad and pencil are thoughtful touches. For safety's sake, prohibit smoking in the bedroom. Besides, the odor of tobacco clings forever. Always spray the bedroom with air freshener a few minutes before the guest arrives. On warm or humid days, turn on the air conditioner as well.

From time to time sleep in each guest room yourself. It's the best test.

**The Breakfast:** Breakfast time can be the most pleasant part of a guest's stay. It is at the breakfast table with you and the other guests that suggestions are made as to what to see and do, and exchanges of experiences are enjoyed. From a guest's point of view, the only expected offering is what is known as a Continental breakfast, which usually consists of juice, roll, and coffee or tea.

Breakfast fare is entirely up to you. If you are a morning person who whips out of bed at the crack of dawn with special recipes for muffins dancing in your head, muffins to be drenched with your homemade preserves followed by eggs Benedict, an assortment of imported coffees or exotic teas—hop to it! You will play to a most appreciative audience. If, however, morning represents an awful intrusion on sleep, and the idea of talking to anyone before noon is difficult, the least you should do is to prepare the breakfast table the night before with the necessary mugs, plates, and silverware. Fill the electric coffeepot and leave instructions that the first one up should plug it in; you can even hook it up to a timer so that it will brew automatically!

Most of us fall somewhere in between these two extremes. Remember that any breakfast at "home" is preferable to getting dressed, getting into a car, and driving to some coffee shop. Whether you decide upon a Continental breakfast or a full American breakfast, consisting of juice or fruit, cereal or eggs, possibly bacon or sausage, toast, rolls, and coffee or tea, is up to you. It is most important that whatever the fare, it be included in your room rate. It is most awkward, especially after getting to know and like your guests, to present an additional charge for breakfast.

With so many of us watching calories, caffeine, and cholesterol, be prepared to offer unsweetened and/or whole grain breads, oat-bran cereals and muffins, and brewed decaf coffee or tea. It is also thoughtful to inquire about your guests' dietary restrictions and allergies. Whatever you serve, do have your table attractively set.

## Some Suggestions

- Don't have a messy kitchen. If you have pets, make sure their food dishes are removed after they've eaten. If you have cats, make sure they don't walk along the countertops, and be certain that litter boxes are cleaned without fail. Sparkling clean surroundings are far more important than the decor.
- Let guests know when breakfast will be served. Check to see if they have any allergies, diet restrictions, or dislikes. Vary the menu if guests are staying more than one night.
- Do offer one nonsweet bread for breakfast.
- Consider leaving a breakfast order sheet in each room with a request that it be returned before guests retire. It might read:

We serve breakfast between 7 AM and 10 AM. Please check your preference and note the time at which you plan to eat.

☐ Coffee ☐ Tea ☐ Decaf ☐ Milk ☐ Toast ☐ Muffins
☐ Sweet Rolls ☐ Orange Juice ☐ Tomato Juice ☐ Fruit Cup

**The Bath:** This really is the third B in B&B. If you are blessed with an extra bathroom for the exclusive use of a guest, that's super. If guests will have to share the facilities with others, that really presents no problem. If it's being shared with your family, the family must always be "last in line." Be sure that they are aware of the guest's importance; the guest, paying or otherwise, always comes first. No retainers, used Band-Aids, or topless toothpaste tubes are to be carelessly left on the sink. The tub, shower, floor, and toilet bowl are to be squeaky clean. The mirrors and chrome should sparkle, and a supply of toilet tissue, fresh soap, and unfrayed towels goes a long way in reflecting a high standard of cleanliness. Make sure that the grout between tiles is free of mildew and that the shower curtain is unstained; add nonskid tape to the tub. Cracked ceilings should be repaired. Paint should be free of chips, and if your bath is wallpapered, make certain no loose edges mar its beauty.

Although it is your responsibility to check out the bath at least twice a day, most guests realize that in a share-the-bath situation they should leave the room ready for the next person's use. It is a thoughtful reminder for you to leave tub cleanser, a cleaning towel or sponge, and bathroom deodorant handy for this purpose. A wastepaper basket, paper towels, and paper cups should be part of your supplies. Needless to say, your hot water and septic systems should be able to accommodate the number of guests you'll have without being overtaxed. Call the plumber to fix any clogged drains or dripping faucets. Make sure that there are enough towel bars and hooks to accommodate the towels of all guests. Extra bathroom touches:

- Use liquid soap dispensers in lieu of bar soap on the sink.
- Provide a place for guests' personal toilet articles; shelves add convenience and eliminate clutter.
- Give different colored towels to each guest.
- Supply each guest room with its own bath soap in a covered soap dish.
- Provide guests with one-size-fits-all terry robes.

## The B&B Business

**Money Matters:** Before embarking upon any business, it's a good idea to discuss it with an accountant and possibly an attorney. Since you'll be using your home for a business enterprise there are things with which they are familiar that are important for you to know. For instance, you may want to incorporate, so find out what the pros and cons are. Ask about depreciation. Deductible business expenses may include refurbishing, furnishings, supplies, printing costs, postage, etc. An accountant will be able to guide you with a simple system of recordkeeping. Accurate records will help you analyze income and expense, and show if you are breaking even or operating at a profit or a loss.

**Taxes:** Contact your state department of taxation requesting specific written information regarding tax collection and payment schedules. Get a sales tax number from your county clerk. If you rent rooms less than 15 days a year, you need not report the B&B income on your federal return. Income after the fourteenth day is taxable, and you can take deductions and depreciation allowances against it. If the revenues from running the B&B are insignificant, you can call it "hobby income" and avoid taxes. However, you can't qualify as a business and may lose other tax advantages.

**Record Keeping:** Open a B&B checking account and use it to pay expenses and to deposit all income, including sales tax associated with the B&B. Write checks whenever possible for purchases; get dated receipts when you can. Estimate the cost of serving breakfast and multiply it by the number of guests you feed annually; keep track of extra expenses for household supplies and utilities.

**The Case for Credit Cards:** Many guests prefer to stay now and pay later; business travelers like the easy record keeping for their expense sheets. Even if you don't wish to accept them on a regular basis, credit cards give you the opportunity to take a deposit over the phone when there isn't time to receive one by mail. The cost is negligible, generally 4 percent.

If you do accept a last-minute reservation without a credit card number to guarantee it, make certain the caller understands that if they don't show up, and you have held the room for them, you will have lost a night's rent. You may also remind the caller that if they aren't there by a mutually agreed-upon time, you may rent the room to someone else. Needless to say, it is equally important for you to remain at home to receive the guests or to be on hand for a phone call should they get lost en route to your home.

**Insurance:** It is important to call your insurance broker. Some homeowner policies have a clause covering "an occasional overnight paying guest." See if you will be protected under your existing coverage and, if not, what the additional premium would be.

Every home should be equipped with smoke detectors and fire extinguishers. All fire hazards should be eliminated; stairways and halls should be well lit and kept free of clutter. If you haven't already done so, immediately post prominently the emergency numbers for the fire department, police, and ambulance service.

**Safety Reminders:** Equip guest bedrooms and bathrooms with nightlights. Keep a flashlight (in working order!) in each bedroom, in case of power failure. Bathrooms should have nonslip surfaces in the tub and shower, and handholds should be installed in bathtubs. Keep a well-stocked first aid kit handy and know how to use it. Learn the Heimlich Maneuver and CPR (cardiopulmonary resuscitation). Periodically test smoke detectors and fire extinguishers to make certain they are in working order.

**Regulations:** If you have read this far and are still excited about the concept of running a B&B, there are several steps to take at this point. As of this writing, there don't seem to be any specific laws governing B&Bs. Since guests are generally received on an irregular basis, B&Bs do not come under the same laws governing hotels and motels. And since B&Bs aren't inns where emphasis is on food rather than on lodging, no comparison can really be made in that regard either. As the idea grows, laws and regulations will probably be passed. Refer to the back of *Bed & Breakfast U.S.A., West and Midwest* to write to your state's office of tourism for information. The address and phone number are listed for your convenience. You might even call or write to a few B&Bs in your state and ask the host about his or her experience in this regard. Most hosts will be happy to give you the benefit of their experience, but keep in mind that they are busy people and it would be wise to limit your intrusion upon their time.

If you live in a traditional, residential area and you are the first in your neighborhood to consider operating a B&B, it would be prudent to examine closely the character of houses nearby. Do physicians, attorneys, accountants, or psychologists maintain offices in their residences? Do dressmakers, photographers, cosmeticians, or architects receive clients in their homes? These professions are legally accepted in the most prestigious communities as "customary house occupations." Bed and breakfast has been tested in many communities where the question was actually brought to court. In towns from La Jolla, California, to Croton-on-Hudson, New York, bed and breakfast has been approved and accepted.

Zoning boards are not always aware of the wide acceptance of the B&B concept. Possibly the best evidence that you could present to them is a copy of *Bed & Breakfast U.S.A., West and Midwest*, which indicates that it is an accepted practice throughout the entire country. It illustrates the caliber of the neighborhoods, the beauty of the homes, and the fact that many professionals are also hosts. Reassure the zoning board that you will accept guests only by advance reservation. You will not display any exterior signs to attract attention to your home. You will keep your home and grounds properly maintained, attractive, and in no way detract from the integrity of your neighborhood. You will direct guests to proper parking facilities and do nothing to intrude upon the privacy of your neighbors.

After all, there is little difference between the visit of a family friend and a B&B guest, because that is the spirit and essence of a B&B. Just as a friend would make prior arrangements to be a houseguest, so will a B&B guest make a reservation in advance. Neither would just drop in for an overnight stay. We are happy to share letters from hosts attesting to the high caliber, honesty, and integrity of B&B guests that come as a result of reading about their accommodations in this book. There are over 12,000 B&Bs extending our kind of hospitality throughout the United States, and the number is increasing geometrically every day.

You should also bring along a copy of *Bed & Breakfast U.S.A., West and Midwest* when you go to visit the local chamber of commerce. Most of them are enthusiastic, because additional visitors mean extra business for local restaurants, shops, theaters, and businesses. This is a good time to inquire what it would cost to join the chamber of commerce.

**The Name:** The naming of your B&B is most important and will take some time and consideration because this is the moment when dreams become reality. It will be used on your brochures, stationery, and bills. (If you decide to incorporate, the corporation needs a name!) It should somehow be descriptive of the atmosphere you wish to convey.

**Brochure:** Once you have given a name to your house, design a brochure. The best ones include a reservation form and can be mailed to your prospective guests. The brochure should contain the name of your B&B, address, phone number, best time to call, your name, a brief description of your home, its ambience, a brief history of the house if it is old, the number of guest rooms, whether or not baths are shared, the type of breakfast served, rates, required deposit, minimum stay requirement if any, dates when you'll be closed, and your cancellation policy. Although widely used, the phrase "Rates subject to change without notice" should be avoided. Rather, state the specific dates when the rates will be valid. A deposit of one night's stay is acceptable, and the promise of a full refund if cancellation is received at least two weeks prior to arrival is typical. If you have reduced rates for a specific length of stay, for families, for senior citizens, etc., mention it.

The Rate Sheet should be a separate insert so that if rates change, the entire brochure need not be discarded. Mention your smoking policy. If you do allow smoking inside the house, do you reserve any bedrooms for nonsmokers? Don't forget to mention the ages of your children, and describe any pets in residence. If you don't accept a guest's pet, be prepared to supply the name, address, and phone number of a reliable local kennel.

If you can converse in a foreign language, say so, because many visitors from abroad seek out B&Bs; it's a marvelous plus to be able to chat in their native tongue. Include your policy regarding children, pets, or smokers, and whether you offer the convenience of a guest refrigerator or barbecue. It is helpful to include directions from a major route and a simple map for finding your home. It's a good idea to include a line or two about yourself and your interests, and do mention what there is to see and do in the area as well as proximity to any major university. A line drawing of your house is a good investment since the picture can be used not only on the brochure but on your stationery, postcards, and greeting cards as well. If you can't have this taken care of locally, write the Tourist House Association. We have a service that can handle it for you.

Take your ideas to a reliable printer for his professional guidance. Don't forget to keep the receipt for the printing bill since this is a business expense.

**Confirmation Letter:** Upon receipt of a paid reservation, do send out a letter confirming it. You can design a form letter and have it offset-printed by a printer, since the cost of doing so is usually nominal. Include the dates of the stay; number of people expected; the rate, including tax; the cancellation policy; as well as explicit directions by car and, if applicable, by public transportation. A simple map reflecting the exact location of your home in relation to major streets and highways is most useful. It is a good idea to ask your guests to call you if they will be traveling and unavailable by phone for the week prior to their expected arrival. You might even want to include any of the house rules regarding smoking, pets, or whatever.

## Successful Hosting

**The Advantage of Hosting:** The nicest part of being a B&B host is that you aren't required to take guests every day of the year. Should there be times when having guests would not be convenient, you can always say you're full and try to arrange an alternate date. But most important, keep whatever date you reserve. It is an excellent idea at the time reservations are accepted to ask for the name and telephone number of an emergency contact should you have to cancel unexpectedly. However, *never* have a guest come to a locked door. If an emergency arises and you cannot reach your prospective guests in time, do make arrangements for someone to greet them, and make alternate arrangements so that they can be accommodated.

**House Rules:** While you're in the thinking stage, give some thought to the rules you'd like your guests to adhere to. The last thing you want for you or your family is to feel uncomfortable in your own home. Make a list of House Rules concerning arrival and departure during the guests' stay, and specify when breakfast is served. If you don't want guests coming home too late, say so. Most hosts like to lock up at a certain hour at night, so arrange for an extra key for night owls. If that makes you uncomfortable, have a curfew on your House Rules list. If smoking disturbs you, confine the area where it's permitted.

Some guests bring a bottle of their favorite beverage and enjoy a drink before going out to dinner. Many hosts enjoy a cocktail hour too, and often provide cheese and crackers to share with guests. B&Bs cannot sell drinks to guests since this would require licensing. If you'd rather no drinks be consumed in your home, say so.

Many hosts don't mind accommodating a well-behaved pet. If you don't mind, or have pets of your own, discuss this with your guests before they pack Fido's suitcase. Your House Rules can even be included in your brochure. That way, both host and guest are aware of each other's likes and dislikes, and no hard feelings are made.

**Entertaining:** One of the most appealing features of being a guest at a B&B is the opportunity to visit in the evening with the hosts. After a day of sightseeing or business, it is most relaxing and pleasant to sit around the living room and chat. For many hosts, this is the most enjoyable part of having guests. However, if you are accommodating several people on a daily basis, entertaining can be tiring. Don't feel you'll be offending anyone by excusing yourself to attend to your own family or personal needs. The situation can be easily handled by having a room to which you can retreat, and offering your guests the living room, den, or other area for games, books, magazines, and perhaps the use of a television or bridge table. Most guests enjoy just talking to one another since this is the main idea of staying at a B&B.

**The Telephone:** This is a most important link between you and your prospective guests. As soon as possible, have your telephone number included under your B&B name in the white pages. It is a good idea to be listed in the appropriate section in your telephone directory yellow pages. If your home phone is used for a lot of personal calls, ask the local telephone company about call-waiting service, or think about installing a separate line for your B&B. If you are out a lot, give some thought to using a telephone answering device to explain your absence and time of return, and record the caller's message. There is nothing more frustrating to a prospective guest than to call and get a constant busy signal, or no answer at all. Request that the caller leave his or her name and address so that you can mail a reservation form. This will help eliminate the necessity of having to return long-distance calls. If the caller wants further information, he or she will call again at the time you said you'd be home.

B&B guests don't expect a phone in the guest room. However, there are times when they might want to use your phone for a long-distance call. In your House Rules list, suggest that any such calls be charged to their home telephone. Business travelers often have telephone charge cards for this purpose. In either case, you should keep a telephone record book and timer near your instrument. Ask the caller to enter the city called, telephone number, and length of call. Thus, you will have an accurate record should a charge be inadvertently added to your bill. Or, if you wish, you can add telephone charges to the guest bill. A telephone operator will quote the cost of the per-minute charge throughout the country for this purpose.

**Maid Service:** If you have several guest rooms and bathrooms, you may find yourself being a chambermaid as part of the business. Naturally, each guest gets fresh linens upon arrival. If a guest stays up to three days, it isn't expected that bed linen be changed every day. What is expected is that the room be freshened and the bath be cleaned and towels replaced every day. If you don't employ a full-time maid you may want to investigate the possibility of hiring a high school student on a part-time basis to give you a hand with the housekeeping. Many guests, noticing the absence of help, will voluntarily lend a hand, although they have the right to expect some degree of service, particularly if they are paying a premium rate.

**Keys:** A great many hosts are not constantly home during the day. Some do "hosting" on a part-time basis, while involved with regular jobs. There are times when even full-time hosts have to be away during the day. If guests are to have access to the house while you are not on the premises, make extra keys and attach them to an oversize key chain. It is also wise to take a key deposit of $50 simply to assure return of the key. Let me add that in the 16 years of my personal experience, as well as in the opinions of other hosts, B&B guests are the most honest people you can have. No one has ever had even a washcloth stolen, let alone the family treasures. In fact, it isn't unusual for the guest to leave a small gift after a particularly pleasant visit. On the other hand, guests are sometimes forgetful and leave belongings behind. For this reason it is important for you to have their names and addresses so that you can return their possessions. They will expect to reimburse you for the postage.

**Registering Guests:** You should keep a regular registration ledger for the guest to complete before checking in. The information should include the full name of each guest, home address, phone number, business address and telephone, and auto license number. It's a good idea to include the name and phone number of a friend or relative in case of an emergency. This information will serve you well for other contingencies, such as the guest leaving some important article behind, an unpaid long-distance phone call, or the rare instance of an unpaid bill. You may prefer to have this information on your guest bill, which should be designed as a two-part carbon form. You will then have a record and the guest has a ready receipt. (Receipts are very important to business travelers!)

**Settling the Bill:** The average stay in a B&B is two nights. A deposit equal to one night's lodging is the norm; when to collect the balance is up to you. Most guests pay upon leaving, but if they leave so early that the settling of the bill at that time is inconvenient, you can request the payment the previous night. You might want to consider the convenience of accepting a major credit card, but contact the sponsoring company first to see what percentage of your gross is expected for this service. If you find yourself entertaining more business visitors than vacationers, it might be something you should offer. Most travelers are aware that cash or traveler's checks are the accepted modes of payment. Accepting a personal check is rarely risky, but again, it's up to you. You might include your preference in your brochure.

**Other Meals:** B&B means that only breakfast is served. If you enjoy cooking and would like to offer other meals for a fee, make sure that you investigate the applicable health laws. If you have to install a commercial kitchen, the idea might be too expensive for current consideration. However, allowing guests to store fixings for a quick snack or to use your barbecue can be a very attractive feature for families traveling with children or for people watching their budget. If you can offer this convenience, be sure to mention it in your brochure. (And be sure to add a line to your House Rules that the guest is expected to clean up.) Some hosts keep an extra guest refrigerator on hand for this purpose.

It's an excellent idea to keep menus from your local restaurants on hand. Try to have a good sampling, ranging from moderately priced to expensive dining spots, and find out if reservations are required. Your guests will always rely heavily upon your advice and suggestions. After all, when it comes to your town, you're the authority! It's also a nice idea to keep informed of local happenings that might be of interest to your visitors. A special concert at the university or a local fair or church supper can add an extra dimension to their visit. If parents are visiting with young children they might want to have dinner out without them; try to have a list of available baby-sitters. A selection of guidebooks covering your area is also a nice feature.

**The Guest Book:** These are available in most stationery and department stores, and it is important that you buy one. It should contain designated space for the date, the name of the guest, home address, and a blank area for the guest's comments. They generally sign the guest book before checking out. The guest book is first of all a permanent record of who came and went. It will give you an idea of what times during the year you were busiest and which times were slow. Second, it is an easy way to keep a mailing list for your Christmas cards and future promotional mailings. You will also find that thumbing through it in years to come will recall some very pleasant people who were once strangers but now are friends.

**Advertising:** Periodically distribute your brochures to the local university, college, and hospital, since out-of-town visitors always need a place to stay. Let your local caterers know of your existence since wedding guests are often from out of town. If you have a major corporation in your area, drop off a brochure at the personnel office. Even visiting or relocating executives and salespeople enjoy B&Bs. Hotels and motels are sometimes overbooked; it wouldn't hurt to leave your brochure with the manager for times when there's no room for their last-minute guests. Local residents sometimes have to put up extra guests, so it's a good idea to take an ad out in your local school or church newspaper. The cost is usually minimal. Repeat this distribution process from time to time so that you can replenish the supply of brochures.

Check the back of this book for the address of your state tourist office. Write to them, requesting inclusion in any brochures listing B&Bs in the state.

The best advertising is being a member of the Tourist House Association since all member B&Bs are fully described in this book, which is available in bookstores, libraries, and B&Bs throughout the United States and Canada. In addition, it is natural for THAA members to recommend one another when guests inquire about similar accommodations in other areas. The most important reason for keeping your B&B clean, comfortable, and cordial is that we are all judged by what a guest experiences in any individual Tourist House Association home. The best publicity will come from your satisfied guests, who will recommend your B&B to their friends.

## Additional Suggestions

**Extra Earnings:** You might want to consider a few ideas for earning extra money in connection with being a host. If guests consistently praise your muffins and preserves, you might sell attractively wrapped extras as take-home gifts. If you enjoy touring, you can plan and conduct a special outing, off the beaten tourist track, for a modest fee. In major cities, you can do such things as acquiring tickets for theater, concert, or sports events. A supply of *Bed & Breakfast U.S.A., West and Midwest* for sale to guests is both a source of income and gives every THAA member direct exposure to the B&B market. Think about offering the use of your washer and dryer. You may, if you wish, charge a modest fee to cover the service. Guests who have been traveling are thrilled to do their wash or have it done for them "at home" rather than wasting a couple of hours at the laundromat.

Several hosts tell me that a small gift shop is often a natural offshoot of a B&B. Items for sale might include handmade quilts, pillows, potholders, and knitted items. One host has turned his hobby of woodworking into extra income. He makes lovely picture frames, napkin rings, and footstools that many guests buy as souvenirs to take home. If you plan to do this, check with the Small Business Administration to inquire about such things as a resale license and tax collection; a chamber of commerce can advise in this regard.

**Transportation:** While the majority of B&B guests arrive by car, there are many who rely on public transportation. Some hosts, for a modest fee, are willing to meet arriving guests at airports, train depots, or bus stations. Do be knowledgeable about local transportation schedules in your area, and be prepared to give explicit directions for your visitors' comings and goings. Have phone numbers handy for taxi service, as well as information on car rentals.

**Thoughtful Touches:** Guests often write to tell us of their experiences at B&Bs as a result of learning about them through this book. These are some of the special touches that made their visit special: fresh flowers in the guest room; even a single flower in a bud vase is pretty. One hostess puts a foil-wrapped piece of candy on the pillow before the guest returns from dinner. A small decanter of wine and glasses, or a few pieces of fresh fruit in a pretty bowl on the dresser are lovely surprises. A small sewing kit in the bureau is handy. Offer guests the use of your iron and ironing board, rather than having them attempt to use the bed or dresser. Writing paper and envelopes in the desk invite the guest to send a quick note to the folks at home. If your house sketch is printed on it, it is marvelous free publicity. A pre-bed cup of tea for adults and cookies and milk for children are always appreciated.

By the way, keep a supply of guest-comment cards in the desk, both to attract compliments as well as to bring to your attention the flaws in your B&B that should be corrected.

**Join the Tourist House Association:** If you are convinced that you want to be a host, and have thoroughly discussed the pros and cons with your family and advisers, complete and return the membership application found at the back of this book. Our dues are $45 annually. The description of your B&B will be part of the next edition of *Bed & Breakfast U.S.A.*, *West and Midwest*, as well as in the interim supplement between printings. Paid-up members receive complimentary copies of the three *Bed & Breakfast U.S.A.* regional guides: *Northeast*, *Southeast*, and *West and Midwest*. You will also receive the THAA's newsletter; regional seminars and conferences are held occasionally and you might enjoy attending. And, as an association, we will have clout should the time come when B&B becomes a recognized industry.

**Affiliating with a B&B Reservation Agency:** There are 111 agencies listed in our three *Bed & Breakfast U.S.A.* books. If you do not care to advertise your house directly to the public, consider joining one in your area. Membership and reservation fees, as well as the degree of professionalism, vary widely from agency to agency, so do check carefully.

**Prediction of Success:** Success should not be equated with money alone. If you thoroughly enjoy people, are well organized, enjoy sharing your tidy home without exhausting yourself, then the idea of receiving compensation for the use of an otherwise dormant bedroom will be a big plus. Your visitors will seek relaxing, wholesome surroundings, and unpretentious hosts who open their hearts as well as their homes. Being a B&B host or guest is an exciting, enriching experience.

# 3

# *B&B Recipes*

The recipes that follow are B&B host originals. They've been chosen because of the raves they've received from satisfied B&B guests. The most important ingredient is the heartful of love that goes into each one.

We always have a good response to our request for favorite breakfast recipes. Although we could not publish them all this time, we will use most of them in future editions.

## Hewick B&B Pecan Coffee Cake

¾ c. brown sugar
1 pkg. of vanilla pudding (not instant)
1 tbsp. cinnamon
6 tbsp. margarine

1 c. pecans
1 12-oz. package refrigerated, unbaked dinner rolls

Preheat the oven to 350°F. Mix together the sugar, pudding, and cinnamon and set aside. Grease a Bundt pan with some of the margarine then coat it with the pecans. Put the rolls in the pan and sprinkle the dry mix over them. Dot with the remaining margarine and let the cake stand covered overnight. Remove the cover and bake for 30 minutes.

*Hewick B&B, Urbana, Virginia*

## Baked Apples New England

6 baking apples (Cortland or MacIntosh)
6 heaping tsp. sugar mixed with 1 tsp. cinnamon

3 tbsp. butter
2 tbsp. water
½ cup raisins (optional)
2 tbsp. rum (optional)

Preheat the oven to 350°F. Core the apples and make a slit through the skin with a knife all the way around, stopping about a third of the way from the top; this keeps the apples from exploding. Place the apples in glass pie plate. Spoon a heaping teaspoon of the sugar-cinnamon mixture into the center of each apple and top with a dab of butter. Pour water into pie plate. Bake 1 hour, basting after 30 minutes. Add water if necessary. You may add raisins to the center of apple or a tablespoon of dark rum to the water for a slightly different flavor.

*The Captain Ezra Nye House, Sandwich, Massachusetts*

## Peach Stratta

6 oz. peach baby food, no water added
1½ c. fresh peaches, diced
1⅓ c. sugar
¼ tsp. nutmeg
¾ tsp. cinnamon
4 eggs
7 c. French bread, crusts removed
   and cubed

Preheat the oven to 350°F. Mix the first six ingredients together until well blended. Pour over the bread and stir gently. Pour the mixture into a 1-quart casserole dish that has been sprayed with vegetable cooking spray. Bake for 50 to 60 minutes.

## Joyce's Blueberry Muffins

1¾ c. flour
⅓ c. sugar
1 tbsp. baking powder
¾ c. milk
⅓ c. oil
1 tsp. grated lemon peel
1 egg, slightly beaten
18 oz. pkg. cream cheese, cut into
   ½-inch cubes
¾ c. fresh or frozen blueberries
1 tbsp. lemon juice
3 tbsp. sugar

Preheat the oven to 400°F. Mix the flour, sugar, and baking powder in a large bowl and set aside. Add the milk, oil, and grated lemon peel to the egg. Add the egg mixture to the flour mixture, blending until just moistened. Fold in the cream cheese and blueberries. Spoon the batter into greased or lined muffin tins until two-thirds full. Bake for 20 minutes. Mix together the lemon juice and sugar and brush over the muffins. Makes 12 muffins.

*Miller's of Montana B&B Inn, Bozeman, Montana*

## Eggs Benedict Caledonia

1 pkg. Hollandaise sauce mix
3 tbsp. lemon juice
2 English muffins
2 tbsp. butter or margarine

4 slices Canadian bacon or ham
4 eggs
Garnish of choice

Preheat the oven to 160°F. Prepare Hollandaise sauce according to package directions, replacing 3 tablespoons of water with lemon juice and set aside. Toast or broil muffin halves and spread with the butter. Top with slices of the Canadian bacon or ham and keep warm in the oven. Poach the eggs for 3½ minutes in cups sprayed with vegetable oil. When the whites are set but the yolks are still loose, invert the eggs onto muffins. Cover the eggs with the sauce. Garnish with fresh parsley, kiwi slice, strawberry half, or a favorite garnish of your choice. Makes 2 servings.

*Caledonia Farm B&B, Flint Hill, Virginia*


## Banana Butter

4 large ripe bananas, peeled and sliced
3 tbsp. lemon juice

1 tsp. pumpkin pie spice
1½ c. sugar

Place the bananas and lemon juice in a blender and process until smooth. Transfer to a large saucepan and stir in the pumpkin pie spice and sugar. Bring the mixture to a boil, lower the heat and simmer for 15 minutes, stirring frequently. Pour into sterilized jars and store in tightly covered containers in the refrigerator. Makes 3 cups.

*Bannick's Bed & Breakfast, Dimondale, Michigan*


## Mountain Top Bacon

½ c. flour
¼ c. brown sugar

1 tsp. black pepper
1 lb. bacon, sliced

Preheat the oven to 300°F. Mix the flour, brown sugar, and pepper in a plastic bag. Add bacon slices one at a time and shake to coat. Lay the slices out in a baking pan. Bake for 20 to 25 minutes, or until crisp. Serves 4.

*Von-Bryan Inn, Sevierville, Tennessee*

## Health Cereal

5 c. old-fashioned oats
2 c. wheat germ
½ c. sesame seeds, ground
1 c. shredded coconut (optional)
1 c. almonds or other nuts, chopped
   finely

½ tsp. cinnamon
¼ tsp. ground cloves
½ tsp. salt
1 c. brown sugar, or to taste
1 c. corn oil, or to taste
1 c. raisins

Preheat the oven to 350°F. In a large bowl, mix together all the ingredients except the raisins. Pour the mixture into a shallow pan and bake 30 minutes, stirring occasionally. Remove from the oven and stir in the raisins. Serve warm or at room temperature.

*Honeysuckle Hill B&B, Madison, Connecticut*

## Aunt Dolly's Almost in the Country Quiche

¾ c. all-purpose flour
½ c. whole wheat flour
Pinch of salt
6 tbsp. butter
4 to 5 tbsp. ice water
5 slices bacon
1 large onion, chopped
2 large potatoes, thinly sliced
2 eggs

⅔ c. heavy cream
1 tbsp. each chopped parsley and
   chives
½ tsp. salt
¼ tsp. black pepper
½ sweet red pepper, seeded and
   chopped
¾ c. grated cheddar cheese

Preheat the oven to 375°F. In a large bowl, combine the flours and the pinch of salt and cut in the butter until the mixture turns to fine crumbs. Add enough water to make a firm dough. Knead lightly. On a lightly floured surface, roll out the pastry to a 10-inch circle. Ease the pastry into a 9-inch quiche pan, pressing evenly around the side; trim the edge. Prick all over with a fork; refrigerate for 30 minutes, or until the dough is firm. Line with foil, fill with dried beans and bake until set, 12 to 15 minutes. Remove the foil and beans and return the pastry to the oven for another 5 minutes. In a large frying pan, cook the bacon until crisp; remove it with a slotted spoon, allow it to cool, and crumble it. Add the onion and potatoes to the bacon drippings and cook until browned. Drain and set aside. Beat the eggs and cream together. Stir in the parsley, chives, the ½ teaspoon salt, and the black pepper and set aside. Spoon the potatoes and onion into the pastry shell and sprinkle

with the bacon and red pepper. Pour in the egg mixture and
sprinkle with the cheese. Bake for 20 to 25 minutes. Serve hot
or cold.

*Aunt Dolly's Attic B&B, Austin, Texas*

## Garden Harvest Muffins

4 c. all-purpose flour
2½ c. sugar
4 tsp. baking soda
4 tsp. cinnamon
1 tsp. salt
2 c. grated carrots
2 c. grated zucchini
1 c. raisins

1 c. chopped pecans
1 c. coconut
2 tart apples, peeled and grated
6 large eggs
1 c. vegetable oil
1 c. buttermilk
2 tsp. vanilla

Preheat the oven to 375°F. In a large bowl, sift together the flour,
sugar, baking soda, cinnamon, and salt. Stir in the carrots,
zucchini, raisins, pecans, coconut, and apples. In another bowl,
whisk together the remaining ingredients and add to the flour-
vegetable mixture. Stir the batter until just blended. Spoon the
batter into well-buttered muffin tins (or use paper liners). Bake on
the middle rack for 25 to 30 minutes, or until the muffins are
springy to the touch. Let the muffins cool in the tins for 5 minutes,
then turn them out onto a rack. Makes about 30 muffins.

*Leland House, Durango, Colorado*

## Sausage en Croute

1 sheet frozen Pepperidge Farm puff
    pastry
1 lb. pork sausage
½ c. chopped onion
½ c. chopped green pepper

6 large mushrooms, sliced
1 large tomato, diced
1 c. total shredded Swiss and
    Cheddar cheese
3 tbsp. chopped parsley

Preheat the oven to 425°F. Thaw the puff pastry about 20 minutes.
Meanwhile, brown the sausage in a skillet, breaking it into bits.
Add the onion, green pepper, and mushrooms and cook until
tender. Remove from the heat and pour off the drippings. Add the
tomato, cheese, and parsley. Unfold the pastry sheet and roll it
out on a lightly floured board to a 13- × -10-inch rectangle. Transfer

to a baking sheet lined with brown paper (a grocery bag works well). Spread the sausage mixture on pastry. Roll up from the long side, jelly-roll fashion, and pinch the edges to seal. Bake for 20 minutes, or until golden brown. Serves 6 to 8 guests.

*Grand Avenue Inn, Carthage, Missouri*

# 4
# Wheelchair Accessible Listings

Although this chapter is small, within a few years *Bed & Breakfast U.S.A., West and Midwest* hopes to have listings from all fifty states and Canada. The requirements are fairly simple. To be listed in this section, all B&Bs must have easy-access entrances and exits. Doorways must be wide enough to admit a wheelchair—36 inches should be wide enough. Toilets and tubs must have reach bars. If the bathroom has a shower, reach bars and a built-in seat are preferable. Wheelchairs should be able to fit under the breakfast table; 26 inches is high enough. It's also a good idea to check to see what kind of activities are available. Many parks, restaurants, shopping areas, museums, beaches, etc. have wheelchair accessibility. If you or someone you know has a B&B that is wheelchair accessible, please turn to page 325 for further details.

## Kern River Inn Bed & Breakfast ✪
### P.O. BOX 1725, 119 KERN RIVER DRIVE, KERNVILLE, CALIFORNIA 93238

| | |
|---|---|
| Tel: **(619) 376-6750; (800) 986-4382** | Open: **All year** |
| Best Time to Call: **8 AM–8 PM** | Reduced Rates: **Available** |
| Hosts: **Jack and Carita Prestwich** | Breakfast: **Full** |
| Location: **50 mi. NE of Bakersfield** | Credit Cards: **MC, VISA** |
| No. of Rooms: **1** | Pets: **No** |
| No. of Private Baths: **1** | Children: **Welcome** |
| Double/pb: **$89–$99** | Smoking: **No** |
| Single/pb: **$79–$89** | Social Drinking: **Permitted** |

Stay in a charming riverfront B&B in a quaint Western town within Sequoia National Forest. Jack and Carita specialize in romantic, relaxing getaways. Their accessible room has a queen bed and a Piute-style, wood-burning fireplace. (Your hosts provide the wood.) Native American pictures and macrame wall hangings accent the room's Southwestern color scheme of beige, mauve, and sage green. The bath has grab bars; the full-size, mirror-doored closet has shelving that can be reached from a wheelchair.

## Little Valley Inn
**3483 BROOKS ROAD, MARIPOSA, CALIFORNIA 95338**

Tel: **(209 742-6204; (800) 889-5444**
Hosts: **Kay and Robert Hewitt**
Location: **8 mi. S of Mariposa**
Suite: **$100**
Open: **All year**
Reduced Rates: **Available**

Breakfast: **Continental**
Credit Cards: **AMEX, MC, VISA**
Pets: **No**
Children: **Welcome**
Smoking: **No**
Social Drinking: **Permitted**

Little Valley Inn's accommodations were designed with the help of a wheelchair-bound friend. This wheelchair-accessible suite has a full kitchen, ramp, grab bars, 36-inch interior door, bath seat, and low switch plates. Guests can enjoy panning for gold in a big cattle trough filled with water; your hosts provide the dirt. If you don't know how to pan, Kay & Robert will be happy to show you!

## Redwood Reflections
**4600 SMITH GRADE, SANTA CRUZ, CALIFORNIA 95060 ✪**

Tel: **(408) 423-7221**
Best Time to Call: **Evenings**
Hosts: **Ed and Dory Strong**
Location: **70 mi. S of San Francisco**
No. of Rooms: **1**
No. of Private Baths: **1**
Suites: **$85**
Open: **All year**

Reduced Rates: **10% Seniors, disabled**
Breakfast: **Full**
Credit Cards: **MC, VISA**
Pets: **No**
Children: **Welcome, over 7**
Smoking: **No**
Social Drinking: **Permitted**

Nestled on 10 private acres of giant redwoods, Redwood Reflections offers one wheelchair-accessible room with a private bath and patio. A romantic Roman tub for two has a transfer seat and adjustable shower head. Grab bars for toilet and tub, 36-inch doors and a roll-in vanity provide accessibility and safety. Guests are invited to concoct favorite goodies and listen to old-time piano music in an ice cream parlor featuring 1920s collectibles and a 100-year-old potbelly stove. A full breakfast is served and dietary restrictions can be observed. Santa Cruz is a wheelchair-friendly town and offers an amusement park, wharf with fine restaurants and a 2-mile coastline sidewalk. The Monterey Bay Aquarium and two state parks are great accessible day excursions.

## Ferncourt Bed and Breakfast
**150 CENTRAL AVENUE, SAN MATEO, FLORIDA 32187**

Tel: **(904) 329-9755**
Best Time to Call: **Evenings**

Hosts: **Jack and Dee Morgan**
Location: **25 mi. W of St. Augustine**

No. of Rooms: **1**
No. of Private Baths: **1**
Double/pb: **$45–$65**
Open: **All year**
Breakfast: **Full**

Pets: **No**
Children: **No**
Smoking: **No**
Social Drinking: **Permitted**
Station Pickup: **Yes**

Ferncourt is a restored 1800s farm home, located in a tiny historic hamlet just a few minutes drive from St. Augustine and Daytona Beach. Guests have use of several rooms and the wraparound veranda. Close by, restaurants serve excellent food. Cookies and tea are offered in the evening. Jack does woodworking and upholstery and many examples of his craft are on display throughout the inn. Dee dabbles in painting and loves antiques and flea markets, but her real passion is food, evidenced by the gourmet breakfast she serves. Discover North Central Florida, then retire to all the charm and hospitality of the Victorian era with your hosts. There is a long concrete wheelchair ramp, and one room is set up for the disabled, with a private bath and handrails installed. For hearing-impaired guests, a smoke alarm has been installed.

## Amanda's B&B Reservation Service ○
**1428 PARK AVENUE, BALTIMORE, MARYLAND 21217**

Tel: **(410) 225-0001; fax: 728-8957**
Best Time to Call: **8:30 AM–5:30 PM Mon.–Fri.**
Coordinator: **Betsy Grater**
States/Regions Covered: **Annapolis, Baltimore, Delaware, District of Columbia, Maryland, New Jersey, Pennsylvania, Virginia, West Virginia**

Descriptive Directory: **$5**
Rates (Double):
　Modest: **$60**
　Luxury: **$75–$125**
Credit Cards: **AMEX, DISC, MC, VISA**

The roster of this reservation service includes eight sites designed for visitors with disabilities—five in downtown Baltimore, two in Annapolis, and one in Chesapeake City.

## Bed & Breakfast Associates—Bay Colony, Ltd. ○
**P.O. BOX 57166, BABSON PARK, BOSTON, MASSACHUSETTS 02157-0166**

Tel: **(617) 449-5302; (800) 347-5088;** fax: **(617) 449-5958**
Best Time to Call: **9:30 AM–12:30 PM; 1:30–5 PM Mon.–Fri.**
Coordinators: **Arline Kardasis and Marilyn Mitchell**
States/Regions Covered:

**Massachusetts—Boston (Beacon Hill and Back Bay)**
Descriptive Directory: **Free**
Rates (Single/Double)
　Luxury: **$89–$135　$95–$135**
Credit Cards: **AMEX, CB, DC, MC, VISA**

Arline and Marilyn offer five accommodations for disabled travelers. All have private baths. Some are convenient to major colleges and universities.

## Blue Goose Inn ✪
### ROUTE 103B, P.O. BOX 2117, MT. SUNAPEE, NEW HAMPSHIRE 03255

| | |
|---|---|
| Tel: **(603) 763-5519** | Breakfast: **Full** |
| Best Time to Call: **Before noon** | Credit Cards: **MC, VISA** |
| Hosts: **Meryl and Ronald Caldwell** | Pets: **No** |
| Location: **10 mi. from I-89** | Children: **Welcome** |
| No. of Rooms: **1** | Smoking: **Permitted** |
| No. of Private Baths: **1** | Social Drinking: **Permitted** |
| Double/pb: **$50** | Airport/Station Pickup: **Yes** |
| Open: **All year** | |

This cozy nineteenth-century Colonial farmhouse is located on scenic Lake Sunapee, at the base of Mt. Sunapee. Meryl and Ronald offer one wheelchair-accessible room adorned with handmade quilts and attractive antiques. Breakfast specialties—such as a maple-flavored biscuit stuffed with bacon, eggs, and cheese—are served on the enclosed porch. Each evening, you're invited to join your hosts on the porch, or by the fireplace in the living room, for wine, fruit, and cheese.

## Jemez River Bed & Breakfast Inn ✪
### 16445 HIGHWAY 4, JEMEZ SPRINGS, NEW MEXICO 87025

| | |
|---|---|
| Tel: **(505) 820-3262** | Breakfast: **Full** |
| Best Time to Call: **Evenings** | Other Meals: **Available** |
| Hosts: **Larry and Roxe Ann Clutter** | Credit Cards: **AMEX, CB, DC, DISC,** |
| Location: **40 mi. NW of Albuquerque** | **MC, VISA** |
| No. of Rooms: **2** | Pets: **Sometimes** |
| No. of Private Baths: **2** | Children: **Welcome** |
| Double/pb: **$99–$109** | Smoking: **No** |
| Open: **All year** | Social Drinking: **Permitted** |
| Reduced Rates: **10% seniors** | |

A new, adobe-style home completed in 1994, Jemez River Bed & Breakfast Inn is nestled on 3½ acres in a valley below the Jemez Mountains Virgin Mesa. At night, the murmuring of the Jemez River— located in the B&B's backyard—will lull you to sleep. As you enjoy a hearty breakfast, you'll feast your eyes on breathtaking mountain views through the grand kitchen windows. Authentic Indian pottery, rugs, paintings, arrowheads, and kachina dolls decorate the bedrooms, which have individual access to a spacious garden plaza; there, a spring-fed birdbath draws hummingbirds and other wildlife. Stone-lined trails follow the spring around cottonwood trees, large rocks and crevices to secluded riverside rest spots. Two rooms are completely accessible for wheelchair users.

## Harborlight Guest House ✪
### 332 LIVE OAK DRIVE, CAPE CARTERET, NORTH CAROLINA 28584

| | |
|---|---|
| Tel: **(919) 393-6868; (800) 624-VIEW [8439]** | Open: **All year** |
| Best Time to Call: **12 noon–9:30 PM** | Reduced Rates: **Available** |
| Hosts: **Bobby and Anita Gill** | Breakfast: **Full** |
| Location: **15 mi. from 70E, exit 24W** | Credit Cards: **AMEX, MC, VISA** |
| No. of Rooms: **1** | Pets: **No** |
| No. of Private Baths: **1** | Children: **No** |
| Double/pb: **$75** | Smoking: **No** |
| Single/pb: **$60** | Social Drinking: **Permitted** |
| | Minimum Stay: **2 nights weekends** |

Located on a secluded waterfront on the North Carolina coast, Harbor Light Guest House offers one waterview room on the first floor that can accommodate wheelchair guests. The bed is queen-size and has a standard bed frame. The bath meets all state specifications. And the outside entrance has a ramp. The room also has a remote color TV and in-room coffee and tea service. In the morning enjoy a gourmet breakfast consisting of egg and cheese dishes, fresh fruits, and fresh breads. Afterwards, explore the waterfront villages of Beaufort and Swansboro, which offer unique gift shops and intimate restaurants. Later in the day experience the waterfront sunset amidst graceful palms and the tranquility of our guest house.

## McGillivray's Log Home and Bed and Breakfast ✪
### 88680 EVERS ROAD, ELMIRA, OREGON 97437

| | |
|---|---|
| Tel: **(503) 935-3564** | Open: **All year** |
| Best Time to Call: **8 AM–8 PM** | Breakfast: **Full** |
| Host: **Evelyn McGillivray** | Credit Cards: **MC, VISA** |
| Location: **14 mi. W of Eugene** | Pets: **No** |
| No. of Rooms: **1** | Children: **Welcome** |
| No. of Private Baths: **1** | Smoking: **No** |
| Double/pb: **$60–$70** | Social Drinking: **Permitted** |
| Single/pb: **$50** | Airport/Station Pickup: **Yes** |

Fir trees cover the five-acre property surrounding this massive home built with six types of wood and featuring both a split-log staircase and an entry ramp. One room, decorated in a classic Americana motif, has a king-size bed and doorways wide enough for wheelchairs. In the bathroom, there is a six-inch step in the shower stall, which has two grab bars and an adjustable height stool; another grab bar is placed near the toilet. Evelyn usually prepares buttermilk pancakes on an antique griddle her mother used. She also offers fresh-squeezed juice, farm-grown apples and grapes, fresh bread, eggs, and all the breakfast trimmings. This B&B is located only three miles from a vineyard, while country roads and a reservoir for fishing and boating are nearby.

## Bed & Breakfast—The Manor ✪

830 VILLAGE ROAD, P.O. BOX 416, LAMPETER, PENNSYLVANIA 17537

| | |
|---|---|
| Tel: **(717) 464-9564; (800) 461-6BED [6233]** | Open: **All year** |
| Best Time to Call: **9 AM–9 PM** | Reduced Rates: **Available** |
| Hosts: **Mary Lou Paolini and Jackie Curtis** | Breakfast: **Full** |
| | Other Meals: **Available** |
| Location: **3 mi. SE of Lancaster** | Credit Cards: **MC, VISA** |
| No. of Rooms: **2** | Pets: **No** |
| No. of Private Baths: **1** | Children: **Welcome** |
| Double/pb: **$75** | Smoking: **No** |
| Double/sb: **$65** | Social Drinking: **No** |
| | Airport/Station Pickup: **Yes** |

Set on 4½ acres of lush Amish farmland, this cozy farmhouse is just minutes away from Lancaster's historic sites and attractions. Guests delight in Mary Lou's delicious breakfasts, with specialties like eggs mornay, apple cobbler, and homemade breads and jams. This cozy inn features two ground-floor bedrooms decorated with country charm and antique beds. Both rooms are easily accessible to the parking area; no steps involved. Guests may join an Old Order Amish family for dinner. A conference room is available for groups. In summer a swim in the pool or a nap under one of the many shade trees is the perfect way to cap a day of touring.

## The Cookie Jar B&B ✪

64 KINGSTOWN ROAD, ROUTE 138, WYOMING, RHODE ISLAND 02898

| | |
|---|---|
| Tel: **(401) 539-2680; (800) 767-4262** | Single/sb: **$58.50** |
| Best Time to Call: **After 5 PM** | Open: **All year** |
| Hosts: **Dick and Madelein Sohl** | Reduced Rates: **Available** |
| Location: **7/10 mi. off I-95, exit 3A** | Breakfast: **Full** |
| No. of Rooms: **2** | Pets: **No** |
| No. of Private Baths: **1** | Children: **Welcome** |
| Max. No. Sharing Bath: **4** | Smoking: **No** |
| Double/pb: **$75** | Social Drinking: **Permitted** |
| Double/sb: **$65** | |

The heart of this house, the living room, was a blacksmith's shop built in 1732; the original ceiling, hand-hewn beams and granite walls are still in use. Fittingly, Dick and Madelein have furnished their home with a mixture of antique, country, and contemporary pieces. You'll enjoy looking around their property, which includes a barn, flower garden, and lots of fruit trees, berry bushes, and grapevines. Two rooms, each with a sink, are ideal for visitors with disabilities. The bathroom has a wall-mounted grab bar at the toilet and a large shower stall (3 by 4 feet) with a built-in fiberglass seat. Despite the rural setting, it's only a short drive to the University of Rhode Island and cities like Mystic and Providence. All guest rooms have color TV and air conditioning.

## Selby House Bed & Breakfast ✪
**226 PRINCESS ANNE STREET, FREDERICKSBURG, VIRGINIA 22401**

Tel: **(703) 373-7037**
Hosts: **Jerry and Virginia Selby**
Location: **54 mi. S of Washington, D.C.**
No of Rooms: **4**
No. of Private Baths: **4**
Double/pb: **$75**
Single/pb: **$65**
Open: **All year**

Reduced Rates: **Available**
Breakfast: **Full**
Credit Cards: **MC, VISA**
Pets: **No**
Children: **Welcome**
Smoking: **No**
Social Drinking: **Permitted**
Station Pickup: **Yes**

Selby House has two barrier-free, ground-level rooms. In 1986, Jerry designed and built this annex to fulfill his dream of extending hospitality to physically challenged guests. All doorways are 36 inches wide. The bedrooms have large baths with grab bars and other necessary adaptations. Both guest rooms connect to a large community area as well as the dining room, and their cement patios provide easy access to all inn facilities.

## The Iris Inn ✪
**191 CHINQUAPIN DRIVE, WAYNESBORO, VIRGINIA 22980**

Tel: **(540) 943-1991**
Best Time to Call: **10 AM–8 PM**
Hosts: **Wayne and Iris Karl**
Location: **25 mi. W of Charlottesville**
No. of Rooms: **1**
No. of Private Baths: **1**
Double/pb: **$75–$95**
Single/pb: **$65**
Open: **All year**
Reduced Rates: **Corporate, Sun.–Thurs.**

Breakfast: **Full**
Credit Cards: **MC, VISA**
Pets: **No**
Children: **Welcome, by arrangement**
Smoking: **No**
Social Drinking: **Permitted**
Minimum Stay: **2 nights weekends**
Airport Pickup: **Yes**

Southern charm and grace in a totally modern facility overlooking the historic Shenandoah Valley from the Blue Ridge Mountains' wooded western slope—that's what awaits you at the Iris Inn. It's ideal for a weekend retreat, a refreshing change for the business traveler, and a tranquil spot for tourists to spend a night or more. The wheelchair-accessible room is comfortably furnished and delightfully decorated with nature and wildlife motifs. The bathroom has a lavatory without a vanity, for easier use. There are grab bars at the toilet and on the sides of the shower, which also has a seat. A pocket door connects the bathroom and bedroom. For your convenience, a ramp leads from the parking lot level to the porch.

---

**For key to listings, see inside front or back cover.**

○ This star means that rates are guaranteed through December 31, 1996, to any guest making a reservation as a result of reading about the B&B in *Bed & Breakfast U.S.A.—1996* edition.

Important! To avoid misunderstandings, always ask about cancellation policies when booking.

Please enclose a self-addressed, stamped, business-size envelope when contacting reservation services.

For more details on what you can expect in a B&B, see Chapter 1.

Always mention *Bed & Breakfast U.S.A.* when making reservations!

If no B&B is listed in the area you'll be visiting, use the form on page 323 to order a copy of our "List of New B&Bs."

We want to hear from you! Use the form on page 325.

# 5

# *State-by-State Listings*

# ALASKA

Fairbanks

Anchorage

## Alaska Bed & Breakfast Association
### 369 SOUTH FRANKLIN, SUITE 200, JUNEAU, ALASKA 99801

Tel: (907) 586-2959; fax: (907) 463-4453
Best Time to Call: **10 AM–5 PM, weekdays**
Coordinators: **Betty Lou and Karla Hart**
States/Regions Covered: **Alaska**

Descriptive Directory: **$5**
Rates (Single/Double):
  Modest: **$65–$70**
  Average: **$60–$70 / $70–$85**
  Luxury: **$85+ / $95+**
Credit Cards: **AMEX, MC, VISA**

Visit cities, towns, and villages throughout the state: you can choose among historic buildings, modern homes, log cabins, and a few "Alaskana rural" sites. Your hosts include artists, teachers, retirees, homemakers, and government employees. Some B&Bs have amenities like saunas and barbecues, others offer splendid hiking and wildlife viewing. To make it easier to plan your trip, Betty Lou and Karla can arrange railroad, air taxi, ferry, and tour bookings.

## Alaska Private Lodgings
### P.O. BOX 200047, ANCHORAGE, ALASKA 99520–0047

Tel: (907) 258-1717; fax: (907) 258-6613
Best Time to Call: 9 AM–6 PM
Coordinator: Mercy Dennis
States/Regions Covered: Anchorage, Denali, Fairbanks, Girdwood, Homer, Hope, Kenai, Palmer, Seward, Talkeetna, Wasilla, Willow

Descriptive Directory of B&Bs: $3
Rates (Single/Double):
  Modest: $45 / $50
  Average: $50 / $75
  Luxury: $75 / $125
Credit Cards: AMEX, MC, VISA

Alaskan hosts are this state's warmest resource! Mercy's accommodations range from an original log house of a pioneer's homestead, where the host is in the antique-doll business, to a one-bedroom apartment with a view of Mt. Denali. Many are convenient to the University of Alaska and Alaska Pacific University. There's a $5 surcharge for one-night stays.

## A Garden House Bed and Breakfast ✪
### 1511 WOO BOULEVARD, ANCHORAGE, ALASKA 99515

Tel: (907) 344-3312
Best Time to Call: Mornings
Hosts: Hersh and Karen Kendall
Location: 10 mi. S of Anchorage
No. of Rooms: 3
No. of Private Baths: 1
Max. No. Sharing Bath: 4
Double/sb: $75
Single/sb: $65
Suites: $75–$95

Open: All year
Reduced Rates: 10% seniors;
  Oct.–Apr. $65–$85
Breakfast: Full
Credit Cards: MC, VISA
Pets: No
Children: Welcome
Smoking: No
Social Drinking: Permitted

A Garden House Bed and Breakfast is a two-story redwood home, situated on 1½ acres with beautiful grounds and a garden. Flowers abound inside and outside the house, and the garden provides gourmet fare. Hersh and Karen serve Alaskan specialties for breakfast, such as Alaskan wild berry jams and reindeer sausage. Your hosts are 22-year residents of Alaska and delight in sharing their knowledge and love of the area. Their hobbies include hunting, fishing, and gardening. Located a short distance from shopping, bike trails, golf course, airport, and the zoo.

## The Green Bough ✪
### 3832 YOUNG STREET, ANCHORAGE, ALASKA 99508

Tel: (907) 562-4636; fax: (907) 562-0445
Best Time to Call: 10 AM–9 PM

Hosts: Jerry and Phyllis Jost
Location: 15 min. from airport/train
No. of Rooms: 4

| | |
|---|---|
| Max. No. Sharing Bath: **4** | Breakfast: **Continental, plus** |
| Double/pb: **$65–$75** | Pets: **No** |
| Double/sb: **$55** | Children: **Welcome** |
| Open: **All year** | Smoking: **No** |
| Reduced Rates: **Families, off-season** | Social Drinking: **No** |

Since 1981, Anchorage's oldest bed and breakfast has been offering a special blend of gracious, unpretentious hospitality. Guest rooms are spacious and reflect a country atmosphere, featuring freshly-ironed sheets, king, full or twin beds and upon request, room phones. The aromas of coffee and cinnamon will start you off to a full day of sightseeing, shopping, fishing, or hiking. You can expect to meet guests from around the world including the backyards of Alaska. The Green Bough is centrally located, near buses, hospitals, universities, and bike trails. Freezer and storage are available for your fish and extra gear. Jerry and Phyllis have been transplanted Alaskans since 1967, and want to share their experience and enthusiasm about the area with you.

## Lakeside B&B ✪
**5031 WEST 80TH AVENUE, ANCHORAGE, ALASKA 99502-4112**

| | |
|---|---|
| Tel: **(907) 248-2249** | Open: **All year** |
| Best Time to Call: **8 AM–6 PM** | Reduced Rates: **Available** |
| Hosts: **Ann and Tim Rittal** | Breakfast: **Continental** |
| Location: **6 mi. S of Anchorage** | Pets: **No** |
| No. of Rooms: **1** | Children: **Welcome** |
| No. of Private Baths: **1** | Smoking: **No** |
| Double/pb: **$75** | Social Drinking: **Permitted** |
| Suites: **$85** | Minimum Stay: **2 nights** |

Lakeside B&B is a little piece of country in the middle of metropolitan Anchorage. This quiet retreat is a secluded getaway in an awesome location, which makes it ideal for visitors and businesspeople. Tim and Ann are self-employed and have 46 years of combined Alaskan experiences. Guests are within an hour of Portage Glacier and Matanuska Valley; Anchorage International Airport is five minutes away. The trip to downtown takes 15 minutes, while Alaska's wildlife is just a glance out the window. Also available are a stationary bike, fax machine and office supplies.

## Snug Harbor Inn ✪
**1226 WEST 10TH AVENUE, ANCHORAGE, ALASKA 99501**

| | |
|---|---|
| Tel: **(907) 272-6249**; fax: **(907) 272-7100** | No. of Private Baths: **5** |
| | Double/pb: **$75** |
| Hosts: **Kenneth and Laurine "Sis" Hill** | Single/pb: **$75** |
| Location: **Downtown Anchorage** | Open: **All year** |
| No. of Rooms: **5** | Reduced Rates: **Families** |

Breakfast: **Full**
Other Meals: **Available**
Credit Cards: **VISA**
Pets: **Sometimes**
Children: **Yes**

Smoking: **Permitted**
Social Drinking: **Permitted**
Minimum Stay: **2 nights**
Airport/Station Pickup: **Yes**
Foreign Languages: **Spanish**

This homey cottage is minutes from bus routes serving downtown Anchorage, with its parks, sports facilities, shopping areas, museum, and performing arts center. Entrance to the Coastal Bike Path—which leads to Earthquake Park—is only three blocks away; your hosts will supply bicycles. You'll get energy for expeditions from Ken's ample breakfasts; the menu ranges from eggs and pancakes to homemade muffins, with juice and coffee or tea.

## The Blue Goose Bed & Breakfast ○
### 4466 DARTMOUTH, FAIRBANKS, ALASKA 99709

Tel: **(907) 479-6973;**
  **(800) 478-6973, within Alaska only;**
  fax: **(907) 457-6973**
Hosts: **Susan and Ken Risse**
Location: **5 mi. W of Fairbanks**
No. of Rooms: **3**
No. of Private Baths: **1**
Max. No. Sharing Bath: **4**
Double/pb: **$75**
Double/sb: **$55–$65**

Single/sb: **$50**
Open: **All year**
Reduced Rates: **Labor Day–Memorial Day**
Breakfast: **Full**
Credit Cards: **MC, VISA, DC, DISC**
Pets: **No**
Children: **Welcome**
Smoking: **No**
Social Drinking: **Permitted**

Susan and Ken's trilevel frame house is a modern home with historic accents, thanks to the antique furniture and other old-time treasures. It's convenient, too: city buses stop one block away and the ride to the airport takes all of ten minutes. For diversion, you may want to visit the Riverboat Discovery and the historic Pump House Restaurant. Breakfast is special at the Blue Goose, with blue-ribbon Alaska rhubarb pie baked each morning and served warm. Your hosts may also dish out homemade bread, muffins with Alaska blueberries, or freshly picked low-bush cranberries. The Risses met while working on the pipeline. Ken, a civil engineer, dabbles in woodworking, while Susan is a full-time hostess and mother interested in needlework.

## Minnie Street B&B ○
### 345 MINNIE STREET, FAIRBANKS, ALASKA 99701

Tel: **(907) 456-1802**
Hosts: **Marnie and Lambert Hazelaar**
Location: **In Fairbanks**
No. of Rooms: **4**
No. of Private Baths: **2**
Max. No. Sharing Bath: **4**
Double/pb: **$85**

Double/sb: **$70**
Single/sb: **$65**
Suites: **$95**
Open: **All year**
Reduced Rates: **Winter**
Breakfast: **Full**
Credit Cards: **AMEX, MC, VISA**

Pets: **No**                                   Social Drinking: **Permitted**
Children: **Welcome**                           Airport/Station Pickup: **Yes**
Smoking: **No**

This bed and breakfast is located within walking distance of the train depot and only five minutes from downtown, where you will find the post office, banks, gift shops, and restaurants. En route you will cross the beautiful Chena River. The cozy, comfortably decorated guest rooms have queen-size beds. Ample parking is provided with plenty of room for RVs; rental cars are available next door. To save money, grill your dinner on Marnie's barbecue. Her sumptuous breakfasts include homemade breads, omelettes, and fruit salad.

## 7 Gables Inn ✪
### P. O. BOX 80488, FAIRBANKS, ALASKA 99708

Tel: **(907) 479-0751; fax: (907) 479-2229**
Best Time to Call: **7 AM–10 PM**
Hosts: **Paul and Leicha Welton**
Location: **2 mi. W of Fairbanks**
No. of Rooms: **9**
No. of Private Baths: **9**
Double/pb: **$50–$120**
Single/pb: **$50–$95**
Suites: **$75–$180**
Open: **All year**

Reduced Rates: **30%, Oct.–Apr.**
Breakfast: **Full**
Other Meals: **Available**
Credit Cards: **AMEX, DC, DISC, MC, VISA**
Pets: **Sometimes**
Children: **Welcome**
Smoking: **No**
Social Drinking: **Permitted**
Airport/Station Pickup: **Yes**
Foreign Languages: **Spanish**

The Weltons' large Tudor-style home is central to many city attractions—Riverboat Discovery, Cripple Creek Resort, University Museum, Alaskaland, Gold Dredge #8—and within walking distance of the University of Alaska's Fairbanks campus. Paul designed and built the house, a worthy destination in its own right. You'll enter through a floral solarium, which leads to a foyer with antique stained glass and indoor waterfall. Party planners take note: 7 Gables has a wine cellar and a wedding chapel. Guests can use the laundry facilities, library, Jacuzzis, canoe, and bikes. All rooms have telephones, cable TV, and VCR and 8 rooms have private Jacuzzi baths. One room is accessible to wheelchair users. Ample breakfasts feature dishes like salmon quiche, crab casserole, and peachy pecan crêpes.

# ARIZONA

Williams •
Flagstaff •
• Sedona

• Camp Verdé
Mayer •

Phoenix • • Scottsdale
Tempe• • Mesa

• Tucson
Tubac •
Patagonia •
• Bisbee

## Mi Casa–Su Casa Bed & Breakfast ✪
### P.O. BOX 950, TEMPE, ARIZONA 85280-0950

Tel: (602) 990-0682; (800) 456-0682;
  fax: (602) 990-3390
Best Time to Call: 8 AM–8 PM
Coordinator: **Ruth T. Young**
States/Regions Covered:
  **Arizona**—Ajo, Bisbee, Cave Creek,
  Flagstaff, Fountain Hills, Mesa, Page,
  Phoenix, Prescott, Scottsdale,
Sedona, Tempe, Tucson, Wickenburg,
Yuma; **Nevada**—Las Vegas; **New
Mexico; Utah**
Rates (Single/Double):
  Modest:  $35–$45
  Average: $45–$65
  Luxury:  $75–$175
Descriptive Directory: **$9.50**

Ruth's guest houses are located statewide; the cities listed above are
only a partial listing. They are located in cities, suburbs, and rural
settings, all of which are within easy driving range of canyons,
national parks, Indian country, Colorado River gem country, the
Mexican border area, historic mining towns, and water recreation
areas. Send $9.50 for her detailed directory. Arizona State University

and the University of Arizona are convenient to many B&Bs. There is a $5 surcharge for one-night stays.

## The Judge Ross House ✪
### 605 SHATTUCK STREET, BISBEE, ARIZONA 85603

| | |
|---|---|
| Tel: **(520) 432-5597 days; 432-4120 evenings and weekends** | Open: **All year** |
| | Breakfast: **Full** |
| Best Time to Call: **Evenings** | Other Meals: **Available** |
| Hosts: **Jim and Bonnie Douglass** | Credit Cards: **MC, VISA** |
| Location: **25 mi. SE of Tombstone** | Pets: **No** |
| No. of Rooms: **3** | Children: **Welcome, over 12** |
| No. of Private Baths: **3** | Smoking: **No** |
| Double/pb: **$65** | Social Drinking: **Permitted** |
| Single/pb: **$60** | Airport/Station Pickup: **Yes** |

A two-story, brick home built at the turn of the century and named for its first owner, a superior court judge, the Judge Ross House has a charmingly old-fashioned look enhanced by decorative moldings, lavish wood trim, and period furniture. Jim and Bonnie are gracious hosts, welcoming visitors with fresh flowers, wine, candy, and magazines. Breakfast varies from day to day, with specialties such as Belgian waffles and eggs Benedict. Bisbee was once the Southwest's largest copper mining area, and the open pit mine remains a major attraction. Browsers will enjoy visiting the town's galleries and antique stores.

## B's B&B ✪
### 94 COPPINGER STREET, P.O. BOX 2019, CAMP VERDE, ARIZONA 86322

| | |
|---|---|
| Tel: **(520) 567-6215** | Double/sb: **$60** |
| Hosts: **Beatrice Richmond** | Open: **All year** |
| Location: **90 mi. N of Phoenix** | Breakfast: **Full** |
| No. of Rooms: **2** | Pets: **No** |
| No. of Private Baths: **1** | Children: **Welcome** |
| Max. No. Sharing Bath: **3** | Smoking: **No** |
| Double/pb: **$60** | Social Drinking: **Permitted** |
| Single/pb: **$50** | Foreign Languages: **French, Spanish** |

B's B&B sits on a hillside; a huge redwood deck has a panoramic view of the water flowing below. Set on an acre of natural landscaping, this bed and breakfast seems isolated, but is very close to the center of town. Things to do include excursions to Fort Verde State Park, Captain King's boat rides, outback tours, horseback riding, and much more. Breakfast may feature B's blintzes, homemade granola and yogurt. Beatrice is a retired elementary school teacher and teaches English as a second language one evening a week. She also enjoys foreign languages and travel.

# Dierker House
**423 WEST CHERRY, FLAGSTAFF, ARIZONA 86001**

| | |
|---|---|
| Tel: **(520) 774-3249** | Breakfast: **Full** |
| Host: **Dorothea Dierker** | Pets: **No** |
| No. of Rooms: **3** | Children: **Welcome, over 12** |
| Max. No. Sharing Bath: **4** | Smoking: **No** |
| Double/sb: **$45** | Social Drinking: **Permitted** |
| Open: **All year** | |

This lovely old home in Flagstaff's historic section is located high in the mountains, at an elevation of 7000 feet. Flagstaff is the hub of wonderful day trips to the Grand Canyon, Native American ruins and reservations, Lake Powell, Monument Valley, and many more sites. The second-floor accommodations are extremely comfortable and include many amenities. In the morning, Dorothea serves an excellent and sociable breakfast in the dining room.

# Serenity House ✪
**P.O. BOX 1254, THIRD STREET AND MAIN, MAYER, ARIZONA 86333**

| | |
|---|---|
| Tel: **(520) 632-4430** | Reduced Rates: **$10 less, Nov.–Apr.** |
| Host: **Sue Ward** | Breakfast: **Continental** |
| Location: **25 mi. E of Prescott; 65 mi.** | Pets: **No** |
| **N of Phoenix** | Children: **Welcome, over 12** |
| No. of Rooms: **2** | Smoking: **No** |
| Max. No. Sharing Bath: **4** | Social Drinking: **Permitted** |
| Double/sb: **$50** | Airport/Station Pickup: **Yes** |
| Open: **All year** | |

This comfortable, country Victorian home is located in an old mining town north of Phoenix and east of Prescott. Built around 1905 by one of the Mayer brothers, who gave this town its name, the home has twelve-foot gabled ceilings, two fireplaces, hardwood floors, original copper and brass door and light fixtures, stained glass, a front porch swing, many large trees, and a pool and hot tub. One guest room has a private entrance to the pool area. There are many antique shops and historical buildings both in Mayer and Prescott. Popular pastimes include gold panning, hiking, rock hounding, and horse racing at Prescott Downs. Special sugar-free diets can easily be accommodated. Locally-grown vegetables and fruits are a summer treat.

# Casa Del Sol ✪
**6951 E. HOBART, MESA, ARIZONA 85207**

| | |
|---|---|
| Tel: **(602) 985-5956** | Max. No. Sharing Bath: **4** |
| Hosts: **Ray and Barb Leo** | Double/sb: **$50–$55** |
| Location: **20 mi. E of Phoenix** | Single/sb: **$45** |
| No. of Rooms: **2** | Open: **All year** |

| | |
|---|---|
| Reduced Rates: **Available** | Children: **Welcome** |
| Breakfast: **Full** | Smoking: **No** |
| Pets: **Sometimes** | Social Drinking: **Permitted** |

This luxurious Southwestern home sits on an acre of property with desert landscaping, fruit trees, and a solar-heated swimming pool. The guest rooms emphasize comfort with queen-size beds and Southwest decor. The word for breakfast is fresh, from ground coffee and fresh-squeezed juice to home-baked breads, muffins and croissants, special omelettes, and waffles. Guests are welcome to enjoy the pool, Jacuzzi, fireplace, and VCR. Nearby attractions include beautiful state parks, the Salt River recreation area, Cactus League spring training, great shopping, golf, and restaurants.

## The Little House ✪
### P.O. BOX 461, 341 SONOITA AVENUE, PATAGONIA, ARIZONA 85624

| | |
|---|---|
| Tel: **(520) 394-2493** | Open: **All year** |
| Hosts: **Don and Doris Wenig** | Breakfast: **Full** |
| Location: **60 mi. S of Tucson** | Pets: **No** |
| No. of Rooms: **2** | Children: **Sometimes** |
| No. of Private Baths: **2** | Smoking: **No** |
| Double/pb: **$80** | Social Drinking: **Permitted** |
| Single/pb: **$60** | |

The Wenigs' home is located close to the Mexican border in a small mountain town at an elevation of 4000 feet. Comfort and privacy are assured in the adobe guest house separated from the main house by a charming courtyard. One of the bedrooms has a queen-size bed; the other has twin beds and is wheelchair accessible. Each bedroom has a fireplace, sitting area, and adjacent patio. Coffee or tea is brought to your room to start the day. Afterward, join Don and Doris for a breakfast of sausage and waffles, eggs from local hens, and home-baked breads. Bird-watching, a visit to a ghost town or silver mine, and shopping in Nogales, Mexico, are pleasant pastimes available.

## Maricopa Manor ✪
### P.O. BOX 7186, 15 WEST PASADENA AVENUE, PHOENIX, ARIZONA 85011

| | |
|---|---|
| Tel: **(602) 274-6302** | Open: **All year** |
| Hosts: **Mary Ellen and Paul Kelley** | Breakfast: **Continental, plus** |
| Location: **5 mi. N of downtown** | Credit Cards: **AMEX, DISC, MC, VISA** |
| Phoenix | Pets: **No** |
| No. of Rooms: **6 suites** | Children: **Welcome** |
| No. of Private Baths: **6** | Smoking: **No** |
| Suites: **$79–$159** | Social Drinking: **Permitted** |

Inside this Spanish-style manor house built in 1928, you'll find beautiful art, antiques, and warm Southwestern hospitality. The five private suites, spacious public rooms, decks, and gazebo spa create an intimate, Old World atmosphere in an elegant urban setting. Maricopa Manor is in the heart of the Valley of the Sun, convenient to shops, restaurants, museums, churches, and civic and government centers. Advance reservations are required.

## Bed & Breakfast Inn Arizona—Arizona Accommodations Reservations
**8900 EAST VIA LINDA, SUITE 101, SCOTTSDALE, ARIZONA 85258**

Tel: **(602) 860-9338; (800) 266-STAY**
  **[7829]; fax: (602) 314-1193**
Best Time to Call: **10 AM–6 PM**
Coordinator: **Scott Stuart**
States/Regions Covered: **Ajo, Bisbee, Clifton, Flagstaff, Globe, Lake Havasu City, Lakeside, Oracle, Page, Phoenix, Prescott, Scottsdale, Sedona, Tombstone, Tucson; Northern California; New Mexico**

Descriptive Directory: **$3**
Rates (Single/Double):
  Modest:   **$35–$50**
  Average:   **$51–$75**
  Luxury:    **$76–$499**
Credit Cards: **AMEX, MC, VISA**
Minimum Stay: **Holidays; 2 nights**

Representing over 200 B&B inns, homestays, vacation apartments, and ranches throughout the state, Scott's unique reservation service can make your getaway a memorable experience. In business for 12 years, this service takes pride in its growing roster of inspected and friendly hosts.

## Bed & Breakfast Southwest Reservation Service ○
**6916 EAST MARIPOSA, SCOTTSDALE, ARIZONA 85251**

Tel: **(602) 947-9704; (800) 762-9704**
Best Time to Call: **10 AM–5 PM**
Coordinators: **Jo and Jim Cummings**
States/Regions Covered: **Arizona, New Mexico, Southern California, Southern Colorado, Southern Nevada**

Descriptive Directory: **$3, SASE**
Rates (Single/Double):
  Modest: **$40–$60**
  Average: **$50–$65**
  Luxury: **$65–up**

Specializing in unique homestays with private suites and guest houses, this company offers an exciting experience to the traveler coming to the Southwest. Hosts, as residents of the area, can give you firsthand information about sports activities, dining opportunities, art exhibits, and answer your questions about the great Southwest. The Cummingses will be happy to help you plan your vacation with gracious hosts throughout the Southwest. B&B Southwest is currently seeking both unique hosts and enthusiastic guests.

## Casa de Mariposa ✪
**6916 EAST MARIPOSA, SCOTTSDALE, ARIZONA 85251**

| | |
|---|---|
| Tel: **(602) 947-9704** | Open: **All year** |
| Best Time to Call: **10 AM–5 PM** | Breakfast: **Continental** |
| Hosts: **Jo and Jim Cummings** | Pets: **No** |
| Location: **15 mi. N of I-10** | Children: **Welcome** |
| No. of Rooms: **1** | Smoking: **No** |
| No. of Private Baths: **1** | Social Drinking: **Permitted** |
| Double/pb: **$95** | Airport/Station Pickup: **Yes** |

This very special guest suite has a deluxe king canopy bed, Southwest decor, private entrance, French doors to the patio, kitchenette, and private bath. Located in the original Sunkist orchards, Casa de Mariposa offers golden grapefruit fresh from the tree. This quiet residential neighborhood is in the heart of beautiful Scottsdale, within walking distance of numerous shops, restaurants, theaters, and golf courses. Guests are welcome to soak in the spa, use the hosts' golf clubs or their box seats at the Giants' spring training games.

## Valley o' the Sun Bed & Breakfast ✪
**P.O. BOX 2214, SCOTTSDALE, ARIZONA 85252**

| | |
|---|---|
| Tel: **(602)941-1281; (800) 689-1281** | Open: **All year** |
| Best Time to Call: **After 5:30 PM** | Reduced Rates: **Seniors** |
| Host: **Kay Curtis** | Breakfast: **Continental** |
| Location: **Tempe** | Pets: **No** |
| No. of Rooms: **3** | Children: **Welcome, over 10** |
| No. of Private Baths: **1** | Smoking: **Permitted** |
| Max. No. Sharing Bath: **4** | Social Drinking: **Permitted** |
| Double/pb: **$40** | Minimum Stay: **2 nights** |
| Double/sb: **$35** | Airport/Station Pickup: **Yes** |
| Single/sb: **$25** | |

The house is ideally located in the college area of Tempe, but is close enough to Scottsdale to enjoy its fine shops and restaurants. From the patio, you can enjoy a beautiful view of the Papago Buttes and McDowell Mountains. Local attractions include swimming at Big Surf, the Phoenix Zoo, and the Scottsdale Center for the Arts.

## Cathedral Rock Lodge ✪
**61 LOS AMIGOS LANE, SEDONA, ARIZONA 86336**

| | |
|---|---|
| Tel: **(520) 282-7608; fax: (520) 282-4505** | Suite: **$110** |
| | Cabin: **$105** |
| Host: **Carol Shannon and family** | Open: **All year** |
| Location: **2.7 mi. from Rte. 89A** | Reduced Rates: **Available** |
| No. of Rooms: **3** | Breakfast: **Full** |
| No. of Private Baths: **3** | Credit Cards: **MC, VISA** |
| Double/pb: **$70–$75** | Pets: **No** |

Children: **Welcome (crib)**          Social Drinking: **Permitted**
Smoking: **No**

Set in rock terrace gardens surrounded by tall shade trees, this rambling country home boasts spectacular views of the surrounding mountains. The suite has its own deck, built against a giant pine tree. Guest bedrooms feature family treasures and handmade quilts. Each day starts with Carol's hot breads and homemade jams; fresh fruits from local orchards are summertime treats. Lovers of the great outdoors will delight in the natural scenic beauty of the area, and browsers will enjoy the many galleries and shops. In the evening, curl up in front of the fireplace, borrow a book, or select a videotape from your host's collection.

## Kennedy House ✪
**HC 30, BOX 785K, 2075 UPPER RED ROCK LOOP ROAD, SEDONA, ARIZONA 86336**

Tel: **(602) 282-1624**
Best Time to Call: **10 AM–10 PM**
Hosts: **Tonya and Chuck Kennedy**
Location: **116 mi. N of Phoenix**
No. of Rooms: **2**
No. of Private Baths: **2**
Double/pb: **$94**
Suites: **$89**
Open: **Feb.–Dec.; closed Thanksgiving and Christmas**
Reduced Rates: **$10 less per night, after 3rd day**

Breakfast: **Full**
Credit Cards: **MC, VISA**
Pets: **No**
Children: **Welcome**
Smoking: **No**
Social Drinking: **Permitted**
Minimum Stay: **2 nights weekends, except Dec. and Feb.**
Airport/Station Pickup: **Yes**

This attractively furnished contemporary home lies within walking distance of Red Rock Crossing, the most photographed spot in Arizona. Chuck, a retired wildlife biologist, offers guests a guided nature hike and will cheerfully assist in planning picnics or giving directions to the area's many famous monuments. After a full day of sightseeing, relax with a beverage on the large deck, or in the heated spa, and watch Cathedral Rock perform her magic.

## Moestly Wood Bed & Breakfast ✪
**2085 UPPER RED ROCK LOOP ROAD, SEDONA, ARIZONA 86336**

Tel: **(520) 204-1461**
Best Time to Call: **8 AM–8 PM**
Hosts: **Roger and Carolyn Moe**
Location: **110 mi. N of Phoenix**
No. of Rooms: **2**
No. of Private Baths: **2**
Suite: **$75–$85**
Open: **All year**

Breakfast: **Full**
Other Meals: **Available**
Credit Cards: **MC, VISA**
Pets: **No**
Children: **Welcome**
Smoking: **No**
Social Drinking: **Permitted**
Minimum Stay: **2 nights on weekends**

This contemporary home is located in the beautiful Arizona red rock country. Just 4 miles out of town you can enjoy spectacular views of Cathedral Rock and the surrounding area, or take a short hike to Red Rock Crossing, one of the state's most photographed sites. Roger and Carolyn enjoy visitors and are happy to help with touring plans, hiking, golfing, or just browsing through Sedona's many shops and galleries. Their large redwood deck is very inviting. Relaxing by the fire is also a comfy, cozy way to spend the evening.

## Tubac Country Inn ✪
### 409 BURRUEL STREET, P.O. BOX 1540, TUBAC, ARIZONA 85646

| | |
|---|---|
| Tel: **(520) 398-3178** | Breakfast: **Continental** |
| Best Time to Call: **Anytime** | Pets: **No** |
| Hosts: **Ruth and Jim Goebel** | Children: **Welcome** |
| Location: **41 mi. S of Tucson** | Smoking: **No** |
| No. of Rooms: **4** | Social Drinking: **Permitted** |
| Suites: **$80** | Airport Pickup: **Yes** |
| Open: **Closed August** | |

This adorable two-story Inn located in the center of Tubac will steal your heart away. Choose a one- or two-bedroom suite; two units have full kitchens for longer stays. Tubac, founded in 1752, is the oldest European settlement in Arizona. Today Tubac is the place where art and history meet. Visit galleries, boutiques, and restaurants all within walking distance of the Inn. Within a few minutes you can drive to shopping in Old Mexico, or see missions, museums, and national parks. The area boasts six outstanding golf courses.

## Casa Tierra Adobe Bed and Breakfast Inn
### 11155 WEST CALLE PIMA, TUCSON, ARIZONA 85743

| | |
|---|---|
| Tel: **(602) 578-3058**; fax: **(602) 578-3058** | Open: **Sept.–May** |
| | Reduced Rates: **10% after 7 days** |
| Best Time to Call: **Mornings** | Breakfast: **Full** |
| Hosts: **Karen and Lyle Hymer-Thompson** | Pets: **No** |
| | Children: **Welcome, over 3** |
| Location: **15 mi. W of Tucson** | Smoking: **No** |
| No. of Rooms: **3** | Social Drinking: **Permitted** |
| No. of Private Baths: **3** | Minimum Stay: **2 nights** |
| Double/pb: **$75–$85** | Foreign Languages: **Spanish** |

Casa Tierra is located on five acres of beautiful Sonoran desert thirty minutes from downtown Tucson. This secluded desert area has hundreds of saguaro cactus, spectacular mountain views, and brilliant sunsets. Built and designed by owners Lyle and Karen, the all-adobe house features entryways with vaulted brick ceilings, an interior arched courtyard, Mexican furnishings, and a Jacuzzi. Each guest room has a private bath, queen-size bed, microwave, small refrigerator, and private patio and entrance. Nearby attractions include the Desert Museum, the Saguaro National Monument, and Old Tucson. Karen is an artist/photographer; Lyle is a designer/builder who takes tours into Mexico.

## Ford's Bed & Breakfast ✪
**1202 NORTH AVENIDA MARLENE, TUCSON, ARIZONA 85715**

| | |
|---|---|
| Tel: **(520) 885-1202** | Suites: **$100; sleeps 4** |
| Best Time to Call: **8–10 AM** | Open: **All year** |
| Hosts: **Sheila and Tom Ford** | Breakfast: **Continental** |
| Location: **In Tucson** | Pets: **No** |
| No. of Rooms: **2** | Children: **No** |
| No. of Private Baths: **1** | Smoking: **No** |
| Double/pb: **$50** | Social Drinking: **Permitted** |
| Single/pb: **$40** | Airport/Station Pickup: **Yes** |

A warm welcome awaits you at this air-conditioned ranch-style home in a quiet residential cul-de-sac on Tucson's northeast side. Walk through your private entrance and enjoy a bird's-eye view of the mountains from your own garden patio. Your English-born hostess, a retired nanny and dog breeder, has lived here for 35 years and can direct you to the attractions of the area: Sabino Canyon, Mount Lemmon, Saguaro National Monument, hiking trails, and the like. For easy access, city bus lines run nearby. Guests have use of a microwave, a refrigerator, and the sitting room with a TV.

## The Gable House ✪
**2324 NORTH MADELYN CIRCLE, TUCSON, ARIZONA 85712**

| | |
|---|---|
| Tel: **(520) 326-1150** | Open: **All year** |
| Hosts: **Albert Cummings and Phyllis Fredona** | Reduced Rates: **10% seniors; 7th day free** |
| Location: **6 mi. from I-10, exit Grant Road** | Breakfast: **Continental, plus** |
| No. of Rooms: **3** | Pets: **No** |
| No. of Private Baths: **2** | Children: **Welcome, over 10** |
| Max. No. Sharing Bath: **4** | Smoking: **No** |
| Double/pb: **$85** | Social Drinking: **Permitted** |
| Double/sb: **$55–$60** | Minimum Stay: **2 nights Feb.–Mar.** |

This Santa Fe pueblo-style home is named for its most famous resident—Clark Gable—who lived here in the early 1940s, some ten years after the house was built. Centrally located on a one-acre lot in a quiet residential neighborhood, this B&B is within walking distance of shops, restaurants, and a bus stop. It's one mile to Tucson Botanical Gardens and three miles to a large city park with golf, tennis, and other recreational facilities. Albert is a semi-retired real estate broker;

Phyllis is a licensed massage therapist. Massage is available on the premises. One-night stays have a $10 surcharge.

## Hideaway B&B ✪
**4344 EAST POE STREET, TUCSON, ARIZONA 85711**

| | |
|---|---|
| Tel: **(520) 323-8067** | Reduced Rates: **Weekly** |
| Best Time to Call: **After 5 PM** | Breakfast: **Continental** |
| Hosts: **Dwight and Ola Parker** | Pets: **No** |
| No. of Rooms: **1** | Children: **No** |
| No. of Private Baths: **1** | Smoking: **No** |
| Guest Cottage: **$45–$60** | Minimum Stay: **3 nights** |
| Open: **Oct.–June; special** | Airport/Station Pickup: **Yes** |
| **arrangements for the rest of year** | |

A cozy bungalow with its own entrance, Hideaway B&B is located in the hosts' backyard in central Tucson, just minutes from two major shopping centers. One mile away, a city park provides lots of diversions, with two golf courses, a driving range, tennis courts, and a zoo. Pima Air Museum, Davis Monthan Air Force Base, the University of Arizona, Colossal Cave, the Old Tucson movie set, and Mt. Lemmon Ski Resort are among the many sights of interest. The air-conditioned accommodations include a private bath, a bedroom, and a sitting room equipped with a TV, VCR, and stereo. Your hosts, a retired art teacher and an engineer/insurance man, enjoy big band music, gardening, and their clown ministry.

## Katy's Hacienda ✪
**5841 EAST 9TH STREET, TUCSON, ARIZONA 85711**

| | |
|---|---|
| Tel: **(602) 745-5695** | Double/pb: **$55** |
| Host: **Katy Gage** | Single/pb: **$45** |
| Location: **8 mi. from Rte. 10, Grant or** | Double/sb: **$55** |
| **Kolb exit** | Single/sb: **$45** |
| No. of Rooms: **2** | Open: **All year** |
| No. of Private Baths: **1** | Reduced Rates: **10% weekly** |
| Max. No. Sharing Bath: **3** | Breakfast: **Full** |

| | |
|---|---|
| Pets: **No** | Social Drinking: **Permitted** |
| Children: **Welcome, over 8** | Minimum Stay: **2 nights** |
| Smoking: **Permitted** | Airport/Station Pickup: **Yes** |

An ornamental iron guard protects this adobe brick house filled with charming antiques and glass. Guests can unwind in the backyard and the patio area, or come inside and enjoy the living room and television room. Katy's Hacienda is within walking distance of the bus line, fine restaurants, theaters, and a hospital. The El Con shopping area, the Randolph Golf Course, and the zoo are three miles away.

## Natural Bed and Breakfast ✪
### 3150 EAST PRESIDIO ROAD, TUCSON, ARIZONA 85716

| | |
|---|---|
| Tel: **(602) 881-4582** | Open: **All year** |
| Best Time to Call: **Mornings** | Reduced Rates: **5% seniors** |
| Host: **Marc Haberman** | Breakfast: **Full** |
| No. of Rooms: **2** | Other Meals: **Available** |
| No. of Private Baths: **1** | Pets: **Sometimes** |
| Max. No. Sharing Bath: **2** | Children: **Welcome** |
| Double/pb: **$65** | Smoking: **No** |
| Single/pb: **$55** | Social Drinking: **Permitted** |
| Double/sb: **$55** | |

Marc Haberman is a holistic health practitioner, and his B&B is natural in all senses of the word: it's a simply furnished, water-cooled home that provides a nontoxic, nonallergenic environment. The grounds are landscaped with palm and pine trees. Only whole-grain and natural foods are served here and the drinking water is purified. Soothing professional massages are available by request.

## Quail's Vista Bed & Breakfast ✪
### 826 EAST PALISADES DRIVE, TUCSON, ARIZONA 85737

| | |
|---|---|
| Tel: **(602) 297-5980** | Reduced Rates: **10% weekly** |
| Host: **Barbara Jones** | Breakfast: **Continental** |
| Location: **10 mi. NW of Tucson** | Pets: **No** |
| No. of Rooms: **3** | Children: **No** |
| No. of Private Baths: **2** | Smoking: **No** |
| Double/pb: **$65–$85** | Social Drinking: **Permitted** |
| Open: **All year** | Airport/Station Pickup: **Yes** |

Native American artifacts and Mexican tile make this modern, solar-heated adobe an attractive blend of the local cultures. Fiestaware dishes, a player piano, and grandmother's furniture in the guest room evoke memories of an older generation. From a seat on the redwood deck you can watch the gorgeous sunset and stargaze in the evening. The swim-stream hot tub is available for swimming or soaking. Breakfasts include a cereal buffet with several toppings, coffee, tea, juices, and baked goods. Light snacks may be put in the refrigerator. Your hostess, a professional Tucson tour guide, can help you discover the area's highlights, and maps, brochures, and restaurant menus are always on hand.

## Redbud House Bed & Breakfast
**7002 EAST REDBUD ROAD, TUCSON, ARIZONA 85715**

| | |
|---|---|
| Tel: (520) 721-0218 | Open: **All year** |
| Hosts: **Ken and Wanda Mayer** | Breakfast: **Full** |
| Location: **7 mi. from Rte. 10** | Pets: **No** |
| No. of Rooms: **1** | Children: **No** |
| No. of Private Baths: **1** | Smoking: **No** |
| Double/pb: **$50** | Social Drinking: **Permitted** |
| Single/pb: **$40** | |

The Mayers' comfortable ranch-style brick home is on a residential street bordered by tall pines and palm trees. There is a view of the Catalina Mountains from the porch. Local attractions are the Saguaro National Monument, the Arizona Sonora Desert Museum, Kitt Peak National Observatory, and Sabino Canyon. You are welcome to use the bicycles, barbecue, and TV, or to just relax on the patio. Several fine restaurants and a recreation complex with Olympic-size swimming pool are nearby.

## The Johnstonian B&B ✪
**321 WEST SHERIDAN AVENUE, WILLIAMS, ARIZONA 86046**

| | |
|---|---|
| Tel: (520) 635-2178 | Double/sb: **$50** |
| Best Time to Call: **Before 8 AM; after** | Single/sb: **$45** |
| **1 PM MST** | Suites: **$108** |
| Hosts: **Bill and Pidge Johnston** | Open: **All year** |
| Location: **55 mi. S. of Grand Canyon** | Breakfast: **Full** |
| **National Park** | Pets: **No** |
| No. of Rooms: **4** | Children: **Welcome** |
| Max. No. Sharing Bath: **4** | Smoking: **No** |
| Double/pb: **$65** | Social Drinking: **Permitted** |
| Single/pb: **$60** | |

As old as the century, this two-story Victorian has been carefully restored and decorated in period style. You'll admire the antique oak furniture and the lovely floral wallpapers. In the winter, guests cluster around the wood-burning stove. Pidge's breakfast specialties include Ukrainian potato cakes, blueberry pancakes, and homemade breads.

# CALIFORNIA

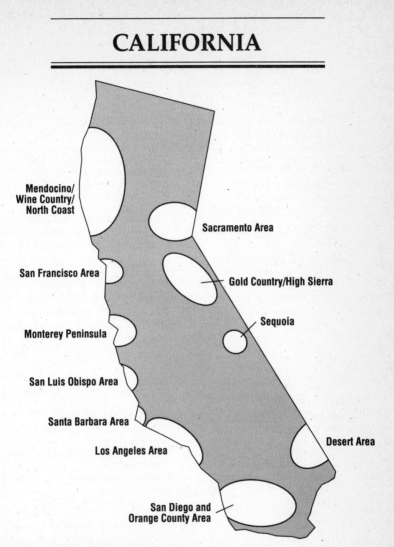

Mendocino/
Wine Country/
North Coast

Sacramento Area

San Francisco Area

Gold Country/High Sierra

Monterey Peninsula

Sequoia

San Luis Obispo Area

Santa Barbara Area

Desert Area

Los Angeles Area

San Diego and
Orange County Area

## Bed & Breakfast California ✪
**3924 EAST 14TH STREET, LONG BEACH, CALIFORNIA 90804**

Tel: (310) 989-0119; (800) 383-3513
Best Time to Call: **Evenings**
Coordinators: **Robin Nahin and Pam
  Hatch**
States/Regions Covered: **Carmel,
  Laguna Beach, Los Angeles,
  Mendocino, Napa, Palm Springs, San**

**Diego, San Francisco, Santa Barbara,
  Yosemite, Tahoe**
Descriptive Directory: **$4**
Rates (Single/Double):
  Modest: **$45 / $75**
  Average: **$76 / $95**
  Luxury: **$96 / Up**

Bed & Breakfast California has 220 listings on their roster. You may choose a beach house in Malibu, a Victorian in San Francisco, a casa in Palm Springs, or an ocean-view suite in Mendocino. Robin and Pam will be glad to help with special occasions, such as parties, honeymoons, weddings, and family reunions. We can also accommodate the handicapped and travelers with pets.

## Eye Openers Bed & Breakfast Reservations ✪
P.O. BOX 694, ALTADENA, CALIFORNIA 91001

Tel: (213) 684-4428; fax: (818) 798-3640
Best Time to Call: 9 AM–5 PM Mon.–Fri.
Coordinators: Ruth Judkins and Betty Cox
States/Regions Covered: Cambria, Laguna Beach, Los Angeles, Palm Springs, Pasadena, San Diego, San Francisco, Santa Barbara, Santa Monica, Yosemite
Descriptive Directory: $2
Rates (Single/Double):
  Modest: $35–$50 / $40–$55
  Average: $50–$85 / $55–$95
  Luxury: $85–$150 / $100–$200
Credit Cards: MC, VISA

Eye Openers Bed & Breakfast Reservations offers accommodations in a variety of beautiful homes, with warm friendly hosts. Ruth and Betty are longtime residents of the Los Angeles/Pasadena area and pride themselves on the personal attention given to guests. They promise to select homes especially for your comfort.

## *DESERT AREA*

## Travellers Repose ✪
P.O. BOX 655, 66920 FIRST STREET, DESERT HOT SPRINGS, CALIFORNIA 92240

Tel: (619) 329-9584
Hosts: Marian and Sam Relkoff
Location: 12 mi. N of Palm Springs
No. of Rooms: 3
No. of Private Baths: 1
Max. No. Sharing Bath: 4
Double/pb: $75
Double/sb: $55–$60
Single/sb: $50–$54
Open: Sept. 1–June 30
Reduced Rates: Weekly; 10% families on 2nd room
Breakfast: Continental
Pets: No
Children: Welcome, over 12
Smoking: No
Social Drinking: Permitted
Airport/Station Pickup: Yes
Foreign Languages: Russian

Bay windows, gingerbread trim, stained-glass windows, and a white picket fence decorate this charming Victorian home. The warm look of oak predominates in floors, wainscoting, and cabinetry. Guest rooms are decorated with hearts, dolls, and teddy bears everywhere. There's a rose bedroom with antiques and lace, a blue-and-white room with a heart motif, and a green room decorated with pine furniture handcrafted by Sam. A patio, pool, and spa complete the amenities. Golf, tennis, museums, galleries, and posh Palm Springs are nearby. Marian graciously serves tea at 4 PM.

## Old Trails Inn
**304 BROADWAY, NEEDLES, CALIFORNIA 92363**

| | |
|---|---|
| Tel: **(619) 326-3523; (800) 326-3528** | Breakfast: **Continental** |
| Best Time to Call: **9 AM–6 PM** | Credit Cards: **AMEX, DISC, MC, VISA** |
| Hosts: **Hank and Edna Wilde** | Pets: **Sometimes** |
| No. of Rooms: **4** | Children: **Yes** |
| No. of Private Baths: **4** | Smoking: **No** |
| Double/pb: **$55** | Social Drinking: **Permitted** |
| Single/pb: **$50** | Airport/Station Pickup: **Yes** |
| Open: **All year** | |

Old Trails Inn is located in the center of the California-Nevada-Arizona tri-state area, where the many activities include golfing, fishing, swimming, boating, gambling, and ghost town and desert exploring. Rumor has it that a scene in *The Grapes of Wrath* was filmed at this renovated cabin court built in the 1930s. While the exteriors haven't changed much, the individually decorated rooms now boast more luxury and comfort than was the norm in the Depression years. Your hosts are longtime residents—and history, bicycle, and travel buffs. Hank is a retired gas company supervisor and real estate investor, while Edna assists in all family endeavors.

## Hotel Nipton ✪
**72 NIPTON ROAD, NIPTON, CALIFORNIA 92364**

| | |
|---|---|
| Tel: **(619) 856-2335** | Breakfast: **Continental** |
| Best Time to Call: **8 AM–6 PM** | Other Meals: **Available** |
| Hosts: **Jerry and Roxanne Freeman** | Credit Cards: **MC, VISA** |
| Location: **10 mi. from I-15** | Pets: **No** |
| No. of Rooms: **4** | Children: **Welcome** |
| Max. No. Sharing Bath: **4** | Smoking: **No** |
| Double/sb: **$50** | Social Drinking: **Permitted** |
| Open: **All year** | Foreign Languages: **Spanish** |
| Reduced Rates: **Group** | |

The population of Nipton is 30! The recently restored hotel, with its foot-thick adobe walls, was built in 1904 and is located in the Mojave National Preserve. Nipton is in the heart of gold-mining territory, 30 minutes from Lake Mojave's Cottonwood Cove. You are welcome to

relax on the porch or in the outdoor Jacuzzi. Continental breakfast is served in the lobby at your convenience.

## GOLD COUNTRY/HIGH SIERRA

### Silver Spur Bed & Breakfast ✪

**44625 SILVER SPUR TRAIL, AHWAHNEE, CALIFORNIA 93601**

| | |
|---|---|
| Tel: **(209) 683-2896** | Reduced Rates: **Nov. 1–May 1** |
| Best Time to Call: **After 3 PM** |   **Sun.–Thurs. $45, Fri.–Sat. $55** |
| Hosts: **Patty and Bryan Hays** | Breakfast: **Continental** |
| Location: **50 mi. N of Fresno** | Credit Cards: **DISC, MC, VISA** |
| No. of Rooms: **2** | Pets: **Sometimes** |
| No. of Private Baths: **2** | Children: **Welcome** |
| Double/pb: **$50–$60** | Smoking: **No** |
| Open: **All year** | Social Drinking: **Permitted** |

Silver Spur Bed & Breakfast is nestled in the Sierra Nevadas, just off historic Highway 49—key to the California Gold Country near the south and west gates of Yosemite National Park and minutes from many outdoor sports. This contemporary log home was built by Bryan and features beautiful clean rooms with private entrances, comfortable beds, and tasteful Southwestern decor. Outdoor resting and dining areas boast outstanding Sierra views. A healthy Continental breakfast is served daily. Patty is a part-time paralegal and gardening enthusiast and Bryan is a builder. Come enjoy Yosemite, and be treated to old-fashioned hospitality.

# The Matlick House ✪
## 1313 ROWAN LANE, BISHOP, CALIFORNIA 93514

Tel: **(619) 873-3133; (800) 898-3133**
Best Time to Call: **8 AM–8 PM**
Hosts: **Ray and Barbara Showalter**
Location: **1 mi. N of Bishop**
No. of Rooms: **5**
No. of Private Baths: **5**
Suites: **$75–$85**
Open: **All year**

Reduced Rates: **Corporate discounts**
Breakfast: **Full**
Pets: **No**
Children: **Welcome, over 14**
Smoking: **No**
Social Drinking: **Permitted**
Airport/Station Pickup: **Yes**

Hikers, backpackers, fishermen, and skiers are drawn to this turn-of-the-century ranch house in Owens Valley, which separates the White Mountains from the Sierra Nevadas. Energetic guests can reserve picnic lunches and explore the area on their own. Of course, you may not be hungry for hours after a full breakfast of eggs, bacon, sausage, fresh-squeezed orange juice, sweet bread, homemade biscuits, and coffee or tea. This is your home away from home. A gallery showcasing local artists and a fine dinner restaurant are within walking distance.

# The Heirloom ✪
## P.O. BOX 322, 214 SHAKLEY LANE, IONE, CALIFORNIA 95640

Tel: **(209) 274-4468**
Hosts: **Melisande Hubbs and Patricia Cross**
Location: **35 mi. E of Sacramento**
No. of Rooms: **6**
No. of Private Baths: **4**
Max. No. Sharing Bath: **2**
Double/pb: **$75–$92**
Single/pb: **$65–$82**
Double/sb: **$60–$75**

Single/sb: **$55–$70**
Open: **All year**
Reduced Rates: **Weekly**
Breakfast: **Full**
Pets: **No**
Children: **Welcome, over 10**
Smoking: **No**
Social Drinking: **Permitted**
Airport/Station Pickup: **Yes**

Nestled in the Sierra foothills, yet close to the historic gold mines, wineries, antique shops, and museums, this 1863 mansion, with its lovely balconies and fireplaces, is a classic example of antebellum architecture. It is furnished with a combination of family treasures and period pieces. Patricia and Melisande's hearty breakfast includes such delights as quiche, crêpes, soufflé, and fresh fruits. Afternoon refreshments are always offered.

# Little Valley Inn ✪
## 3483 BROOKS ROAD, MARIPOSA, CALIFORNIA 95338

Tel: **(209) 742-6204; (800) 889-5444**
Hosts: **Kay and Robert Hewitt**

Location: **8 mi. S of Mariposa**
No. of Rooms: **3**

| | |
|---|---|
| No. of Private Baths: **3** | Credit Cards: **AMEX, MC, VISA** |
| Double/pb: **$80** | Pets: **No** |
| Suites: **$100, sleeps 4** | Children: **Welcome** |
| Open: **All year** | Smoking: **No** |
| Reduced Rates: **Available** | Social Drinking: **Permitted** |
| Breakfast: **Continental** | |

Little Valley Inn is a special place to stay near Yosemite National Park, in California's Gold Country. Rooms are spacious and modern, with decks, refrigerator, individually controlled heat and air-conditioning and in-room coffee and tea. You may want to hike or picnic on the four acres among the huge old oaks, pines, and historic Indian grinding stones while watching the deer or birds. Or pan for gold on the 1000 feet of creek where the old forty-niners did—Kay and Robert will be happy to show you how. There is a gift shop on the property with gold prospecting items, books, cowboy hats, and authentic Indian handcrafts. Fax service is also available.

## Chaney House ✪
**4725 WEST LAKE BOULEVARD, P.O. BOX 7852, TAHOE CITY, CALIFORNIA 96145**

| | |
|---|---|
| Tel: **(916) 525-7333** | No. of Private Baths: **4** |
| Hosts: **Gary and Lori Chaney** | Double/pb: **$100** |
| Location: **50 mi. W of Reno, Nevada** | Suites: **$105–$110** |
| No. of Rooms: **4** | Guest Apartment: **$115** |

Open: **All year**
Breakfast: **Full**
Pets: **No**
Children: **Welcome, over 12**

Smoking: **No**
Social Drinking: **Permitted**
Minimum Stay: **2 nights, weekends**

Built on the Lake Tahoe shore by Italian stonemasons, Chaney House has an almost medieval quality, with its dramatically arched windows, extra thick walls, and enormous fireplace. The rear of the house faces the waterfront, where the Chaneys' private beach and pier beckon to guests. A water-skiing boat will even be placed at your disposal, by advance arrangement. Winter visitors can choose from 19 nearby ski areas. All the bedrooms have wood paneling and antique furniture. Breakfasts feature such foods as French toast and quiche.

## LOS ANGELES AREA

## Bed & Breakfast Southwest Reservation Service—California ✪
**6916 EAST MARIPOSA, SCOTTSDALE, ARIZONA 85251**

Tel: **(602) 947-9704; (800) 762-9704**
Best Time to Call: **10 AM–8 PM**
Coordinators: **Jo and Jim Cummings**
States/Regions Covered: **Southern California**

Descriptive Directory: **$3, SASE**
Rates (Single/Double):
  Modest: **$40–$60**
  Average: **$50–$65**
  Luxury: **$65–up**

Specializing in unique homestays with private suites and guest houses, this service offers exciting experiences to the traveler coming to the Southwest. Jo and Jim are residents of the area and can give firsthand information about sport activities, dining opportunities, art exhibits, and answer your questions about the great Southwest. The Cummingses will be happy to help you plan your vacation with gracious hosts throughout the region. Bed & Breakfast Southwest is always looking for unique hosts and enthusiastic guests.

## El Camino Real Bed & Breakfast
**P.O. BOX 5598, SHERMAN OAKS, CALIFORNIA 91403-5598**

Tel: **(818) 501-8218**
Best Time to Call: **Evenings**
Coordinator: **Lisa Reinstein**
States/Regions Covered: **Anaheim, Beverly Hills, Malibu, Palm Springs, San Diego, San Fernando Valley; Sun Valley, ID; Zion, UT**

Rates (Single/Double):
  Modest: **$40–45 / $45–50**
  Average: **$50–$60 / $55–$75**
  Luxury: **$60 / $115**
Credit Cards: **No**
Minimum Stay: **2 nights**

This service brings the tradition of California hospitality begun with the Franciscan missions to the present-day traveler. Homes are in beach communities conveniently located to such attractions as Disneyland, Knotts Berry Farm, and the movie studios. Average accommodations are in upper-middle-class homes with swimming pools/spas, except in hilly areas. Lisa offers modest apartments with simple furnishings and a luxurious private guest house on an estate with a hot tub and swimming pool. All hosts are longtime residents of California, familiar with the restaurants, tourist attractions, and the best ways of getting to them.

## Fran's Around a Corner Country Cottage ○

**1584 NORTH CYPRESS STREET, LA HABRA HEIGHTS, CALIFORNIA 90631**

| | |
|---|---|
| Tel: **(310) 690-6422** | Breakfast: **Continental** |
| Best Time to Call: **After 7 PM,** | Pets: **No** |
| **weekdays** | Children: **Welcome** |
| Host: **Fran Cooper** | Smoking: **No** |
| Location: **20 mi. E of Los Angeles** | Social Drinking: **Permitted** |
| Guest cottage: **$150, sleeps 4** | Minimum Stay: **2 days** |
| Open: **All year** | Airport Pickup: **Yes** |
| Reduced Rates: **10% seniors; 10%** | |
| **families** | |

Just around the corner, on a country road, sits this private one-bedroom cottage; its kitchenette is fully equipped, with a refrigerator, microwave, coffeemaker, cooking pans, and eating utensils. The quiet location puts the attractions of southern California at your feet—Disneyland, Knotts Berry Farm, Movieland Wax Museum, and shopping malls are nearby, and it's a 45-minute drive to the beach.

## Casablanca Villa ○

**449 NORTH DETROIT STREET, LOS ANGELES, CALIFORNIA 90036**

| | |
|---|---|
| Tel: **(213) 938-4794** | Breakfast: **Continental** |
| Host: **Suzanne Moultout** | Pets: **No** |
| No. of Rooms: **1** | Children: **No** |
| Double/sb: **$60** | Smoking: **No** |
| Single/sb: **$50** | Social Drinking: **No** |
| Open: **All year** | Foreign Languages: **French** |

Suzanne Moultout welcomes you to her Spanish-style house located on a quiet, attractive street. Here, guests can enjoy the convenience of being close to West Hollywood, downtown, and Beverly Center, while having a comfortable home base. Your hostess offers an attractive guest room and a shady yard with fruit trees. She will gladly direct you to such nearby sights as Hollywood Hills, CBS Studios, and the beaches. Even if you don't have a car, the area is quite convenient, with a bus stop located within walking distance.

## Laurel Bed and Breakfast ✪
P.O. BOX 67854, LOS ANGELES, CALIFORNIA 90067

| | |
|---|---|
| Tel: **(310) 475-6159** | Open: **All year** |
| Hosts: **Fred and Fredi Daitch** | Breakfast: **Continental** |
| No. of Rooms: **1** | Pets: **Sometimes** |
| No. of Private Baths: **1** | Children: **Welcome** |
| Double/pb: **$60–$80** | Smoking: **No** |
| Single/pb: **$55–$75** | Social Drinking: **No** |

Laurel Bed and Breakfast was named in honor of Stan Laurel, with whom one of the owners had a correspondence when she was a child; copies of their letters line the walls. The charming basement guest room has a private entrance. Laurel B&B is ideally located in a great residential area, within two miles of UCLA and UCLA Medical Center, Beverly Hills, and Century City. It's four miles to Santa Monica beach—be sure to ride the 1915 carousel featured in movies, including *The Sting*. An eighteen-hole golf course, numerous restaurants, and a shopping mall are all within walking distance. Laurel Bed and Breakfast is also an excellent base for visiting L.A.'s numerous world-class museums, movie studios, theme parks and other attractions.

## Hideaway House ✪
8441 MELVIN AVENUE, NORTHRIDGE, CALIFORNIA 91324

| | |
|---|---|
| Tel: **(818) 349-5421** | Open: **All year** |
| Best Time to Call: **6–10 PM** | Breakfast: **Full** |
| Hosts: **Dean and Dorothy Dennis** | Pets: **Sometimes** |
| Location: **20 mi. NW of Los Angeles** | Children: **No** |
| No. of Rooms: **1** | Smoking: **No** |
| No. of Private Baths: **1** | Social Drinking: **Permitted** |
| Double/pb: **$55–$60** | Airport/Station Pickup: **Yes** |

Located in a beautiful Los Angeles suburb, this country ranch home on over an acre in the San Fernando Valley is a good base for exploring southern California. It's 30 minutes to the beach, and 50 minutes to Disneyland. Freeways, shops, and restaurants are nearby. Dean and Dorothy welcome you to their art- and antique-filled home, and will provide local guide service by prior arrangement.

## The Whites' House ✪
17122 FAYSMITH AVENUE, TORRANCE, CALIFORNIA 90504

| | |
|---|---|
| Tel: **(310) 324-6164** | Open: **All year** |
| Host: **Margaret White** | Reduced Rates: **Weekly, monthly** |
| Location: **5 mi. S of Los Angeles Intl.** | Breakfast: **Continental** |
| **Airport** | Pets: **No** |
| No. of Rooms: **2** | Children: **No** |
| No. of Private Baths: **2** | Smoking: **No** |
| Double/pb: **$30–$35** | Social Drinking: **Permitted** |
| Single/pb: **$25** | |

This contemporary home, with its fireplaces, deck, and patio, is located on a quiet street in an unpretentious neighborhood. The airport and lovely beaches are 15 minutes away. Disneyland, Knotts Berry Farm, Universal Studio Tours, and Hollywood are 30 minutes from the door. Use the laundry facilities or kitchen; Margaret wants you to feel perfectly at home.

## Coleen's California Casa ✪
### BOX 9302, WHITTIER, CALIFORNIA 90608

| | |
|---|---|
| Tel: **(310) 699-8427** | Open: **All year** |
| Best Time to Call: **7 AM–7 PM** | Reduced Rates: **5% families; weekly** |
| Host: **Coleen Davis** | Breakfast: **Full** |
| Location: **8 mi. E of Los Angeles** | Other Meals: **Available** |
| No. of Rooms: **7** | Pets: **Sometimes** |
| No. of Private Baths: **6** | Children: **Welcome, over 5** |
| Double/pb: **$85** | Smoking: **No** |
| Single/pb: **$75** | Social Drinking: **Permitted** |
| Double/sb: **$75** | Miniumum Stay: **2 nights** |
| Single/sb: **$65** | Airport/Station Pickup: **Yes** |
| Suites: **$110, sleeps 5** | Foreign Languages: **Spanish** |

Find your own paradise at this hilltop B&B in a historic Quaker town. Enjoy sunshine and serenity as you sit on the luxuriant patio sampling the full breakfast prepared by your host, a home economist. Dinners are available by prior arrangement. Coleen will be happy to direct you to Disneyland, Knotts Berry Farm, and many other nearby Los Angeles attractions. Tennis courts, jogging and hiking paths, and Whittier College are also close at hand. After sightseeing, refresh yourself with wine and cheese and watch the sunset and the city lights illuminate the sky.

## *MENDOCINO/WINE COUNTRY/NORTH COAST*

## Hillcrest B&B ✪
### 3225 LAKE COUNTY HIGHWAY, CALISTOGA, CALIFORNIA 94515

| | |
|---|---|
| Tel: **(707) 942-6334** | Double/sb: **$45–$70** |
| Best Time to Call: **After 8 PM** | Open: **All year** |
| Host: **Debbie O'Gorman** | Breakfast: **Continental** |
| Location: **2 mi. N of Calistoga** | Pets: **Welcome** |
| No. of Rooms: **6** | Children: **No** |
| No. of Private Baths: **4** | Smoking: **Permitted** |
| Max. No. Sharing Bath: **4** | Social Drinking: **Permitted** |
| Double/pb: **$60–$90** | |

Hillcrest has a breathtaking valley view of Mt. St. Helena, in an area famed for its wineries and spas. Without leaving the B&B's 36-acre property, guests can hike, swim, fish, or stay indoors and play the

Steinway grand piano. The house was built by Debbie's great-great-grandfather, and you'll see cherished family heirlooms at every turn. An elegant Continental breakfast of juice, coffee, fresh fruit, and baked goods is served on antique china and silver. For those of you who do not mind paying a higher rate, 3 rooms are available.

## Scarlett's Country Inn ✪
### 3918 SILVERADO TRAIL NORTH, CALISTOGA, CALIFORNIA 94515

Tel: **(707) 942-6669**
Best Time to Call: **9 AM–5 PM**
Host: **Scarlett Dwyer**
Location: **75 mi. N of San Francisco;**
   **30 mi. from I-80, Napa exit**
No. of Rooms: **3**
No. of Private Baths: **3**
Double/pb: **$95**
Single/pb: **$80**

Suites: **$115–$150**
Guest Cottage: **$305; sleeps 6**
Open: **All year**
Breakfast: **Full**
Pets: **No**
Children: **Welcome**
Smoking: **No**
Social Drinking: **Permitted**
Foreign Languages: **Spanish**

This Inn is an intimate retreat tucked away in a small canyon in the heart of the famed Napa Valley, just minutes away from wineries and spas. Tranquility, green lawns, and a refreshing swimming pool await you in this peaceful woodland setting. An ample breakfast, featuring freshly squeezed juice, sweet rolls, and freshly ground coffee, is served on the deck, at poolside, or in your own sitting room. All rooms have separate entrances, queen-size beds, and luxurious linens.

## Muktip Manor ✪
### 12540 LAKESHORE DRIVE, CLEARLAKE, CALIFORNIA 95422

Tel: **(707) 994-9571**
Hosts: **Jerry and Nadine Schiffman**
Location: **101 mi. N of San Francisco**
No. of Rooms: **1 suite**
No. of Private Baths: **1**
Suite: **$65**

Open: **All year**
Breakfast: **Full**
Pets: **Welcome**
Children: **Sometimes**
Smoking: **Permitted**
Social Drinking: **Permitted**

Nadine and Jerry traded the often-frenzied San Francisco lifestyle for an uncomplicated existence by the largest lake in the state. They do not offer Victoriana, priceless antiques, or gourmet food. They do provide comfortable accommodations in an unpretentious beach house, a place to relax on the deck, and the use of their private beach and bicycles. They enjoy windsurfing and canoeing, and have been known to give instruction to interested guests. The motto of Muktip Manor is, "If you wish company, we are conversationalists; if you wish privacy, we're invisible."

# Inn Oz ✪

**13311 LAKESHORE DRIVE, P.O. BOX 1046, CLEARLAKE PARK, CALIFORNIA 95424**

Tel: **(707) 995-0853**
Best Time to Call: **Between 8 AM and 6 PM PST**
Hosts: **Pauline and Charley Stephanski**
Location: **100 mi. N of San Francisco**
No. of Rooms: **1**
No. of Private Baths: **1**
Double/pb: **$60**

Open: **All year**
Reduced Rates: **10% seniors**
Breakfast: **Full, Continental**
Pets: **Yes**
Children: **Welcome**
Smoking: **Permitted**
Social Drinking: **Permitted**

On the shores of California's largest freshwater lake, two hours north of San Francisco by automobile (and faster by house in a cyclone), you'll find country so beautiful it could have inspired L. Frank Baum's tales of the land of Oz. Savor unsurpassed sunsets, full moons, and starry heavens over Clear Lake from your bed or on your private patio. Your spacious chamber has a private entrance, a wood-burning fireplace, and a fully equipped kitchenette; the bathroom has a shower and a tub with a portable whirlpool. Pianists are encouraged to tickle the ivories of the upright Steinway. For additional fun, ask your hosts to show you the doll's house Pauline's grandfather built in 1938.

# "An Elegant Victorian Mansion" Bed & Breakfast Experience

**1406 'C' STREET, EUREKA, CALIFORNIA 95501**

Tel: **(707) 444-3144, 442-5594**
Best Time to Call: **2–12 PM EST**
Hosts: **Doug and Lily Vieyra**
No. of Rooms: **4**
No. of Private Baths: **2**
Max. No. Sharing Bath: **4**
Double/pb: **$95–$115**
Double/sb: **$75–$110**
Single/sb: **$65–$85**
Suite: **$95–$145**
Open: **All year**

Reduced Rates: **Available**
Breakfast: **Full**
Credit Cards: **MC, VISA**
Pets: **No**
Children: **Welcome, over 15**
Smoking: **No**
Social Drinking: **Permitted**
Airport/Station Pickup: **Yes**
Foreign Languages: **Dutch, French, German**

Just a few blocks from Eureka's historic Old Town, on a rise overlooking the city and Humboldt Bay, sits "An Elegant Victorian Mansion." Opulent and gracious, it is one of Eureka's most luxurious homes, offering spirited camaraderie and five-star service. A visit here is like

a festive vacation with one's best friends. Warm and friendly hosts serve breakfast in the regal splendor of a National Historic Landmark.

## Gingerbread Mansion Inn
**400 BERDING STREET, FERNDALE, CALIFORNIA 95536**

| | |
|---|---|
| Tel: **(707) 786-4000; (800) 952-4136** | Reduced Rates: **Available** |
| Host: **Ken Torbert** | Breakfast: **Full** |
| Location: **15 mi S of Eureka** | Credit Cards: **AMEX, MC, VISA** |
| No. of Rooms: **9** | Pets: **No** |
| No. of Private Baths: **9** | Children: **Welcome, over 10** |
| Double/pb: **$90–$185** | Smoking: **No** |
| Single/pb: **$75–$170** | Social Drinking: **Permitted** |
| Suites: **$120–$185** | Minimum Stay: **2 nights Saturday,** |
| Open: **All year** | **holidays, and special events** |

Painted peach and yellow, surrounded by English gardens, this striking Victorian landmark is one of northern California's most photographed homes. Guests have a choice not only of bedrooms, but of parlors as well: two are stocked with books and games, a third is set up for afternoon tea, and the fourth displays the Inn's own 1000-piece jigsaw puzzle in various stages of completion. In your bedroom there are a bathrobe in the dresser and a hand-dipped chocolate by the bedside. Forgot your raingear? Not to worry, umbrellas are available. In good weather, borrow a house bicycle. For breakfast, homemade muffins, fruit, local cheeses, homemade granola, baked egg dishes, and beverages are served in the formal dining room overlooking the garden.

# Campbell Ranch Inn ✪
## 1475 CANYON ROAD, GEYSERVILLE, CALIFORNIA 95441

| | |
|---|---|
| Tel: **(707) 857-3476; (800) 959-3878** | Open: **All year** |
| Best Time to Call: **10 AM–8 PM** | Breakfast: **Full** |
| Hosts: **Mary Jane and Jerry Campbell** | Credit Cards: **AMEX, MC, VISA** |
| Location: **1.6 mi. from Rte. 101,** | Pets: **No** |
| **Canyon Road exit** | Children: **Welcome, over 10** |
| No. of Rooms: **5** | Smoking: **No** |
| No. of Private Baths: **5** | Social Drinking: **Permitted** |
| Double/pb: **$85–$145** | Minimum Stay: **2 nights weekends** |
| Guest Cottage: **$165** | Airport/Station Pickup: **Yes** |

"Spectacular!" and "charming!" are expressions most often used when guests describe their stay at this picture-perfect hilltop home surrounded by 35 acres in the heart of the Sonoma County wine country. The spacious bedrooms, each with a king-size bed, are handsomely furnished; several have balconies where views of mountains and vineyards are a backdrop to the colorful flower gardens. Breakfast, beautifully served, features a selection of fresh fruit, choice of gourmet egg dishes, homemade breads and cakes, and a variety of beverages. You can burn off the calories on the Campbells' tennis court or in their swimming pool, or borrow a bike to tour the wineries. Water sports and fishing are less than four miles away. Jerry will be happy to make your dinner reservations at one of the area's fine restaurants, but leave room for Mary Jane's dessert, always served "at home."

# Palisades Paradise B&B ✪
## 1200 PALISADES AVENUE, REDDING, CALIFORNIA 96003

| | |
|---|---|
| Tel: **(916) 223-5305; (800) 382-4649** | Open: **All year** |
| Best Time to Call: **Evenings** | Reduced Rates: **Available** |
| Host: **Gail Goetz** | Breakfast: **Continental, plus weekdays;** |
| Location: **1¼ mi. from Rte. I-5 exit** | **full weekends** |
| **Hilltop Dr.** | Credit Cards: **AMEX, MC, VISA** |
| No. of Rooms: **2** | Pets: **No** |
| Max. No. Sharing Bath: **4** | Children: **Welcome, over 6** |
| Double/sb: **$65–$75** | Smoking: **No** |
| Single/sb: **$60–$70** | Social Drinking: **Permitted** |

Enjoy breathtakingly beautiful views from the patio and spa deck of this contemporary riverside home near Shasta College and Simpson College. Stay in either the Cozy Retreat or the Sunset Suite, both aptly named. In the morning, Gail serves ample breakfasts, with gourmet coffee, pastries, and her own Palisades fruit puffs.

# Hilltop House B&B

**9550 ST. HELENA ROAD, ST. HELENA, CALIFORNIA 94574**

| | |
|---|---|
| Tel: **(707) 944-0880** | Breakfast: **Full** |
| Hosts: **Annette and Bill Gevarter** | Credit Cards: **AMEX, MC, VISA** |
| Location: **5 mi. from Rte. 29** | Pets: **No** |
| No. of Rooms: **3** | Children: **Welcome** |
| No. of Private Baths: **3** | Smoking: **No** |
| Double/pb: **$105–$175** | Social Drinking: **Permitted** |
| Open: **All year** | Minimum Stay: **2 nights weekends,** |
| Reduced Rates: **10% Jan. 1–Apr. 15** | **Apr. 15–Nov. 30** |

Annette and Bill built their contemporary country retreat to follow the contours of the Mayacama Mountains. The house is surrounded by 135 acres at the top of the ridge separating the wine regions of Napa and Sonoma. The unspoiled wilderness includes a garden of native plants, shrubs, and the sounds of hummingbirds and other wildlife. A 2000-square-foot deck with hot tub provides the perfect spot for enjoying the panoramic views. The airy guest rooms are comfortably decorated with a combination of antiques and contemporary pieces, and each has spectacular views and a private entrance onto the deck. Your hosts serve a generous breakfast of fresh fruit, eggs, cheese, and yogurt, with fresh-baked breads and muffins. They also welcome you for afternoon snacks and a glass of sherry in the evening. Hilltop House is 12 minutes from St. Helena, and 30 minutes from Napa. The historic town of Calistoga, popular for its restorative hot mineral water, mud baths, massages, and fine restaurants, is located nearby.

# Vichy Hot Springs

**2605 VICHY SPRINGS ROAD, UKIAH, CALIFORNIA 95482**

| | |
|---|---|
| Tel: **(707) 462-9515** | Open: **All year** |
| Best Time to Call: **9 AM–9 PM** | Breakfast: **Continental** |
| Hosts: **Gilbert and Marjorie Ashoff** | Credit Cards: **AMEX, DC, MC, VISA** |
| Location: **105 mi. N of San Francisco** | Pets: **No** |
| No. of Rooms: **14** | Children: **Welcome** |
| No. of Private Baths: **14** | Smoking: **No** |
| Double/pb: **$130** | Social Drinking: **Permitted** |
| Single/pb: **$85** | Airport Pickup: **Yes** |
| Guest Cottage: **$160–$170** | Foreign Languages: **Spanish** |

Choose between twelve individually decorated rooms and two self-contained cottages at this B&B spa. Vichy features naturally sparkling, 90-degree mineral baths, a 104-degree pool, and an Olympic-size pool, along with 700 private acres with trails and roads for hiking, jogging, picnicking, and mountain biking. Staff members offer Swedish massage, reflexology, herbal facials, and acupressure. Set amid native oak, madrone, manzanita, bay, fir, pine, and buckeye, this quiet resort will leave you refreshed and invigorated.

## MONTEREY PENINSULA

# Happy Landing Inn ✪
**P.O. BOX 2619, CARMEL, CALIFORNIA 93921**

| | |
|---|---|
| Tel: **(408) 624-7917** | Credit Cards: **MC, VISA** |
| Best Time to Call: **8:30 AM–9 PM** | Pets: **No** |
| Hosts: **Robert Ballard and Dick Stewart** | Children: **Welcome, over 12** |
| Location: **120 mi. S of San Francisco** | Smoking: **No** |
| No. of Rooms: **7** | Social Drinking: **Permitted** |
| No. of Private Baths: **7** | Minimum Stay: **2 nights weekends** |
| Double/pb: **$90–155** | Foreign Languages: **Japanese,** |
| Open: **All year** | **Portuguese, Spanish** |
| Breakfast: **Continental** | |

Located on Monte Verde between 5th and 6th Streets, this Hansel and Gretel– style inn is a charming and romantic place to stay. Rooms with cathedral ceilings open onto a beautiful garden with gazebo, pond, and flagstone paths. Lovely antiques and personal touches, including breakfast served in your room, make your stay special.

# Babbling Brook Inn ✪
**1025 LAUREL STREET, SANTA CRUZ, CALIFORNIA 95060**

| | |
|---|---|
| Tel: **(408) 427-2437; (800) 866-1131** | Reduced Rates: **Available** |
| Best Time to Call: **7 AM–11 PM** | Breakfast: **Full** |
| Host: **Helen King** | Credit Cards: **AMEX, DISC, MC, VISA** |
| Location: **2 blocks from Hwy. 1** | Pets: **No** |
| No. of Rooms: **12** | Children: **Welcome, over 12** |
| No. of Private Baths: **12** | Smoking: **No** |
| Double/pb: **$85–$165** | Foreign Languages: **French, Spanish** |
| Open: **All year** | |

Cascading waterfalls, a brook, historic waterwheel gardens, and red-wood trees surround this country inn. The oldest part of the house was built in 1909 on what was once a tannery and flour mill. Over the years, the house was changed by a number of owners, including the counsel to a czar and a woman known as the countess, who added several rooms and a balcony. It is a rustic, rambling retreat decorated in French country furnishings. Most rooms have a cozy fireplace, private deck, and outside entrance. Your host has owned restaurants and hotels in South America and is an expert in making 2 people or 100 feel equally at home. Helen is a gourmet cook, as you will see from her breakfast repertoire of omelettes, stratas, and frittatas. This historic inn is walking distance from the ocean, boardwalk, shops, and tennis courts.

## Downeyland Bed & Breakfast ✪
### 4205 VINE HILL LANE, SANTA CRUZ, CALIFORNIA 95065

| | |
|---|---|
| Tel: (408) 425-8065 | Reduced Rates: **Available** |
| Hosts: **Leah and Jim Downey** | Breakfast: **Full** |
| No. of Rooms: **3** | Other Meals: **Available** |
| No. of Private Baths: **3** | Pets: **No** |
| Double/pb: **$75–$85** | Children: **Welcome, over 9** |
| Single/sb: **$45** | Smoking: **No** |
| Suites: **$85–$115** | Social Drinking: **Permitted** |
| Open: **All year** | |

This charming home offers antique furnishings, a parlor where guests can gather, a porch and a deck where you can enjoy a select breakfast. Upon afternoon arrival champagne or a fresh fruit drink along with hors d'oeuvres are served. The gardens surrounding Downeyland are breathtaking, with acres of redwoods and a private grove along a stream with a large table perfect for a picnic, reading or a chess game. Located a short distance from the house are many attractions, including beaches, boardwalk, and the 400-mile sanctuary of Monterey Bay. Leah and Jim provide personal assistance with entertainment, restaurants, and sightseeing.

## Inn Laguna Creek ✪
### 2727 SMITH GRADE, SANTA CRUZ, CALIFORNIA 95060

| | |
|---|---|
| Tel: (408) 425-0692 | Open: **All year** |
| Best Time to Call: **9 AM–8 PM** | Breakfast: **Full** |
| Hosts: **Jim and Gay Holley** | Credit Cards: **AMEX, MC, VISA** |
| Location: **8 mi. N of Santa Cruz** | Pets: **No** |
| No. of Rooms: **3** | Children: **Welcome** |
| Double/pb: **$98–$125** | Smoking: **No** |
| Suite: **$125** | Social Drinking: **Permitted** |

A distinctive modern residence with a curved roof, this B&B nestles in the redwood forests of the Santa Cruz Mountains. The large rooms have queen-size beds, down comforters, a private deck overlooking the creek, and a private entrance. The sitting room boasts a wet bar, stereo, VCR, and games. A sunning deck with a spa, picnic area, and acres of gardens are yours to enjoy. There are lots of things to do, from hiking, biking, surfing, and beachcombing to whale watching, wine tasting, and antiquing. Sightseers will want to add Roaring Camp and Big Trees Railroad, Mystery Spot, Redwood State Parks, Lighthouse Point, and Mission Santa Cruz to their itineraries. A country-style breakfast is served with special attention to dietary restrictions. Herbal tea, cookies, fresh fruit, and popcorn are always available. A vegetarian breakfast is available with advance notice.

# Jasmine Cottage ✪
**731 RIVERSIDE AVENUE, SANTA CRUZ, CALIFORNIA 95060**

Tel: **(408) 429-1415**
Host: **Dorothy Allen**
Location: **1 mi. from Rte 17 or 1 exit from Ocean St.**
No. of Rooms: **1**
No. of Private Baths: **1**
Double/pb: **$65**
Single/pb: **$45**
Open: **All year**

Breakfast: **Full**
Credit Cards: **MC, VISA**
Other Meals: **Available**
Pets: **No**
Children: **Welcome**
Smoking: **No**
Social Drinking: **Permitted**
Airport/Station Pickup: **Yes**

Jasmine Cottage offers easy access to many of Santa Cruz's favorite spots—the boardwalk and Pacific Garden Mall are within walking distance. Summertime presents opportunities to attend the Cabrillo Music Festival and Shakespeare Santa Cruz. Your room, which has a private entrance, is furnished in the style of a 1910 Edwardian bungalow, with a full-size or single bed, TV, stereo, and other modern comforts. Upon arrival, you'll find a complimentary tray of wine and cheese in your room. Dorothy's breakfast specialties include vegetable quiche and buckwheat pancakes.

# Redwood Reflections ✪
**4600 SMITH GRADE, SANTA CRUZ, CALIFORNIA 95060**

Tel: **(408) 423-7221**
Best Time to Call: **Evenings**
Hosts: **Ed and Dory Strong**
Location: **70 mi. S of San Francisco**
No. of Rooms: **2**
No. of Private Baths: **2**
Double/pb: **$75**
Suite: **$85**

Open: **All year**
Reduced Rates: **10% seniors, disabled**
Breakfast: **Full**
Credit Cards: **MC, VISA**
Pets: **No**
Children: **Welcome, over 7**
Smoking: **No**
Social Drinking: **Permitted**

Nestled in the Santa Cruz Mountains, Redwood Reflections offers ten unspoiled acres of giant redwoods and trails. The rambling, rustic home is paneled throughout, with lots of windows, and furnished in country antiques. Each secluded room provides a sitting area, private bath, TV, queen-size bed, down comforters, and a romantic fountain and fireplace. Guests may enjoy the spa and fulfill childhood fantasies concocting delicious treats from the antique soda fountain. Things to do include hiking, wine tasting, and exploring nearby beaches and numerous state parks in the area. A country-style breakfast is prepared on an antique wood stove. Waffles piled high with fresh berries and country hash browns are favorites of guests.

# Knighttime Bed and Breakfast ✪

**890 CALABASAS ROAD, WATSONVILLE, CALIFORNIA 95076**

| | |
|---|---|
| Tel: **(408) 684-0528** | Open: **All year** |
| Best Time to Call: **8–10 AM; 5–7 PM** | Breakfast: **Full** |
| Hosts: **Diane Knight and Ray Miller** | Other Meals: **Available** |
| Location: **90 mi. S of San Francisco** | Pets: **Sometimes** |
| No. of Rooms: **1** | Children: **Welcome** |
| No. of Private Baths: **1** | Smoking: **No** |
| Double/pb: **$60** | Social Drinking: **Permitted** |
| Single/pb: **$50** | |

A wooden home with a pitched roof and wide porches, Knighttime is set on 26 wooded acres just a few minutes' drive from the beaches between Santa Cruz and Monterey. Sunlight bathes the interior filled with art, pine cabinetry, and country comforts. Eclectic furnishings include some antiques as well as reproductions and wicker. The main floor has a country French flavor while the upper floor—the private guest area—is strongly influenced by shells and the sea. This spacious guest area consists of a sitting room, large bath, large bedroom, and a second bedroom that can sleep two additional people in the same party.

# *NORTH CENTRAL/SACRAMENTO/REDDING AREA*

# Tin Roof Bed & Breakfast ✪

**24741 FORESTHILL ROAD, FORESTHILL, CALIFORNIA 95631**

| | |
|---|---|
| Tel: **(916) 367-4466** | Reduced Rates: **Available** |
| Hosts: **Clyde and Judith Larrew** | Breakfast: **Continental** |
| No. of Rooms: **3** | Credit Cards: **AMEX, MC, VISA** |
| No. of Private Baths: **1** | Pets: **Sometimes** |
| Max. No. Sharing Bath: **4** | Children: **By arrangement** |
| Double/pb: **$85** | Smoking: **No** |
| Double/sb: **$85** | Social Drinking: **Permitted** |
| Open: **All year** | Airport/Station Pickup: **Yes** |

Visit the Tin Roof Bed & Breakfast and experience the mountain air and friendly people. Enjoy white-water rafting, fishing at a nearby mountain lake, hiking, gold panning tours with Clyde, or relax in the oak rocking chairs on the porch. Winter sports include snowmobiling, cross-country skiing, snowshoeing, and snowplay at the China Wall Recreation Area. The house was built in 1875 and the charm of days gone by is still evident from the tin roof, wraparound porch, and creaky stairs. Inside, you'll find a wood stove in the kitchen, knotty pine walls, antique furniture, and interesting memorabilia throughout.

# The Inn at Shallow Creek Farm ✪
## 4712 ROAD DD, ORLAND, CALIFORNIA 95963

Tel: (916) 865-4093; (800) 865-4093
Best Time to Call: Evenings
Hosts: Mary and Kurt Glaeseman
Location: 3 mi. from I-5
No. of Rooms: 4
No. of Private Baths: 2
Max. No. Sharing Bath: 4
Double/pb: $65
Double/sb: $55
Guest Cottage: $75; sleeps 2–4
Open: All year

Reduced Rates: $10 less after 3rd night
Breakfast: Continental
Pets: No
Children: Sometimes
Smoking: No
Social Drinking: Permitted
Airport/Station Pickup: Yes
Foreign Languages: French, German, Spanish

The orchards of Shallow Creek Farm are known for mandarin and navel oranges and sweet grapefruit. Luscious berries, fresh garden produce, and a collection of exotic poultry, including rare silver guinea hens and African geese, are quite extraordinary. The Inn, a gracious turn-of-the-century farmhouse, offers airy, spacious rooms furnished with carefully chosen antiques and family heirlooms, combining nostalgia with country comfort. Breakfast features homemade baked goods and jams, and a generous assortment of fresh fruits or juices and hot beverages.

# The Feather Bed ✪
## 542 JACKSON STREET, QUINCY, CALIFORNIA 95971

Tel: (916) 283-0102; (800) 696-8624
Hosts: Bob and Jan Janowski
Location: 70 mi. NW of Reno, Nevada
No. of Rooms: 7
No. of Private Baths: 7
Double/pb: $75
Single/pb: $70
Suite: $85
Separate Cottages: $120

Open: All year
Reduced Rates: 10% less on 3rd night
Breakfast: Full
Credit Cards: AMEX, DC, MC, VISA
Pets: No
Children: Welcome
Smoking: No
Social Drinking: Permitted
Airport/Station Pickup: Yes

This charming Queen Anne was built in 1893 and renovated at the turn of the century. The rooms feature vintage wallpaper, antique furnishings, and charming baths; most have clawfoot tubs. Enjoy a glass of cider in the parlor, or a cool iced tea on the front porch. A full three-course breakfast is served on the patio or in the dining room. The inn is convenient to water sports, snowmobiling, hiking, tennis, and skiing. Your hosts offer complimentary bicycles to help you explore beautiful Plumas National Forest and historic downtown Quincy. Restaurants and the county museum are close by.

## SAN DIEGO AND ORANGE COUNTY AREA

### Coronado Village Inn ✪
**1017 PARK PLACE, CORONADO, CALIFORNIA 92118**

| | |
|---|---|
| Tel: **(619) 435-9318** | Open: **All year** |
| Best Time to Call: **To 10 PM** | Reduced Rates: **Winter weekly** |
| Hosts: **Brent and Elizabeth Bogh** | **rate—7th night free** |
| Location: **3 mi. W of San Diego** | Breakfast: **Continental** |
| No. of Rooms: **14** | Credit Cards: **AMEX, MC, VISA** |
| No. of Private Baths: **14** | Pets: **No** |
| Double/pb: **$50–$70** | Children: **Welcome** |
| Single/pb: **$50–$70** | Smoking: **Yes** |
| Suites: **$70–$80; sleeps 4** | Social Drinking: **Permitted** |

Enjoy the ambience of yesteryear at this small, European-style hotel. Within easy walking distance are tennis courts, golf courses, boating facilities, quaint shops, fine restaurants, and the white sandy beaches of the Pacific Ocean. San Diego and Mexico are just a short drive away, boasting numerous attractions.

### The Blue Door ✪
**13707 DURANGO DRIVE, DEL MAR, CALIFORNIA 92014**

| | |
|---|---|
| Tel: **(619) 755-3819** | Open: **All year** |
| Best Time to Call: **Anytime** | Breakfast: **Full** |
| Hosts: **Bob and Anna Belle Schock** | Pets: **No** |
| Location: **20 mi. N of San Diego** | Children: **Welcome, over 16** |
| No. of Rooms: **1 suite** | Smoking: **No** |
| No. of Private Baths: **1** | Social Drinking: **Permitted** |
| Suite: **$60–$70** | |

Enjoy New England charm in a quiet southern California setting overlooking exclusive Torrey Pines State Reserve. A garden-level two-room suite with wicker accessories and king or twin beds is yours. The sitting room has a couch, a desk, and a color TV. Breakfast is served in the spacious country kitchen or in the dining room warmed by the fire on chilly days. Anna Belle prides herself on creative breakfast menus featuring homemade baked goods. Breakfast specialties include blueberry muffins, Swedish oatmeal pancakes, and Blue Door orange French toast. Your hosts will gladly direct you to the nearby racetrack, beach, zoo, or University of California at San Diego. There is a $10 surcharge for one-night stays.

### Gulls Nest ✪
**12930 VIA ESPERIA, DEL MAR, CALIFORNIA**
**(MAILING ADDRESS: P.O. BOX 1056, DEL MAR, CALIFORNIA 92014)**

| | |
|---|---|
| Tel: **(619) 259-4863** | Location: **20 mi. N of San Diego** |
| Best Time to Call: **Before 8:30 AM** | No. of Rooms: **2** |
| Hosts: **Connie and Mike Segel** | No. of Private Baths: **2** |

| | |
|---|---|
| Double/pb: **$75** | Pets: **No** |
| Suite: **$95** | Children: **Welcome, over 6** |
| Open: **All year** | Smoking: **No** |
| Breakfast: **Full** | Social Drinking: **Permitted** |

Gulls Nest is a contemporary wood home surrounded by pine trees. The house boasts a beautiful view of the ocean and a bird sanctuary from two upper decks. Guest accommodations consist of a comfortable, quiet room with queen-size bed, TV, private bath, and patio. The suite has a king-size bed and a sitting room that can accommodate a third person for $10 more. Breakfast is served outdoors, weather permitting, and features fresh-squeezed juice, eggs, homemade breads, and coffee cake. Great swimming and surfing are three blocks away at Torrey State Beach. Golf, shops, and restaurants are a 5-minute drive, and Tijuana and the international border are 40 minutes away.

## At Your Leisure Bed and Breakfast ✪
**525 SOUTH THIRD STREET, EL CAJON, CALIFORNIA 92019**

| | |
|---|---|
| Tel: **(619) 444-3124** | Open: **All year** |
| Best Time to Call: **Evenings** | Reduced Rates: **10% seniors, weekly** |
| Hosts: **Ron and Joan Leasure** | Breakfast: **Continental** |
| Location: **18 mi. E of San Diego Airport** | Credit Cards: **MC, VISA** |
| No. of Rooms: **2** | Pets: **No** |
| Max. No. Sharing Bath: **4** | Children: **Welcome** |
| Double/sb: **$58** | Smoking: **No** |
| Single/sb: **$55** | Social Drinking: **Permitted** |

A warm welcome awaits you at this comfortable and historic 1928 home, decorated with antiques and vintage clothing. Guests can enjoy a glass of iced tea or a cup of hot chocolate in the game room, by the swimming pool or on the front porch or patio. At Your Leisure Bed and Breakfast is located on the bus route, only one mile from the major freeways, and just minutes from the airport and train station. Places of interest include San Diego Zoo, Balboa Park, universities, golf courses, convention centers, stadium, beaches, mountains, deserts and many sites in between, including fine restaurants and shopping.

## Sea Breeze B&B ✪
**121 NORTH VULCAN, ENCINITAS, CALIFORNIA 92024**

| | |
|---|---|
| Tel: **(619) 944-0318** | Double/sb: **$90** |
| Host: **Kirsten Richter** | Suite: **$150** |
| Location: **23 mi. N of San Diego** | Open: **All year** |
| No. of Rooms: **5** | Reduced Rates: **10% weekly, seniors,** |
| No. of Private Baths: **5** | **families** |
| Double/pb: **$75–150** | Breakfast: **Continental** |

Pets: **No**
Children: **Welcome (playpen)**

Smoking: **Permitted**
Social Drinking: **Permitted**

Choose among a separate apartment, three queen bedrooms, and a penthouse with a private spa, whirlpool tub, and shower in this contemporary two-story home filled with custom, one-of-a-kind furnishings. Sunbathe in privacy on the deck overlooking the Pacific, or stroll down to Moonlight Beach for a refreshing ocean dip. It's a short walk to downtown Encinitas, which boasts many fine restaurants. Mt. Palomar Observatory, Sea World, Del Mar Race Track, and the Mexican border are about a half hour away by car. Guests have use of a kitchenette. Continental breakfasts consist of muffins, fresh fruit, yogurt, and coffee, tea, or hot chocolate.

## Hidden Village Bed & Breakfast ✪
### 9582 HALEKULANI DRIVE, GARDEN GROVE, CALIFORNIA 92641

Tel: **(714) 636-8312**
Best Time to Call: **8 AM–9 PM**
Hosts: **Dick and Linda O'Berg**
Location: **3 mi. S of Anaheim**
No. of Rooms: **4**
No. of Private Baths: **2**
Max. No. Sharing Bath: **2**
Double/pb: **$55**
Single/pb: **$45**
Double/sb: **$50**

Single/sb: **$40**
Suites: **$75**
Open: **All year**
Reduced Rates: **$10 less, Sun.–Thurs.**
Breakfast: **Full**
Pets: **Sometimes**
Children: **Welcome (crib)**
Smoking: **No**
Social Drinking: **Permitted**
Airport/Station Pickup: **Yes**

Linda has decorated this large Colonial home with lacy draperies and handmade quilts; she's a professional weaver, and guests are welcome to browse in her studio. When you're done looking at fabrics, Disneyland, the Anaheim Convention Center, and Orange County's lovely beaches are just minutes away. Couch potatoes can watch tapes on the VCR, while the energetic can borrow the O'Bergs' bicycles and go for a spin. In the mornings, you'll savor a full breakfast of fresh fruit, homemade apple muffins, and quiche or omelettes.

## Country Comfort Bed and Breakfast ✪
### 5104 EAST VALENCIA DRIVE, ORANGE, CALIFORNIA 92669

Tel: **(714) 532-2802 or 532-4010**
Best Time to Call: **Evenings**
Hosts: **Geri Lopker and Joanne Angell**
Location: **5 mi. E of Anaheim**
No. of Rooms: **3**
No. of Private Baths: **3**
Double/pb: **$65**
Single/pb: **$60**
Open: **All year**

Reduced Rates: **10% less after 3rd night**
Breakfast: **Full**
Other Meals: **Available**
Pets: **By arrangement**
Children: **Welcome**
Smoking: **No**
Social Drinking: **Permitted**

Located in a quiet residential area, Geri and Joanne have furnished their home with your comfort and pleasure in mind. It is disabled-accessible with adaptive equipment available. Amenities include a swimming pool, cable TV and VCR, an atrium, fireplace, and the use of Jacuzzi for two. Breakfast often features delicious Scotch eggs, stuffed French toast and hash, along with fruits and assorted beverages. Vegetarian selections are also available. Disneyland and Knotts Berry Farm are less than seven miles away.

## Blom House Bed & Breakfast ✪
**1372 MINDEN DRIVE, SAN DIEGO, CALIFORNIA 92111**

| | |
|---|---|
| Tel: **(619) 467-0890** | Reduced Rates: **$59 Sun.–Thurs.** |
| Hosts: **Bette and John Blom** | **double or single** |
| Location: **In San Diego** | Breakfast: **Full** |
| No. of Rooms: 3 | Pets: **No** |
| No. of Private Baths: 3 | Children: **Welcome (crib/high chair)** |
| Double/pb: **$75** | Smoking: **No** |
| Single/pb: **$65** | Social Drinking: **Permitted** |
| Suite: **$85** | Minimum Stay: **2 nights** |
| Open: **All year** | |

Blom House is a charming one-story cottage located on a bluff in a residential neighborhood, less than ten minutes from the beach, downtown, and all local tourist attractions. The 65-foot deck has a spa and offers a view of the lights from the Hotel Circle below. Guest areas have 14-foot ceilings and antique furnishings, as well as cookies and chocolates. You'll find lots of extras in your room, from the color TV, VCR, phone, and refrigerator, to bathrobes, a hair dryer, an iron and ironing board, and complimentary wine and cheese. A four-course gourmet breakfast is served each morning. And for dining, Bette and John have two-for-one coupons for a large variety of neighborhood restaurants. The Blom House Bed & Breakfast is fully air-conditioned.

## The Cottage ✪
**3829 ALBATROSS STREET, SAN DIEGO, CALIFORNIA 92103**

| | |
|---|---|
| Tel: **(619) 299-1564** | Open: **All year** |
| Best Time to Call: **9 AM–5 PM** | Breakfast: **Continental** |
| Hosts: **Robert and Carol Emerick** | Credit Cards: **AMEX, MC, VISA** |
| Location: **1 mi. from Rte. 5** | Pets: **No** |
| No. of Rooms: 2 | Children: **Welcome** |
| No. of Private Baths: 2 | Smoking: **No** |
| Double/pb: **$49–$80** | Social Drinking: **Permitted** |
| Guest Cottage: **$75–$95; sleeps 3** | |

Located in the Hillcrest section, where canyons and old houses dot the landscape, this private hideaway offers a cottage with a king-size

bed, full bath, and fully equipped kitchen. Decorated with turn-of-the-century furniture, the wood-burning stove and oak pump organ evoke memories of long ago. It's two miles to the zoo, less to Balboa Park, and it is within easy walking distance of restaurants, shops, and theater. The University of California and the University of San Diego are nearby.

## Vera's Cozy Corner
### 2810 ALBATROSS STREET, SAN DIEGO, CALIFORNIA 92103

Tel: **(619) 296-1938**
Best Time to Call: **Before 10 AM; after 5 PM**
Host: **Vera V. Warden**
No. of Rooms: **1**
No. of Private Baths: **1**
Double/pb: **$50**
Single/pb: **$40**

Open: **All year**
Reduced Rates: **Weekly; 10% seniors**
Breakfast: **Continental**
Pets: **No**
Children: **No**
Smoking: **No**
Social Drinking: **Permitted**
Foreign Languages: **French, German**

This crisp white Colonial with black shutters sits on a quiet cul-de-sac overlooking San Diego Bay. Guest quarters consist of a separate cottage with private patio entrance. Vera offers fresh-squeezed juice from her own fruit trees in season as a prelude to breakfast, served in Vera's old-world dining room. The house is convenient to local shops and restaurants, and is a mile from the San Diego Zoo.

## SAN FRANCISCO AREA

### Bed and Breakfast San Francisco ✪
P.O. BOX 420009, SAN FRANCISCO, CALIFORNIA 94142

Tel: (415) 479-1913
Best Time to Call: 9:30 AM–5 PM
  Mon.–Fri.
Coordinators: Susan and Richard
  Kreibich
States/Regions Covered: Carmel,
  Marin County, Monterey, Napa, San
  Francisco, Sonoma (wine country)

Descriptive Directory: $2
Rates (Double):
  Modest:   $55–$65
  Average:  $75–$95
  Luxury:   $100–$125
Credit Cards: AMEX, DC, MC, VISA
Minimum Stay: 2 nights

The San Francisco locations are near all of the famous sights, such as Fisherman's Wharf and Chinatown. Many are historic Victorian houses. Some homes offer hot tubs and sundecks; a few are on yachts and houseboats.

### Burlingame B&B ✪
1021 BALBOA AVENUE, BURLINGAME, CALIFORNIA 94010

Tel: (415) 344-5815
Hosts: Joe and Elnora Fernandez
Location: ½ mi. from Rte. 101
No. of Rooms: 1
No. of Private Baths: 1
Double/pb: $50
Single/pb: $40
Open: All year

Breakfast: Continental
Pets: No
Children: Welcome
Smoking: No
Social Drinking: No
Airport/Station Pickup: Yes
Foreign Languages: Italian, Spanish

Located in a pleasantly quiet neighborhood, with San Francisco only minutes away by good public transportation. The house offers the privacy of upstairs guest quarters with a view of a creek and native flora and fauna. It's all very clean and cheerfully decorated. Joe and Elnora will direct you to restaurants and shops to suit your budget.

### Lore's Haus ✪
22051 BETLEN WAY, CASTRO VALLEY, CALIFORNIA 94546

Tel: (510) 881-1533
Host: Lore Bergman
Location: 25 mi. SE of San Francisco
No. of Rooms: 2
No. of Private Baths: 1
Max. No. Sharing Bath: 4
Double/pb: $60
Single/pb: $55
Double/sb: $55
Single/sb: $50

Open: All year
Breakfast: Full
Pets: No
Children: Welcome, over 14
Smoking: Permitted
Social Drinking: Permitted
Airport/Station Pickup: Yes
Foreign Languages: French, German
Minimum Stay: 2 nights

Lore's Haus is an attractive ranch home on a quiet street, with a large, beautiful garden. Lore was born in Germany and has spent the last 30 years in Castro Valley. She prides herself on offering Americans a true European atmosphere, with a lot of plants, books, comfortable furnishings, and oriental rugs. Breakfast includes French Brie, fresh German black bread, homemade jams, cold cuts, and eggs. If you like, tours of the Bay Area, Napa Valley, or anyplace else are available in German, French, or English. If you'd like to venture out on your own, the city center is 25 minutes away via car or rapid transit. After a day of touring, come back to Lore's and enjoy a glass of wine.

## Old Thyme Inn ✪
### 779 MAIN STREET, HALF MOON BAY, CALIFORNIA 94019

| | |
|---|---|
| Tel: (415) 726-1616 | Open: All year |
| Best Time to Call: 8 AM–10 PM | Breakfast: Full |
| Hosts: Marcia and George Dempsey | Credit Cards: MC, VISA |
| Location: 30 mi. S of San Francisco | Pets: No |
| No. of Rooms: 3 | Children: Welcome, over 12 |
| No. of Private Baths: 3 | Smoking: No |
| Double/pb: $65–$85 | Social Drinking: Permitted |
| Single/pb: $60–$85 | Minimum Stay: Holiday weekends |
| Suites: $145–$210 | Foreign Languages: French |

The Old Thyme Inn is a restored Victorian house located on the Pacific coast just 35 minutes south of San Francisco. Some rooms have fireplaces, some have baths with double-size whirlpool tubs, and all are decorated with antiques. Your hosts invite you to stroll in George's herb garden; if you like, you can have a cutting kit and take samples home for your own use. George's breakfast includes his justly celebrated buttermilk scones. For those of you who don't mind paying a higher rate, 4 rooms are available.

## Zaballa House ✪
### 324 MAIN STREET, HALF MOON BAY, CALIFORNIA 94019

| | |
|---|---|
| Tel: (415) 726-9123 | Reduced Rates: Mon.–Thurs. |
| Best Time to Call: 7 AM–8 PM | Breakfast: Full |
| Host: Kerry Pendercast | Credit Cards: AMEX, DISC, MC, VISA |
| Location: 35 mi. S of San Francisco | Pets: By arrangement |
| No. of Rooms: 9 | Children: Welcome, over 8 |
| No. of Private Baths: 9 | Smoking: No |
| Double/pb: $65–$165 | Social Drinking: Permitted |
| Open: All year | |

Built in 1859 by Estanislao Zaballa, the community's first city planner, this bed-and-breakfast inn is the oldest house in Half Moon Bay. The inn is located on the same block as two of the coast's finest restaurants and enjoys a wonderful garden setting. The local gardens provide the inn with an abundance of flowers for all the rooms. Kerry is an expert in neighborhood lore—ask her to tell you about the ghost. In the evenings, guests are invited to share complimentary drinks around the fireplace; in the mornings, all-you-can-eat breakfasts are served.

## Goose & Turrets B&B ✪
### 835 GEORGE STREET, P.O. BOX 937, MONTARA, CALIFORNIA 94037-0937

| | |
|---|---|
| Tel: **(415) 728-5451** | Reduced Rates: **15% Mon.–Thurs.,** |
| Best Time to Call: **10 AM–9 PM** | **10% after 5th night** |
| Hosts: **Raymond and Emily Hoche-** | Breakfast: **Full** |
| **Mong** | Credit Cards: **AMEX, DISC, MC, VISA** |
| Location: **23 mi. SW of San Francisco** | Pets: **No** |
| No. of Rooms: **5** | Children: **Welcome** |
| No. of Private Baths: **5** | Smoking: **No** |
| Double/pb: **$85–$110** | Social Drinking: **Permitted** |
| Open: **All year** | Foreign Languages: **French** |

Located only 20 minutes from San Francisco Airport and half a mile from the beach, Goose & Turrets B&B is a convenient headquarters for day excursions to San Francisco, Silicon Valley, Berkeley, Monterey Aquarium and Carmel. Nearby are restaurants, galleries, tidepools, fishing, golf, hiking, horseback riding, shops, and remnants of the area's lurid past during Prohibition. Enjoy delicious four-course breakfasts, comfortable beds, quiet gardens with courting swing, hammock, fountains, bocce ball court, and meet the three mascot geese. English tea and tasty snacks are served every afternoon. Raymond and Emily are well-traveled pilots who have lived in the South and in Europe, at places whose customs and cuisines are reflected in the food and the hospitality provided at the inn.

## Adella Villa B&B ✪
### P.O. BOX 4528, PALO ALTO, CALIFORNIA 94309

| | |
|---|---|
| Tel: **(415) 321-5195**; fax: **(415) 325-** | Breakfast: **Full** |
| **5121** | Credit Cards: **AMEX, DC, MC, VISA** |
| Host: **Tricia Young** | Pets: **No** |
| Location: **30 mi. S of San Francisco** | Children: **Welcome, over 8** |
| No. of Rooms: **5** | Smoking: **No** |
| No. of Private Baths: **5** | Social Drinking: **Permitted** |
| Double/pb: **$95** | Airport/Station Pickup: **Yes** |
| Suites: **$110** | Foreign Languages: **German, Spanish** |
| Open: **All year** | |

This gorgeous, restored 1920s Italian villa is located in an exclusive area near Stanford University and Silicon Valley. The B&B, a pink stucco mansion with white trim, stands on an acre of lush park-like grounds with a Japanese koi pond, an aviary, and a swimming pool. The music foyer boasts a Steinway grand piano crafted in the 1930s.

Fans of antiques will find much to admire, including an English dining room set, a five-foot nineteenth-century Imari vase, and a French marble commode. But there's nothing old-fashioned about the guest room amenities, such as bathrobes, down comforters, cable TV, sherry and wine, and cooked-to-order breakfasts.

## Casa Arguello
### 225 ARGUELLO BOULEVARD, SAN FRANCISCO, CALIFORNIA 94118

Tel: **(415) 752-9482**
Best Time to Call: **10 AM–6 PM**
Hosts: **Emma Baires and Marina McKenzie**
No. of Rooms: **4**
No. of Private Baths: **2**
Max. No. Sharing Bath: **3**
Double/pb: **$70–$77**
Double/sb: **$55**

Open: **All year**
Breakfast: **Continental, plus**
Pets: **No**
Children: **Welcome, over 7**
Smoking: **No**
Social Drinking: **Permitted**
Minimum Stay: **2 nights**
Foreign Languages: **Spanish**

This spacious duplex has an elegant living room, dining room, and cheerful bedrooms that overlook neighboring gardens. Tastefully decorated with modern and antique furnishings, it is convenient to Golden Gate Park, Golden Gate Bridge, Union Square, and fine shops and restaurants. The University of California Medical School is nearby. Excellent public transportation is close by.

## Casita Blanca ✪
### 330 EDGEHILL WAY, SAN FRANCISCO, CALIFORNIA 94127

Tel: **(415) 564-9339**
Host: **Joan Bard**
No. of Rooms: **1 cottage**
No. of Private Baths: **1**
Guest Cottage: **$80; sleeps 2**
Open: **All year**
Breakfast: **Continental**

Pets: **No**
Children: **No**
Smoking: **No**
Social Drinking: **Permitted**
Minimum Stay: **2 nights**
Foreign Languages: **French, Spanish**

Casita Blanca is a guest cottage perched high on a hill, not far from Golden Gate Park. In this delightful hideaway, nestled among giant trees, you'll find twin beds, a private bath with a stall shower, and a complete kitchen stocked for your convenience with all the necessary items. If you tire of sightseeing and shopping, then just curl up in front of the little fireplace, have a glass of wine, and listen to the birds singing outside. Joan also offers accommodations in Carmel-by-the-Sea, Lake Tahoe, Sonoma, Palm Desert, and Maui.

## Chez Duchene ✪
### 1075 BROADWAY, SAN FRANCISCO, CALIFORNIA 94133

| | |
|---|---|
| Tel: **(415) 441-3160** | Breakfast: **Continental** |
| Host: **Jay Duchene** | Pets: **No** |
| No. of Rooms: **1** | Children: **Welcome** |
| No. of Private Baths: **1** | Smoking: **No** |
| Double/pb: **$90** | Social Drinking: **Permitted** |
| Open: **All year** | Minimum Stay: **2 nights** |

Located in the Russian Hill district of San Francisco, this charming three-story Victorian home is two blocks from the famous cable car lines and within walking distance to North Beach, Fisherman's Wharf, the financial district, Union Square, Chinatown, Ghirardelli Square and the Embarcadero. City bus lines are also close by. This quaint home overlooks San Francisco Bay and has a panoramic view of the city from the upstairs deck and bedroom windows. Chez Duchene is furnished entirely in a combination of modern and antique pieces, including oriental rugs. Original woodwork highlights every room in the house.

## Rancho San Gregorio ✪
### ROUTE 1, BOX 54, SAN GREGORIO, CALIFORNIA 94074

| | |
|---|---|
| Tel: **(415) 747-0810**; fax: **(415) 747-0184** | Open: **All year** |
| | Reduced Rates: **Available** |
| Hosts: **Bud and Lee Raynor** | Breakfast: **Full** |
| Location: **35 mi. S of San Francisco** | Pets: **No** |
| No. of Rooms: **3** | Children: **Welcome** |
| No. of Private Baths: **3** | Smoking: **No** |
| Double/pb: **$70–$90** | Social Drinking: **Permitted** |
| Suite: **$145** | Airport/Station Pickup: **Yes** |

Graceful arches and bright stucco characterize this Spanish Mission home set on 15 wooded acres. Rooms are decorated with American antiques and family pieces. Your hosts, Bud and Lee, are glad to share a snack and a beverage. A full feast features eggs or pancakes, fresh fruit and breads, and a variety of meats. The atmosphere is relaxing, and guests are welcome to borrow a book from the library, or play the organ. Rancho San Gregorio is close to the beach, horseback riding, and golf. San Francisco, Half Moon Bay, and a variety of state parks and recreational areas are within an hour's drive. For those of you who don't mind paying a higher rate, 2 rooms are available.

## Madison Street Inn ✪
### 1390 MADISON STREET, SANTA CLARA, CALIFORNIA 95050

| | |
|---|---|
| Tel: **(800) 491-5541**; **(408) 249-5541**; fax: **(408) 249-6676** | Location: **1½ mi. from Rte. 880** |
| | No. of Rooms: **5** |
| Hosts: **Theresa and Ralph Wigginton** | No. of Private Baths: **3** |

Max. No. Sharing Bath: **4**
Double/pb: **$75–$85**
Double/sb: **$60**
Single/sb: **$60**
Open: **All year**
Reduced Rates: **20% seniors**
Breakfast: **Full**

Other Meals: **Available**
Credit Cards: **AMEX, DC, MC, VISA**
Pets: **No**
Children: **Welcome**
Smoking: **No**
Social Drinking: **Permitted**

This restored, vintage Queen Anne is furnished with oriental rugs and museum-quality antiques, including brass beds and tubs-for-two. Landscaped gardens, a swimming pool, and a hot tub grace the grounds, and a sunny meeting room is available for business gatherings. Belgian waffles or eggs Benedict are often on the breakfast menu. Exciting dinners can be arranged, prepared by Ralph, an accomplished cook. It is convenient to Santa Clara University and San Jose State University and San Jose Airport.

## SAN LUIS OBISPO AREA

### Baywood Bed & Breakfast Inn ✪
**1370 SECOND STREET, BAYWOOD PARK, CALIFORNIA 93402**

Tel: **(805) 528-8888**
Best Time to Call: **8 AM–8 PM**
Hosts: **Pat and Alex Benson and Barbie Porter**
Location: **12 mi. W of San Luis Obispo**
No. of Rooms: **15**
No. of Private Baths: **15**
Double/pb: **$80–$140**
Suites: **$120–$140**
Open: **All year**

Reduced Rates: **Available**
Breakfast: **Full**
Other Meals: **Available**
Credit Cards: **MC, VISA**
Pets: **No**
Children: **Welcome**
Smoking: **No**
Social Drinking: **Permitted**
Minimum Stay: **2 days on holiday weekends**

This waterfront establishment lies on a tiny peninsula that projects into Morro Bay. Outdoor types will find plenty to do here; the options include kayaking, golfing, hiking, bicycling, and picnicking. Several shops and restaurants are right in town, and Montano De Oro State Park, San Luis Obispo, and Hearst Castle are only minutes away. Each Baywood suite has bay views, cozy seating areas, and a wood-burning fireplace. Guests are treated to afternoon wine and cheese, room tours, and breakfast in bed.

### Kraemers Kozy Kastle ✪
**360 WORCESTER DRIVE, CAMBRIA, CALIFORNIA 93428**

Tel: **(805) 927-8270**
Best Time to Call: **8 AM–8 PM**
Hosts: **Margaret and Eddie Kraemer**
Location: **35 mi. N of San Luis Obispo**
No. of Rooms: **1**

No. of Private Baths: **1**
Double/pb: **$65**
Open: **All year**
Breakfast: **Continental**
Pets: **No**

| | |
|---|---|
| Children: **No** | Social Drinking: **Permitted** |
| Smoking: **No** | Minimum Stay: **2 nights, holidays** |

Kraemers Kozy Kastle is located in an interesting coastal village between Los Angeles and San Francisco, about six miles south of Hearst Castle. Guests will enjoy this beautiful studio apartment with its own entrance. There are twin beds, a color TV, and a minikitchen suitable for preparing light meals. Cambria, known for its community of artists, has more than 25 art galleries and boutique shops. The surrounding areas have wineries for touring and tasting. The restaurants are excellent and your hosts can provide insight into where the locals dine. Enjoy white-water ocean views from a picture window as you enjoy a gourmet Continental breakfast.

## Gerarda's Bed & Breakfast ✪
**1056 BAY OAKS DRIVE, LOS OSOS, CALIFORNIA 93402-4006**

| | |
|---|---|
| Tel: **(805) 534-0834** | Single/sb: **$26.50** |
| Host: **Gerarda Ondang** | Open: **All year** |
| Location: **10 mi. from Hwy. 101** | Breakfast: **Full** |
| No. of Rooms: **3** | Pets: **Welcome** |
| No. of Private Baths: **1** | Children: **Welcome** |
| Max. No. Sharing Bath: **4** | Smoking: **No** |
| Double/pb: **$41.34** | Social Drinking: **Permitted** |
| Single/pb: **$26.50** | Airport/Station Pickup: **Yes** |
| Double/sb: **$41.34** | Foreign Languages: **Dutch, Indonesian** |

When you stay at Gerarda's, you are in for a veritable Dutch treat! Located in a pleasant, quiet neighborhood, the house is surrounded by interesting landscaping and lovely flower beds. This is a simple home comfortably furnished, with charm and warmth. Breakfast features Dutch delicacies such as honeycake, jams, and breads. Hearst Castle, Morro Bay, and San Luis Obispo are within a half hour's drive. Gerarda has thoughtfully placed a TV in each guest bedroom.

## *SANTA BARBARA AREA*

## Carpinteria Beach Condo ✪
**1825 CRAVENS LANE, CARPINTERIA, CALIFORNIA 93013**

| | |
|---|---|
| Tel: **(805) 684-1579** | Breakfast: **Continental** |
| Best Time to Call: **7 AM–9 PM** | Pets: **No** |
| Hosts: **Bev and Don Schroeder** | Children: **Welcome** |
| Location: **11 mi. SE of Santa Barbara** | Smoking: **No** |
| Guest Condo: **$60–$75; sleeps 2 to 4** | Social Drinking: **Permitted** |
| Open: **All year** | Station Pickup: **Yes** |
| Reduced Rates: **Available** | |

You may view majestic mountains from this one-bedroom condo across the street from the beach. If you tire of the ocean, there is also a swimming pool. Play a set of tennis at the local Polo and Racquet

Club, visit your hosts' avocado and lemon ranch less than two miles away, or take a ten-minute drive into Santa Barbara. Breakfast is a do-it-yourself affair in the condo's complete minikitchen.

## Cliff Drive Guest House:
## An Ocean View Bed and Breakfast ✪
**1405 CLIFF DRIVE, SANTA BARBARA, CALIFORNIA 93109**

| | |
|---|---|
| Tel: (805) 963-3525 | Open: **All year** |
| Best Time to Call: **7 AM–9 PM** | Breakfast: **Continental** |
| Hosts: **Bob and Phyllis Adams** | Credit Cards: **MC, VISA** |
| Location: **100 mi. NW of Los Angeles** | Pets: **No** |
| No. of Rooms: 2 | Children: **Welcome** |
| Max. No. Sharing Bath: **4** | Smoking: **No** |
| Double/sb: $85 | Social Drinking: **Permitted** |

Cliff Drive Guest House is located three blocks from a secluded beach. Guests will enjoy a full ocean view from the ⅔-acre grounds studded with giant oaks and artful landscaping. The house is a 1940s Spanish hacienda with a red tile roof, typical of what one expects to see in Santa Barbara. A deluxe Continental breakfast is served in a picnic basket, and can be enjoyed in the gazebo, dining room, ocean-view porch or rooftop deck. Whether you are strolling the nearby wooded ocean trails or relaxing in the spa with a glass of chardonnay, you will enjoy the charming ambiance that is truly Santa Barbara.

## Long's Seaview Bed & Breakfast ✪
**317 PIEDMONT ROAD, SANTA BARBARA, CALIFORNIA 93105**

| | |
|---|---|
| Tel: (805) 687-2947 | Open: **All year** |
| Best Time to Call: **Before 6 PM** | Breakfast: **Full** |
| Host: **LaVerne Long** | Pets: **No** |
| Location: **1½ mi. from Hwy. 101** | Children: **No** |
| No. of Rooms: 1 | Smoking: **No** |
| No. of Private Baths: 1 | Social Drinking: **Permitted** |
| Double/pb: $75–$79 | Airport/Station Pickup: **Yes** |
| Single/pb: $75 | |

Overlooking Santa Barbara's prestigious north side, this ranch-style home is in a quiet, residential neighborhood. Breakfast is usually served on the patio, where you can see the ocean, Channel Islands, and the small family citrus orchard and garden. Convenient to the beach, Solvang, and Santa Ynez Valley, the large, airy bedroom is cheerfully furnished with antiques and king-size bed. The breakfast menu varies from Southern dishes to Mexican specialties.

## Ocean View House ✪
### P.O. BOX 3373, SANTA BARBARA, CALIFORNIA 93130-3373

Tel: **(805) 966-6659**
Best Time to Call: **8 AM–5 PM**
Hosts: **Bill and Carolyn Canfield**
Location: **2 mi. from Hwy. 101**
No. of Rooms: **2**
No. of Private Baths: **1**
Double/pb: **$70**
Suite: **$90 for 4**

Open: **All year**
Breakfast: **Continental**
Pets: **Sometimes**
Children: **Welcome**
Smoking: **No**
Social Drinking: **Permitted**
Airport/Station Pickup: **Yes**
Minimum Stay: **3 nights**

This California ranch house features a guest room furnished with a queen-size bed and antiques. The adjoining paneled den, with double-bed divan and TV, is available together with the guest room as a suite. While you relax on the patio, you can look out at the sailboats on the ocean. It's a short walk to the beach and local shops.

## *SEQUOIA AREA/SIERRA FOOTHILLS*

## Kern River Inn Bed & Breakfast ✪
### P.O. BOX 1725, 119 KERN RIVER DRIVE, KERNVILLE, CALIFORNIA 93238

Tel: **(619) 376-6750; (800) 986-4382**
Best Time to Call: **10 AM–9 PM**
Hosts: **Jack and Carita Prestwich**
Location: **50 mi. NE of Bakersfield**
No. of Rooms: **6**
No. of Private Baths: **6**
Double/pb: **$89–$99**
Single/pb: **$79–$89**

Open: **All year**
Reduced Rates: **Available**
Breakfast: **Full**
Credit Cards: **MC, VISA**
Pets: **No**
Children: **Welcome**
Smoking: **No**
Social Drinking: **Permitted**

Stay in a charming riverfront B&B in a quaint Western town within Sequoia National Forest. Carita and Jack specialize in romantic, relaxing getaways. Nearby activities include golf, hiking, biking, whitewater rafting, downhill skiing, and year-round fishing in front of the Inn. It's an easy stroll to shops, restaurants, and parks, and a short drive to the giant redwood trees. Your hosts love to fish and hike and can direct you to some of their favorite locations.

## Cort Cottage ✪
### P.O. BOX 245, THREE RIVERS, CALIFORNIA 93271

| | |
|---|---|
| Tel: **(209) 561-4671** | Breakfast: **Continental** |
| Best Time to Call: **Before 9 PM** | Pets: **No** |
| Hosts: **Gary and Catherine Cort** | Children: **Welcome** |
| Location: **5 mi. W of Sequoia National Park** | Smoking: **No** |
| | Social Drinking: **Permitted** |
| Guest Cottage: **$75; sleeps 2** | Minimum Stay: **2 nights** |
| Open: **All year** | |

Hidden in the Sierra foothill village of Three Rivers, you will find this private guest cottage ten minutes away from the entrance to Sequoia National Park. Built by Gary and Catherine as a house for Grandma, the cottage fits snugly into the hillside and has a panoramic view of mountains and sky. It offers an outdoor hot tub, a fully equipped kitchen, and full bath with step-down tub. Your hosts work as an architect/artist and a part-time nurse, have interests in gardening, crafts, and photography, and own a local art gallery.

# COLORADO

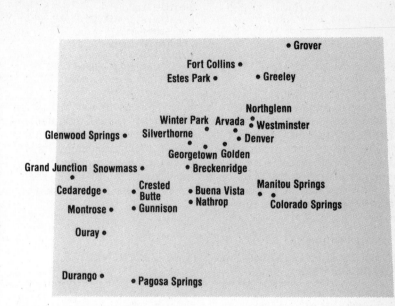

## Bed & Breakfast Southwest Reservation Service—Southern Colorado ✪
**6916 EAST MARIPOSA, SCOTTSDALE, ARIZONA 85251**

Tel: **(602) 947-9704; (800) 762-9704**
Best Time to Call: **10 AM–8 PM**
Coordinators: **Jo and Jim Cummings**
States/Regions Covered: **Southern Colorado**

Descriptive Directory: **$3, SASE**
Rates (Single/Double):
Modest: **$40–$60**
Average: **$50–$65**
Luxury: **$65–up**

Specializing in unique homestays with private suites and guest houses, this service offers exciting experiences to the traveler coming to the Southwest. Jo and Jim are residents of the area and can give firsthand information about sport activities, dining opportunities, and art exhibits and answer your questions about the great Southwest. The Cummingses will be happy to help you plan your vacation with gracious hosts throughout the region. Bed & Breakfast Southwest is always looking for unique hosts and enthusiastic guests.

## On Golden Pond Bed & Breakfast
**7831 ELDRIDGE, ARVADA, COLORADO 80005**

| | |
|---|---|
| Tel: **(303) 424-2296** | Open: **All year** |
| Best Time to Call: **Anytime** | Reduced Rates: **10% weekly, seniors** |
| Hosts: **John and Kathy Kula** | Breakfast: **Full** |
| Location: **15 mi. W of Denver** | Credit Cards: **AMEX, DISC, MC, VISA** |
| No. of Rooms: **5** | Pets: **Sometimes** |
| No. of Private Baths: **5** | Children: **Welcome** |
| Double/pb: **$50–$80** | Smoking: **No** |
| Single/pb: **$40–$70** | Social Drinking: **Permitted** |
| Suites: **$80–$100** | Foreign Languages: **German** |

A secluded retreat tucked into the Rocky Mountain foothills, this custom-built, two-story brick home has dramatic views of mountains, prairies, and downtown Denver. Birds and other wildlife are drawn to the ten-acre grounds, which have a fishing pond and hiking trails. After a full breakfast, stroll along the garden path, bicycle by the creek, swim laps in the pool, or ride horses into the foothills. Then join John and Kathy for a late afternoon kaffeeklatsch. Conclude the day with a soak in the hot tub.

## Cotten House ✪
**102 SOUTH FRENCH STREET, P.O. BOX 387, BRECKENRIDGE, COLORADO 80424**

| | |
|---|---|
| Tel: **(970) 453-5509** | Open: **All year** |
| Hosts: **Peter and Georgette Contos** | Breakfast: **Full** |
| Location: **85 mi. W of Denver** | Other Meals: **Available** |
| No. of Rooms: **2** | Pets: **No** |
| No. of Private Baths: **1** | Children: **Welcome** |
| Max. No. Sharing Bath: **4** | Smoking: **No** |
| Double/pb: **$65–$95** | Social Drinking: **Permitted** |
| Double/sb: **$50–$85** | Foreign Languages: **Greek, French** |

Get the feel of Breckenridge's mining days in this restored 1886 Victorian listed on the National Historic Register. Peter and Georgette can tell you about their town's past with the help of period photographs mounted on their walls. The common room—equipped with a TV, VCR, books, and games—is a favorite gathering place, but shopping, restaurants, and evening entertainments will lure you to Main Street, two blocks away. Breckenridge's stunning mountain setting is appealing throughout the year. Admire wildflowers in the spring, attend special summer events, see the aspens change color in the fall; higher rates apply in the winter, when you have access to cold weather activities from the free shuttle bus that stops at the B&B's front door.

# Trout City Inn ✪
BOX 431, BUENA VISTA, COLORADO 81211

Tel: (719) 495-0348
Best Time to Call: After 6 PM
Hosts: Juel and Irene Kjeldsen
Location: 5 mi. E of Buena Vista on
 Hwy. 24
No. of Rooms: 4
No. of Private Baths: 4
Double/pb: $35–$40

Open: June 15–Sept. 15
Breakfast: Full
Other Meals: Available
Credit Cards: MC, VISA
Pets: No
Children: Welcome, over 10
Smoking: No
Social Drinking: Permitted

Trout City Inn is a historic site on the famous South Park Narrow Gauge Railroad, and is located at the edge of a trout stream. It is an accurate reconstruction of a mountain railroad depot, with authentic private rail cars containing Pullman berths. The depot rooms feature Victorian decor, high ceilings, and four-poster or brass beds. Glass doors open onto a deck with views of the 14,000-foot peaks of the Continental Divide. Hiking, biking, panning for gold, and fly-fishing are within steps of the front door; white-water rafting is minutes away.

# Cedars' Edge Llamas Bed and Breakfast ✪
2169 HIGHWAY 65, CEDAREDGE, COLORADO 81413

Tel: (970) 856-6836
Hosts: Ray and Gail Record
Location: 50 mi. E of Grand Junction
No. of Rooms: 4
No. of Private Baths: 4
Double/pb: $50–$75
Single/pb: $40–$65

Open: All year
Breakfast: Full
Pets: No
Children: Welcome
Smoking: No
Social Drinking: Permitted
Airport/Station Pickup: Yes

Nestled on the southern slope of the Grand Mesa, this modern cedar home offers a panoramic view of several mountain ranges, plus the unique opportunity to share life on a llama-breeding ranch. The accommodations are immaculate. Cheerful rooms are tastefully decorated in pastel shades, with exposed beams, hanging plants, and light streaming in from many windows. Sportsmen and sportswomen can fish for trout, hunt deer and elk, or go cross-country and downhill skiing. After a filling breakfast, guests can join Ray and Gail in feeding or grooming well-behaved four-footed friends—a rewarding experience for all.

# Timberline Bed & Breakfast ✪
2457 U50 ROAD, CEDAREDGE, COLORADO 81413

Tel: (970) 856-7379
Best Time to Call: Mornings or
 evenings

Hosts: Al and Shirley Richardson
Location: 60 mi. E of Grand Junction
No. of Rooms: 1

No. of Private Baths: **1**
Double/pb: **$40**
Single/pb: **$30**
Open: **All year**
Breakfast: **Continental**

Pets: **Yes**
Children: **Welcome**
Smoking: **No**
Social Drinking: **Permitted**
Airport/Station Pickup: **Yes**

Set on a hillside at the foot of Grand Mesa, this B&B occupies the ground floor of a country home surrounded by pinyon, oak, and juniper trees. The three-room suite has a queen-size bed, living room, woodburning stove, and a fully equipped kitchen. Guests may while away the hours with fishing, hiking, boating, and cross-country and downhill skiing. Timberline lies within easy driving distance of Powderhorn Ski Resort, Black Canyon of the Gunnison, Colorado National Monument, and Curecanti National Recreation Area.

## Holden House—1902 Victorian Bed & Breakfast Inn
**1102 WEST PIKES PEAK AVENUE, COLORADO SPRINGS, COLORADO 80904**

Tel: **(719) 471-3980**
Best Time to Call: **9 AM–9 PM**
Hosts: **Sallie and Welling Clark**
No. of Rooms: **6**
No. of Private Baths: **6**
Double/pb: **$75**
Suites: **$100–$110**
Open: **All year**

Breakfast: **Full**
Credit Cards: **AMEX, DC, DISC, MC, VISA**
Pets: **No**
Children: **No**
Smoking: **No**
Social Drinking: **Permitted**

Built by Isabel Holden, this 1902 storybook Victorian, 1906 carriage house, and adjacent 1898 Victorian are centrally located near historic Old Colorado City. The inn, lovingly restored by the Clarks in 1985, is filled with antiques and family heirlooms. Named for mining towns, guest rooms are furnished with queen beds, period furnishings, and down pillows. The inn also boasts four romantic suites with tubs for two, mountain views, fireplaces, and more! Gourmet breakfasts, served in the elegant formal dining room, might include carob chip muffins, Sallie's famous Southwestern Eggs Fiesta, fresh fruit, gourmet coffee, tea, and juice. Complimentary refreshments, homemade cookies, and turn-down service are just some of Holden House's special touches. Sallie and Welling will be happy to help in planning your itinerary around the many activities in the Pikes Peak region. Friendly resident cats Mingtoy and Muffin will greet you.

## The Painted Lady Bed & Breakfast Inn ✪
**1318 WEST COLORADO AVENUE, COLORADO SPRINGS, COLORADO 80904**

Tel: **(719) 473-3165**
Best Time to Call: **After 5 PM**

Hosts: **Valerie and Zan Maslowski**
No. of Rooms: **3**

No. of Private Baths: **3**
Double/pb: **$65–$115**
Open: **All year**
Reduced Rates: **10% seniors**
Breakfast: **Full**

Credit Cards: **DISC, MC, VISA**
Pets: **No**
Children: **Welcome, Over 10**
Smoking: **No**
Social Drinking: **Permitted**

This restored 1894 Victorian home is complete with gingerbread trim, wraparound porches, coach lights, and wonderful mountain views. Inside, the guest rooms feature lace curtains and period furnishings. One room includes a clawfooted "tub for two" for that extra bit of pampering. The common rooms are bright and inviting. A hearty breakfast will ready you for a full day of business, sightseeing in the Pikes Peak area, or for shopping and browsing just blocks away in historic Old Colorado City. The resident cat will be on hand to greet you, provide a homey atmosphere, and of course, beg for a tummy rub!

## The Elizabeth Anne B&B ✪
### P.O. BOX 1051, CRESTED BUTTE, COLORADO 81224

Tel: **(970) 349-0147**
Hosts: **Carl and Judy Jones**
Location: **225 mi. SW of Denver**
No. of Rooms: **4**
No. of Private Baths: **4**
Double/pb: **$69–$85**
Single/pb: **$65–$80**
Open: **May 25–Oct. 10; Nov. 15–
  Apr. 15**

Breakfast: **Full**
Credit Cards: **AMEX, MC, VISA**
Pets: **No**
Children: **Welcome, (large room only)**
Smoking: **No**
Social Drinking: **Permitted**
Minimum Stay: **2 days winter
  weekends**
Airport Pickup: **Yes**

The Elizabeth Anne is in the National Historic District of Crested Butte, an 1880s mining town. This new Victorian home echoes the warmth and charm of Crested Butte's past. The common areas are decorated with Queen Anne furniture, and the bedrooms have a Victorian appeal of their own. Other amenities are a soothing hot tub, guest refrigerator, and bicycle and ski storage. Recreational opportunities abound, with Nordic and Alpine skiing in the winter. Summer offers mountain biking, hiking, fishing, golfing, and horseback riding. Crested Butte also has a myriad of shops and gourmet restaurants. Your hosts, Carl and Judy, who recently retired from engineering and nursing careers, invite you to come and share their mountain experience.

## Queen Anne Bed & Breakfast Inn ✪
### 2147 TREMONT PLACE, DENVER, COLORADO 80205

Tel: **(303) 296-6666; (800) 432-INNS
  [4667]; fax: 296-2151**
Best Time to Call: **Until 9 PM**

Host: **Tom King**
No. of Rooms: **14**
No. of Private Baths: **14**

Double/pb: **$75–$155**
Open: **All year**
Breakfast: **Full**
Credit Cards: **AMEX, DC, DISC, MC, VISA**

Pets: **No**
Children: **Welcome, over 12**
Smoking: **No**
Social Drinking: **Permitted**

Located in the residential Clements Historic District, these two side-by-side Victorians built in 1879 and 1886 face Benedict Fountain Park. Decorated in the Queen Anne style, the luxurious bedrooms offer mountain or city views along with such touches as heirloom antiques, air-conditioning, and writing desks. Fine art, good books, and unobtrusive chamber music provide a lovely backdrop. A generous breakfast is served, including seasonal fruits, assorted breads, juice, granola, and a special blend of coffee. The Central Business District, museums, shopping, and diverse restaurants are within walking distance. You are always welcome to help yourself to fruit, candy, and soft drinks.

## Country Sunshine B&B
**35130 HIGHWAY 550 NORTH, DURANGO, COLORADO 81301**

Tel: **(970) 247-2853; (800) 383-2853**
Best Time to Call: **9 AM–6 PM**
Hosts: **Beanie and Gary Archie**
No. of Rooms: **7**
No. of Private Baths: **7**
Double/pb: **$85**
Open: **All year**

Breakfast: **Full**
Credit Cards: **AMEX, DC, DISC, MC, VISA**
Pets: **No**
Children: **Welcome, over 5**
Smoking: **No**
Social Drinking: **Permitted**

This ranch-style home sits on three acres overlooking the Animas River Valley. Beanie and Gary offer guests a leisure room with a massive lava-rock fireplace and a large outdoor spa. Wildlife is abundant and the views are spectacular. A hearty breakfast is served each morning and a wide variety of refreshments are always available. Purgatory Ski Area, Mesa Verde National Park and the Durango & Silverton Narrow Gauge Train are all nearby. Country Sunshine is a comfortable, casual, get-away-from-it-all kind of place. Families are especially welcome.

## The Leland House Bed & Breakfast Suites
**721 EAST SECOND AVENUE, DURANGO, COLORADO 81301**

Tel: **(303) 385-1920; (800) 664-1920**
Best Time to Call: **Days**
Host: **Kirk Komick**
Location: **350 mi. NW of Denver**
No. of Rooms: **10**
No. of Private Baths: **10**
Double/pb: **$85–$95**

Suites: **$125–$175**
Open: **All year**
Reduced Rates: **Available**
Breakfast: **Full**
Other Meals: **Available**
Credit Cards: **MC, VISA**
Pets: **No**

Children: **Welcome**                    Social Drinking: **Permitted**
Smoking: **No**

Originally built in 1927 as an apartment house, the Leland House was restored by the Komicks as a B&B in 1993. All rooms have cable TV and telephone service. Six suites have separate living rooms, bedrooms, and full service kitchens; four studios have kitchenettes. The interior is decorated with rustic antiques, accented by photos, memorabilia, and biographies of historic figures associated with the property. Leland House is steps away from Durango's historic downtown district and the Durango-Silverton Narrow Gauge Railroad Station. Gourmet breakfasts consist of fresh-baked goods, homemade granola, and may include fruit-filled French toast or a Southwestern breakfast burrito.

## Lightner Creek Inn Bed and Breakfast ✪
999 C.R. 207, DURANGO, COLORADO 81301

| | |
|---|---|
| Tel: **(303) 259-1226**; fax: **(303) 259-0732** | Open: **All year** |
| Best Time to Call: **9 AM–9 PM** | Reduced Rates: **20% Nov. 1–Apr. 30** |
| Hosts: **Richard and Julie Houston** | Breakfast: **Full** |
| Location: **4 mi W of Durango** | Credit Cards: **DISC, MC, VISA** |
| No. of Rooms: **8** | Pets: **No** |
| No. of Private Baths: **5** | Children: **Welcome 10 and over** |
| Max. No. Sharing Bath: **4** | Smoking: **No** |
| Double/pb: **$95–$150** | Social Drinking: **Permitted** |
| Double/sb: **$85–$95** | Minimum Stay: **2 Nights Holiday Weekends** |

Nestled among rugged peaks, shimmering streams, and grazing llamas and horses, Lightner Creek Inn's 20-acre pastoral setting deserves to be discovered. This 1903 French countryside home has been exquisitely renovated, providing a casual but elegantly romantic retreat. The Inn combines charming Victorian detail with antique furnishings and cozy fireplaces, gourmet breakfasts, and the warmth and hospitality of Julie and Richard. While only four miles from Durango (home of the Durango-Silverton Narrow Gauge train) and an easy ride to Mesa Verde, Purgatory, Telluride, and Wolf Creek, the Inn offers excellent mountain trails, trout fishing, and spectacular vistas, making a stay here truly memorable.

## Logwood—The Verheyden Inn ✪
35060 HIGHWAY 550, DURANGO, COLORADO 81301

| | |
|---|---|
| Tel: **(303) 259-4396**; **(800) 369-4082** | No. of Rooms: **6** |
| Best Time to Call: **After 10 AM** | No. of Private Baths: **6** |
| Hosts: **Debby and Greg Verheyden** | Double/pb: **$75–$130** |
| Location: **212 mi. NW of Albuquerque, New Mexico** | Single/pb: **$55–$120** |
| | Open: **All year** |

Reduced Rates: **$10 less winter
single occupancy**
Breakfast: **Full**
Credit Cards: **MC, VISA**
Pets: **No**

Children: **Welcome, over 7**
Smoking: **No**
Social Drinking: **Permitted**
Minimum Stay: **2 nights holidays**

This luxurious red cedar log home is located in the Animas River Valley. The house has a large wraparound deck with plenty of comfortable areas where guests can make themselves at home. Rooms are decorated with home-stitched quilts. A new suite has been added, complete with a fireplace, VCR, TV, and a view of the river. Guests can enjoy downhill or cross-country skiing, taking a sleigh ride or relaxing by the fireplace with a cup of hot chocolate. A full country breakfast and award-winning desserts are served for your enjoyment.

### River House B&B ✪
**495 ANIMAS VIEW DRIVE, DURANGO, COLORADO 81301**

Tel: **(303) 247-4775; (800) 254-4775**
Hosts: **Crystal Carroll and Kate and
Lars Enggren**
No. of Rooms: **7**
No. of Private Baths: **7**
Double/pb: **$65–$95**
Single/pb: **$55–$80**
Open: **All year**
Reduced Rates: **10% Mar. and Oct.**

Breakfast: **Full**
Other Meals: **Available**
Credit Cards: **DISC, MC, VISA**
Pets: **No**
Children: **Welcome**
Smoking: **No**
Social Drinking: **Permitted**
Airport/Station Pickup: **Yes**

Healthful gourmet breakfasts are served in this B&B's spectacular, 900-square-foot atrium featuring eight skylights, a hot tub, a goldfish pond, and a cascading waterfall. From the bedrooms, views of the Animas River Valley often include elk, deer, geese, and eagles. Skiers enjoy the warmth of three fireplaces, while the large-screen TV is alive with nature videos. The house is often reserved for weddings, reunions, and retreats. Massage and hypnotherapy are offered by appointment.

### Scrubby Oaks Bed & Breakfast ✪
**P.O. BOX 1047, DURANGO, COLORADO 81302**

Tel: **(303) 247-2176**
Best Time to Call: **Early mornings;
evenings**
Host: **Mary Ann Craig**
Location: **4 mi. from junction 160 and
550**
No. of Rooms: **7**
No. of Private Baths: **3**
Max. No. Sharing Bath: **4**
Double/pb: **$75**

Single/pb: **$60**
Double/sb: **$65**
Single/sb: **$50**
Open: **Apr. 30–Oct. 31**
Breakfast: **Full**
Pets: **No**
Children: **Welcome**
Smoking: **No**
Social Drinking: **Permitted**

There's a quiet country feeling to this two-story home set on 10 acres overlooking the spectacular Animas Valley and surrounding mountains. Trees and gardens frame the patios where breakfast is apt to be served. All breads and preserves are homemade, and strawberry Belgian waffles are a specialty. On chilly mornings, the kitchen fireplace is the cozy backdrop for your wake-up cup of coffee or cocoa. You are made to feel part of the family and are welcome to play pool, take a sauna, read a book, watch a VCR movie, or simply take in the crisp air.

## Eagle Cliff House
### BOX 4312, ESTES PARK, COLORADO 80517

| | |
|---|---|
| Tel: (303) 586-5425 | Open: All year |
| Best Time to Call: Early morning | Breakfast: Full |
| Hosts: Nancy and Mike Conrin | Pets: No |
| Location: 2½ mi. W of Estes Park | Children: Welcome |
| No. of Rooms: 3 | Smoking: No |
| No. of Private Baths: 3 | Social Drinking: Permitted |
| Double/pb: $80 | Minimum Stay: 2 nights, weekends |
| Guest Cottage: $95 | Airport/Station Pickup: Yes |

Nancy and Mike are dedicated hikers who live within walking distance of Rocky Mountain National Park, so don't be surprised if they invite you for an afternoon's exploration of their favorite "backyard" trails. Saturday evening get-togethers are commonplace, especially in the summer. Recreational opportunities abound throughout the year, from golf, tennis, and horseback riding, to cross-country and downhill skiing. One guest room of this woodsy retreat is decorated with mementos of Mexico and the American Southwest; the cottage and the second guest room are furnished in Victorian style.

## Elizabeth Street Guest House ✪
### 202 EAST ELIZABETH, FORT COLLINS, COLORADO 80524

| | |
|---|---|
| Tel: (970) 493-BEDS [2337] | Single/sb: $45–$50 |
| Best Time to Call: 10 AM–7 PM | Open: All year |
| Hosts: John and Sheryl Clark | Breakfast: Full |
| Location: 65 mi. N of Denver | Credit Cards: AMEX, MC, VISA (for |
| No. of Rooms: 3 | deposits only) |
| Max. No. Sharing Bath: 4 | Pets: No |
| Double/pb: $85–$90 | Children: Welcome, over 8 |
| Single/pb: $65–$70 | Smoking: No |
| Double/sb: $65–$70 | Social Drinking: Permitted |

This completely renovated and restored 1905 brick American four-square has leaded windows and oak woodwork. Family antiques, plants, old quilts, and handmade touches add to its charm. All of the bedrooms have sinks. It is close to historic Old Town Square, Estes

Park, Rocky Mountain National Park, and a block away from Colorado State University. John and Sheryl will spoil you with their special brand of hospitality and homemade treats.

## Hardy House
**605 BROWNELL STREET, GEORGETOWN, COLORADO 80444**

| | |
|---|---|
| Tel: **(303) 569-3388; (800) 490-4802** | Suite: **$82–$112** |
| Best Time to Call: **10 AM–8 PM** | Open: **All year** |
| Hosts: **Carla and Michael Wagner** | Breakfast: **Full** |
| Location: **50 mi. W of Denver** | Other Meals: **Available** |
| No. of Rooms: **4** | Pets: **No** |
| No. of Private Baths: **4** | Children: **No** |
| Double/pb: **$73–$82** | Smoking: **No** |
| Single/pb: **$63–$72** | Social Drinking: **Permitted** |

Back in the 1870s this bright red Victorian, surrounded by a white picket fence, was the home of a blacksmith. Inside you can relax by the potbelly parlor stove, sleep under feather comforters, and wake up to candlelight breakfast dishes such as waffle cheese strata and coffee cake. Guest quarters range from a two-bedroom suite to rooms with king-size or twin beds. In the evening, the Wagners serve coffee and tea. Hardy House is located in the heart of the Historic District, half a block from the shops of Main Street. It is also close to hiking, skiing, and is walking distance from the Loop Railroad. Perhaps the best way to explore the town is on a six-speed tandem mountain bike, which your hosts will gladly lend.

## The Kaiser House ✪
**932 COOPER AVENUE, GLENWOOD SPRINGS, COLORADO 81601**

| | |
|---|---|
| Tel: **(303) 945-8827** | Breakfast: **Full** |
| Best Time to Call: **9 AM–5 PM** | Credit Cards: **DISC, MC, VISA** |
| Hosts: **Ingrid and Glen Eash** | Pets: **No** |
| Location: **160 mi. W of Denver** | Children: **Welcome, over 8** |
| No. of Rooms: **7** | Smoking: **No** |
| No. of Private Baths: **7** | Social Drinking: **Permitted** |
| Double/pb: **$62–$122** | Minimum Stay: **Weekends and holidays** |
| Single/pb: **$42–$92** | Station Pickup: **Yes** |
| Open: **All year** | |
| Reduced Rates: **10% for 4 nights or more** | |

Located in the center of Glenwood Springs, the "Spa of the Rockies," Kaiser House combines turn-of-the-century charm and modern comforts. Each bedroom, decorated in Victorian style, has a private bath. In the winter, before hitting the ski slopes, savor a gourmet breakfast in either the spacious dining room or the sunny breakfast nook. In the summer, enjoy brunch on the private patio. From Kaiser House, it's an easy walk to parks, shopping, fine restaurants, and the hot-springs pool and vapor caves.

## The Dove Inn
### 711 14TH STREET, GOLDEN, COLORADO 80401-1906

| | |
|---|---|
| Tel: **(303) 278-2209** | Open: **All year** |
| Hosts: **Sue and Guy Beals** | Reduced Rates: **10% weekly** |
| Location: **10 mi. W of downtown Denver** | Breakfast: **Full** |
| | Credit Cards: **AMEX, DC, MC, VISA** |
| No. of Rooms: **6** | Pets: **No** |
| No. of Private Baths: **6** | Children: **Welcome (crib)** |
| Double/pb: **$55–$77** | Smoking: **No** |
| Single/pb: **$48–$70** | Social Drinking: **Permitted** |

The Dove Inn is a charming Victorian on grounds beautifully landscaped with decks, walkways, and huge trees. The house has many bay windows, dormers, and angled ceilings; each room is individually decorated with pretty wallpapers and Victorian touches. Breakfast specialties such as cinnamon rolls and fresh fruit compotes are served. This delightful inn is located in the foothills of West Denver in one of the state's most beautiful valleys, yet it is just minutes from downtown Denver, historic Golden, and many other Rocky Mountain attractions. No unmarried couples, please.

## The Cider House ✪
### 1126 GRAND AVENUE, GRAND JUNCTION, COLORADO 81501

| | |
|---|---|
| Tel: **(303) 242-9087** | Open: **All year** |
| Host: **Helen Mills** | Reduced Rates: **Available** |
| Location: **2 mi. from I-70** | Breakfast: **Full** |
| No. of Rooms: **3** | Other Meals: **Available** |
| No. of Private Baths: **1** | Credit Cards: **MC** |
| Max. No. Sharing Bath: **4** | Pets: **Sometimes** |
| Double/pb: **$48** | Children: **Welcome** |
| Single/pb: **$35** | Smoking: **Permitted** |
| Double/sb: **$45** | Social Drinking: **Permitted** |
| Single/sb: **$30** | Airport/Station Pickup: **Yes** |

Nestled in the heart of Grand Junction is this two-story frame house built at the start of the century. It is comfortably decorated with period furnishings, old-fashioned wallpapers, and nostalgic touches. Lace curtains and French doors add to the elegance of the living room. Sumptuous breakfasts of locally grown fruit, homemade breads, jams, special waffles, and beverages are served in the adjoining dining room. Nearby attractions include the Grand Mesa, river rafting, dinosaur digs, and some of the best winter skiing in the country.

## Sterling House Bed & Breakfast Inn ✪
**818 12TH STREET, GREELEY, COLORADO 80631**

| | |
|---|---|
| Tel: **(303) 351-8805** | Breakfast: **Full** |
| Host: **Lillian Peeples** | Credit Cards: **MC, VISA** |
| Location: **55 mi. N of Denver** | Other Meals: **Available** |
| No. of Rooms: **2** | Pets: **No** |
| No. of Private Baths: **2** | Children: **Welcome, over 10** |
| Double/pb: **$49** | Smoking: **Restricted** |
| Single/pb: **$44** | Social Drinking: **Permitted** |
| Suite: **$170** | Minimum Stay: **2nd week in May only** |
| Open: **All year** | Foreign Languages: **German** |
| Reduced Rates: **Weekly** | |

One of Greeley's pioneers, cattle baron and banker Asa Sterling built this home for his family in 1886. Under its current ownership, the house retains its Victorian charm, thanks to the period decor and furniture. Downtown Greeley and the University of Northern Colorado are within walking distance, and it's an easy drive to Rocky Mountain National Park. Guests rave about Lillian's full breakfasts, with specialties like German apple pancakes and crêpes Benedict. Romantic candlelight dinners can also be arranged.

## West Pawnee Ranch ✪
**29451 WELD COUNTY ROAD 130, GROVER, COLORADO 80729**

| | |
|---|---|
| Tel: **(970) 895-2482** | Open: **All year** |
| Best Time to Call: **8 AM–10 PM** | Breakfast: **Full** |
| Hosts: **Paul and Louanne Timm** | Other Meals: **Available** |
| Location: **50 mi. N of Greeley** | Pets: **No** |
| No. of Rooms: **2** | Children: **Welcome** |
| No. of Private Baths: **2** | Smoking: **No** |
| Double/pb: **$50–$55** | Social Drinking: **Permitted** |
| Single/pb: **$50** | Airport/Station Pickup: **Yes** |
| Suites: **$55** | |

Paul and Louanne invite you to visit their working ranch, located on the peaceful prairie in northeastern Colorado. Try your hand at ranch jobs, checking cattle, fences and water wells. Activities include horseback riding, hiking, bird-watching. Or bring your mountain bike and ride the grassland trails. In the evenings, join your hosts on the patio and enjoy the view of the prairie with the Chalk Bluffs in the background. The ranch is located four miles from Pawnee National Grasslands, thirty miles from Pawnee Buttes and a historic two-story wooden depot/museum.

## Mary Lawrence Inn
**601 NORTH TAYLOR, GUNNISON, COLORADO 81230**

| | |
|---|---|
| Tel: **(303) 641-3343** | Hosts: **Pat and Jim Kennedy** |
| Best Time to Call: **10 AM–10 PM** | Location: **195 mi. W and S of Denver** |

No. of Rooms: **5**
No. of Private Baths: **5**
Double/pb: **$69**
Single/pb: **$69**
Suites: **$85–$135; sleep 2–4**
Open: **All year**
Breakfast: **Full**

Credit Cards: **MC, VISA**
Pets: **No**
Children: **Welcome, over 6**
Smoking: **No**
Social Drinking: **Permitted**
Airport/Station Pickup: **Yes**

An Italianate frame house with spacious, antique-filled guest rooms, and comfortable common areas, the Mary Lawrence Inn is located in a well-kept neighborhood inside Gunnison's city limits. Surrounded by wilderness and Forest Service land, this B&B is a haven for sportspeople of all types; the Black Canyon of the Gunnison, the Alpine Tunnel, the town of Crested Butte, and many spectacular mountain vistas are all within an hour's drive.

## Two Sisters Inn
**TEN OTOE PLACE, MANITOU SPRINGS, COLORADO 80829**

Tel: **(719) 685-9684; (800) 2 SIS-INN
  [274-7466]**
Best Time to Call: **Evenings**
Hosts: **Sharon Smith and Wendy
  Goldstein**
Location: **4 mi. W of Colorado Springs**
No. of Rooms: **5**
No. of Private Baths: **3**
Max. No. Sharing Bath: **4**
Double/pb: **$75**

Double/sb: **$63**
Guest Cottage: **$95**
Open: **All year**
Breakfast: **Full**
Credit Cards: **DISC, MC, VISA**
Pets: **No**
Children: **Welcome, over 10**
Smoking: **No**
Social Drinking: **Permitted**

Built in 1919 as a boardinghouse, this rose-colored Victorian bungalow has been lovingly restored with four bedrooms and a honeymoon cottage in the back garden. Family collectibles, antiques, and fresh flowers fill the sunny rooms. Your hosts, former caterers, set out a gourmet breakfast of home-baked muffins, freshly ground coffee, fresh fruit, and a hot entree. The Inn is located at the base of Pikes Peak, in Manitou Springs' historic district. Nearby attractions include the Garden of the Gods, the cog railway, the U.S. Air Force Academy, and the Olympic Training Center.

## Maria's Bed & Breakfast
**20538 HIGHWAY 550 SOUTH, MONTROSE, COLORADO 81401**

Tel: **(970) 249-8288; fax: (970) 240-
  8281**
Best Time to Call: **8 AM–9 PM**
Hosts: **Maria and Harold LaMar**
Location: **5 mi. S of Montrose**
No. of Rooms: **3**
No. of Private Baths: **3**
Double/pb: **$50**
Open: **Mar. 15–Dec. 31**

Breakfast: **Full**
Pets: **No**
Children: **Welcome**
Smoking: **No**
Social Drinking: **No**
Airport/Station Pickup: **Yes**
Foreign Languages: **French, German,
  Flemish**

Colorful flowers, trees and a beautifully groomed yard surround this gambrel-roofed home. Summer evenings can be spent on the large comfortable porches enjoying the majestic views of the San Juan Mountains while indulging in one of Harold's homemade pies. A few things to do and see include hunting, hiking, fishing, and skiing. Black Canyon National Monument, Ouray Hot Springs, Ridegeway Recreational Area, and Telluride are famous for their summer festivals and skiing. Maria and Harold give all guests special attention and pamper them with home-cooked specialties, such as Belgian waffles with strawberries and whipped topping, eggs Benedict, Quiche Lorraine, blueberry muffins, breads and jams.

## Claveau's Streamside Bed and Breakfast ✪
**18820 C.R. 162, NATHROP, COLORADO 81236**

| | |
|---|---|
| Tel: **(719) 395-2553** | Open: **All year** |
| Best Time to Call: **Before 8 AM; after 6 PM** | Reduced Rates: **Nov.–May** |
| | Breakfast: **Full** |
| Hosts: **Denny and Kathy Claveau** | Pets: **No** |
| Location: **130 mi. SW of Denver** | Children: **Call in advance** |
| No. of Rooms: **3** | Smoking: **No** |
| No. of Private Baths: **3** | Social Drinking: **Permitted** |
| Double/pb: **$64–$69** | Minimum Stay: **Holiday weekends** |

Located within San Isabel National Forest, Claveau's Streamside Bed and Breakfast is in the shadow of the Rockies' Collegiate Peaks. Mt. Princeton, Mt. Yale, Mt. Harvard, Mt. Oxford, and other challenging peaks beckon all to climb their glistening summits. Wildlife abounds here; deer, elk, bighorn sheep, and mountain goats are your hosts' neighbors. Winter offers downhill and cross-country skiing. Summer offers fishing, hiking, white-water rafting, horseback riding, or just relaxing by a stream. Kathy and Denny are environmentally active outdoor advocates. They look forward to helping guests plan their daily adventures, which may range from fine dining to visiting natural hot springs.

## Country Gardens ☼
**1619 EAST 136TH AVENUE, P.O. BOX 33765, NORTHGLENN, COLORADO 80233-0765**

| | |
|---|---|
| Tel: **(303) 451-1724** | Open: **All year** |
| Best Time to Call: **12–9 PM** | Reduced Rates: **5% Seniors** |
| Hosts: **Arlie and Donna Munsie** | Breakfast: **Full** |
| Location: **13 mi. N of Denver, ½ mi. E of I-25** | Credit Cards: **MC, VISA** |
| No. of Rooms: **4** | Pets: **No** |
| No. of Private Baths: **4** | Children: **Welcome, over 12** |
| Double/pb: **$65–$75** | Smoking: **No** |
| Single/pb: **$55–$65** | Social Drinking: **Permitted** |
| Suites: **$100** | Airport/Station Pickup: **Yes** |

Picture a country Victorian home on four acres with lots of natural landscaping and a panoramic mountain view. This B&B is lovingly decorated with family antiques and country furnishings throughout. Enjoy the rock garden with its waterfall, goldfish pond and flowers, as well as other gardens with walking paths and sitting areas. Relax in the outdoor hot tub or lovely Victorian gazebo. Sit or swing on the covered wraparound porch. A typical country breakfast includes cream cheese pecan waffles with fruit toppings, sausage, homemade muffins, and juice. Country Gardens is one block from an 18-hole municipal golf course and walking/riding trails, one hour from many mountain attractions including old mining towns with legalized gambling.

## Ouray 1898 House ☼
**322 MAIN STREET, P.O. BOX 641, OURAY, COLORADO 81427**

| | |
|---|---|
| Tel: **(970) 325-4871** | Open: **May 1–Jan. 5** |
| Best Time to Call: **After 5 PM** | Breakfast: **Full** |
| Hosts: **Kathy and Lee Bates** | Credit Cards: **MC, VISA** |
| Location: **On Hwy. 550** | Pets: **No** |
| No. of Rooms: **3** | Children: **Welcome** |
| No. of Private Baths: **3** | Smoking: **No** |
| Double/pb: **$68–$85** | Social Drinking: **Permitted** |

This 90-year-old house has been carefully renovated and combines the elegance of the 19th century with the comfortable amenities of the 20th. Each guest room features a spectacular view of the San Juan Mountains from its private deck. Breakfast is beautifully served on antique china. Jeep trips, horseback riding, hiking, browsing in the many quaint shops, and relaxing in the hot springs are but a few of the local diversions.

## Broken Arrow B&B & Horse Hotel ☉
### 96 OAKRIDGE DRIVE, PAGOSA SPRINGS, COLORADO 81147

| | |
|---|---|
| Tel: (970) 731-5758 | Open: All year |
| Hosts: Pat, Jim and Misty Milam | Reduced Rates: 10% seniors |
| Location: 11 mi. W of Pagosa Springs | Breakfast: Continental |
| No. of Rooms: 3 | Pets: Welcome |
| No. of Private Baths: 3 | Children: Welcome |
| Double/pb: $40 | Smoking: No |
| Suites: $50–$60 | Social Drinking: Permitted |

The Broken Arrow B&B & Horse Hotel is located in southwest Colorado, in the heart of the San Juan Mountains. Guests will be within driving distance of the famous Narrow Gauge Railroad in both Durango, Colorado, and Chama, New Mexico. You may also want to visit the Anasazi Indian ruins up on Chimney Rock Mountains and in Cortez, Colorado. For the outdoors person, Pagosa Springs offers some of the best hunting, fishing, and skiing in Colorado. And to ease the aches and pains from the outdoors, Pagosa Springs has a natural mineral hot springs downtown.

## Mountain Vista Bed & Breakfast ☉
### P.O. BOX 1398, 358 LAGOON LANE, SILVERTHORNE, COLORADO 80498

| | |
|---|---|
| Tel: (970) 468-7700 | Double/sb: $65–$75 |
| Best Time to Call: Evening | Open: All year |
| Host: Sandy Ruggaber | Reduced Rates: 10% seniors |
| Location: 60 mi. W of Denver | Breakfast: Full, Continental |
| No. of Rooms: 3 | Pets: No |
| No. of Private Baths: 1 | Children: Welcome, over 6 |
| Max. No. Sharing Bath: 4 | Smoking: No |
| Double/pb: $70–$75 | Social Drinking: Permitted |

Mountain Vista offers something for everyone. Since it's surrounded by fine resorts like Keystone, Arapahoe Basin, Copper Mountain, Breckenridge, and Vail, guests can enjoy downhill skiing at its best. In the summer, try hiking, kayaking, cycling, golf, tennis, rafting, and fishing (an outdoor grill is available for you to cook your catch). Visit the factory outlet stores or go to the many concerts, festivals, and cultural events offered throughout Summit County. After a busy day, relax by the fireplace with your favorite drink, watch TV, read, do a puzzle, or retire to a warm comfortable room. You will awaken in the morning to the smell of a hearty homemade breakfast.

# Starry Pines ✪
**2262 SNOWMASS CREEK ROAD, SNOWMASS, COLORADO 81654**

| | |
|---|---|
| Tel: **(303) 927-4202; (800) 527-4202** | Apartment: **$100, for two** |
| Best Time to Call: **7 AM–9 AM,** | Open: **All year** |
| **4 PM–9 PM** | Reduced Rates: **Available** |
| Host: **Shelley Burke** | Breakfast: **Continental** |
| Location: **200 mi. W of Denver** | Children: **Welcome, over 6** |
| No. of Rooms: **2** | Smoking: **No** |
| Max. No. Sharing Bath: **4** | Social Drinking: **Permitted** |
| Double/sb: **$80–$90** | Minimum Stay: **2 nights ski season** |
| Single/sb: **$75–$85** | |

On 70 private acres with its own trout stream and a panoramic view of the Rockies, Starry Pines offers you year-round activities and hospitality. Enjoy the Aspen summer music festival, ballet, and theater. Try hot-air balloon rides landing in the B&B's fields, or biking, hiking, jeeping, and riding in the back country. For quieter moments, there's a secluded picnic site with horseshoes and a hammock by the stream. Fall unveils spectacular aspen foliage. Winter and spring bring world-renowned skiing at four mountains only 25 minutes away, plus snowshoeing and cross-country skiing at Starry Pines's own door. At the end of the day, bathe in the hot tub on the patio, then sit around the living room fireplace or watch a movie on the VCR.

# The Victorian Lady ✪
**4199 WEST 76TH AVENUE, WESTMINSTER, COLORADO 80030**

| | |
|---|---|
| Tel: **(303) 428-9829** | Open: **All year** |
| Best Time to Call: **Anytime** | Breakfast: **Full** |
| Host: **Karen Sanders** | Other Meals: **Available** |
| Location: **10 mi. NW of Denver** | Pets: **No** |
| No. of Rooms: **2** | Children: **Welcome, over 8** |
| Max. No. Sharing Bath: **4** | Smoking: **No** |
| Double/sb: **$60** | Social Drinking: **No** |
| Single/sb: **$50** | Airport/Station Pickup: **Yes** |

You'll step back in time upon entering The Victorian Lady, where the rooms are filled with lovely reminders of another day. This B&B is ideally located for sightseers: just minutes from downtown Denver and public transportation, it's also near I-70, highway to some of the world's best skiing. Breakfast, served in the gazebo during the summer, may consist of cheese strata, almond poppyseed cake with warmed lemon sauce, or an old Western favorite, hearty biscuits and gravy. There's tea in the afternoon and, at bedtime, snacks that are sure to bring on pleasant dreams.

## Alpen Rose ✪
### 244 FOREST TRAIL, P.O. BOX 769, WINTER PARK, COLORADO 80482

| | |
|---|---|
| Tel: **(303) 726-5039; (800) 531-1373** | Reduced Rates: **10% seniors** |
| Best Time to Call: **Mornings; evenings** | Breakfast: **Full** |
| Hosts: **Robin and Rupert Sommeraver** | Credit Cards: **AMEX, MC, VISA** |
| Location: **62 mi. W of Denver** | Pets: **Sometimes** |
| No. of Rooms: **3** | Children: **Welcome, over 10** |
| No. of Private Baths: **3** | Smoking: **No** |
| Double/pb: **$65–$85** | Social Drinking: **Permitted** |
| Single/pb: **$45–$85** | Airport/Station Pickup: **Yes** |
| Open: **All year** | Foreign Languages: **Austrian, German** |

Surrounded by aspen and pine trees, this woodsy retreat is much like the chalets Rupert remembers from his days as an Austrian Ski School instructor. If you want to go skiing, the Winter Park slopes are just 2 miles away. Hiking, fishing, mountain biking, rafting, and golfing are the main summer activities in this area. Throughout the year, a memorable breakfast with Austrian specialties awaits you in the morning; after the day's adventures, a crackling fire, hot tea, and cookies beckon you home. For those of you who don't mind paying a higher rate, 2 rooms are available.

## Engelmann Pines ✪
### P.O. BOX 1305, WINTER PARK, COLORADO 80482

| | |
|---|---|
| Tel: **(303) 726-4632; (800) 992-9512** | Open: **All year** |
| Hosts: **Heinz and Margaret Engel** | Breakfast: **Full** |
| Location: **67 mi. W of Denver** | Credit Cards: **AMEX, DISC, MC, VISA** |
| No. of Rooms: **7** | Pets: **No** |
| No. of Private Baths: **5** | Children: **Welcome** |
| Max. No. Sharing Bath: **4** | Smoking: **No** |
| Double/pb: **$75–$115** | Social Drinking: **Permitted** |
| Single/pb: **$65–$105** | Airport/Station Pickup: **Yes** |
| Double/sb: **$55–$75** | Foreign Languages: **German** |
| Single/sb: **$45–$65** | |

From its Rocky Mountain perch, this spacious modern lodge offers spectacular views of the Continental Divide. Bathrooms are equipped with Jacuzzis, and there is a complete kitchen for guests' use. A free bus ferries skiers from the front door to some of Colorado's best ski slopes; cross-country ski aficionados will find a trail just across the road. When the snow melts, it's time to go golfing, hiking, fishing, and horseback riding. In the morning, eager sportsmen and -women can fill up on marzipan cake, muesli, and fresh fruit crêpes.

# HAWAII

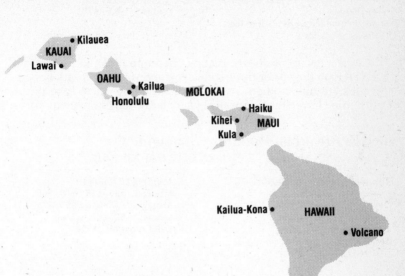

## Babson Reservation Service
**3371 KEHA DRIVE, KIHEI, MAUI, HAWAII 96753**

Tel: **(808) 874-1166; (800) 824-6409;**
  **fax: (808) 879-7906**
Coordinators: **Ann and Bob Babson**
States/Regions Covered: **All Hawaiian
  Islands**

Rates (Double):
  Modest: **$55**
  Average: **$70**
  Luxury: **$95**

Ann and Bob can place you in any of 150 B&Bs or cottages throughout the Hawaiian Islands. Experience the real Hawaii in charming yet economical surroundings. Explore the beautiful white sand beaches and rain forests, snorkel in magical waters, and get to know the real Hawaii. Whatever your interests may be, the Babsons will be happy to direct you.

## Bed & Breakfast—Hawaii
### P.O. BOX 449, KAPAA, HAWAII 96746

| | |
|---|---|
| Tel: **(808) 822-7771; (800) 733-1632;** fax: **(808) 822-2723** | Descriptive Directory: **$10.95** Rates (Single/Double): |
| Best Time to Call: **8:30 AM–4:30 PM** | Modest: **$45 / $55** |
| Coordinators: **Evie Warner (Nancy and Patty)** | Average: **$65 / $85** Luxury: **$85 / $125** |
| States/Regions Covered: **All of the Hawaiian Islands** | Credit Cards: **MC, VISA** Minimum Stay: **2 nights** |

Hawaii is a group of diverse islands offering traditional warmth and hospitality to the visitor through this membership organization. Some are separate units; others are in the main house. Most have private baths. The University of Hawaii at Oahu is convenient to many B&Bs.

## Bed & Breakfast Honolulu Statewide ✪
### 3242 KAOHINANI DRIVE, HONOLULU, HAWAII 96817

| | |
|---|---|
| Tel: **(800) 288-4666; (808) 595-7533;** fax: **(808) 595-2030** | Rates (Single/Double): |
| Best Time to Call: **8 AM–5 PM Mon.–Fri., 8 AM–noon** | Modest: **$40–$55 / $40–$60** Average: **$55–$70 / $55–$75** |
| Coordinator: **Mary Lee** | Luxury: **$75 up / $75 up** |
| States/Regions Covered: **Hawaii: statewide** | Credit Cards: **MC, VISA** |

This home-based family service, started in 1982, pays careful attention to visitors who want to be more than tourists. That's made it Hawaii's largest statewide agency, listing more than 700 rooms, on all islands. Many agencies have membership fees and directories; this one doesn't! When you call the 800 number or fax Bed & Breakfast Honolulu, Mary can match your needs, desires, and pocketbook to her computerized listings. This service's size lets her offer very favorable rates on rental cars and inter-island air.

## Haikuleana B&B, Plantation Style ✪
### 555 HAIKU ROAD, HAIKU, MAUI, HAWAII 96708

| | |
|---|---|
| Tel: **(808) 575-2890** | Reduced Rates: **After 5th night** |
| Best Time to Call: **8 AM–8 PM; HST** | Breakfast: **Full** |
| Host: **Frederick J. Fox, Jr.** | Pets: **No** |
| Location: **12 mi. E of Kahului** | Children: **Welcome, over 6** |
| No. of Rooms: **4** | Smoking: **No** |
| No. of Private Baths: **4** | Social Drinking: **Permitted** |
| Double/pb: **$80–$95** | Minimum Stay: **2 nights** |
| Single/pb: **$65–$80** | Foreign Languages: **Swedish** |
| Open: **All year** | |

Experience the real feelings of "aloha" in an 1850s Hawaiian plantation home. Set in the agricultural district, close to secluded waterfalls and beautiful beaches, Haikuleana is a convenient way station for visitors headed to Hana and Haleakala Crater. Swimming ponds, the world's best windsurfing, and golf courses are all nearby. Fred completely renovated the house; you'll admire its high ceilings, plank floors, porch, and lush Hawaiian gardens. The cool, tropical rooms are furnished with drapes, ticking comforters, wicker, and antiques.

## Pilialoha Bed & Breakfast Cottage ✪
### 2512 KAUPAKALUA ROAD, HAIKU, MAUI, HAWAII 96708

| | |
|---|---|
| Tel: **(808) 572-1440** | Breakfast: **Continental** |
| Best Time to Call: **9 AM–9 PM** | Pets: **No** |
| Hosts: **Bill and Machiko Heyde** | Children: **Welcome** |
| Location: **10 mi. E of Kahului** | Smoking: **No** |
| Guest Cottages: **$85** | Social Drinking: **Permitted** |
| Open: **All year** | Minimum Stay: **2 nights** |
| Reduced Rates: **Weekly** | Foreign Languages: **Japanese** |

*Pilialoha*, in Hawaiian, means "friendship." Located in lush, cool upcountry Maui on a two-acre property, with half-century-old eucalyptus trees and a cottage garden, Pilialoha is convenient to North Shore beaches, Haleakala National Park, and the road to Hana. This is a separate small house for one group of guests, most comfortable for two people but accommodates up to five. The cottage has a fully equipped kitchen with complimentary assortment of coffee and teas, a cable TV, and private telephone in the living room. Bill enjoys ham radio and welcomes other hams to operate his station. Machiko is an artist and avid gardener.

## Bev & Monty's Bed & Breakfast ✪
### 4571 UKALI STREET, HONOLULU, OAHU, HAWAII 96818

| | |
|---|---|
| Tel: **(808) 422-9873** | Open: **All year** |
| Best Time to Call: **7 AM–9 PM; HST** | Reduced Rates: **Weekly** |
| Hosts: **Bev and Monty Neese** | Breakfast: **Continental** |
| Location: **4½ mi. from airport** | Pets: **No** |
| No. of Rooms: **2** | Children: **Welcome** |
| Max. No. Sharing Bath: **4** | Smoking: **Permitted** |
| Double/sb: **$50** | Social Drinking: **Permitted** |
| Single/sb: **$40** | Airport/Station Pickup: **Yes** |

This typical Hawaiian home is convenient to many of Hawaii's most popular attractions. Bev and Monty are just a mile above historic Pearl Harbor, and the Arizona Memorial can be seen from their veranda. They enjoy sharing a Hawaiian aloha for a convenient overnight stay or a long vacation where they can share their favorite places with you. This comfortable home is just off the access road leading east to

Honolulu and Waikiki, or west to the North Shore beaches, sugar plantations, and pineapple fields. Good hiking country as well as city entertainment and shopping centers are located nearby.

## Akamai Bed & Breakfast
**172 KUUMELE PLACE, KAILUA, OAHU, HAWAII 96734**

| | |
|---|---|
| Tel: **(808) 261-2227** | Open: **All year** |
| Best Time to Call: **8 AM–8 PM** | Breakfast: **Full** |
| Host: **Diane Van Ryzin** | Pets: **No** |
| No. of Rooms: **2** | Children: **Welcome, over 7** |
| No. of Private Baths: **2** | Smoking: **Permitted** |
| Double/pb: **$60** | Social Drinking: **Permitted** |
| Single/pb: **$60** | Minimum Stay: **3 nights** |

Guests at Akamai stay in a separate wing of the house; each room has a private entrance, bath, cable TV, and radio. Honolulu and Waikiki are within a half-hour drive, but you may prefer to lounge by your host's pool or take the eight-minute stroll to the beach. No meals are served here, but your refrigerator is stocked with breakfast foods and the kitchen area is equipped with light cooking appliances, dishes, and flatware. Laundry facilities are also available.

## Papaya Paradise ✪
**395 AUWINALA ROAD, KAILUA, OAHU, HAWAII 96734**

| | |
|---|---|
| Tel: **(808) 261-0316**; fax: **(808) 261-0316** | Open: **All year** |
| | Breakfast: **Continental** |
| Best Time to Call: **7 AM–8 PM; HST** | Pets: **No** |
| Hosts: **Bob and Jeanette Martz** | Children: **Welcome, over 6** |
| Location: **10 mi. E of Honolulu** | Smoking: **Permitted** |
| No. of Rooms: **2** | Social Drinking: **Permitted** |
| Double/pb: **$70–$75** | Minimum Stay: **3 nights** |

The Martz paradise is on the windward side of Oahu, miles from the high-rise hotels, but just 20 miles from the Waikiki/Honolulu airport. Each guest room has two beds, a ceiling fan, air-conditioning, cable TV, and its own private entrance. Bob loves to cook, and serves breakfast on the lanai overlooking the pool and Jacuzzi. Kailua Beach, a beautiful white sandy beach four miles long, is within easy walking distance.

## Anne's Three Bears Bed & Breakfast ✪
**72-1001 PUUKALA STREET, KAILUA-KONA, HAWAII 96740**

| | |
|---|---|
| Tel: **(800) 765-0480; (808) 325-7563** | Location: **7 mi. N of Kailua-Kona** |
| Best Time to Call: **AM** | No. of Rooms: **2** |
| Hosts: **Anne, Art and Nanette Stockel** | No. of Private Baths: **2** |

Double/pb: **$65–$75**
Open: **All year**
Reduced Rates: **10% weekly**
Breakfast: **Full**
Credit Cards: **MC, VISA**
Pets: **No**

Children: **Welcome, over 2**
Smoking: **No**
Social Drinking: **Permitted**
Minimum Stay: **2 nights**
Foreign Languages: **German**

Anne's Three Bears Bed and Breakfast features comfortable, friendly accommodations and a spectacular view of the Kona coastline. This beautiful cedar home is close to Kailua town and the many beaches on the Kona coast. A terrific breakfast is served each morning on the lanai, and complimentary beach chairs, coolers, and boogie boards are provided.

Anne and Nanette also have a free reservation service specializing in bed and breakfast accommodations on all Hawaiian Islands. They charge no booking fee; all bed and breakfasts have been inspected. Accommodations range from $55 to $85 for two people.

## Hale Maluhia (House of Peace) B&B Inn
**76-770 HUALALAI ROAD, KAILUA-KONA, HAWAII 96740**

Tel: **(800) 559-6627**
Best Time to Call: **9 AM–5 PM**
Hosts: **Ken and Ann Smith**
Location: **2½ mi. SE of Kailua-Kona**
No. of Rooms: **5**
No. of Private Baths: **5**
Double/pb: **$55–$85**
Single/pb: **$50–$80**
Suites: **$110–$225**
Open: **All year**

Reduced Rates: **10% after 7 nights**
Breakfast: **Full**
Credit Cards: **AMEX, DC, DISC, MC, VISA**
Pets: **Sometimes**
Children: **Welcome**
Smoking: **No**
Social Drinking: **Permitted**
Minimum Stay: **3 nights, or pay 5% surcharge**

From a gentle tropical elevation of 900 feet, this beautiful owner-designed inn surveys an acre of old Hawaii coffee, orchard and ranch lands in the Holualoa fruit belt. Yet the site is only 2.5 miles from Kailua-Kona, the heart of the Big Island Recreational Paradise, with easy airport access. Privacy is a top priority with four decks, a game room with slate pool table and cable TV/VCR movie viewing area, and a great room for relaxing. The stone/tile Japanese spa, gardens with stream, waterfalls, koi ponds, water lilies and turtles bring nature close. Buffet of fresh fruits, juices, cereals, breads, rolls, ham, eggs, tea and 100 percent Kona coffee, to name a few of the daily breakfast specialties, get your day off to a good start. Beach and snorkeling equipment are provided at no extra charge.

## Kona Sunset House
### 72-4008 MAMALAHOA HIGHWAY, KAILUA-KONA, HAWAII 96740

Tel: **(808) 325-5901**
Best Time to Call: **7 AM–9 PM**
Hosts: **Kathy and Bill McKown**
Location: **7 mi. N of Kailua-Kona**
No. of Rooms: **2**
Suites: **$65–$75**
Open: **All year**

Breakfast: **Continental**
Pets: **No**
Children: **Welcome**
Smoking: **No**
Social Drinking: **Permitted**
Minimum Stay: **2 nights**

Comfortable trade-wind temperatures and panoramic views of the ocean and sunsets can be savored from your lanai at this B&B located 1600 feet up the western side of Hualalai. Kathy and Bill offer two suites built in 1991. The White Ginger Suite has a queen-size bed, full kitchen, and utensils that guests can use to prepare other meals. The Plumeria Suite has a queen-size bed, small refrigerator, toaster oven, coffeemaker, and a small sink. A Continental breakfast consisting of tropical fruits, baked goods, tropical granola, fruit juices, tea and coffee, is available in each suite, to eat at your convenience.

## Ann & Bob Babson's Vacation Rentals
### 3371 KEHA DRIVE, KIHEI, MAUI, HAWAII 96753

Tel: **(808) 874-1166; (800) 824-6409**
Hosts: **Ann and Bob Babson**
Location: **15 mi. S of Kahului**
No. of Rooms: **3**
No. of Private Baths: **3**
Double/pb: **$65–$80**
Single/pb: **$65–$80**
Guest Cottage: **$95, for 2—sleeps 6**

Open: **All year**
Reduced Rates: **Available**
Breakfast: **Continental**
Pets: **No**
Children: **Welcome, over 12**
Smoking: **No**
Social Drinking: **Permitted**
Minimum Stay: **3 nights**

This B&B is located in Maui Meadows, just above beautiful Wailea, with a 180-degree view of the Pacific Ocean looking west. You can see the islands of Lanai and Kahoolawe, and the sunsets are spectacular. The Babsons' spacious home (3200 square feet) and their two-bedroom, two-bath cottage (700 square feet) are situated on a half-acre of fully landscaped land. The Bougainvillea Suite and Molokini Master Suite include a wonderful Continental breakfast; the Hibiscus Hideaway Apartment and Sunset Cottage have kitchens. All units include telephone for local calls, cable TV, and washer/dryer facilities. Your hosts encourage long-term stays and offer 10% discount for 7-day stays, 20% discount for 30-day stays for direct bookings.

## Whale Watch House ✪
726 KUMULANI DRIVE, KIHEI, MAUI, HAWAII 96753

Tel: (808) 879-0570; fax: (808) 874-8102
Best Time to Call: 8 AM–8 PM
Hosts: Patricia and Patrick Lowry
No. of Rooms: 4
No. of Private Baths: 4
Double/pb: $65
Single/pb: $60
Guest Cottage: $85, sleeps 2; $100, sleeps 4; studio, $85

Open: All year
Reduced Rates: 10% less June, July, Sept., Oct.
Breakfast: Continental
Pets: No
Children: No
Smoking: Yes
Social Drinking: Permitted
Minimum Stay: 2 nights

Whale Watch House is located at the very edge of Ulupalakua Ranch on Haleakala, Maui's 10,228-foot dormant volcano. At every turn there are wonderful views of the ocean, the mountains, and the neighboring islands, Lanai and Kahoolawe. Your hosts' lush tropical garden is filled with fruits and flowers, and the swimming pool is large enough for laps. Sunbathe on the large decks around the house, cottage, and pool, or drive down to the beach—you'll be there in five minutes.

## Hale Ho'o Maha ✪
P.O. BOX 422, KILAUEA, KAUAI, HAWAII 96754

Tel: (800) 851-0291
Best Time to Call: 7 AM–7 PM
Hosts: Kirby B. Guyer and Toby Searles
Location: 28 mi. N of Lihue Airport
No. of Rooms: 4
No. of Private Baths: 2
Max. No. Sharing Bath: 4
Double/pb: $75–$80
Double/sb: $65

Open: All year
Reduced Rates: 10% after 5th night
Breakfast: Continental
Pets: No
Children: Welcome, over 10
Smoking: Permitted
Social Drinking: Permitted
Foreign Languages: Spanish

Escape to a B&B that lives up to its name, which means "house of rest" in Hawaiian. This single-story home is perched on the cliffs along Kauai's north shore. Sandy beaches, rivers, waterfalls, and riding stables are five minutes away. Ask your hosts to direct you to "Queens Bath"—a natural saltwater whirlpool. Guests have full use of the kitchen, gas grill, cable TV, and boogie boards. When in Rome, do as the Romans: Kirby will teach you to dance the hula and make leis, and Toby will instruct you in scuba diving.

## Kula Cottage ✪
206 PUAKEA PLACE, KULA, MAUI, HAWAII 96790

Tel: (808) 871-6230, 878-2043
Best Time to Call: 8 AM–5 PM

Hosts: Larry and Cecilia Gilbert
Location: 16 mi. SE of Kahului

Guest Cottage: **$85, sleeps 2**
Open: **All year**
Breakfast: **Continental**
Pets: **No**
Children: **Welcome, over 12**

Smoking: **Permitted**
Social Drinking: **Permitted**
Minimum Stay: **2 nights**
Foreign Languages: **Spanish**

Flowers and fruit-bearing trees surround this new, fully-equipped one-bedroom bungalow. There are wonderful views of the ocean and the West Maui Mountains, plus loads of amenities: a wood-burning fireplace, washer and dryer, patio furniture, barbecue, cooler, beach towels, and more. Nearby are restaurants, the beach, a national park, gardens, and a winery. Your hosts can arrange sailing, snorkeling, and helicopter trips for you. The Continental breakfast features home-baked breads, fresh fruit, juice, and coffee or tea.

## Kula View Bed and Breakfast ✪

**140 HOLOPUNI ROAD (MAILING ADDRESS: P.O. BOX 322), KULA, MAUI, HAWAII 96790**

Tel: **(808) 878-6736**
Best Time to Call: **8 AM–6 PM**
Host: **Susan Kauai**
Location: **16 mi. E of Kahului**
No. of Rooms: **1**
No. of Private Baths: **1**
Double/pb: **$85**
Single/pb: **$85**

Open: **All year**
Reduced Rates: **10% weekly**
Breakfast: **Continental**
Pets: **No**
Children: **No**
Smoking: **No**
Social Drinking: **Permitted**
Minimum Stay: **2 nights**

The fragrances of island fruits and flowers fill the fresh mountain air at this B&B 2000 feet above sea level, on the slopes of the dormant volcano Haleakala. The upper-level guest room has its own private entrance and a spacious deck that faces majestic Haleakala Crater, where the sunrises are nothing short of magical. Breakfast is served at a sun-warmed wicker table overlooking a flower and herb garden. Kula View is surrounded by two acres of lush greenery, yet it is close to Kahului Airport, shopping centers, parks, and beaches.

## Hale Keoki Bed & Breakfast ✪

**3264 HUAKA PLACE, LAWAI, KAUAI, HAWAII 96756**

Tel: **(808) 332-9094**
Best Time to Call: **Evenings**
Hosts: **George and Susan Czetwertynski**
Location: **12.3 mi. W of Lihue**
No. of Rooms: **1**
No. of Private Baths: **1**
Double/pb: **$85**
Open: **All year**

Reduced Rates: **$75 per day after 7th day**
Breakfast: **Continental**
Pets: **No**
Children: **No**
Smoking: **No**
Social Drinking: **Permitted**
Minimum Stay: **3 nights**
Foreign Languages: **Polish**

Located on the sunny south shore of Kauai, Hale Keoki Bed & Breakfast is central to sandy beaches, restaurants, championship golf courses and numerous other activities that George and Susan will help you plan and enjoy. The guest room overlooks coffee and sugarcane fields with an unobstructed ocean and mountain view—you can watch the sun rise out of the Pacific in the comfort of your bed. Your room has a private entrance, queen bed, kitchenette with microwave, cable TV and VCR. Guests are welcome to luxuriate in the outdoor spa, located in an attractive garden setting. Breakfast is served on the covered lanai, weather permitting.

## Chalet Kilauea—The Inn at Volcano ✪
P.O. BOX 998, VOLCANO, HAWAII 96785

| | |
|---|---|
| Tel: **(808) 967-7786; (800) 937-7786** | Open: **All year** |
| Hosts: **Lisha and Brian Crawford** | Breakfast: **Full** |
| Location: **2 mi. NE of Hawaii Volcanoes** | Pets: **No** |
| **National Park** | Children: **Welcome, crib** |
| No. of Rooms: **5** | Smoking: **Permitted** |
| No. of Private Baths: **5** | Social Drinking: **Permitted** |
| Double/pb: **$85–$175** | Foreign Languages: **Dutch, French,** |
| Guest Cottage: **$75–$225** | **Portuguese, Spanish** |
| Suites: **$175** | |

Brian and Lisha are international travelers who know the art of hospitality. You can stay in the Out of Africa Room, with a merlot marble bath and Jacuzzi tub; the Oriental Room with a teal marble bath and Jacuzzi tub; the Continental Lace Suite with a separate sitting and dressing room and a double Jacuzzi tub; or the Treehouse Suite. All rooms have cable TV and a video library. There's a large common room, a covered deck, and a six-person Jacuzzi in the garden. Ohia trees, hapu'u ferns and healthy brilliant hydrangeas create a lush, beautiful setting. Enjoy a candlelight gourmet breakfast served on fine china and linen in the dining room that has black-and-white tile floors and French windows looking out onto a flower fringed yard.

## Hale Kilauea ✪
P.O. BOX 28, VOLCANO, HAWAII 96785

| | |
|---|---|
| Tel: **(808) 967-7591; (800) 733-3839** | Reduced Rates: **10% seniors** |
| Best Time to Call: **8 AM–10 PM** | Breakfast: **Continental** |
| Hosts: **Maurice Thomas and Jiranan** | Credit Cards: **AMEX, MC, VISA** |
| Location: **28 mi. NE of Hilo** | Pets: **Sometimes** |
| No. of Rooms: **10** | Children: **Welcome** |
| No. of Private Baths: **10** | Smoking: **Permitted** |
| Double/pb: **$55–$75** | Social Drinking: **Permitted** |
| Open: **All year** | |

Hale Kilauea is a quiet place near the heart of Volcano Village, just outside Hawaii Volcanoes National Park, the world's only "drive-in volcano." Colorful, exotic native birds live in the towering pines and ohia trees that surround this B&B. After a day of climbing mountains and peering into craters, enjoy an evening of conversation around the living room fireplace. Your host Maurice, a lifelong Volcano resident, has neighbors and friends who know about volcano geology and the history and tradition of old Hawaii.

**For key to listings, see inside front or back cover.**

○ This star means that rates are guaranteed through December 31, 1996, to any guest making a reservation as a result of reading about the B&B in *Bed & Breakfast U.S.A.—1996* edition.

Important! To avoid misunderstandings, always ask about cancellation policies when booking.

Please enclose a self-addressed, stamped, business-size envelope when contacting reservation services.

For more details on what you can expect in a B&B, see Chapter 1.

Always mention *Bed & Breakfast U.S.A.* when making reservations!

If no B&B is listed in the area you'll be visiting, use the form on page 323 to order a copy of our "List of New B&Bs."

We want to hear from you! Use the form on page 325.

# IDAHO

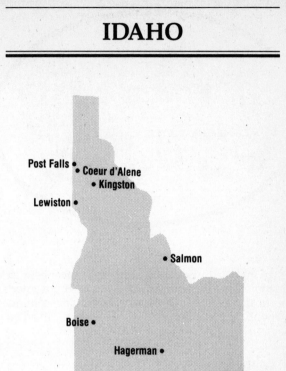

Post Falls •
  • Coeur d'Alene
    • Kingston
Lewiston •

• Salmon

Boise •

Hagerman •

• Fish Haven

## Idaho Heritage Inn
### 109 WEST IDAHO, BOISE, IDAHO 83702

Tel: **(208) 342-8066**
Best Time to Call: **9 AM–8 PM**
Hosts: **Phyllis and Tom Lupher**
No. of Rooms: **6**
No. of Private Baths: **6**
Double/pb: **$59–$69**
Suites: **$79–$89**
Open: **All year**

Breakfast: **Full**
Credit Cards: **AMEX, DISC, MC, VISA**
Pets: **No**
Children: **Welcome, over 5**
Smoking: **No**
Social Drinking: **Permitted**
Station Pickup: **Yes**

The Idaho Heritage Inn is a traditional bed and breakfast located just six blocks from downtown Boise and a short walk from Boise's beautiful greenbelt, a paved river path leading to nature trails, historic museums, art galleries, and Zoo Boise. Many of the city's finest restaurants, shops, and movie theaters are just blocks away. The Inn's guest rooms are gracefully and comfortably appointed with antique

furniture, giving each one its own special atmosphere in which to relax and enjoy. This 1904 inn served as a former governor's mansion and home to the late Senator Frank Church and continues to host guests of political prominence, such as former First Lady Barbara Bush.

## Cricket on the Hearth ✪
### 1521 LAKESIDE AVENUE, COEUR d'ALENE, IDAHO 83814

| | |
|---|---|
| Tel: **(208) 664-6926** | Double/sb: **$50–$60** |
| Best Time to Call: **4 PM–10 PM** | Open: **All year** |
| Hosts: **Al and Karen Hutson** | Reduced Rates: **$5 less after 2nd night** |
| Location: **30 mi. E of Spokane** | Breakfast: **Full** |
| No. of Rooms: **5** | Pets: **No** |
| No. of Private Baths: **3** | Children: **Welcome, over 10** |
| Max. No. Sharing Bath: **4** | Smoking: **No** |
| Double/pb: **$70–$80** | Social Drinking: **Permitted** |

Cricket on the Hearth, Coeur d'Alene's first bed-and-breakfast inn, is a comfortable 1920s cottage with second-story dormer windows and a large front porch. Guests can unwind in the game room; musicians should ask Al about the antique pump organ, which has been in his family since 1916. Lake Coeur d'Alene, just a mile away, is a great place for boating and fishing. The area's many golf courses will lure duffers, and the snow-covered slopes will challenge skiers. Morning meals feature fruit, oven-fresh muffins and breads, and main courses like deep-dish French toast with huckleberry sauce.

## Bear Lake Bed and Breakfast ✪
### 500 LOVELAND LANE, FISH HAVEN, IDAHO 83287

Tel: **(208) 945-2688**
Best Time to Call: **Anytime**
Host: **Esther Harrison**
Location: **125 mi. N of Salt Lake City,
  Utah, on Bear Lake**
No. of Rooms: **4**
No. of Private Baths: **1**
Max. No. Sharing Bath: **4**
Double/pb: **$75**

Double/sb: **$65**
Open: **All year**
Breakfast: **Full**
Credit Cards: **MC, VISA**
Pets: **Sometimes**
Children: **Welcome, over 12**
Smoking: **No**
Social Drinking: **Permitted**

Make yourselves at home in this spacious secluded log home, hand built and designed by the owners. Sitting on the deck you can absorb the peace and beauty of the turquoise blue lake below. The national forest is half a mile behind the B&B and the colors are a sight to behold in the fall with the yellow aspens and red and orange maples mixed with the green pines. With each guest room decorated in a different style, you will find total hospitality here, and yummy aromas coming from the kitchen each morning. Take part in all lake activities, including boat rentals. Apart from the waterfront, there is a tour-guided cave, horseback riding, chuck wagon dinners, and mountain biking. Esther subs at local schools and makes items for the B&B gift shop. She has horses and loves the out-of-doors.

## The Cary House ✪
### 17985 U.S. 30 NORTH, HAGERMAN, IDAHO 83332

Tel: **(208) 837-4848**
Best Time to Call: **8 AM–10 PM**
Hosts: **Darrell and Linda Heinemann**
Location: **90 mi. SE of Boise**
No. of Rooms: **4**
No. of Private Baths: **4**
Double/pb: **$55–$75**

Open: **All year**
Breakfast: **Full**
Pets: **No**
Children: **Welcome, over 12**
Smoking: **No**
Social Drinking: **Permitted**

This beautifully restored two-story farmhouse from the late Victorian era is richly furnished with locally obtained antiques. Your hosts, Idaho natives, combine country-style hospitality with gourmet cooking to ensure that your stay is pleasurable. Cary House is located in the lower portion of the Shoshone Gorge of the Snake River, where the abundance of spring water makes for excellent hiking, fishing, and bird-watching. Several splendid golf courses lie within easy driving distance, and day trips can be made to Sun Valley, Craters of the Moon National Monument, and the Sawtooth National Forest.

## Kingston 5 Ranch Bed & Breakfast ○

P.O. BOX 130-42, 297 SILVER VALLEY ROAD, KINGSTON,
IDAHO 83839

| | |
|---|---|
| Tel: (208) 682-4862; (800) 443-3505 | Suite: **$85** |
| Best Time to Call: **8 AM–8 PM** | Open: **All year** |
| Hosts: **Walt and Pat Gentry** | Breakfast: **Full** |
| Location: **25 mi. E of Coeur d'Alene** | Pets: **By arrangement** |
| No. of Rooms: **2** | Children: **No** |
| No. of Private Baths: **2** | Smoking: **No** |
| Double/pb: **$85** | Social Drinking: **Permitted** |
| Single/pb: **$75** | Minimum Stay: **3 nights suite** |

Kingston 5 Ranch is located in the heart of the Coeur d'Alene Mountains. The luxurious suite has spectacular views of the surrounding mountains and valley and an in-room jetted tub. This 4500-square-foot home offers guests many relaxing options, including an outdoor hot tub. The area is an outdoor paradise. In the winter enjoy skiing and snowmobiling. Summertime, choose from Silver Mountain outdoor concerts, mountain biking, tennis, golfing, hiking, fishing, canoeing and river float trips—all within ten minutes of the property. The biggest summer attraction is on-site horseback riding, your horse or your hosts'. Guests and their horses can be accommodated. A recently retired health care administrator, Walt is an expert horseman who truly enjoys the outdoors. Pat is currently working as a health care administrator and also does clinical research.

## Shiloh Rose B&B ○

3414 SELWAY DRIVE, LEWISTON, IDAHO 83501

| | |
|---|---|
| Tel: (208) 743-2482 | Breakfast: **Full** |
| Best Time to Call: **Before 10 AM** | Credit Cards: **MC, VISA** |
| Host: **Dorthy Mader** | Pets: **Sometimes** |
| Location: **100 mi. S of Spokane, Wash.** | Children: **Welcome, over 10** |
| Suite: **$75** | Smoking: **No** |
| Open: **All year** | Social Drinking: **Permitted** |
| Reduced Rates: **10% seniors** | Airport/Station Pickup: **Yes** |

Shiloh Rose has one spacious suite. Lovely wallpapers, lace curtains, and fine bed linens give the bedroom a warm, country-Victorian feel. The cozy private sitting room has a wood-burning stove, overflowing bookshelves, and an upright grand piano, as well as a TV and VCR. Breakfasts feature fresh fruit, home-baked muffins, gourmet casseroles, and your choice of coffee or tea. On warm summer evenings, you'll share the backyard with quail and pheasant families. Golf and water sports are available much of the year. The surrounding area is a hunting and fishing paradise and the river levees provide eight miles of hiking and biking trails. But top priority should be given to a day-long jet-boat trip up Hells Canyon, the deepest gorge in the Northwest.

## River Cove ✪
P.O. BOX 1862, POST FALLS, IDAHO 83854

Tel: (208) 773-9190
Best Time to Call: After 5 PM
Hosts: Eric and Rosalynd Wurmlinger
Location: 20 mi. E of Spokane, Washington
No. of Rooms: 3
No. of Private Baths: 3
Suites: $89
Open: All year

Reduced Rates: Available
Breakfast: Full
Pets: Sometimes
Children: Welcome, under 5 by arrangement
Smoking: No
Social Drinking: Permitted
Airport Pickup: Yes

At River Cove, guests enjoy a homey atmosphere with privacy. This new contemporary home is situated on a wooded lot overlooking the beautiful Spokane River. Guests can relax and take in the spectacular view from the patio, or stroll along the many scenic trails by the river. Each morning, breakfast is served in the main dining room or out on the terrace. Guests are often invited to join their hosts on a complimentary boat cruise.

## Heritage Inn ✪
510 LENA STREET, SALMON, IDAHO 83467

Tel: (208) 756-3174
Best Time to Call: 8 AM–8 PM
Host: Audrey Nichols
Location: ½ mi. from Hwy. 93
No. of Rooms: 5
Max. No. Sharing Bath: 3
Double/sb: $38–$42
Single/sb: $25–$29

Cottage: $40
Open: All year
Breakfast: Continental, plus
Credit Cards: MC, VISA
Pets: No
Children: Welcome
Smoking: Restricted
Social Drinking: Permitted

This 100-year-old Victorian farmhouse is set in a valley, surrounded by mountains and pine trees. In the old days, this was a cozy stopover for those traveling by stagecoach. The Heritage has since been lovingly restored and decorated with many antiques. Enjoy a cool drink on the glassed-in sun porch while you enjoy the quiet of this pretty neighborhood. The River of No Return is just half a mile away, and it's just a mile to the city park and swimming pool. Your hostess serves homemade muffins and jams in the sunny dining room or on the porch each morning. She is a native of Salmon and can gladly direct you to restaurants within walking distance, nearby ghost towns, and other places of historic or cultural interest.

# ILLINOIS

Galena •    **Mundelein** •   • Winnetka

     **Sycamore** •    • Chicago

Rock Island •     • Oswego

   • **Mossville**

Navuoo •        • **Champaign**

Quincy •

Williamsville •

     • Arcola

Jerseyville •

     • Mt. Carmel

  • Maeystown

## Bed & Breakfast/Chicago, Inc. ✪
P.O. BOX 14088, CHICAGO, ILLINOIS 60614-0088

Tel: **(312) 951-0085**
Coordinator: **Mary Shaw**
States/Regions Covered: **Downtown Chicago, Hyde Park, Near North, North Shore suburbs**

Rates (Single/Double):
   Modest: **$65 / $75**
   Average: **$75 / $85–$95**
Credit Cards: **AMEX, MC, VISA**

Mary welcomes you to Midwestern hospitality in the "windy city" and its North Shore suburbs. Discover Chicago's outdoor sculpture plazas on foot, shop world-famous Marshall Field's, or observe the skyline from the top of the Sears Tower while staying in one of the over 150 different guest rooms, unhosted furnished apartments, or inns represented by this service. There is a two-night minimum on most accommodations.

## B&B Midwest Reservations ✪
### 2223 CRUMP LANE, COLUMBUS, TENNESSEE 47203

Tel: (800) 34 B AND B [342-2632]
Best Time to Call: 9 AM–5 PM
   Mon.–Fri.
Coordinator: Martha McDonald-Swan
States/Regions Covered:
   Illinois—Cairo, Danforth, Elizabeth,
   Franklin Grove, Galena, Geneva,
   Gurnee, Hinsdale, Morrison,
   Mundelein, Oakbrook, Oak Park,
   Oregon, Oswego, Springfield,
   Taylorville, Wadsworth, West

Dundee, Woodstock, Yorkville;
Indiana—Anderson, Bainbridge,
Centerville, Franklin, Knightstown,
Whiteland
Descriptive Directory: Free
Rates (Single/Double):
   Modest:  $45 / $55
   Average:  $50 / $100
   Luxury:   $110 / $179
Credit Cards: AMEX, DISC, MC, VISA

B&B Midwest Reservations (formerly B&B Northwest Suburban–Chicago) has expanded beyond northern Illinois to include southern Illinois and Indiana. Most homes are on historic registers. Hosts enjoy sharing beautiful antiques, handwork, and lots of TLC with their guests. Many also offer numerous special activities and theme weekends, available from suburban locations to country farms.

## Curly's Corner
### RR 2, BOX 590, ARCOLA, ILLINOIS 61910

Tel: (217) 268-3352
Best Time to Call: Anytime
Hosts: Warren and Maxine Arthur
Location: 35 mi. S of Champaign; 5 mi.
   from I-57
No. of Rooms: 4
No. of Private Baths: 2
Max. No. Sharing Bath: 3
Double/pb: $55–$60

Single/sb: $40
Open: All year
Breakfast: Full
Pets: No
Children: Welcome, over 10
Smoking: No
Social Drinking: No
Airport/Station Pickup: Yes

This ranch-style farmhouse is located in a quiet Amish community. Your hosts are dedicated to cordial hospitality and will gladly share information about the area or even take you on a tour. They offer comfortable bedrooms with king- or queen-size beds. In the morning, enjoy a wonderful breakfast of homemade biscuits, apple butter, fresh country bacon, and eggs. Curly's Corner is a half mile from beautiful Rockome Gardens.

## The Golds
### 2065 COUNTY ROAD, 525 E, CHAMPAIGN, ILLINOIS 61821

Tel: (217) 586-4345
Best Time to Call: Evenings
Hosts: Bob and Rita Gold
Location: 6 mi. W of Champaign

No. of Rooms: 3
Max. No. Sharing Bath: 4
Double/sb: $45
Single/sb: $40

Open: **All year**
Reduced Rates: **15% weekly**
Breakfast: **Continental**
Pets: **No**

Children: **Welcome**
Smoking: **No**
Social Drinking: **Permitted**
Airport/Station Pickup: **Available**

One of the most beautiful views in Champaign County is yours from the deck of this restored farmhouse. The house is set on six acres surrounded by prime central Illinois farmland. Inside you'll find country antiques, complemented by beautiful wainscoting. An open walnut stairway leads to bedrooms decorated with four-poster beds, handmade quilts, and oriental rugs. Guests can relax by the living room wood stove or enjoy a glass of wine on the deck. Bob and Rita offer garden fruits and cider for breakfast, served with homemade jams, muffins, and coffee cakes. The Golds is two miles from Lake of the Woods, and 20 minutes from the University of Illinois campus. Shopping and restaurants are also within easy reach.

## A City Bed & Breakfast ✪
**2150 NORTH LINCOLN PARK WEST, CHICAGO, ILLINOIS 60614**

Tel: **(312) 472-0027**
Host: **Susan Barton**
No. of Rooms: **1**
No. of Private Baths: **1**
Double/pb: **$70**
Single/pb: **$60**
Open: **All year**

Reduced Rates: **Available**
Breakfast: **Continental**
Pets: **No**
Children: **Welcome, over 6**
Smoking: **No**
Social Drinking: **Permitted**

Nestled in a vintage apartment building in the heart of Lincoln Park, this bed and breakfast offers a charming yet sophisticated ambiance. Accommodations are spacious and comfortable. Guests are welcomed with a panoramic view of Lincoln Park, Lake Michigan, and Chicago's skyline. A breakfast buffet is Susan's specialty, with a selection of fruit juices, fresh-baked goods, fine jams, and the best coffee. Within walking distance guests can enjoy Lincoln Park's famous zoo, flower conservatory and gardens, jogging and cycling paths, and beaches. Shopping at Water Tower Palace, a visit to the John Hancock Center Observatory, or a tour of the Art Institute are only a short bus ride away. Ask Susan about dinner, theater, or the Chicago Symphony.

## Lake Shore Drive Bed and Breakfast ✪
**CHICAGO, ILLINOIS 60614**

| | |
|---|---|
| Tel: **(312) 404-5500** | Open: **All year** |
| Best Time to Call: **9 AM–11 PM, weekdays** | Reduced Rates: **Available for extended stays** |
| Host: **Barbara Mark** | Breakfast: **Continental, plus** |
| Location: **2 mi. N of center Chicago** | Pets: **No** |
| No. of Rooms: **1** | Children: **No** |
| No. of Private Baths: **1** | Smoking: **No** |
| Double/pb: **$80** | Social Drinking: **Permitted** |
| Single/pb: **$70** | Minimum Stay: **3 nights** |

Barbara welcomes you to her lovely home in the sky, featuring spectacular wraparound views of Lake Michigan, Lincoln Park, and the Chicago skyline. The romantic guest room features cable TV and a dazzling view of the city and the sailboats in Lake Michigan. In good weather, savor a glass of wine and the panoramic views from the rooftop garden. Lake Michigan's beaches, Lincoln Park Zoo, Wrigley Field, jogging and cycling paths, fine dining, jazz and blues clubs, theaters, and great shopping are all within walking distance of this neighborhood. Excellent public transportation provides easy access to downtown, Orchestra Hall, the Art Institute, architectural walking tours, Lake Michigan cruises, Northwestern Memorial Hospital, and McCormick Convention Center. Having hosted guests from all over the world, Barbara gives an extra-special welcome to visitors from abroad. Your gracious and charming hostess can update you on all there is to do and see in Chicago.

## Old Town Bed & Breakfast ✪
**1451 NORTH NORTH PARK AVENUE, CHICAGO, ILLINOIS 60610**

| | |
|---|---|
| Tel: **(312) 440-9268** | Breakfast: **Continental** |
| Best Time to Call: **Anytime** | Credit Cards: **AMEX, MC, VISA** |
| Host: **Michael Serritella** | Pets: **No** |
| No. of Rooms: **2** | Children: **No** |
| Max. No. Sharing Bath: **4** | Smoking: **No** |
| Double/sb: **$75** | Social Drinking: **Permitted** |
| Open: **All year** | |

This modern town house is furnished with fine art and old family photographs. Each guest room has air-conditioning, a phone, and fully cabled TV. For your convenience there is both on-street and off-street parking. Restaurants, major museums, and public transportation are within walking distance. Enjoy breakfast indoors or, weather permitting, in the private, walled garden. Michael, a former teacher and university administrator, is knowledgeable about the city and surrounding countryside, and is eager to help guests make the most of their trip.

## Avery Guest House ✪
### 606 SOUTH PROSPECT STREET, GALENA, ILLINOIS 61036

| | |
|---|---|
| Tel: **(815) 777-3883** | Open: **All year** |
| Best Time to Call: **9 AM–9 PM** | Reduced Rates: **10% Sun.–Thur.** |
| Hosts: **Gerry and Armon Lamparelli** | Breakfast: **Full** |
| Location: **15 mi. E of Dubuque, Iowa** | Credit Cards: **MC, VISA** |
| No. of Rooms: **4** | Pets: **No** |
| Max. No. Sharing Bath: **4** | Children: **Welcome, over 12** |
| Double/sb: **$65** | Smoking: **Restricted** |
| Single/sb: **$60** | Social Drinking: **Permitted** |

Built before the Civil War days and remodeled in the 1920s, the Avery Guest House is located within a few blocks of Galena's main shopping center and historical buildings. After a day of exploring, Avery Guest House is a homey refuge where you can share your experiences with your hosts or other guests. Enjoy the view from our porch swing, watch TV, or join in on a table game. Sleep will come easily on a comfortable queen-size bed in one of our four guest rooms. Breakfast is served in a sunny dining room with a bay window overlooking the Galena River Valley.

## The Homeridge Bed and Breakfast ✪
### 1470 NORTH STATE STREET, JERSEYVILLE, ILLINOIS 62052

| | |
|---|---|
| Tel: **(618) 498-3442** | Reduced Rates: **Corporate rate $10 less Sun.–Thurs.** |
| Best Time to Call: **Anytime** | |
| Hosts: **Sue and Howard Landon** | Breakfast: **Full** |
| Location: **45 mi. N of St. Louis, Mo.** | Credit Cards: **MC, VISA** |
| No. of Rooms: **4** | Pets: **No** |
| No. of Private Baths: **4** | Children: **Welcome, over 14** |
| Double/pb: **$65** | Smoking: **No** |
| Single/pb: **$65** | Social Drinking: **No** |
| Open: **All year** | Airport/Station Pickup: **Yes** |

The Homeridge, built in 1867, is a beautiful, warm, 14-room Italianate Victorian private home on eighteen acres in a comfortable country atmosphere. You'll admire the original woodwork, twelve-foot ceilings and crown molding; a hand-carved, curved stairway leads to the third floor with its 12 × 12 foot cupola or watchtower room. Other details include a 20 × 40 foot swimming pool and an expansive, pillared front porch. Once the estate of Senator Theodore S. Chapman (1891–

1960), this B&B is being reviewed for listing in the National Historic Registry. Homeridge is conveniently located between Springfield, Illinois, and St. Louis, Missouri.

## Corner George Inn ✪
**CORNER OF MAIN AND MILL, P.O. BOX 103, MAEYSTOWN, ILLINOIS 62256**

| | |
|---|---|
| Tel: **(618) 458-6660; (800) 458-6020** | Breakfast: **Full** |
| Best Time to Call: **9 AM–9 PM** | Credit Cards: **MC, VISA** |
| Hosts: **David and Marcia Braswell** | Pets: **No** |
| No. of Rooms: **6** | Children: **Welcome, over 12** |
| No. of Private Baths: **6** | Smoking: **No** |
| Double/pb: **$69–$94** | Social Drinking: **Permitted** |
| Open: **All year** | Foreign Languages: **German** |

A frontier Victorian structure built in 1884—when it was known as the Maeystown Hotel and Saloon—the Corner George Inn has been painstakingly restored. In addition to the six antique-filled guest rooms, there are two sitting rooms, a wine cellar, and an elegant ballroom, where David and Marcia serve breakfast. Maeystown is a quaint 19th-century village; guests can tour it on a bicycle built for two or aboard a horse-drawn carriage. Nearby are St. Louis, Fort de Chartres, Fort Kaskaskia, and the scenic bluff road that hugs the Mississippi.

## Old Church House Inn
**1416 EAST MOSSVILLE ROAD, MOSSVILLE, ILLINOIS 61552**

| | |
|---|---|
| Tel: **(309) 579-2300** | Double/sb: **$69** |
| Best Time to Call: **9 AM–9 PM CST** | Single/sb: **$55** |
| Hosts: **Dean and Holly Ramseyer** | Open: **All year** |
| Location: **5 minutes N of Peoria** | Breakfast: **Continental, plus** |
| No. of Rooms: **2** | Credit Cards: **MC, VISA** |
| No. of Private Baths: **1** | Pets: **No** |
| Max. No. Sharing Bath: **4** | Children: **Welcome, over 10** |
| Double/pb: **$99** | Smoking: **No** |
| Single/pb: **$69 (Mon.–Thurs. only)** | Social Drinking: **No** |

Nestled in the scenic Illinois River Valley 5 miles north of Peoria, Old Church House Inn welcomes you to the plush warmth of the Victorian era. Curl up to a crackling fire, take tea in the flower garden, sink deep into the queen-size featherbeds, and enjoy being pampered. Listed on the National Historic American Building Survey, this 1869 church still boasts soaring 18-foot ceilings, tall arched windows, and an "elevated library." Victorian antiques, period furnishings, pedestal sinks, colorful quilts, thick robes, and fine soaps allow guests to relax in luxury. Swiss chocolates, a house specialty, are placed on pillows during chamber service. Bicycling and cross-country skiing on the Rock Island Trail is just five minutes away, while nearby Peoria

features riverboat cruises, cultural attractions, antiquing, and a full range of dining choices to suit your taste!

## The Poor Farm Bed & Breakfast ✪
**POOR FARM ROAD, MOUNT CARMEL, ILLINOIS 62863**

Tel: **(800) 646-3276; (618) 262-4663;**
 fax: **(618) 262-8199**
Hosts: **Liz and John Stelzer**
Location: **1 mi. N of Mount Carmel**
No. of Rooms: **4**
No. of Private Baths: **4**
Double/pb: **$45–$55**
Single/pb: **$45–$55**
Suites: **$85–$95**
Open: **All year**

Reduced Rates: **Available**
Breakfast: **Full**
Other Meals: **Available**
Credit Cards: **AMEX, DISC, MC, VISA**
Pets: **No**
Children: **Welcome**
Smoking: **Permitted**
Social Drinking: **Permitted**
Airport Pickup: **Yes**

Named for its previous use—as a nineteenth-century shelter for the homeless—this stately, 35-room brick landmark is sure to enchant you with its quiet, country charm. Poor Farm is adjacent to a 25-acre county park and within sight of an 18-hole golf course. Red Hill State Park, Beall Woods Conservation Area and Nature Preserve, a swimming pool, driving range, tennis courts, boating, and fishing are only minutes away. These amenities, plus your hosts' Midwestern hospitality, make this B&B the "inn" place to stay.

# Round-Robin Guesthouse ✪
## 231 EAST MAPLE AVENUE, MUNDELEIN, ILLINOIS 60060

Tel: **(708) 566-7664**
Hosts: **George and Laura Loffredo**
Location: **38 mi. NW of Chicago**
No. of Rooms: **6**
No. of Private Baths: **3**
Max. No. Sharing Bath: **4**
Double/pb: **$65**
Double/sb: **$45–$55**
Suite: **$115**

Open: **All year**
Reduced Rates: **10% seniors, families**
Breakfast: **Full**
Credit Cards: **MC, VISA**
Pets: **No**
Children: **Welcome**
Smoking: **No**
Social Drinking: **Permitted**

This handsome red Victorian with white trim takes its name from the letters circulated by your hosts' relatives for more than 70 years; to encourage you to write friends and family, George and Laura will provide you with paper, pen, and stamps. The many local diversions ensure that you'll have plenty to write about. Six Flags Great America, the Volo Auto Museum, and the antique village of Long Grove are barely fifteen minutes away by car, and you're never far from golf, swimming, and horseback riding. During the summer, the Chicago Symphony is in residence at nearby Ravinia Park. Or you can enjoy Laura's renditions of classical and ragtime music on the piano. You'll wake up to the aroma of fresh-brewed coffee; coffee cake, muffins, and homemade jam are served between 7:30 and 9 AM.

# The Ancient Pines Bed & Breakfast
## 2015 PARLEY STREET, NAUVOO, ILLINOIS 62354

Tel: **(217) 453-2767**
Best Time to Call: **9 AM–9 PM**
Host: **Genevieve Simmens**
Location: **225 mi. SW of Chicago**
No. of Rooms: **3**
Max. No. Sharing Bath: **3**
Double/sb: **$45**
Single/sb: **$35**

Open: **All year**
Reduced Rates: **15% weekly**
Breakfast: **Full**
Pets: **Sometimes**
Children: **Welcome**
Smoking: **No**
Social Drinking: **Permitted**

This turn-of-the-century brick home is rich in detail inside and out, from the stained-glass windows and etched-glass front door to the tin ceilings, open staircase, and carved woodwork. Wander through herb and flower gardens, play badminton on the lawn, or listen to music in the library. Local attractions include wineries (Nauvoo holds its own grape festival), Civil War reenactments, historic Mormon homes, and Nauvoo State Park. Whatever your itinerary, you'll wake to the aroma of baking bread, served with eggs and sausage or ham. Special low-cholesterol menus are available upon request.

## The Gilbert Gaylord House ✪
**1542 PLAINFIELD ROAD, OSWEGO, ILLINOIS 60543**

Tel: **(708) 554-1865**
Best Time to Call: **8 AM–9 PM**
Hosts: **Robert and Candice Hadley Johnson**
Location: **45 mi. SW of Chicago**
No. of Rooms: **2**
No. of Private Baths: **1**
Max. No. Sharing Bath: **4**
Double/pb: **$85**
Single/pb: **$75**
Double/sb: **$75**

Single/sb: **$65**
Suites: **$120**
Open: **All year**
Reduced Rates: **10% 2 nights or more, 5% seniors**
Breakfast: **Continental**
Pets: **Sometimes**
Children: **Welcome**
Smoking: **No**
Social Drinking: **Permitted**
Foreign Languages: **French**

The Gilbert Gaylord House is a stately brick Italianate built in 1865. This intimate B&B offers rural seclusion on an old farm. Nearby is southern Fox River Valley, antiquing, bicycling, cross-country skiing, hiking, fishing, golfing, canoeing, shopping, and riverboat gambling in Aurora and Joliet. Robert, Candice, and infant son Samuel will make you feel at home with the comfortable furnishings, including Victorian antiques. Breakfast is served either in front of a blazing fire or on the Victorian screen porch. Bob works in foreign exchange and Candice runs an advertising sales business from home.

## The Kaufmann House
**1641 HAMPSHIRE, QUINCY, ILLINOIS 62301**

| | |
|---|---|
| Tel: **(217) 223-2502** | Single/sb: **$40–$45** |
| Best Time to Call: **Noon–9 PM** | Reduced Rates: **10% 3 nights or more** |
| Hosts: **Emery and Bettie Kaufmann** | Open: **All year** |
| Location: **100 mi. W of Springfield** | Breakfast: **Continental, plus** |
| No. of Rooms: **3** | Pets: **No** |
| No. of Private Baths: **1** | Children: **Welcome (crib)** |
| Max. No. Sharing Bath: **4** | Smoking: **No** |
| Double/pb: **$65** | Social Drinking: **No** |
| Single/pb: **$60** | Airport/Station Pickup: **Yes** |
| Double/sb: **$50–$55** | |

History buffs will remember Quincy, set right on the Mississippi River, as the scene of the famous Lincoln-Douglas debates, while architecture buffs will be attracted to the town's feast of Victorian styles—Greek Revival, Gothic Revival, Italianate, and Richardsonian. The Kaufmann House was built 100 years ago, and the owners have been careful to maintain its "country" feeling. Guests may enjoy breakfast in the Ancestor's Room, on a stone patio, or at a picnic table under the trees. They are invited to play the piano, watch TV, or enjoy popcorn by the fire. The Kaufmanns describe themselves as "Christians who have a love for God, people, nature, and life."

## The Potter House Bed & Breakfast Inn
**1906 7 AVENUE, ROCK ISLAND, ILLINOIS 61201**

| | |
|---|---|
| Tel: **(309) 788-1906; (800) 747-0339** | Credit Cards: **AMEX, DC, DISC, MC, VISA** |
| Best Time to Call: **10 AM–9 PM** | Pets: **No** |
| Hosts: **Gary and Nancy Pheiffer** | Children: **Welcome** |
| No. of Rooms: **5** | Smoking: **No** |
| No. of Private Baths: **5** | Social Drinking: **Permitted** |
| Double/pb: **$65–$95** | Minimum Stay: **Special event weekends and peak seasons** |
| Guest Cottage: **$100, sleeps 4** | Airport Pickup: **Yes** |
| Suites: **$75, sleeps 3** | |
| Open: **All year** | |
| Breakfast: **Full** | |

Stay in either the main house or the adjacent cottage at this turn-of-the-century property listed on the National Register of Historic Places. Look for the old-fashioned details, from porcelain doorknobs to embossed leather wallcovering and stained- and leaded-glass windows.

Even the bathrooms are distinctive: one has its original nickel-plated hardware. You'll notice other historic homes in the neighborhood. Gamblers will want to stroll six blocks to the Mississippi, where a riverboat casino is moored. Those who like less risky games can play croquet or shoot baskets on the inn grounds.

## Top o' the Morning ✪
### 1505 19TH AVENUE, ROCK ISLAND, ILLINOIS 61201

| | |
|---|---|
| Tel: **(309) 786-3513** | Double/pb: **$60–$80** |
| Best Time to Call: **After 5 PM** | Open: **All year** |
| Hosts: **Sam and Peggy Doak** | Breakfast: **Full** |
| Location: **1½ mi. from Rte. 92, 18th Ave. exit** | Pets: **No** |
| | Children: **Welcome** |
| No. of Rooms: **3** | Smoking: **Permitted** |
| No. of Private Baths: **3** | Social Drinking: **Permitted** |

Sam and Peggy welcome you to their country estate, set on a bluff overlooking the Mississippi River, near the center of the Quad Cities area. The 18-room mansion is situated at the end of a winding drive on three acres of lawn, orchards, and gardens. The guest rooms, graced with lovely chandeliers and oriental rugs, command a spectacular view of the cities and river. The parlor, with its grand piano and fireplace, is an inviting place to relax. Local attractions are Mississippi

River boat rides, harness racing, Rock Island Arsenal, Black Hawk State Park, Augustana College, and St. Ambrose University.

## Country Charm Inn ✪
### 15165 QUIGLEY ROAD, SYCAMORE, ILLINOIS 60178

Tel: **(815) 895-5386**
Best Time to Call: **Anytime**
Hosts: **Howard and Donna Petersens**
Location: **55 mi. W of Chicago**
No. of Rooms: **3**
No. of Private Baths: **3**
Double/pb: **$35–$75**
Open: **All year**
Reduced Rates: **On a weekly basis**

Breakfast: **Continental, weekdays; full, weekends**
Pets: **No**
Children: **Welcome**
Smoking: **No**
Social Drinking: **No**
Minimum Stay: **Only for local weekend events**

On a tree-topped knoll in rich farming country stands this rambling, turn-of-the-century stucco home. Howard and Donna's comfortable accommodations blend understated elegance with casual warmth and friendliness. Enjoy a full country breakfast on the cozy front porch; house specialties range from egg-cheese dishes and designer pancakes to peach cobblers and pecan roll rings. Then lounge around the sunken fireplace, watch a movie on the large-screen TV with surround sound, borrow a book from the loft library, or roam around the farm. Champ the trick horse sends personal note cards to children telling about his barnyard pals, including llamas and another horse. For those planning to exchange vows, the Petersens have built a charming wedding chapel on the property.

# Bed and Breakfast at Edie's
## 233 EAST HARPOLE, P.O. BOX 351, WILLIAMSVILLE, ILLINOIS 62693

Tel: **(217) 566-2538**
Best Time to Call: **After 5 PM,**
  **weekends**
Host: **Edith L. Senalik**
Location: **10 mi. N of Springfield**
No. of Rooms: **3**
Max. No. Sharing Bath: **4**
Double/sb: **$45**

Single/sb: **$35**
Open: **All year**
Reduced Rates: **Available**
Breakfast: **Continental**
Pets: **No**
Children: **Welcome**
Smoking: **No**
Social Drinking: **Permitted**

Just ten minutes north of the state capital, Springfield, the friendly village of Williamsville offers the peace, quiet, and safety of a small town. Edie's is a 75-year-old Mission-style house where guests have use of a formal living room, dining room, and a TV room equipped with cable TV and a video library. Springfield offers the Abraham Lincoln attractions, Springfield Theater Centre, Old State Capitol, Lincoln Land Community College, and Sangamon State University. Historic Petersburg and New Salem, 20 miles to the west, are easily accessible.

# Chateau des Fleurs ✪
## 552 RIDGE ROAD, WINNETKA, ILLINOIS 60093

Tel: **(708) 256-7272**
Best Time to Call: **Mornings**
Host: **Sally Ward**
Location: **15 mi. N of Chicago**
No. of Rooms: **3**
No. of Private Baths: **3**
Double/pb: **$95**
Single/pb: **$90**

Open: **All year**
Reduced Rates: **10% weekly**
Breakfast: **Full**
Pets: **No**
Children: **Welcome, over 11**
Smoking: **No**
Social Drinking: **Permitted**

At Chateau des Fleurs, guests may enjoy the elegance of a French country home and still be only 30 minutes from Chicago's Loop. Antique shops, Lake Michigan, and commuter trains are within walking distance. But there's so much to do at this luxurious B&B, you may not want to leave. Swim in the pool, screen movies on Sally's 50-inch television, tickle the ivories of a Steinway baby grand, or admire the terraced yard and carefully tended gardens. Sally serves a full breakfast with homemade breads, and turkey and ham. Guest rooms have TV and phones. Fax and copier are available.

# INDIANA

Chesterton •

• Peru
• Marion

Middletown •
Rockville •        • Knightstown
• Indianapolis

• Grandview

## Gray Goose Inn ✪
### 350 INDIAN BOUNDARY ROAD, CHESTERTON, INDIANA 46304

Tel: **(800) 521-5127; (219) 926-5781**
Best Time to Call: **9 AM–10 PM**
Hosts: **Tim Wilk and Charles Ramsey**
Location: **60 mi. E of Chicago**
No. of Rooms: **8**
No. of Private Baths: **8**
Double/pb: **$80–$95**
Single/pb: **$80–$95**
Suites: **$110–$135**

Open: **All year**
Reduced Rates: **10% seniors**
Breakfast: **Full**
Credit Cards: **AMEX, DISC, MC, VISA**
Pets: **No**
Children: **Welcome, over 12**
Smoking: **Restricted**
Social Drinking: **Permitted**

Elegant accommodations await you in this English country-style house overlooking a 30-acre lake. Guest rooms feature four-poster beds, fine linens, and thick, fluffy towels. Some rooms are decorated in Williamsburg style, some have fireplaces and Jacuzzi. Enjoy a quiet moment in the common rooms, or relax with a cup of coffee in the scenic wicker room. Take long walks beside shady oaks, feed the

Canada geese and wild ducks. The Gray Goose is five minutes from Dunes State and National Lakeshore Parks. Swimming, hiking, and fishing sites on Lake Michigan are all within easy reach. Dining and weekend entertainment are within walking distance.

## The River Belle Bed & Breakfast ✪
### P.O. BOX 669, HIGHWAY 66, GRANDVIEW, INDIANA 47615

| | |
|---|---|
| Tel: (812) 649-2500 | Single/sb: $40 |
| Best Time to Call: 8 AM–1 PM | Guest Cottage: $60, sleeps 4 |
| Hosts: Don and Pat Phillips | Open: All year |
| Location: 33 mi. E of Evansville | Reduced Rates: Weekly |
| No. of Rooms: 6 | Breakfast: Continental |
| No. of Private Baths: 2 | Credit Cards: MC, VISA |
| Max. No. Sharing Bath: 4 | Pets: No |
| Double/pb: $65 | Children: Welcome |
| Single/pb: $60 | Smoking: No |
| Double/sb: $45–$55 | Social Drinking: Permitted |

Guests may choose from a selection of accommodations in an 1866 white painted brick steamboat-style house, an 1898 redbrick Italianate house, or an 1860 cottage with full kitchen. These adjacent beauties on the Ohio River have been carefully restored by Pat and Don to serve as their B&B complex. The guest rooms are large and airy, furnished with timeless heirlooms and graced by lace curtains and oriental rugs. You may choose to walk along the riverfront, sit quietly and watch the white squirrels play among the magnolia, pecan, and dogwood trees, or take a side trip to the nearby Lincoln Boyhood National Memorial, Lincoln State Park, the "Young Abe Lincoln" Drama, and Holiday World (the nation's oldest theme amusement park).

## The Tranquil Cherub
### 2164 NORTH CAPITOL AVENUE, INDIANAPOLIS, INDIANA 46202-1251

| | |
|---|---|
| Tel: (317) 923-9036 | Suite: $80–$85 |
| Best Time to Call: 8 AM–10 AM; 6 PM–10 PM | Open: All year |
| | Reduced Rates: Weekly |
| Hosts: Thom and Barbara Feit | Breakfast: Full |
| Location: ½ mi. from I-65 exit 115 | Credit Cards: AMEX, MC, VISA |
| No. of Rooms: 4 | Pets: No |
| No. of Private Baths: 2 | Children: Welcome, over 14 |
| Max. No. Sharing Bath: 4 | Smoking: Restricted |
| Double/pb: $65–$75 | Social Drinking: Permitted |
| Double/sb: $55 | Airport Pickup: Yes |
| Single/sb: $50 | |

From the central location of this B&B, you are only minutes from downtown. As you enter the foyer, the beautifully crafted oak staircase and pier mirror will draw your eye. Lace curtains, Battenburg lace comforters, wicker furniture, Beardsley prints, and Art Deco furniture decorate the rooms. In the morning, the aroma of freshly brewed coffee—served from an English sideboard in the upstairs hall—will waft to your room. Ease into your day with juice and the paper in the upstairs sitting room. Breakfast is served in the dining room, where beveled glass and a sparkling chandelier accent the oak paneling and fireplace. Weather permitting, you may have your meal on the rear deck overlooking the lily ponds. There is a $5 surcharge for one-night stays.

## Old Hoosier House ✪
### 7601 SOUTH GREENSBORO PIKE, KNIGHTSTOWN, INDIANA 46148

Tel: (317) 345-2969; (800) 775-5315
Hosts: **Tom and Jean Lewis**
Location: **30 mi. E of Indianapolis**
No. of Rooms: **4**
No. of Private Baths: **4**
Double/pb: **$60–$70**
Single/pb: **$55–$65**
Open: **All year**

Reduced Rates: **10% seniors**
Breakfast: **Full**
Pets: **No**
Children: **Welcome**
Smoking: **No**
Social Drinking: **Permitted**
Airport/Station Pickup: **Yes**

The Old Hoosier House takes you back more than 100 years, when the livin' was easier. The rooms are large, with high ceilings, arched windows, antiques, and mementos. A library and patio are available for your pleasure. In the morning you'll wake to the aroma of homemade rolls and coffee. Golfers will enjoy the adjoining golf course, while antique buffs will be glad to know there are hundreds of local dealers in the area. The cities of Anderson and Richmond are close by, and the Indianapolis 500 is within an hour's drive.

## Olde Country Club ✪
### 8544 SOUTH COUNTY ROAD, 575 WEST,
### P.O. BOX 115, KNIGHTSTOWN, INDIANA 46148

Tel: (317) 345-5381
Best Time to Call: **Noon–5 PM**
Hosts: **Dick and Norma Firestone**
Location: **35 mi. E of Indianapolis**
No. of Rooms: **2**
No. of Private Baths: **2**
Double/pb: **$65**
Single/pb: **$60**

Open: **All year**
Reduced Rates: **Available**
Breakfast: **Full**
Pets: **No**
Children: **No**
Smoking: **No**
Social Drinking: **Permitted**

Dick and Norma, who own one of Knightstown's antique shops, purchased this property in 1961 and expanded it over the years, adding a family room, greenhouse, herb garden, and fish pond. The house once belonged to the Knightstown golf course, and you can practice your chip shots on your hosts' short par three. Rooms are decorated with paisley and floral wallpapers, lace curtains, and, of course, antique furniture. When you're not prowling for antiques of your own—there are lots of shops in town—you can play golf on an eighteen-hole course or ride an old-fashioned train.

## Golden Oak Bed & Breakfast
**809 WEST FOURTH STREET, MARION, INDIANA 46952**

| | |
|---|---|
| Tel: **(317) 651-9950** | Open: **All year** |
| Best Time to Call: **9 AM–9 PM** | Breakfast: **Full** |
| Hosts: **Lois and Dave Lutes** | Credit Cards: **AMEX, MC, VISA** |
| Location: **60 mi. N of Indianapolis** | Pets: **No** |
| No. of Rooms: **4** | Children: **Welcome** |
| No. of Private Baths: **4** | Smoking: **No** |
| Double/sb: **$65** | Social Drinking: **Permitted** |
| Single/sb: **$60** | |

Enjoy the elegance of this beautifully restored two-story home built in the 1890s. Inside, the rooms glow with the rich oak woodwork that inspires this B&B's name. Throughout the house, you'll see hand-crocheted items; similar ones are for sale in your hosts' gift shop. The James Dean Gallery and Historical Museum, the Mississinewa Battlefield, beaches, golf courses, and antique shops are among the area's attractions. For your dining pleasure, the Hostess House of Marion is within walking distance.

## Country Rose B&B ✪
**5098 NORTH MECHANICSBURG ROAD,**
**MIDDLETOWN, INDIANA 47356**

| | |
|---|---|
| Tel: **(317) 779-4501; (800) 395-6449** | Open: **All year** |
| Hosts: **Rose and Jack W. Lewis** | Breakfast: **Full** |
| Location: **40 mi. NE of Indianapolis** | Pets: **No** |
| No. of Rooms: **2** | Children: **Welcome** |
| Max. No. Sharing Bath: **3** | Smoking: **No** |
| Double/sb: **$55** | Social Drinking: **No** |
| Single/sb: **$45** | Minimum Stay: **2 nights Memorial** |
| Suites: **$65–$105** | **Day, NASCAR** |

Country Rose is a small-town, garden B&B in historic Raintree County, home of the Indiana Basketball Hall of Fame. Middletown lies 50 minutes from the Indy 500, 30 minutes from Castleton Mall, and 20 minutes from both Ball State and Anderson Universities. You won't drive off on an empty stomach. Rose prepares a full breakfast each morning, featuring specialties like fried mush, fried apples, and country Tennessee biscuits.

## Rosewood Mansion ✪
### 54 NORTH HOOD, PERU, INDIANA 46970

Tel: **(317) 472-7151; fax: (317) 472-5575**
Best Time to Call: **8 AM–9 PM**
Hosts: **Lynn and Dave Hausner**
No. of Rooms: **8**
No. of Private Baths: **8**
Double/pb: **$70–$75**
Single/pb: **$55–$65**
Suites: **$85**
Open: **All year**

Reduced Rates: **10% weekly, seniors, families, business travelers (midweek)**
Breakfast: **Full**
Other Meals: **Available by request**
Credit Cards: **AMEX, DISC, MC, VISA**
Pets: **No**
Children: **Welcome**
Smoking: **Restricted**
Social Drinking: **Permitted**
Airport/Station Pickup: **Yes**

Rosewood Mansion is a stately brick Georgian residence constructed in 1872. A winding wooden staircase connects each floor, and stained-glass windows accent each landing. The house is decorated in period style, with floral wallpaper and antique furniture. Because this B&B is located three blocks from downtown Peru, restaurants, shops, public parks, and numerous sports facilities are just minutes away. Guests breakfast on coffee, tea, juice, fresh fruit, freshly baked breads or muffins, and quiche or eggs Benedict. Each room has a TV and phone.

## Suits Us
### 514 NORTH COLLEGE, ROCKVILLE, INDIANA 47872

Tel: **(317) 569-5660**
Hosts: **Bob and Ann McCullough**
Location: **50 mi. W of Indianapolis**
No. of Rooms: **4**
No. of Private Baths: **4**
Double/pb: **$50–$65**
Suite: **$125, sleeps 2–6**

Open: **All year**
Breakfast: **Continental, plus**
Pets: **No**
Children: **Welcome**
Smoking: **No**
Social Drinking: **Permitted**

This classic plantation-style home, with its widow's walk and generous front porch, dates to the early 1880s. The Strausses, a locally prominent family, bought the house about twenty years later; their overnight guests included Woodrow Wilson, Annie Oakley, James Whitcomb Riley, and John L. Lewis. Today, Ann and Bob extend their hospitality to you. There are books and a color TV in each room, and some even have stereos. Turkey Run Park is ten miles away, while five universities—Indiana State, DePauw, Wabash, St. Mary-of-the-Woods, and Rose-Hulman—are within a thirty-mile radius. Also, Rockville sponsors its own annual event, the Covered Bridge Festival.

---

**For key to listings, see inside front or back cover.**

✪ This star means that rates are guaranteed through December 31, 1996, to any guest making a reservation as a result of reading about the B&B in *Bed & Breakfast U.S.A.*—1996 edition.

Important! To avoid misunderstandings, always ask about cancellation policies when booking.

Please enclose a self-addressed, stamped, business-size envelope when contacting reservation services.

For more details on what you can expect in a B&B, see Chapter 1.

Always mention *Bed & Breakfast U.S.A.* when making reservations!

If no B&B is listed in the area you'll be visiting, use the form on page 323 to order a copy of our "List of New B&Bs."

We want to hear from you! Use the form on page 325.

# IOWA

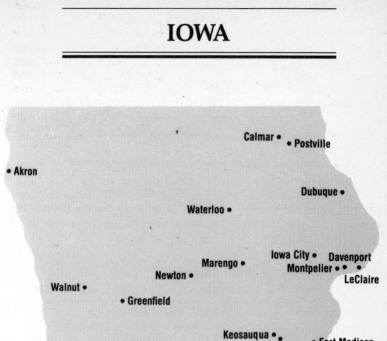

## Wildflower Log Cabin Bed & Breakfast ✪
**501 HIGHWAY 12, RR3, BOX 1, AKRON, IOWA 51001**

Tel: **(800) 257-6642; (712) 568-2206**
Best Time to Call: **Evenings**
Hosts: **Jeanne and CJ Hinrichsen**
Location: **28 mi. N of Sioux City**
No. of Rooms: **3**
No. of Private Baths: **1**
Max. No. Sharing Bath: **4**
Double/pb: **$45**
Double/sb: **$40**

Single/sb: **$35**
Open: **All year**
Reduced Rates: **10% after 2nd night**
Breakfast: **Full**
Pets: **No**
Children: **No**
Smoking: **No**
Social Drinking: **Permitted**

This cozy log cabin on the prairie provides a delightful break for travelers. Jean and CJ welcome you to their handcrafted log home lovingly decorated with antiques and collectibles. Enjoy the porch swing in the living room, soak in the hot tub, stargaze around the backyard, or stroll among the abundant flowers. Breakfasts are country style, and guests are invited to help themselves to soft drinks and

fresh baked cookies. Wildflower Log Cabin Bed & Breakfast is located at the northernmost point of Iowa's Loess Hills Scenic Byway and adjoins a 29-acre prairie preserve, the only approved Volkswalk site in Western Iowa.

## Hillcrest House of Bonaparte ✪
### P.O. BOX 186, FIFTH & WEST STREET, BONAPARTE, IOWA 52620

| | |
|---|---|
| Tel: **(319) 592-3373** | Open: **All year** |
| Host: **Mary V. Hart** | Reduced rates: **10% seniors, AARP** |
| Location: **60 mi. S of Iowa City** | Breakfast: **Full** |
| No. of Rooms: **5** | Other Meals: **Available** |
| No. of Private Baths: **2** | Pets: **Sometimes** |
| Max No. Sharing Bath: **4** | Children: **Welcome** |
| Double/pb: **$65** | Smoking: **No** |
| Double/sb: **$60** | Social Drinking: **Permitted** |
| Single/sb: **$50** | Station Pickup: **Yes** |

Hillcrest House is located in a quiet little river town of five hundred people. The house sits on the town's highest hill next to a four-hundred-acre farm, and features a magnificent oak staircase and beautiful woodwork that has been exquisitely maintained since 1865. Bonaparte is on the historical register as are many of the surrounding towns, giving guests much to see and visit. Mary has a degree in Hotel Management and Culinary Arts and her greatest desire is to delight your palate after a restful night's sleep. You may have your breakfast served in a sunny parlor on an iron and glass table or in the formal dining room in front of an arched stained glass window with walnut trim. A tin of homemade candy is on the night table of each clean, airy guest room. A trip to the Hillcrest House is a return to grace and hospitality of another era with enough modern amenities to make it a relaxing, memorable visit.

## Calmar Guesthouse ✪
**103 NORTH STREET, R.R. 1, BOX 206, CALMAR, IOWA 52132**

| | |
|---|---|
| Tel: **(319) 562-3851** | Breakfast: **Full** |
| Hosts: **Art and Lucille Kruse** | Pets: **No** |
| Location: **10 mi. S of Decorah** | Children: **Welcome** |
| No. of Rooms: **5** | Smoking: **No** |
| Max. No. Sharing Bath: **5** | Social Drinking: **Permitted** |
| Double/sb: **$40–$45** | Airport/Station Pickup: **Yes** |
| Open: **All year** | |

A recent guest reports that "The Calmar Guesthouse is a spacious, lovely, newly remodeled Victorian home located on the edge of town. The atmosphere is enhanced by the friendly, charming manner of Lucille, who made us feel right at home. The rooms were comfortable, private, and pretty. After a peaceful night's sleep, we were served a delicious breakfast of fresh farm eggs with ham and cheeses, croissants with butter and jam, homemade cinnamon rolls, and coffee. I would recommend it to anyone visiting the area." Nearby points of interest include Lake Meyer, the world's smallest church, and Spillville, home of hand-carved Bily Bros. Clocks.

## Fulton's Landing Guest House
**1206 EAST RIVER DRIVE, DAVENPORT, IOWA 52803**

| | |
|---|---|
| Tel: **(319) 322-4069** | No. of Rooms: **5** |
| Hosts: **Bill and Pat Schmidt** | No. of Private Baths: **3** |
| Location: **150 mi. W of Chicago** | Max. No. Sharing Bath: **4** |

Double/pb: **$75–$85**
Double/sb: **$55**
Suites: **$100**
Open: **All year**
Reduced Rates: **Available**
Breakfast: **Full**

Credit Cards: **AMEX, DISC, MC, VISA**
Pets: **No**
Children: **Welcome**
Smoking: **No**
Social Drinking: **Permitted**

Pat and Bill recently restored this house as a bed and breakfast, with cut-glass windows, wide hallways, carved woodwork, curved ceilings, and many of the original gas and electrical fixtures. Sixteen columns frame the front porch where guests can relax in comfortable chairs while enjoying the view of the Mississippi River. Guest rooms are furnished with antique walnut beds and floral wallcoverings, and terry robes are supplied. Breakfast specialties include juice, fruit, apple cinnamon French toast, and egg cheese sausage casserole. Bill and Pat have created a sophisticated yet comfortable environment from the beds to the meals.

## River Oaks Inn ✪
**1234 EAST RIVER DRIVE, DAVENPORT, IOWA 52803**

Tel: **(319) 326-2629; (800) 352-6016**
Best Time to Call: **9 AM–9 PM**
Hosts: **Bill and Suzanne Pohl; Ron and Mary Jo Pohl**
Location: **2 mi. from I-80**
No. of Rooms: **5**
No. of Private Baths: **5**
Double/pb: **$49–$69**
Suites: **$99**
Carriage House: **$125–$175**

Open: **All year**
Reduced Rates: **Available**
Breakfast: **Full**
Credit Cards: **MC, VISA**
Pets: **Sometimes**
Children: **Welcome**
Smoking: **Restricted**
Social Drinking: **Permitted**
Airport/Station Pickup: **Yes**
Foreign Languages: **Spanish**

Abner Davison combined Italianate, Victorian, and Prairie architecture when he built his home back in the 1850s. The house is situated on a rolling lot that still shows evidence of the original carriage drive. Choose from a suite with king-size bed, sun porch, and dressing room; the Ambrose Fulton Room, with double bed and garden view; the Mississippi Room, with queen-size bed and window seat; or the Abner Davison Room, which has twin beds or a king-size bed and a bay window. Breakfast is served in the dining room, or out on the deck in warm weather. The Inn is located one block from riverboat rides, and is convenient to many area attractions, such as Historic Rock Island Arsenal and the village of East Davenport.

## The Richards House
**1492 LOCUST STREET, DUBUQUE, IOWA 52001**

Tel: **(319) 557-1492**
Best Time to Call: **Anytime**
Host: **Michelle Delaney**

No. of Rooms: **6**
No. of Private Baths: **4**
Max. No. Sharing Bath: **2**

Double/pb: **$45–$75**
Single/pb: **$45–$75**
Double/sb: **$40–$55**
Single/sb: **$40–$55**
Suites: **$50–$85**
Open: **All year**
Reduced Rates: **10% Nov.–Apr.; 40%
  Sun.–Thurs.**

Breakfast: **Full**
Credit Cards: **AMEX, DC, DISC, MC,
  VISA**
Pets: **Sometimes**
Children: **Welcome (crib)**
Smoking: **Restricted**
Social Drinking: **Permitted**
Airport/Station Pickup: **Yes**

Inside and out, this four-story Victorian is a feast for the eyes, with its gabled roof, stained-glass windows, gingerbread trim, and elaborate woodwork. Rooms are furnished in period style. Guests can continue their journey back in time with a ride on the Fenelon Place Cable Car, the shortest inclined railway in the country. Then it's time to pay respects to another form of transportation at the Woodward Riverboat Museum. You're welcome to use the kitchen for light snacks; in the morning, Michelle takes over, setting out fresh fruit, waffles, pancakes, sausage, and homemade breads.

## Kingsley Inn ✪
**707 AVENUE H, FORT MADISON, IOWA 52627**

Tel: **(319) 372-7074; (800) 441-2327**
Best Time to Call: **Before 10 PM**
Host: **Mrs. Myrna Reinhard**
Location: **On U.S. Highway 61**

No. of Rooms: **14**
No. of Private Baths: **14**
Double/pb: **$70–$115**
Open: **All year**

Reduced Rates: **Available**
Breakfast: **Continental, plus**
Other Meals: **Available**
Credit Cards: **AMEX, DC, DISC, MC, VISA**
Pets: **No**

Children: **Welcome, over 12**
Smoking: **No**
Social Drinking: **Permitted**
Minimum Stay: **Holidays**
Station Pickup: **Yes**

Relax in 1860s Victorian luxury—these spacious rooms are furnished in period antiques with today's modern comforts. Awaken to the aroma of "Kingsley Blend" coffee and enjoy the specialty breakfast in the elegant morning room. Then stroll to the replica 1808 Fort, museum, parks, shops, and antique malls, Catfish Riverbend Casino. Historic Nauvoo, Illinois, is 15 minutes away. Treat yourselves to a unique lunch or dinner at Alpha's on the Riverfront. Amenities include private baths (some whirlpools), CATV, AC, and telephones.

## Kountry Klassics ✪
**2002 295TH AVENUE, FORT MADISON, IOWA 52627**

Tel: **(319) 372-5484**
Hosts: **Sonny and Judy Holmes**
Location: **2 mi. N of Fort Madison**
No. of Rooms: **3**
No. of Private Baths: **2**
Max. No. Sharing Bath: **2**
Double p/b: **$55**
Double s/b: **$50**

Open: **All year**
Breakfast: **Full**
Other Meals: **Available**
Pets: **No**
Children: **Welcome**
Smoking: **No**
Airport/Station Pickup: **Yes**

If you like a quiet restful sleep in a farm country setting, Kountry Klassics is just the place for you. This B&B is decorated with antiques and lots of linen and lace. You will have your own private entry that is wheelchair accessible. In the morning, you'll be treated to a hearty, hot country breakfast served on grandma's favorite dishes that conjure memories of the past. Judy's floral designs, displayed throughout the home, create a country-Victorian look that will enhance your peaceful stay.

## Mississippi Rose and Thistle Inn ✪
**532 AVENUE F, FORT MADISON, IOWA 52627**

Tel: **(319) 372-7044**
Best Time to Call: **Anytime**
Hosts: **Bill and Bonnie Saunders**
Location: **20 mi. S of Burlington**
No. of Rooms: **4**
No. of Private Baths: **4**
Double p/b: **$70–$90**
Single p/b: **$65–$90**
Open: **All year**

Reduced Rates: **Available**
Breakfast: **Full**
Other Meals: **Available**
Credit Cards: **AMEX, MC, VISA**
Pets: **No**
Children: **Welcome, over 12**
Smoking: **No**
Social Drinking: **Permitted**
Airport/Station Pickup: **Yes**

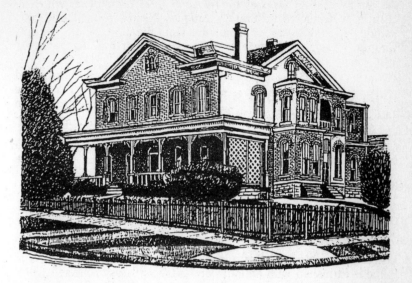

A prominent local businessman built this three-story, Italianate Victorian mansion in 1881; more than a hundred years later, the details remain gorgeous, from the brick home's extra-large windows and wraparound porch to the marble fireplaces and hand-carved black walnut staircase. In your room you'll find period antiques, a miniature park bench bookcase and, for a nightcap, a crystal decanter of cream sherry. By prior arrangement, candlelight dinners are served in the private alcove on the first floor. Bill and Bonnie promise that after waking up from a great night's sleep on one of their custom-made beds, you'll be treated to a Victorian culinary excursion featuring egg dishes, fruit, and fresh-baked delicacies.

## The Wilson Home ✪
**RR 2, BOX 132-1, GREENFIELD, IOWA 50849**

| | |
|---|---|
| Tel: **(515) 743-2031** | Double/pb: **$65–$85** |
| Best Time to Call: **5–10 PM** | Open: **All year** |
| Hosts: **Wendy and Henry Wilson** | Breakfast: **Full** |
| Location: **1 mi. E of Greenfield on Hwy. 92** | Pets: **Sometimes** |
| | Children: **Welcome (crib)** |
| No. of Rooms: **2** | Smoking: **Restricted** |
| No. of Private Baths: **2** | Social Drinking: **Permitted** |

Enjoy the quiet, simple life at The Wilson Home, set in the rolling countryside. The poolhouse encloses a huge indoor pool; a two-level deck filled with plants, wicker and iron furniture, a beverage-stocked kitchenette; and two spacious guest rooms. Breakfasts are served in the sunny dining room of the Wilsons' 1918 farmhouse, which is beautifully decorated with family antiques. Nearby you will find golf, fishing, antiquing, an airplane museum, the Bridges of Madison County, and John Wayne's birthplace. Pheasant hunting packages available.

## Bella Vista Place Bed & Breakfast ✪
**2 BELLA VISTA PLACE, IOWA CITY, IOWA 52245**

| | |
|---|---|
| Tel: **(319) 338-4129** | Open: **All year** |
| Host: **Daissy P. Owen** | Reduced Rates: **Available** |
| Location: **1 mi. from Highway 80,** | Breakfast: **Full** |
| **Exit 244** | Pets: **No** |
| No. of Rooms: **4** | Children: **Welcome** |
| Max. No. Sharing Bath: **4** | Smoking: **No** |
| Double/pb: **$65–$75** | Social Drinking: **Permitted** |
| Double/sb: **$55** | Airport Pickup: **Yes** |
| Single/sb: **$45–$50** | Foreign Languages: **Spanish** |

Listed on the National Register of Historic Places, this lovely 1920s home is furnished with antiques and artifacts Daissy collected while traveling through Europe and Latin America. Guests can relax in a comfortable air-conditioned room, share the company of other guests in the living room or enjoy the view of the Iowa River from the deck. You will savor Daissy's hearty breakfast and delicious coffee. Downtown Iowa City and the University of Iowa are within walking distance. The Hoover Library, Amana Colonies, and the Amish center of Kalona are nearby.

## The Golden Haug ✪
**517 EAST WASHINGTON, IOWA CITY, IOWA 52240**

| | |
|---|---|
| Tel: **(319) 338-6452; 354-4284** | Open: **All year** |
| Best Time to Call: **Anytime** | Reduced Rates: **Available** |
| Hosts: **Nila Haug and Dennis Nowotny** | Breakfast: **Full** |
| Location: **2 mi. from I-80, Exit 244** | Pets: **No** |
| No. of Rooms: **4** | Children: **Welcome** |
| No. of Private Baths: **4** | Smoking: **No** |
| Double/pb: **$68–$95** | Social Drinking: **Permitted** |
| Single/pb: **$68–$95** | Airport Pickup: **Yes** |
| Suites: **$80–$95** | |

Nila and Dennis's 1920s Arts-and-Crafts house has been restored and updated to provide comfortable accommodations and modern conveniences. Guests can retreat to the comfort of their suites or enjoy the camaraderie of other visitors. With refreshments upon your arrival, evening snacks, and brunch-size breakfasts, you won't go away hungry. The convenient Iowa City location puts you within walking distance of the University of Iowa, restaurants, stores, and houses of worship.

## Mason House Inn of Bentonsport ✪
ROUTE 2, BOX 237, KEOSAUQUA, IOWA 52565

| | |
|---|---|
| Tel: (319) 592-3133 | Single/sb: $39–$49 |
| Hosts: Sheral and William McDermet | Open: All year |
| Location: 40 mi. SE of Ottumwa | Breakfast: Full |
| No. of Rooms: 9 | Other Meals: Available |
| No. of Private Baths: 5 | Credit Cards: MC, VISA |
| Max. No. Sharing Bath: 3 | Pets: Sometimes |
| Double/pb: $74 | Children: Welcome |
| Single/pb: $54 | Smoking: No |
| Double/sb: $49–$59 | Social Drinking: Permitted |

Mason House Inn was built next to the Des Moines River by Mormon artisans en route to Salt Lake City. The three-story Georgian house contains 26 rooms. It is the only steamboat inn, built as such, still hosting persons in Iowa. The Inn has the only fold-down copper bathtub in the state. Sheral and Bill purchased the Inn in 1989 and have done extensive remodeling, allowing for ground-level rooms with private baths. Guests will find a full cookie jar in every room. The entire village is on the National Registry of Historic Places. Iowa's oldest courthouse is six miles to the east. Bill served as a pastor for local congregations for 29 years, and Sheral was a manager for a deli before moving to Bentonsport.

## Mississippi Sunrise Bed & Breakfast ✪
18950 GREAT RIVER ROAD, LECLAIRE, IOWA 52753

| | |
|---|---|
| Tel: (319) 332-9203 | Open: Apr.-Oct. |
| Hosts: Ted and Eloise Pfeiff | Reduced Rates: Weekly |
| Location: 11 mi. E of Davenport | Breakfast: Full |
| No. of Rooms: 2 | Pets: No |
| Max. No. Sharing Bath: 4 | Children: Welcome, over 12 |
| Double/sb: $45–$50 | Smoking: No |
| Single/sb: $40–$45 | Social Drinking: No |

You'll be captivated by the superb panoramic view of the Mississippi River from the dining room, living room, enclosed porch, and large deck of this B&B. This lovely hillside brick home is surrounded by trees, flowers, and birds on one acre of land. It is conveniently located on Highway 67 near Interstate 80. Two bedrooms with a large shared bath, air-conditioning, fireplace, and furnishings designed and built by the hosts provide for your comfort. A full home-cooked breakfast including seasonal fruits and jams from the garden is served. Enjoy the wildlife, the flowers, and the beautiful Mississippi River.

## Loy's Farm Bed & Breakfast ✪
### 2077 KK AVENUE, MARENGO, IOWA 52301

| | |
|---|---|
| Tel: (319) 642-7787 | Double/sb: **$50–$60** |
| Best Time to Call: **7 AM, 9:30 PM** | Single/sb: **$45** |
| Hosts: **Loy and Robert Walker** | Open: **All year** |
| Location: **3 mi. from I-80 exit 216 N** | Breakfast: **Full** |
| No. of Rooms: **3** | Other Meals: **Available** |
| No. of Private Baths: **1** | Pets: **If caged** |
| Max. No. Sharing Bath: **4** | Children: **Welcome** |
| Double/pb: **$50–$60** | Smoking: **No** |
| Single/pb: **$45** | Social Drinking: **Permitted** |

The Walkers invite you to visit their contemporary farm home in the heartland of rural Iowa. Enjoy the peaceful surroundings of a large lawn, gardens, and patio. The rooms are furnished in modern and refinished pieces. Guests are welcome to relax in the family room by the fire or to stop by the recreation room for a game of shuffleboard or pool and a treat from the snack bar. A farm tour gives you the chance to see the farm facilities and operations, maybe even hold a baby pig. Each morning enjoy a typical farm breakfast with a gourmet touch. Visit the historic villages of the Amana Colonies, developed as a communal system. The Amana Colonies are Iowa's largest tourist attraction. Tanger Mall, 64 designer outlet stores, and twelve restaurants (six that serve German food) are all located nearby. Herbert Hoover's birthplace, the Kalona Amish, Brucemore Mansion, and Iowa City are all just a short drive away.

## Varners' Caboose Bed & Breakfast ✪
### 204 EAST SECOND STREET, P.O. BOX 10, MONTPELIER, IOWA 52759

| | |
|---|---|
| Tel: (319) 381-3652 | Open: **All year** |
| Best Time to Call: **Afternoons** | Breakfast: **Full** |
| Hosts: **Bob and Nancy Varner** | Pets: **Sometimes** |
| Location: **11 mi. W of Davenport** | Children: **Welcome** |
| No. of Rooms: **1** | Smoking: **No** |
| No. of Private Baths: **1** | Social Drinking: **Permitted** |
| Double/pb: **$55** | Airport/Station Pickup: **Yes** |

Bob and Nancy offer their guests the unique experience of staying in a genuine Rock Island Line caboose. Their home, located close to the Mississippi, was the original Montpelier Depot, and the caboose is a self-contained unit with bath, shower, and kitchen set on its own track behind the house. It sleeps four, with a queen-size bed and two singles in the cupola. The rate is increased to $65 when more than two occupy the caboose. A fully prepared egg casserole, fruit, homemade breads, juice, and coffee or tea are left in the kitchen to be enjoyed at your leisure. Enjoy this quiet town while being a few minutes downstream from the heart of the Quad Cities.

# LaCorsette Maison Inn
## 629 FIRST AVENUE EAST, NEWTON, IOWA 50208

Tel: **(515) 792-6833**
Host: **Kay Owen**
Location: **25 mi. E of Des Moines**
No. of Rooms: **7**
No. of Private Baths: **7**
Double/pb: **$70–$175**
Suites: **$85–$165**
Open: **All year**

Breakfast: **Full**
Other Meals: **Available**
Pets: **Sometimes**
Children: **By Arrangement**
Smoking: **No**
Social Drinking: **Permitted**
Airport/Station Pickup: **Yes**

Bringing a touch of Spanish architecture to the American heartland, this 21-room mansion has all the hallmarks of the Mission style, from its stucco walls and red-tiled roof to its interior oak woodwork. Certain nights of the week, Kay doubles as a chef, preparing elaborate six-course dinners for as many as 57 scheduled guests; the first caller to make reservations selects the entree, and a house tour precedes the meal. Overnight guests wake up to a full breakfast accented by the herbs and vegetables Kay grows in the backyard. If you want to work off the calories, tennis courts and a pool are in the area.

# Old Shepherd House ✪
## 256 W. TILDEN STREET, BOX 251, POSTVILLE, IOWA 52162

Tel: **(319) 864-3452**
Best Time to Call: **10 AM–10 PM**
Host: **Rosalyn Krambeer**
Location: **25 mi. SE of Decorah**
No. of Rooms: **4**
No. of Private Baths: **4**
Double/pb: **$45–$50**

Single/sb: **$30**
Open: **All year**
Breakfast: **Full**
Pets: **Sometimes**
Children: **Welcome**
Smoking: **Restricted**
Social Drinking: **Permitted**

Postville, a town of 1500 with four quaint crafts shops and a fabulous antique emporium, is in northeast Iowa in an area known as the state's

Little Switzerland. Within a thirty-mile radius you can canoe the Iowa River, or visit sites like the Vesterheim Museum, Effigy Mounds, Villa Louis, Spook Cave, and Bily Brothers clock museum. Shepherd House, built in the early 1880s, is furnished entirely with antique and Victorian pieces. Your hostess is an interior decorator, and she's filled her home with unusual window treatments, restored trunks, and crafts work.

## Antique City Inn B&B ✪
### 400 ANTIQUE CITY DRIVE, P.O. BOX 584, WALNUT, IOWA 51577

| | |
|---|---|
| Tel: (712) 784-3722; (800) 714-3722 | Breakfast: **Full** |
| Host: **Sylvia Reddie** | Other Meals: **Available** |
| Location: **52 mi. E of Omaha, Nebraska** | Credit Cards: **MC, VISA** |
| No. of Rooms: **5** | Pets: **No** |
| No. of Private Baths: **1** | Children: **Welcome, over 12** |
| Max. No. Sharing Bath: **3** | Smoking: **No** |
| Double/pb: **$42** | Social Drinking: **Permitted** |
| Open: **All year** | |

This 1911 Victorian residence has been restored to its original state and furnished in period style. You'll admire all the old-fashioned features, such as the wraparound porch, beautiful woodwork, French doors, butler pantry, and dumbwaiter. A block away, in a neighborhood of turn-of-the century brick streets and globed streetlights, you'll find antique shops with more than 200 dealers, plus the restored opera house—home of a country music museum and Iowa's Country Music Hall of Fame. Sylvia's full breakfasts typically consist of juice, fruit, fried potatoes, casseroles, and pecan rolls.

## The Daisy Wilton Inn ✪
### 418 WALNUT STREET, WATERLOO, IOWA 50703

| | |
|---|---|
| Tel: (319) 232-0801 | Reduced Rates: **10% seniors; 10% families** |
| Best Time to Call: **Afternoons** | Breakfast: **Full** |
| Hosts: **Sue and Al Brase** | Pets: **No** |
| Location: **100 mi. NE of Des Moines** | Children: **Welcome, over 12** |
| No. of Rooms: **3** | Smoking: **No** |
| Max. No. Sharing Bath: **4** | Social Drinking: **Permitted** |
| Double/sb: **$55–$65** | Airport/Station Pickup: **Yes** |
| Single/sb: **$50–$60** | |
| Open: **All year** | |

The Daisy Wilton Inn is a Queen Anne–style Victorian, rich in turn-of-the-century detail. Stained and beveled glass windows adorn the turreted home. Your hosts' cherished antiques and Victorian art nouveau decor complement the interior, which has oak woodwork and a dramatic winding staircase. The parlor, with its bookcase and fireplace, is an inviting room for conversation, music, reading, or games. Stately guest chambers offer luxurious accommodations. Savor the elegant surroundings and pleasant pastimes of the Victorian age.

# KANSAS

- WaKeeney
  - Victoria    Abilene •
- Marienthal                                    Tonganoxie •

                    Wichita •

                                            Fort Scott •

## Balfours' House
### ROUTE 2, ABILENE, KANSAS 67410

Tel: **(913) 263-4262**
Best Time to Call: **Anytime**
Hosts: **Gilbert and Marie Balfour**
Location: **2¼ mi. S of Abilene**
Suites: **$50–$150**
Open: **All year**
Breakfast: **Full**

Credit Cards: **AMEX, MC, VISA**
Pets: **Sometimes**
Children: **Welcome**
Smoking: **Restricted**
Social Drinking: **Permitted**
Airport/Station Pickup: **Sometimes**

Gilbert and Marie Balfour welcome you to their modern, cottage-style home, set on a hillside. The house is located on just over two acres, and has a spacious yard. Guests have their own private entrance into the family room, which includes a fireplace, piano, and TV. The main attraction of the house is a hexagonal recreation room that has a built-in swimming pool, spa, and dressing area with shower. A separate Southwestern-style bungalow is also available. Your hosts will gladly direct you to the Eisenhower Museum, Greyhound Hall of Fame, and old historic mansions.

## Old Glory Guest House ✪
### 600 NORTH SPRUCE, ABILENE, KANSAS 67410

Tel: **(913) 263-3225**
Best Time to Call: **Anytime**
Hosts: **Sam and Linda Hawes**
Location: **85 mi. W of Topeka**
No. of Rooms: **1**
No. of Private Baths: **1**
Double/pb: **$55**
Single/pb: **$45**
Open: **All year**

Reduced Rates: **Dec.–Feb.**
Breakfast: **Full, Continental**
Credit Cards: **MC, VISA**
Pets: **No**
Children: **Welcome, over 6**
Smoking: **No**
Social Drinking: **Permitted**
Airport/Station Pickup: **Yes**

Old Glory Guest House is a nostalgic 1884 Italianate-style bed and breakfast with a touch of patriotic pride. Located one mile south of Interstate 70 in a quiet residential neighborhood, it is convenient to downtown Abilene, a town of historic mansions, museums, and antique/crafts shops. Old Glory features tall ceilings, elegant woodwork, pocket doors, and a wraparound side porch. The five-star guest room, honoring Abilene native Dwight D. Eisenhower, is furnished with a full-size antique bed with matching furniture and modern bath. Eggs Benedict is the breakfast specialty served in the sunny bay-windowed dining room.

## Country Quarters ✪
### ROUTE 5, BOX 80, FORT SCOTT, KANSAS 66701

Tel: **(316) 223-2889**
Best Time to Call: **After 5 PM**
Host: **Marilyn McQuitty**
Location: **2 mi. S of Fort Scott**
No. of Rooms: **2**
Max. No. Sharing Bath: **4**
Double/sb: **$30**

Open: **All year**
Breakfast: **Full**
Pets: **No**
Children: **Welcome**
Smoking: **Permitted**
Social Drinking: **Permitted**

Marilyn McQuitty welcomes you to a real working farm located outside a charming Victorian town. Her 100-year-old farmhouse is furnished with comfortable family pieces. While you're sitting by the fire, ask to hear the story behind the 100-year-old hearth and hand-carved mantelpiece. Guests are welcome to relax on the porch or visit the ceramic shop located on the premises. There is easy access to the Fort Scott Lake, Gunn Park, and the Fort Scott National Historic Site, an authentically restored military fort dating back to 1892. Downtown you can drive past the magnificent old homes, browse through antique stores, and visit a one-room schoolhouse.

## Krause House ✪
### ROUTE 1, BOX 42, MARIENTHAL, KANSAS 67863

Tel: **(316) 379-4627**
Hosts: **Paul and Merilyn Krause**
Location: **13 mi. W of Scott City**
No. of Rooms: **2**
No. of Private Baths: **1**
Max. No. Sharing Bath: **4**
Double/pb: **$40**
Single/pb: **$35**
Double/sb: **$35**

Single/sb: **$30**
Open: **All year**
Reduced Rates: **Families**
Breakfast: **Full**
Pets: **Sometimes**
Children: **Welcome**
Smoking: **No**
Social Drinking: **No**

Experience a working grain farm in the western Kansas countryside. Paul and Merilyn Krause have a remodeled farmhouse surrounded by tall shade trees. Breakfast specialties such as egg casseroles, home-made breads, and cinnamon rolls are served on the glassed-in patio overlooking the flowers and greenery. Krause House is 25 miles from Scott County State Park, where you may fish, boat, hunt for fossils, and see Indian ruins.

## Almeda's Bed and Breakfast Inn ✪
### 220 SOUTH MAIN, TONGANOXIE, KANSAS 66086

Tel: **(913) 845-2295**
Best Time to Call: **Before 9 AM;**
  **evenings**

Hosts: **Almeda and Richard Tinberg**
Location: **20 mi. W of Kansas City**
No. of Rooms: **6**

No. of Private Baths: **2**
Max. No. Sharing Bath: **4**
Double/pb: **$40**
Single/pb: **$35**
Double/sb: **$30**
Single/sb: **$25**
Suite: **$65**

Open: **All year**
Breakfast: **Continental, plus**
Pets: **No**
Children: **Welcome**
Smoking: **Restricted**
Social Drinking: **Permitted**

This small-town B&B has a tranquil, friendly atmosphere. An inn for decades—during World War I it attained coast-to-coast fame as the Myers Hotel—it was designated a historic landmark in 1983. The rooms are decorated with country flair, accented by antiques from Almeda's collection. Guests may sip a cup of coffee by the stone bar in the room used as a bus stop in the thirties; the movie *Bus Stop* was inspired by this site. A plaque outside the dining room tells the story of the hotel.

## Das Younger Haus ✪
**1202 HICKORY, VICTORIA, KANSAS 67671**

Tel: **(913) 735-2760**
Hosts: **Tom and Det Younger**
Location: **3 mi. from I-70, exit 168**
No. of Rooms: **4**
No. of Private Baths: **1**
Max. No. Sharing Bath: **4**
Double/pb: **$60**
Single/pb: **$50**
Double/sb: **$45**
Single/sb: **$40**

Open: **All year**
Breakfast: **Full**
Credit Cards: **MC, VISA**
Pets: **No**
Children: **Welcome**
Smoking: **No**
Social Drinking: **Permitted**
Airport/Station Pickup: **Yes**
Foreign Languages: **German**

Victoria is a community of approximately 1300 people. Many of the residents are direct descendants of Volga German immigrants and speak German fluently. Victoria is best known for its Catholic church, the Cathedral of the Plains, which is a National Historic Site. Das Younger Haus was built in 1979 of native field stone and wood. Tom and Bernadette will be there to greet you upon arrival. You'll get the feeling of being home when you kick off your shoes and curl up by the fireplace or go out to the flower-laden deck for a beverage and German cookies. Breakfast will include fresh fruit or juice, homemade German sausage, fresh country eggs, and homemade rolls. Denver is 350 miles west and Kansas City is 275 miles east.

## Thistle Hill
**ROUTE 1, BOX 93, WAKEENEY, KANSAS 67672**

Tel: **(913) 743-2644**
Best Time to Call: **6–8 AM; evenings**
Hosts: **Dave and Mary Hendricks**

Location: **1½ mi. from I-70 exit 120**
No. of Rooms: **4**
No. of Private Baths: **3**

Max. No. Sharing Bath: **4**
Double/pb: **$55–$65**
Single/pb: **$45**
Double/sb: **$55**
Single/sb: **$45**
Open: **All year**

Breakfast: **Full**
Pets: **No**
Children: **Welcome**
Smoking: **Restricted**
Social Drinking: **Permitted**
Airport/Station Pickup: **Yes**

The entry of this weathered wood country house sets the hospitable tone of this B&B located 325 miles west of Kansas City, or the same distance east of Denver, Colorado. Seasonal wreaths, an Early American bench, antique lanterns, and a big sign saying, "Welcome to Thistle Hill" are the Hendrickses' way of saying they're glad you've come to visit. They're anxious to share with you the pleasures of their rural life, which include cooking, restoring antiques, and working with their team of draft horses. A varied breakfast often includes country fresh eggs, breakfast meats, fresh-baked breads, or hotcakes made with whole wheat from their own wheat fields. On chilly mornings it is served near the fireplace. Cedar Bluff Reservoir, for fishing, is 30 miles away; pheasant, waterfowl, and deer roam 10,000 acres of public hunting land nearby.

## Vermilion Rose—A Bed and Breakfast Place ✪

**1204 NORTH TOPEKA AVENUE,
WICHITA, KANSAS 67214-2843**

Tel: **(316) 267-7636; fax: (316) 267-7642**
Best Time to Call: **Anytime**
Hosts: **Marietta Anderson and Ken Kern**
Location: **1 mi. N of Downtown Wichita**
No. of Rooms: **4**
No. of Private Baths: **4**
Double/pb: **$60–$90**

Single/pb: **$45–$75**
Open: **All year**
Breakfast: **Continental, plus**
Other Meals: **Available**
Credit Cards: **MC, VISA**
Pets: **No**
Smoking: **No**
Social Drinking: **Permitted**
Airport/Station Pickup: **Yes**

Vermilion Rose is a new owner-occupied bed and breakfast in a turn-of-the-century home in Wichita's Historic Midtown District. The immediate area had the nickname "lumberman's row," since the proprietors of many early Wichita lumber businesses built their residences here. Guests are invited to enjoy the common room, dining and library areas; for a small additional fee, a fax machine and copier can be at your disposal. Breakfast specialties include fresh fruit, juices, breads, pastries, and seasonal surprises.

# MICHIGAN

Calumet •

Champion • • Au Train
• Blaney Park

Harbor Springs •
• Petoskey
Traverse City • • Eastport
• Beulah

Sebewaing •
Laingsburg • • Frankenmuth
Holland • Rochester • • Port Sanilac
Saugatuck • Dimondale Hills • Lexington
Fennville • • Martin
Allen • • Dearborn
• • Ann Arbor
Hillsdale Brooklyn

## The Olde Bricke House ✪
### P.O. BOX 211, ALLEN, MICHIGAN 49227

Tel: **(517) 869-2349**
Host: **Erma Jones**
Location: **On Rte. 12**
No. of Rooms: **4**
Max. No. Sharing Bath: **4**
Double/sb: **$50**
Single/sb: **$40**
Open: **Mar. 1–Dec. 15**
Reduced Rates: **10% Sun.–Thurs.**
Breakfast: **Continental**

Credit Cards: **MC, VISA**
Pets: **No**
Children: **Welcome, over 13**
Smoking: **Permitted**
Social Drinking: **Permitted**
Minimum Stay: **2 nights during Hillsdale College special weekends (Homecoming, Parents' Weekends, Graduation)**

This Victorian house, built in 1873, was recently renovated. If you are an antiques buff, spend the day browsing the fabulous shops (75 at last count) that have made Allen the Antiques Capital of Michigan. Several lakes for boating, swimming, and fishing are nearby, and Hillsdale College is 10 miles away. You are welcome to join your host for afternoon refreshments on the porch or in the library or living room.

## The Urban Retreat ✪
### 2759 CANTERBURY ROAD, ANN ARBOR, MICHIGAN 48104

| | |
|---|---|
| Tel: **(313) 971-8110** | Double/sb: **$55–$60** |
| Best Time to Call: **5–10 PM** | Single/sb: **$45** |
| Hosts: **Andre Rosalik and Gloria Krys** | Open: **All year** |
| Location: **40 mi. W of Detroit** | Breakfast: **Full** |
| No. of Rooms: **2** | Pets: **No, cats on premises** |
| Max. No. Sharing Bath: **4** | Children: **No** |
| Double/pb: **$60–$65** | Smoking: **Restricted** |
| Single/pb: **$50** | Social Drinking: **Permitted** |

This 1950s ranch-style house is located on a quiet, tree-lined street, 10 minutes from downtown and the University of Michigan campus. The home is decorated with antiques and collectibles from the early 1900s, with an abundance of bird's-eye maple furniture. Adjacent to the property is the County Farm Park, 127 acres of meadowland with walking and jogging paths and a 13-box bluebird trail. The Retreat has been designated as a Backyard Wildlife Habitat by the National Wildlife Federation. Andre and Gloria emphasize a quiet, relaxed atmosphere and assure their guests a peaceful visit and personal attention.

## Pinewood Lodge ✪
### P.O. BOX 176, M28 WEST, AU TRAIN, MICHIGAN 49806

| | |
|---|---|
| Tel: **(906) 892-8300** | Single/sb: **$55** |
| Best Time to Call: **9 AM–9 PM** | Open: **All year** |
| Hosts: **Jerry and Jenny Krieg** | Breakfast: **Full** |
| Location: **24 mi. E of Marquette** | Credit Cards: **DISC, MC, VISA** |
| No. of Rooms: **8** | Pets: **No** |
| No. of Private Baths: **6** | Children: **No** |
| Max. No. Sharing Bath: **4** | Smoking: **No** |
| Double/pb: **$70–$85** | Social Drinking: **Permitted** |
| Double/sb: **$55–$60** | Airport/Station Pickup: **Yes** |

This B&B is a pine log home on the shores of Lake Superior. Pictured Rocks National Shoreline is right down the highway, and you can see the Grand Islands from the living room. Guests can enjoy activities year-round, from swimming, diving, and boating to ice fishing, snowmobiling, and downhill and cross-country skiing.

## The Windermere Inn ✪
### 7723 CRYSTAL DRIVE, BEULAH, MICHIGAN 49617

| | |
|---|---|
| Tel: **(616) 882-9000** | Hosts: **Anne Fitch-Clark and Cameron** |
| Best Time to Call: **8 AM–11 PM** | **Clark** |

Location: **35 mi. SW of Traverse City**
No. of Rooms: **4**
No. of Private Baths: **4**
Double/pb: **$69**
Single/pb: **$59**
Open: **All year**
Breakfast: **Continental**

Credit Cards: **MC, VISA**
Pets: **Sometimes**
Children: **Welcome, over 10**
Smoking: **No**
Social Drinking: **Permitted**
Minimum Stay: **2 nights on weekends
June–Aug.**

Whether you sip lemonade on the screened porch in summer or enjoy a hot toddy by the fire in winter, The Windermere Inn on beautiful Crystal Lake makes comfort its top priority. Situated in scenic Benzie County, the Inn has Sleeping Bear National Lakeshore to its north, Crystal Mountain ski resort to its south, Interlochen Arts Academy to its east, Lake Michigan and its beaches to its west, and golf courses all around. Anne and Cameron can help make your stay as eventful or relaxing as you wish. Your day begins with native fruits and muffins in summer, breakfast casseroles and breads in winter.

## Celibeth House ✪

**ROUTE 1, BOX 58A, M-77 BLANEY PARK ROAD, BLANEY PARK, MICHIGAN 49836**

Tel: **(906) 283-3409**
Host: **Elsa Strom**
Location: **60 mi. W of Mackinac Bridge**
No. of Rooms: **7**
No. of Private Baths: **7**
Double/pb: **$45–$50**
Single/pb: **$40–$45**

Open: **May 1–Dec. 1**
Reduced Rates: **10% after 2nd night**
Breakfast: **Continental**
Credit Cards: **MC, VISA**
Pets: **No**
Children: **Welcome**
Smoking: **No**
Social Drinking: **Permitted**

This lovely house, built in 1895, is situated on 85 acres overlooking a small lake. Many of the scenic attractions of Michigan's Upper Peninsula lie within an hour's drive. Guests may enjoy a cozy living room, a quiet reading room, a comfortably furnished porch, an outdoor deck, and lots of nature trails. Elsa is a retired personal manager who enjoys reading, gardening, traveling, and collecting antiques.

## Dewey Lake Manor Bed & Breakfast ✪

**11811 LAIRD ROAD, BROOKLYN, MICHIGAN 49230**

Tel: **(517) 467-7122**
Best Time to Call: **Before 11 PM**
Hosts: **Joe, Barb, Barry, and Tandy Phillips**
Location: **45 mi. SW of Ann Arbor**
No. of Rooms: **5**
No. of Private Baths: **5**
Double/pb: **$55–$75**
Single/pb: **$50–$70**
Open: **All year**

Reduced Rates: **Available**
Breakfast: **Continental, plus**
Other Meals: **Available, picnic baskets**
Credit Cards: **MC, VISA**
Pets: **No**
Children: **Welcome**
Smoking: **No**
Social Drinking: **Permitted**
Minimum Stay: **3 nights on race weekends, 2 nights holiday weekends**

This 1870s Italianate home sits on the shore of Dewey Lake in the Irish Hills of southern Michigan. Four spacious, airy rooms are furnished with antiques and old-fashioned wallpapers. Guests may linger over a Continental-plus breakfast in the formal dining room or on the porch overlooking the lake. Picnics, bonfires, volleyball, or croquet may be enjoyed on the large lawn. Nearby is the Stagecoach Stop Dinner Theater, as well as golf courses, quaint towns, and many antique shops. Come experience the country with the Phillips family.

## The Calumet House ✪
**1159 CALUMET AVENUE, P.O. BOX 126, CALUMET, MICHIGAN 49913**

| | |
|---|---|
| Tel: **(906) 337-1936** | Open: **All year** |
| Hosts: **George and Rose Chivses** | Breakfast: **Full** |
| Location: **10 mi. N of Hancock-Houghton** | Pets: **No** |
| | Children: **No** |
| No. of Rooms: **2** | Smoking: **No** |
| Max. No. Sharing Bath: **4** | Social Drinking: **Permitted** |
| Double/sb: **$30** | Airport/Station Pickup: **Yes** |
| Single/sb: **$25** | Foreign Languages: **Finnish** |

The Calumet House is set in a historic old mining town, known for its clean air and scenic vistas. Built in 1895, the house boasts its original woodwork and is filled with local antique furnishings. In the morning, you're in for a treat with Rose's home cooking. Breakfast specialties include English scones, pancakes, local berries in season, and homemade jam. Calumet House is within walking distance of the village, with its opera house, museum, and antique shops. Your hosts will also direct you to local hunting and fishing, as well as to places that any botanist would call paradise. It's 10 miles north of Michigan Technological University and Suomi College.

## Michigamme Lake Lodge ✪
**BOX 97, CHAMPION, MICHIGAN 49814**

| | |
|---|---|
| Tel: **(800) 358-0058** | Open: **All year** |
| Hosts: **Frank and Linda Stabile** | Reduced Rates: **Available** |
| Location: **30 mi. W of Marquette on US 41** | Breakfast: **Continental** |
| | Credit Cards: **MC, VISA** |
| No. of Rooms: **9** | Pets: **No** |
| No. of Private Baths: **3** | Children: **Welcome** |
| Max. No. Sharing Bath: **2** | Smoking: **No** |
| Double/pb: **$59–$125** | Social Drinking: **Permitted** |

Built in 1934, listed on the State and National Historical Register, this two-and-a-half-story lodge is a fine representative of the "great camps" that punctuated Michigan's Upper Peninsula. Guests can relax by a crackling fire in the massive stone fireplace gracing the large central hall. Lake Michigamme provides opportunities for canoeing, swimming, fishing, and boating. Depending on the season, you may go cross-country skiing, snowshoeing, hiking, and biking. With a cup of coffee in hand, enjoy sunrise from the porch, which has a panoramic view of the lake. Outside, birch trees line the walkways that lead to a secluded area with beautiful flower gardens. For those of you who don't mind paying a higher rate, 3 rooms are available.

## York House ☉
### 1141 NORTH YORK, DEARBORN, MICHIGAN 42128

| | |
|---|---|
| Tel: **(313) 561-2432** | Single/pb: **$55** |
| Best Time to Call: **Afternoons, evenings** | Open: **All year** |
| | Breakfast: **Continental** |
| Host: **Joan Schnell** | Pets: **No** |
| Location: **15 mi. W of Detroit** | Children: **Welcome** |
| No. of Rooms: **2** | Smoking: **No** |
| No. of Private Baths: **2** | Social Drinking: **No** |
| Double/pb: **$65** | Airport/Station Pickup: **Yes** |

This unique 1927 yellow brick home with red tile roof is furnished in the period of the 1920s and 1930s, and is perfect for a getaway weekend. The Charles Lindbergh room and the Old Car room have been furnished by Joan with antiques and other mementos from the past, adding to the house's charm and your comfort. York House is located five minutes from the Henry Ford Museum, Greenfield Village, and Fairlane Town Mall with 220 stores. Sports fans will be close to the Detroit Tigers, Pistons, Red Wings, and Lions. For an international adventure, it's just twenty minutes to the casinos in Windsor, Ontario, Canada.

## Bannicks B&B ☉
### 4608 MICHIGAN ROAD, M-99, DIMONDALE, MICHIGAN 48821

| | |
|---|---|
| Tel: **(517) 646-0224** | Open: **All year** |
| Hosts: **Pat and Jim Bannick** | Breakfast: **Full** |
| Location: **5 mi. SW of Lansing** | Pets: **No** |
| No. of Rooms: **2** | Children: **Welcome** |
| Max. No. Sharing Bath: **3** | Smoking: **No** |
| Double/sb: **$35** | Social Drinking: **Permitted** |
| Single/sb: **$25** | |

This large ranch-style home features a stained-glass entry, nautical-style basement, and a Mona Lisa bathroom. Guest accommodations consist of comfortable bedrooms and a den-TV room. Your hosts invite you to share a cup of coffee anytime. They will be happy to advise on the sights of Michigan's capital city, just five minutes away. Michigan State University is eight miles away.

## Torch Lake Sunrise Bed and Breakfast ☉
**BOX 52, EASTPORT, MICHIGAN 49627**

| | |
|---|---|
| Tel: **(616) 599-2706** | Reduced Rates: **Available** |
| Host: **Betty A. Collins** | Breakfast: **Full** |
| Location: **35 mi. N of Traverse City** | Pets: **Sometimes** |
| No. of Rooms: **3** | Children: **Welcome** |
| No. of Private Baths: **3** | Smoking: **No** |
| Double/pb: **$75–$95** | Social Drinking: **Permitted** |
| Open: **All year** | |

This B&B overlooks what *National Geographic* calls the third most beautiful lake in the world. All rooms are furnished with antiques and have decks and private baths. Close at hand are several golf courses, tennis courts, gourmet restaurants, and ski resorts. For summer activities, a canoe, a rowboat, and paddleboards are available. In winter, cross-country skiing awaits you just outside. Wake up seeing the sunrise over the lake and smelling the wonderful aroma of fresh muffins baking! Perhaps you'll be served a frittata, or strawberry pancakes, or eggs Benedict, but always fresh fruit of the season.

## The Kingsley House
**626 WEST MAIN STREET, FENNVILLE, MICHIGAN 49408**

| | |
|---|---|
| Tel: **(616) 561-6425** | Reduced Rates: **10% after 4th night;** |
| Hosts: **David and Shirley Witt** | **10% seniors** |
| Location: **8 mi. SE of Saugatuck** | Breakfast: **Full** |
| No. of Rooms: **6** | Pets: **No** |
| No. of Private Baths: **6** | Smoking: **No** |
| Double/pb: **$65–$85** | Social Drinking: **Permitted** |
| Suites: **$125** | Airport/Station Pickup: **Yes** |
| Open: **All year** | Foreign Languages: **Dutch, Friesian** |

This elegant Queen Anne Victorian takes its name from the locally prominent family who built it in 1886. Furnished and decorated in period style, the inn reflects the warmth and charm of a bygone era. Full family-style breakfasts are served in the formal dining room. Honeymoon suites with whirlpool baths and fireplaces are available. Saugatuck, Holland, and the sandy beaches of Lake Michigan are only minutes away.

## Bed & Breakfast at The Pines ☉
**327 ARDUSSI STREET, FRANKENMUTH, MICHIGAN 48734**

| | |
|---|---|
| Tel: **(517) 652-9019** | Double/sb: **$45** |
| Hosts: **Richard and Donna Hodge** | Single/sb: **$35** |
| Location: **60 mi. N of Detroit** | Open: **All year** |
| No. of Rooms: **2** | Breakfast: **Continental, plus** |
| Max. No. Sharing Bath: **4** | Pets: **Sometimes** |

Children: **Welcome**                                  Social Drinking: **Permitted**
Smoking: **No**

Enjoy the casual atmosphere of this brick, ranch-style home with a secluded yard surrounded by evergreen trees. German Bavarian heritage is the main theme of the town and its specialty shops. Bed & Breakfast at The Pines is located in a quiet residential area within walking distance to restaurants and tourist attractions. Guest rooms are beautifully furnished with heirloom quilts, ceiling fans, herbal accents, and fresh flowers. Morning specialties include homemade breads, rolls, muffins, granola, and fresh fruits. Their motto is "Come as a stranger—leave as a friend."

## Mottls Getaway ✪
**1021 BIRCHCREST COURT, HARBOR SPRINGS, MICHIGAN 49740**

Tel: **(616) 526-9682**
Host: **Carol Mottl**
Location: **3½ mi. W of Harbor Springs**
No. of Rooms: **2**
Max. No. Sharing Bath: **4**
Suites: **$50**
Open: **All year**
Reduced Rates: **15% weekly; 25% families**

Breakfast: **Full**
Pets: **Sometimes**
Children: **Welcome**
Smoking: **Permitted**
Social Drinking: **Permitted**
Airport Pickup: **Yes**

Located in the prestigious northern Michigan vacation area on Lake Michigan's beautiful blue Little Traverse Bay, Mottls Getaway suites include a kitchenette with a refrigerator, stove, and oven; a large stone fireplace in the furnished living room; two bedrooms with twin beds; a bathroom; and a private outside entrance. Nearby attractions for sports enthusiasts include several good public golf courses; the ski areas of Nubs Nob, Boyne Highlands, and Boyne Mountain; a dozen marked and groomed cross-country ski trails; and sandy swimming beaches on Little Traverse Bay and other inland lakes. A daily help-yourself breakfast features home-baked breads.

## Shadowlawn Manor ✪
**84 UNION STREET, HILLSDALE, MICHIGAN 49242**

Tel: **(517) 437-2367**
Hosts: **Art Young and Al Paskevich**
Location: **90 mi. SW of Detroit**
No. of Rooms: **4**
No. of Private Baths: **4**
Double/pb: **$63**
Single/pb: **$58**
Open: **All year**

Reduced Rates: **10% Jan., Feb.; weekly; 10% seniors**
Credit Cards: **DISC, MC, VISA**
Breakfast: **Full**
Pets: **No**
Smoking: **No**
Social Drinking: **Permitted**

Built in 1860, Shadowlawn Manor has been restored and refurbished with your comfort in mind. Art and Al have been collecting furniture, silverware, crystal, and antique accessories for years, and they have used it all to great advantage at Shadowlawn. They will be happy to direct you to the lake, beach, golf course, or Hillsdale College's arboretum. You are welcome to relax on the screened-in porch, where, in springtime, the lilacs perfume the air.

## Dutch Colonial Inn
### 560 CENTRAL AVENUE, HOLLAND, MICHIGAN 49423

| | |
|---|---|
| Tel: **(616) 396-3664; fax: (616) 396-0461** | Open: **All year** |
| | Breakfast: **Full** |
| Hosts: **Bob, Pat, Ellen, and Jan Elenbaas** | Pets: **No** |
| Location: **30 mi. W of Grand Rapids** | Children: **Welcome, over 10** |
| No. of Rooms: **5** | Smoking: **No** |
| No. of Private Baths: **5** | Social Drinking: **No** |
| Double/pb: **$55–$95** | Airport/Station Pickup: **Yes** |
| Suites: **$105–$150** | |

Bob and Pat invite you to experience Dutch hospitality in their spacious Colonial Inn. The house is set in a quiet residential area and has a lovely yard and sun porch. Rooms are furnished with traditional family antiques, some dating back to the 1830s. Choose from a bedroom with lovely candlewicking on the drapes, comforters and pillow shams, or the Jenny Lind room with antique beds and raspberry and dusty rose accents. Amenities include air-conditioning, TVs, in-room phones, and whirlpool tubs for two, for that special romantic touch. Breakfast specialties include quiche, homemade rolls and muffins, served in the formal dining room. The Inn is centrally located in a beautiful city famous for its tulip festival, original Dutch windmill, and miles of sandy beaches on Lake Michigan. Business travelers are welcome.

## Seven Oaks Farm ✪
### 7891 HOLLISTER ROAD, LAINGSBURG, MICHIGAN 48848

| | |
|---|---|
| Tel: **(517) 651-5598** | Open: **All year** |
| Best Time to Call: **Evening** | Breakfast: **Continental** |
| Host: **Mary C. Pino** | Pets: **Yes** |
| Location: **15 mi. NE of East Lansing** | Children: **Welcome** |
| No. of Rooms: **1** | Smoking: **Permitted** |
| No. of Private Baths: **1** | Social Drinking: **Permitted** |
| Double/pb: **$50** | Airport/Station Pickup: **Yes** |
| Single/pb: **$35** | |

This beautiful country home with antique furnishings, built in 1847, is located on 100 acres of peaceful woods and farmland pleasant for walking. Golf, auctions, antique stores, an elegant restaurant and

Sleepyhollow State Park (for swimming and cross-country skiing) are only two miles away. An outlet and other shopping malls, as well as music, theater, and sports at Michigan State University, are just fifteen minutes away. The State Capital is twenty-five minutes away. Your hostess, an attorney, raises sheep and has two children. Children and pets are welcome. Come enjoy country comfort and refreshments.

## Governor's Inn ✪
### LEXINGTON, MICHIGAN 48450

| | |
|---|---|
| Tel: **(810) 359-5770** | Open: **All year** |
| Hosts: **Marlene and Jim Boyda** | Breakfast: **Continental** |
| Location: **20 mi. N of Port Huron** | Pets: **No** |
| No. of Rooms: **3** | Children: **Welcome** |
| No. of Private Baths: **3** | Smoking: **No** |
| Double/pb: **$55** | Social Drinking: **Permitted** |
| Single/pb: **$50** | |

A handsome residence built in 1859, the Inn is located near the shore of Lake Huron. It has been refurbished to its original "summer home" style. Wicker furniture, rag rugs, iron beds, and green plants accent the light, airy decor. You can stroll to the nearby beach, browse through interesting shops, fish from the breakwater, or play golf or tennis. Marlene and Jim look forward to sharing their quaint village surroundings with you.

## Pine Manor Bed & Breakfast ✪
### 1436 TENTH STREET, MARTIN, MICHIGAN 49070

| | |
|---|---|
| Tel: **(616) 672-9164** | Single/pb: **$45** |
| Host: **Patricia L. Peden** | Open: **All year** |
| Location: **2 mi. from route US 131,** | Breakfast: **Continental** |
| **Exit 55** | Pets: **No** |
| No. of Rooms: **2** | Children: **Welcome, over 10** |
| No. of Private Baths: **2** | Smoking: **No** |
| Double/pb: **$55** | Social Drinking: **Permitted** |

This century-old farmhouse, lovingly restored over the last 20 years, sits back from the main road amid landscaped lawns and old pines. Breakfast is served in the bright, wrought-iron breakfast room or in the formal dining room. Accommodations are private, with an upstairs sitting room offering a TV, VCR, books, and games. Patricia, who is retired, enjoys cooking, entertaining, and gardening, and will happily direct you to antique shops, golf and skiing facilities, and local restaurants.

## Benson House B&B ✪
### 618 EAST LAKE STREET, PETOSKEY, MICHIGAN 49770

| | |
|---|---|
| Tel: **(616) 347-1338** | Breakfast: **Full** |
| Best Time to Call: **After 10 AM** | Credit Cards: **MC, VISA** |
| Hosts: **Rod and Carol Benson** | Pets: **No** |
| No. of Rooms: **3** | Children: **Welcome, over 6** |
| No. of Private Baths: **3** | Smoking: **No** |
| Double/pb: **$85–$95** | Social Drinking: **Permitted** |
| Suite: **$120** | Airport/Station Pickup: **Yes** |
| Open: **All year** | |

From the beautiful veranda of Benson House, you can admire Lake Michigan's Little Traverse Bay, just as guests did in 1878 when this Victorian inn first opened its doors. Petoskey is in the heart of Michigan's Little New England; the town's Gaslight District offers excellent shopping and dining. Mackinac Island is just a short drive away, as are numerous beaches, lakes, and other points of interest. The area's scenic roads wind through forests, valleys, and upland meadows. Five major ski resorts provide the Midwest's best downhill and cross-country skiing. For those of you who don't mind paying a higher rate, one other room is available.

## Raymond House Inn ✪
### 111 SOUTH RIDGE STREET, M-25, PORT SANILAC, MICHIGAN 48469

| | |
|---|---|
| Tel: **(810) 622-8800; (800) 622-7229** | Reduced Rates: **10% seniors** |
| Hosts: **The Denisons** | Breakfast: **Full** |
| Location: **30 mi. N of Port Huron** | Pets: **No** |
| No. of Rooms: **7** | Children: **Welcome, over 12** |
| No. of Private Baths: **7** | Smoking: **No** |
| Double/pb: **$65–$75** | Social Drinking: **Permitted** |
| Open: **Mar. 1–Dec. 31** | |

Shirley will put you right at ease in her antique-filled inn with the conveniences of today and the ambience of 1895. Each bedroom is furnished with period furniture, brightly colored spreads, and lace curtains. There's an old-fashioned parlor and a dining room where you are served breakfast. Sport fishermen and sailboat enthusiasts will enjoy this area; cultural activities, quilting bees, and the annual summer festival are longtime traditions here. There is an antique and gift shop in the Inn.

## Paint Creek B&B ✪
### 971 DUTTON ROAD, ROCHESTER HILLS, MICHIGAN 48306

| | |
|---|---|
| Tel: **(810) 651-6785** | No. of Rooms: **3** |
| Hosts: **Loren and Rea Siffring** | Max. No. Sharing Bath: **3** |
| Location: **35 mi. N of Detroit** | Double/sb: **$40–$45** |

| | |
|---|---|
| Single/sb: **$35–$40** | Pets: **Sometimes** |
| Open: **All year** | Children: **Welcome** |
| Reduced rates: **Available** | Smoking: **No** |
| Breakfast: **Full** | Social Drinking: **Permitted** |

Located on 3½ woodsy acres, this B&B brings guests close to nature. During the day, sit in the family room and watch the birds and squirrels; at night, check out the raccoons and opossums that gather on the feeding platform. For those who want to experience the great outdoors, there's hiking, biking, and cross-country skiing on the trail adjoining the property, plus four recreational parks less than fifteen minutes away. Sightseers will want to visit the Stoney Creek historic district, Oakland University, Pontiac Silverdome, the Palace (home of the Detroit Pistons), and Pine Knob Ski Hill and its outdoor concert facility.

## Sherwood Forest Bed & Breakfast ✪
**938 CENTER STREET, P.O. BOX 315, SAUGATUCK, MICHIGAN 49453**

| | |
|---|---|
| Tel: **(800) 838-1246** | Other Meals: **Available** |
| Best Time to Call: **9 AM–10 PM** | Credit Cards: **MC, VISA** |
| Hosts: **Keith and Sue Charak** | Pets: **No** |
| Location: **40 mi. SW of Grand Rapids** | Children: **Welcome, over 12** |
| No. of Rooms: **5** | Smoking: **No** |
| No. of Private Baths: **5** | Social Drinking: **Permitted** |
| Double p/b: **$60–$140** | Minimum Stay: **2 nights, weekends;** |
| Open: **All year** | **May 1–Oct. 31** |
| Breakfast: **Continental** | Airport/Station Pickup: **Yes** |

Woods surround this beautiful, 1890s Victorian home with a large wraparound porch. All guest rooms are furnished with antiques; one has a Jacuzzi and another has a fireplace. Outside is a heated swimming pool and deck, along with a separate cottage that sleeps seven. Lake Michigan and a public beach are half a block away. The area's wide white sandy beaches are the perfect place for strolling, swimming, or watching spectacular sunsets. Saugatuck's attractions include chamber music, art galleries, summer theater, charming gift shops, golf, charter boats, sailing, cross-country skiing, and fine dining.

## Rummel's Tree Haven ○
**41 NORTH BECK STREET, M-25, SEBEWAING, MICHIGAN 48759**

| | |
|---|---|
| Tel: **(517) 883-2450** | Open: **All year** |
| Best Time to Call: **Afternoons; evenings** | Breakfast: **Full** |
| | Pets: **Sometimes** |
| Hosts: **Carl and Erma Rummel** | Children: **Welcome (crib)** |
| Location: **28 mi. NE of Bay City** | Smoking: **Permitted** |
| No. of Rooms: **2** | Social Drinking: **Permitted** |
| Double/pb: **$45** | Airport/Station Pickup: **Yes** |
| Single/pb: **$30** | |

A tree grows right through the porch and roof of this charming old home that was built by the Beck family in 1878. Guests can relax in large, airy rooms furnished with twin beds and comfortable family pieces. City dwellers are sure to enjoy the small-town friendliness and the quiet of the countryside. Saginaw Bay offers fine fishing, hunting, boating, bird-watching, or just plain relaxing. Carl and Erma offer color TV, videocassettes, and the use of the barbecue and refrigerator. They love having company and will do all they can to make you feel welcome and relaxed.

## Linden Lea, A B&B on Long Lake
**279 SOUTH LONG LAKE ROAD, TRAVERSE CITY, MICHIGAN 49684**

| | |
|---|---|
| Tel: **(616) 943-9182** | Breakfast: **Full** |
| Hosts: **Jim and Vicky McDonnell** | Pets: **No** |
| Location: **9 mi. W of Traverse City** | Children: **Welcome, by arrangement** |
| No. of Rooms: **2** | Smoking: **No** |
| No. of Private Baths: **2** | Social Drinking: **Permitted** |
| Double/sb: **$90** | Minimum Stay: **Holiday weekends** |
| Open: **All year** | Airport/Station Pickup: **Yes** |
| Reduced Rates: **$75 Nov.–April** | |

Linden Lea is an extensively remodeled and expanded 1900 lakeside cottage set on a private sandy beach surrounded by woods. The bedrooms are comfortably furnished in country style, accented with antiques. You are certain to enjoy the window seats and the panoramic views of Long Lake. The area offers the Interlochen Center for the

Arts National Music Camp, a PGA golf course, and local wineries. Breakfast features local specialties, such as smoked bacon, maple syrup, and berries that make the home-baked muffins so delicious.

## Bed & Breakfast Reservations of Michigan
### 4655 CHAREST, WATERFORD, MICHIGAN 48327

Tel: **(810) 682-2665**
Best Time to Call: **6–10 PM**
Coordinators: **Tom and Denise Erhart**
States/Region Covered: **Bayview, Detroit, Eaton Rapids, Fennville, Fruitport, Ludington, Marquette, St. Clair, St. Ignace, Traverse City**

Rates (Single/Double):
  Modest:  **$40 / $50**
  Average:  **$60 / $75**
  Luxury:  **$80 /$80–$220**
Credit Cards: **MC, VISA**

Tom and Denise represent more than fifty B&B homes and inns throughout the entire state. Choices include a large country inn in a charming nineteenth-century fairy tale village, a recently renovated Victorian mansion overlooking International Waterway, and a Bavarian-style country home with authentic German decor and a delightful German host.

# MINNESOTA

Fergus Falls •

• Stacy
• Minneapolis/St. Paul
• Dundas

Round Lake •   • Sherburn   • Spring Valley

## Martin Oaks B&B ✪
### 107 FIRST STREET, DUNDAS, MINNESOTA 55019

Tel: **(507) 645-4644**
Best Time to Call: **Before noon or after 6 PM**
Hosts: **Marie and Frank Gery**
Location: **35 mi. S of Minneapolis and St. Paul**
No. of Rooms: **2**
Max. No. Sharing Bath: **4**
Double/sb: **$69**
Single/sb: **$55**
Open: **All year**

Breakfast: **Full**
Other Meals: **Available**
Credit Cards: **MC, VISA**
Pets: **No**
Children: **Sometimes**
Smoking: **No**
Social Drinking: **Permitted**
Minimum Stay: **2 nights during college events**
Airport/Station Pickup: **Yes**

Built in 1869 by the treasurer of the thriving Archibald Mill just across the Cannon River, Martin Oaks is listed on the National Register of Historic Places. The architecture combines elements of Italianate and Greek Revival styles. Some rooms have their original pine floors, and all are furnished with comfortable antiques. Local activities abound, with options like golf, tennis, skiing, biking, hiking, canoeing, antiquing, and bookstore browsing. St. Olaf and Carleton colleges are minutes away. After serving you fresh fruit, egg dishes, and home-baked goodies, your hostess, a storyteller, will probably end breakfast by regaling you with an episode or two of local history.

## Bergerud B's ✪

### ROUTE 5, BOX 61, FERGUS FALLS, MINNESOTA 56537

| | |
|---|---|
| Tel: **(218) 736-4720** | Breakfast: **Full** |
| Hosts: **James and Sylvia Bergerud** | Other Meals: **Available** |
| Location: **12 mi. S of Fergus Falls** | Pets: **No** |
| No. of Rooms: **3** | Children: **Welcome, over 8** |
| Max. No. Sharing Bath: **6** | Smoking: **No** |
| Double/sb: **$35** | Social Drinking: **Permitted** |
| Single/sb: **$30** | Foreign Languages: **Norwegian** |
| Open: **All year** | |

This home was built by the host's grandfather in 1895, on the century farm homesteaded in 1881. Jim and Sylvia have modernized the house, but the original structure remains much the same. Located twelve miles from the city, Bergerud B's offers a peaceful night of rest and relaxation. Take a walk in the country, play a game of pool, or just sit by one of the two fireplaces on a cool night with a good book and a cup of hot cider. Awake to the smell of flavored coffee and a sumptuous hearty breakfast. Upon your departure Jim and Sylvia will fill your thermos and send you on your way with a baked goody. Your hosts enjoy meeting new people and will make your stay at Bergerud's a memorable experience.

## The Prairie House on Round Lake ✪

### RR 1, BOX 105, ROUND LAKE, MINNESOTA 56167

| | |
|---|---|
| Tel: **(507) 945-8934** | Single/sb: **$45** |
| Hosts: **Ralph and Virginia Schenck** | Open: **All year** |
| No. of Rooms: **4** | Breakfast: **Full** |
| No. of Private Baths: **1** | Pets: **Welcome** |
| Max. No. Sharing Bath: **4** | Children: **Welcome** |
| Double/pb: **$55** | Smoking: **No** |
| Single/pb: **$55** | Social Drinking: **Permitted** |
| Double/sb: **$45** | Airport/Station Pickup: **Yes** |

Built in 1879 by a prominent Chicago businessman, this farmhouse is a retreat from the bustle of city life. It's a working horse farm: American paint horses roam the pasture, and three barns house both young stock in training and show horses that are exhibited all over the world. A cupola rising from the central stairway is circled by four dormer bedrooms on the second floor. Antique furniture accented with equine touches reflects the spirit of the farm. Fishing, hiking, swimming, boating, and tennis are at the doorstep.

## The Garden Gate ✪
### 925 GOODRICH AVENUE, ST. PAUL, MINNESOTA 55105

| | |
|---|---|
| Tel: **(612) 227-8430; (800) 967-2703** | Open: **All year** |
| Hosts: **Mary and Miles Conway** | Breakfast: **Continental** |
| Location: **1 mi. from I-94 exit** | Credit Cards: **No** |
| **Lexington Parkway** | Pets: **Sometimes** |
| No. of Rooms: **3** | Children: **Welcome** |
| Max. No. Sharing Bath: **3** | Smoking: **No** |
| Double/sb: **$60** | Social Drinking: **Permitted** |
| Single/sb: **$50** | Airport/Station Pickup: **Yes** |

A garden of delights awaits you at this Victorian duplex in the heart of St. Paul's Victoria Crossing neighborhood, within easy reach of downtown, the airport, the capitol, and the Mall of America. The Gladiola, Rose, and Delphinium rooms are as beautiful as their namesakes. A typical breakfast may include fresh fruit, baked pastries, cereal, and yogurt. To pamper the body as well as the palate, guests may arrange to have a therapeutic massage.

## Four Columns Inn ✪
### RT. 2, BOX 75, SHERBURN, MINNESOTA 56171

| | |
|---|---|
| Tel: **(507) 764-8861** | Doulbe s/b: **$50** |
| Best Time to Call: **Anytime** | Single s/b: **$50** |
| Hosts: **Norman and Pennie Kittleson** | Open: **All year** |
| Location: **150 mi. W of Minneapolis** | Reduced Rates: **10% families** |
| No. of Rooms: **4** | Breakfast: **Full** |
| No. of Private Baths: **3** | Pets: **No** |
| Max. No. Private Baths: **3** | Children: **Sometimes** |
| Max. No. Sharing Bath: **4** | Smoking: **No** |
| Double p/b: **$60–$70** | Social Drinking: **Permitted** |
| Single p/b: **$60–$70** | Airport/Station Pickup: **Yes** |

Built as a guest house in 1884, this former stagecoach stop now welcomes the modern-day traveler. Lovingly remodeled by the Kittlesons during the last forty-five years, this Victorian mansion offers four rooms—including the very popular Bridal Suite. Throughout, the house is filled with antiques and musical instruments, including a player piano and a 1950s jukebox. A walnut-paneled den, two working fireplaces, circular stairway, and a library complete your home-away-from-home. A full breakfast served with warm hospitality rounds out your stay in the country. Four Columns is located in south central Minnesota, just two miles from I-90.

## Chase's Bed & Breakfast
**508 NORTH HURON, SPRING VALLEY, MINNESOTA 55975**

| | |
|---|---|
| Tel: (507) 346-2850 | Reduced Rates: **15% weekly** |
| Hosts: **Bob and Jeannine Chase** | Breakfast: **Full** |
| Location: **26 mi. S of Rochester** | Credit Cards: **DISC, MC, VISA** |
| No. of Rooms: **5** | Pets: **No** |
| No. of Private Baths: **5** | Children: **Sometimes** |
| Double/pb: **$75** | Smoking: **No** |
| Single/pb: **$60** | Social Drinking: **Permitted** |
| Open: **Feb.–Dec.** | Airport/Station Pickup: **Yes** |

William H. Strong built this Second Empire–style home in 1879 for $8,000. At the time, it was considered to be the most handsome home in the county. Over the years, the house has been an office, motel, and rest home, and is now listed on the National Register of Historic Places. Guests will find elegant rooms furnished in period antiques, many of which are for sale. Bob and Jeannine serve a hearty breakfast and offer snacks and setups in the evening. Nearby activities include swimming, tennis, golf, trout fishing, and hiking. Chase's is 18 miles from the airport, and 28 miles from the Mayo Clinic. The Amish area is nearby.

## Kings Oakdale Park Guest House ✪
**6933 232 AVENUE NORTHEAST, STACY, MINNESOTA 55079**

| | |
|---|---|
| Tel: (612) 462-5598 | Suites: **$35** |
| Hosts: **Donna and Charles Solem** | Open: **All year** |
| Location: **38 mi. N of St. Paul** | Breakfast: **Continental** |
| No. of Rooms: **3** | Pets: **Sometimes** |
| No. of Private Baths: **2** | Children: **No** |
| Double/pb: **$32** | Smoking: **Permitted** |
| Single/pb: **$26** | Social Drinking: **Permitted** |
| Double/sb: **$30** | Foreign Languages: **French** |
| Single/sb: **$25** | |

This comfortable home is situated on four landscaped acres on the banks of Typo Creek. The picnic tables, volleyball net, and horseshoe game are sure signs of a hospitable country place. It is a serene retreat for people on business trips to the Twin Cities. The Wisconsin border and the scenic St. Croix River, where boat trips are offered, are minutes from the house. Charles and Donna will direct you to the most reasonable restaurants in town. For late snacks, refrigerators in the bedrooms are provided.

# MISSOURI

## Bed & Breakfast Kansas City—Missouri & Kansas
P.O. BOX 14781, LENEXA, KANSAS 66285

Tel: **(913) 888-3636**
Coordinator: **Edwina Monroe**
States/Regions Covered:
  **Kansas—Lenexa, Overland Park,
  Wichita; Missouri—Grandview,
  Independence, Kansas City, Lee's**

**Summit, Parkville, St. Joseph,
Springfield, Warrensburg, Weston**
Rates (Single/Double):
  Average:   **$35 / $40–$50**
  Luxury:    **$60 / $65–$130**
Credit Cards: **No**

You will enjoy visiting such places as the Truman Library and home, Crown Center, Country Club Plaza, Arrowhead Stadium, Royals Stadium, Kemper Arena, the Missouri Repertory Theatre, and the American Heartland Theater, Nelson Art Gallery, New Theatre Restaurant, Toy & Miniature Museum.

## Borgman's Bed & Breakfast ✪
**ARROW ROCK, MISSOURI 65320**

---

Tel: **(816) 837-3350**
Best Time to Call: **7–9 AM**
Hosts: **Helen and Kathy Borgman**
Location: **100 mi. E of Kansas City**
No. of Rooms: **4**
Max. No. Sharing Bath: **4**
Double/sb: **$45–$50**
Single/sb: **$40**

Open: **All year**
Reduced Rates: **10% 3 nights**
Breakfast: **Continental**
Other Meals: **Dinner (winter only)**
Pets: **Sometimes**
Children: **Welcome**
Smoking: **No**
Social Drinking: **Permitted**

This 1860 home is spacious and comfortable, and it is furnished with cherished family pieces. Helen is a seamstress, artisan, and baker. Wait till you taste her fresh breads! Daughter Kathy is a town tour guide, so you will get firsthand information on this National Historic Landmark town at the beginning of the Santa Fe Trail. A fine repertory theater, the Lyceum, is open in summer. Crafts shops, antique stalls, and the old country store are fun places to browse in. Good restaurants are within walking distance.

## The Wildflower Inn
**ROUTE 2, BOX 101, BOURBON, MISSOURI 65441**

---

Tel: **(314) 468-7975**
Best Time to Call: **4–7 PM**
Hosts: **Mary Lou and Jerry Hubble**

Location: **65 mi. from St. Louis**
No. of Rooms: **4**
No. of Private Baths: **4**

Double/pb: **$60–$75**
Open: **All year**
Breakfast: **Full**
Pets: **No**

Children: **No**
Smoking: **No**
Social Drinking: **Permitted**

The Wildflower Inn sits graciously on 42 acres in the foothills of the Ozarks. Surrounded by natural springs and abundant wildlife, the setting is private and relaxing. Amenities include color TVs, central heating and air-conditioning for year-round comfort. Guests are invited to relax in the gathering room in front of an old-fashioned fireplace. There, you can enjoy a book, games, or visit with other guests while sipping complimentary coffee or tea. Things to do include fishing, canoeing, rafting, antiquing, or visiting the wineries, Meramec Caverns, Meramec State Park, and Meramec Springs. A full country breakfast is served. Specialties include Belgian waffles, Western omelettes, orange muffins, angel flake biscuits, sausage gravy and apple quiche.

## Ozark Mountain Country B&B Service
**BOX 295, BRANSON, MISSOURI 65616**

Tel: **(417) 334-4720; (800) 695-1546**
Best Time to Call: **10 AM–4 PM;**
　**7–10 PM**
Coordinator: **Kay Cameron**
States/Regions Covered:
　**Missouri—Branson, Camdenton,**
　**Hollister, Kimberling City,**
　**Marionville, Shell Knob, Springfield;**

**Arkansas—Eureka Springs;**
**Oklahoma—Tulsa–Carthage**
Rates (Single/Double):
　Modest: **$35–$55**
　Average: **$60–$70**
　Luxury: **$150**
Credit Cards: **AMEX, MC, VISA**

After receiving a stamped, self-addressed legal envelope, Kay will send you a complimentary copy of her descriptive listings of more than one hundred carefully selected small inns, private cottages, and luxurious suites. She will also include coupons. Discounts are available for groups and stays of more than three nights.

## The Brass Swan ✪
**H.C.R. 5, BOX 2368-2, BRANSON, MISSOURI 65616**

Tel: **(417) 334-6873; (800) 280-6873**
Best Time to Call: **9 AM–9 PM**
Hosts: **Dick and Gigi House**
Location: **35 mi. S of Springfield**
No. of Rooms: **4**
No. of Private Baths: **4**
Double/pb: **$70–$80**
Single/pb: **$65–$75**

Open: **All year**
Breakfast: **Full**
Credit Cards: **DISC, MC, VISA**
Pets: **No**
Children: **Call ahead**
Smoking: **Restricted**
Social Drinking: **Permitted**

This elegant contemporary home has all the modern conveniences that will make your stay in Branson a wonderful, memorable experience. The Brass Swan is located in a quiet wooded area with a view of beautiful Lake Taneycomo, but it is only 1½ easy-to-travel miles to the Grand Palace and other attractions on 76 Country Boulevard. The spacious guest rooms have sitting areas and private baths; some have private entrances and hot tubs. Use the game room, treadmill, hot tub, microwave, and refrigerator and wet bar, which are stocked with complimentary snacks and beverages. A family-style breakfast is served daily.

## Inn at Fall Creek Country Bed & Breakfast ✪
**391 CONCORD AVENUE, BRANSON, MISSOURI 65616**

| | |
|---|---|
| Tel: **(417) 336-3422; (800) 280-3422;** fax: **(417) 336-5950** | Suites: **$95** |
| | Open: **All year** |
| Host: **J. C. McCracken** | Breakfast: **Full** |
| Location: **4 min. from famous 76 Country Blvd.** | Other Meals: **Available** |
| | Credit Cards: **DISC, MC, VISA** |
| No. of Rooms: **4** | Pets: **No** |
| No. of Private Baths: **4** | Children: **Welcome, over 12** |
| Double/pb: **$75** | Smoking: **Restricted** |
| Single/pb: **$70** | Social Drinking: **Permitted** |

Experience true country splendor! Down a country lane, cozy guest rooms and suites await you. The Chantilly Lace and Sugar Plum Dream suites have fireplaces and private entrances; one has a Jacuzzi tub in the room, the other has a private hot tub on a private deck. Two cozy guest rooms are on the main level, the Quilt Room and Auntie's Attic. All guest rooms have king or queen beds and down-filled comforters. Outside, from the 50-foot deck, relax and enjoy the sights and sounds of the Inn tucked away amidst dogwood trees and alongside a creek. A country breakfast is served in the dining room and may include specialties such as blueberry pancakes or orange French toast. Homemade cookies are always available. Honeymoon and special occasion packages are available for Branson's best—romance or rest!

## Josie's Peaceful Getaway ✪
**H.C.R. 1, BOX 1104, BRANSON, MISSOURI 65616**

| | |
|---|---|
| Tel: **(417) 338-2978; (800) 289-4125** | No. of Private Baths: **3** |
| Best Time to Call: **7 AM–10 PM** | Double/pb: **$55–$75** |
| Hosts: **Bill and JoAnne Coats** | Single/pb: **$50–$70** |
| Location: **50 mi. S of Springfield, Missouri** | Suite: **$95** |
| | Open: **All year** |
| No. of Rooms: **3** | Reduced Rates: **Available** |

Breakfast: **Full**
Credit Cards: **MC, VISA**
Pets: **No**
Children: **Welcome, over 5**

Smoking: **No**
Social Drinking: **Permitted**
Minimum Stay: **2 nights, Oct.–May**

In addition to its spectacular waterfront setting on Table Rock Lake, Josie's features a contemporary design, brown cedar siding, an outdoor Jacuzzi and a veranda with a panoramic view. Inside there are wood-burning fireplaces, cathedral ceilings, antiques, and stained glass, thoughtfully accented by lace and candlelight. One room is a suite with a double whirlpool bath. Nearby attractions include Silver Dollar City, Branson's own music shows, and a marina. JoAnne, a full-time hostess, and Bill, a civil engineer, can tell you all about the local sights.

## Ramblewood Bed and Breakfast ✪
**402 PANORAMIC DRIVE, CAMDENTON, MISSOURI 65020**

Tel: **(314) 346-3410**
Best Time to Call: **After 5 PM**
Host: **Mary Massey**
Location: **90 mi. S of Columbia**
No. of Rooms: **3**
Max. No. Sharing Bath: **4**
Double/sb: **$50**

Single/sb: **$45**
Open: **All year**
Breakfast: **Full**
Pets: **No**
Children: **No**
Smoking: **No**
Social Drinking: **Permitted**

Ramblewood is a Pilgrim-red home with white trim. Set on a quiet, wooded lot, it has the feel of an English country cottage. Spend the night in an attractive, comfortable room and awaken to breakfast served on a sunny deck. Ham-and-cheese omelettes and homemade breads are specialties of the house. The inn is minutes from Lake of the Ozarks, HaHa Tonka State Park and Castle, and antique shops, malls, and restaurants to suit any taste. After a busy day, enjoy a cool drink on the porch.

## Bellevue Bed & Breakfast ✪
**312 BELLEVUE, CAPE GIRARDEAU, MISSOURI 63701**

Tel: **(800) 768-6822; (314) 335–3302**
Hosts: **Fred and Jackie Hoelscher**
Location: **100 mi. S of St. Louis**
No. of Rooms: **2**
No. of Private Baths: **2**
Double/pb: **$55**
Single/pb: **$45**
Open: **All year**

Breakfast: **Full**
Credit Cards: **MC, VISA**
Pets: **No**
Children: **Welcome**
Smoking: **No**
Social Drinking: **Permitted**
Airport/Station Pickup: **Yes**

Built in 1891, this Second Empire Victorian home has been faithfully returned to its turn-of-the-century elegance. The original ceiling stencils have been restored in the dining room and parlor. Both bedrooms, furnished in antiques, have queen-size beds. A full breakfast served in the formal dining room features fresh breads and seasonal fruits. Guests may enjoy a leisurely stroll to the nearby riverfront and shopping at the many nearby antique and specialty shops. Fred is a retired salesman who will make you feel at home and tell you all you want to know about the area.

## Grand Avenue Inn ✪
**1615 GRAND AVENUE, CARTHAGE, MISSOURI 64836**

| | |
|---|---|
| Tel: **(417) 358-7265** | Open: **All year** |
| Best Time to Call: **8 AM–5 PM** | Reduced Rates: **Available** |
| Hosts: **Betty Nisich and Paula Hunt** | Breakfast: **Full** |
| Location: **10 mi. E of Joplin** | Credit Cards: **MC, VISA** |
| No. of Rooms: **4** | Pets: **No** |
| No. of Private Baths: **4** | Children: **Welcome, over 5** |
| Double/pb: **$65–$85** | Smoking: **No** |
| Double/sb: **$55–$65** | Social Drinking: **Permitted** |
| Suites: **$95–$115** | Airport/Station Pickup: **Yes** |

Built in 1893, the Grand Avenue Inn is a breathtaking mansion of the Victorian era, with four stained glass windows, handsome woodwork, and a winding oak staircase. Guests will rest in elegantly furnished rooms and wake to breakfast served in the formal dining room or on the veranda. Afternoons can be spent lounging by the pool. Complimentary beverages and a cheese tray are available between 4 and 6 PM. For your comfort, there is central heating and air-conditioning throughout the house.

## Garth Woodside Mansion
**NEW LONDON GRAVEL ROAD, RR1, HANNIBAL, MISSOURI 63401**

| | |
|---|---|
| Tel: **(314) 221-2789** | Open: **All year** |
| Best Time to Call: **10 AM–7 PM** | Breakfast: **Full** |
| Hosts: **Irv and Diane Feinberg** | Credit Cards: **MC, VISA** |
| Location: **99 mi. N of St. Louis** | Pets: **No** |
| No. of Rooms: **8** | Children: **Welcome, over 12** |
| No. of Private Baths: **8** | Smoking: **No** |
| Double/pb: **$65–$110** | Social Drinking: **Permitted** |

This Second Empire Victorian, built in 1871, has a three-story flying staircase, 14-foot ceilings, and eight hand-carved marble fireplaces. Many of the room furnishings date back to the original owners. Stroll the 39 country acres, then sit down for a leisurely afternoon beverage. Breakfast, served in the formal dining room, features peach French toast, fluted quiche cups, and eggs picante. This location is ideal for touring Mark Twain country or for a romantic getaway. What's more,

your hosts will pamper you with wonderful extras like nightshirts and turn-down service.

## Visages ✪
### 327 NORTH JACKSON, JOPLIN, MISSOURI 64801

| | |
|---|---|
| Tel: **(417) 624-1397; (800) 896-1397** | Double/sb: **$40–50** |
| Best Time to Call: **8 AM–10 PM** | Single/sb: **$35–45** |
| Hosts: **Bill and Marge Meeker** | Open: **All year** |
| Location: **3 mi. W of Rte. 71** | Breakfast: **Full** |
| No. of Rooms: **3** | Credit Cards: **AMEX, DISC** |
| No. of Private Baths: **1** | Pets: **Sometimes** |
| Max. No. Sharing Bath: **4** | Children: **Welcome (crib)** |
| Double/pb: **$60** | Smoking: **No** |
| Single/pb: **$55** | Social Drinking: **Permitted** |

Visages takes its name from the twenty sculptured faces imbedded in the masonry walls surrounding the house, a distinctive chocolate-brown Colonial that dates to 1898. The Meekers bought the house as an abandoned wreck in 1977 and spent the next ten years refurbishing it; not surprisingly, Bill lists woodworking as one of his hobbies. They serve a full Ozark Mountain country breakfast.

## Pridewell ✪
### 600 WEST 50TH STREET, KANSAS CITY, MISSOURI 64112

| | |
|---|---|
| Tel: **(816) 931-1642** | No. of Private Baths: **1** |
| Best Time to Call: **4–9 PM** | Double/pb: **$70** |
| Hosts: **Edwin and Louann White** | Single/pb: **$65** |
| No. of Rooms: **2** | Open: **All year** |

Breakfast: **Full**
Pets: **No**
Children: **Welcome**

Smoking: **No**
Social Drinking: **Permitted**

This fine Tudor residence is situated in a wooded residential area on the battlefield of the Civil War's Battle of Westport. The Nelson Art Gallery, the University of Missouri at Kansas City, and the Missouri Repertory Theatre are close by. It is adjacent to the Country Club Plaza shopping district, which includes several four-star restaurants, tennis courts, and a park.

## The Dickey House Bed & Breakfast Inn ✪
**331 SOUTH CLAY STREET, MARSHFIELD, MISSOURI 65706**

Tel: **(417) 468-3000**
Hosts: **William and Dorothy Buesgen**
Location: **22 mi. NE of Springfield**
No. of Rooms: **6**
No. of Private Baths: **6**
Double/pb: **$55–$95**
Open: **All year**
Reduced Rates: **Available**

Breakfast: **Full**
Credit Cards: **DISC, MC, VISA**
Pets: **No**
Children: **Welcome, over 12**
Smoking: **No**
Social Drinking: **Permitted**
Airport Pickup: **Yes**
Foreign Languages: **German**

As you approach this lovely Colonial Revival mansion, named for the prominent lawyer who built it in 1908, the Ionic columns, widow's walk, and front entrance with beveled glass will transport you to a bygone era. Each bedroom is furnished with antiques and reproductions. Outside, oak trees and benches punctuate the lawns and gardens. An Amish settlement, the Buena Vista Exotic Animal Park, Laura Ingalls Wilder Museum, and Bass Pro Shop are among the nearby points of interest. Branson and Silver Dollar City are one hour to the south. To revive you after the day's activities, your hosts offer complimentary beverages and snacks.

## Gramma's House
**1105 HIGHWAY D, MARTHASVILLE, MISSOURI 63357**

Tel: **(314) 433-2675**
Best Time to Call: **8 AM–5 PM**
Hosts: **Judy and Jim Jones**
Location: **50 mi. W of St. Louis**
No. of Rooms: **4**
No. of Private Baths: **4**
Double/pb: **$75**
Single/pb: **$50**

Guest Cottage: **$90**
Open: **All year**
Breakfast: **Full**
Credit Cards: **MC, VISA**
Pets: **Sometimes**
Children: **Welcome**
Smoking: **No**
Social Drinking: **Permitted**

At this romantic 150-year-old farmhouse, morning starts with a full, hearty breakfast like grandma used to make. You can relax and maybe hear the bobwhite's call, reminding you of special times you spent at your own grandparents' home. Accommodations range from bedrooms to snug cottages with their own fireplaces. There are antique shops in Marthasville and Washington, and wineries in Augusta, Dutzow, and Hermann. Close by is the Missouri River hiking and biking trail. The historic Daniel Boone home and burial site are also in the area.

## Bartlett Farm B&B ✪
### 3473 HIGHWAY Y, NORWOOD, MISSOURI 65717

| | |
|---|---|
| Tel: **(417) 746-4161** | Open: **All year** |
| Hosts: **Burt and Betty Bartlett** | Breakfast: **Full** |
| Location: **50 mi. E of Springfield** | Pets: **Sometimes** |
| No. of Rooms: **1** | Children: **Welcome, over 5** |
| No. of Private Baths: **1** | Smoking: **Permitted** |
| Double/pb: **$50** | Social Drinking: **Permitted** |

Bartlett Farm occupies its own 80-acre valley in the Ozarks, with plenty of farm animals in residence. There are a fishing pond on the property and more fishing sites nearby, plus deer and turkey hunting in season. Burt, a retired real estate broker, and Betty, a registered nurse, like to share their casual, friendly lifestyle, as well as their screened-in porch, fireplace, and large heated spa. The B&B is convenient to such attractions as old mills, float trips, and the Laura Ingalls Wilder Museum and Home in Mansfield.

## Dear's Rest B&B ✪
### 1408 CAPP HILL RANCH ROAD, OZARK, MISSOURI 65721

| | |
|---|---|
| Tel: **(800) 588-2262; (417) 581-3839** | Breakfast: **Full** |
| Best Time to Call: **Before 10:30 PM** | Credit Cards: **MC, VISA** |
| Hosts: **Linda and Allan Schilter** | Pets: **No** |
| Location: **10 mi. S of Ozark** | Children: **Welcome, crib** |
| Suite: **$90** | Smoking: **No** |
| Open: **All year** | Social Drinking: **Permitted** |

When was the last time you walked through a forest, saw wildlife, over 150 species of birds, wildflowers, explored the crystal-clear waters of a spring-fed creek or relaxed in a hot tub surrounded by the natural beauty of the Ozark Hills? Dear's Rest makes it all a reality when you stay in this new rustic Amish-built home, decorated with a fireplace and family antiques that give guests a comfortable homey feeling. This B&B is located adjoining the Mark Twain National Forest, 45 minutes from Branson, Springfield, the famous Bass Pro Shops and Museum, and a major Civil War battlefield. Downtown Ozark is an

antique shoppers' haven. A breakfast of simple country fare—often described as the "no lunch breakfast"—is served in the sunroom or on the deck. Linda and Allan entertain one party at a time, consisting of 1 through 6 people, to ensure your comfort and privacy.

## Down-to-Earth Lifestyles
### 12500 NORTHWEST CROOKED ROAD, PARKVILLE, MISSOURI 64152

| | |
|---|---|
| Tel: **(816) 891-1018** | Open: **All year** |
| Hosts: **Lola and Bill Coons** | Reduced Rates: **Families** |
| Location: **15 mi. N of downtown Kansas City** | Breakfast: **Full** |
| | Pets: **No** |
| No. of Rooms: **4** | Children: **Welcome** |
| No. of Private Baths: **4** | Smoking: **Restricted** |
| Double/pb: **$75** | Social Drinking: **Permitted** |
| Single/pb: **$65** | Airport/Station Pickup: **Yes** |

This spacious new earth-integrated home, with its picture windows and skylights, emphasizes close contact with nature. It's located on an 85-acre ranch, where there are horses and cows, a fishing pond, and lots of space for mind and soul. The furnishings complement the country setting, and the heated indoor pool, exercise room, and jogging and walking trails will keep you in shape. Lola and Bill will be pleased to suggest nearby places of interest if you can bear to tear yourself away from this restorative haven.

## Charlotte's Apple Blossom Inn ✪
### 200 WEST BROADWAY, PLATTSBURG, MISSOURI 64477

| | |
|---|---|
| Tel: **(816) 539-3243** | Open: **All year** |
| Hosts: **Darrell and Charlotte Apple** | Reduced Rates: **7th night free** |
| Location: **30 mi. N of Kansas City** | Breakfast: **Full** |
| No. of Rooms: **3** | Pets: **No** |
| No. of Private Baths: **3** | Children: **By arrangement** |
| Double/pb: **$50** | Smoking: **No** |

Darrell and Charlotte lovingly restored this 1910 home with lighting, color, and a warm interior that says "welcome." After a day of exploring the Pony Express and Jesse James attractions or the Amish settlement, relax in their comfortable parlor with an evening apple dessert. In the morning enjoy a full breakfast consisting of an apple specialty with freshly-ground coffee from a local shop and home-baked breads and muffins. For early risers, coffee is served upstairs. Each room's decor has a distinctive personality with antique wicker, claw-footed tub or handmade quilts. Visit local shops for antiques and specialty gifts. Restaurants are within walking distance. Afterward, enjoy a stroll down the quiet tree-lined streets to see other period homes.

## Cameron's Crag ✪
### P.O. BOX 526, POINT LOOKOUT, MISSOURI 65726

| | |
|---|---|
| Tel: **(417) 335-8134; (800) 933-8529** | Breakfast: **Full** |
| Host: **Glen Cameron** | Other Meals: **Available** |
| Location: **3 mi. S of Branson** | Pets: **No** |
| Suites: **$95; sleeps 2** | Children: **Welcome, infants, over 6** |
| Open: **All year** | Smoking: **No** |
| Reduced Rates: **$10 less Jan.–Mar.,** | Social Drinking: **Permitted** |
| **after 1st night** | Airport Pickup: **Yes** |

Enjoy your choice of three delightful accommodations in this striking contemporary home perched high on a bluff overlooking Lake Taney-como. All three suites have private entrances, king-size beds, and a deck with a spa. You'll savor one of your host's hearty breakfasts before you explore area attractions like Silver Dollar City, Table Rock State Park, and Mutton Hollow Craft Village.

## Doelling Haus ✪
### 4817 TOWNE SOUTH, ST. LOUIS, MISSOURI 63128

| | |
|---|---|
| Tel: **(314) 894-6796** | Single/sb: **$50** |
| Best Time to Call: **8 AM–10 PM** | Open: **All year** |
| Hosts: **David and Carol Doelling** | Breakfast: **Full** |
| Location: **7 mi. S of St. Louis** | Children: **Welcome** |
| No. of Rooms: **2** | Smoking: **No** |
| No. of Private Baths: **1** | Social Drinking: **Permitted** |
| Double/pb: **$60–$65** | |

Doelling Haus captures the spirit of a European country home with Bavarian antiques, family heirlooms, and collectibles amidst a background of rich color. Bedrooms are appointed with antique furniture, linens and quilts, yet sacrifice nothing to 20th-century comfort. Specially prepared Irish cream truffles await you beside your bed each night. Enjoy the peaceful patio, or walk around the friendly neighborhood. Many points of interest are nearby, such as the Arch, zoo, Grant's Farm, major sports, riverboat casinos and cruises, antique malls, shopping, fine restaurants, and historic Kimmswick. But before you head out, you'll fortify yourself with a sumptuous breakfast featuring European delicacies, homemade breads, and fresh-ground coffee. Experience "gemutlichkeit," a sense of well-being, and rediscover Old World hospitality.

## The Dreamcatcher ☉
### 4 GREENDALE DRIVE, ST. LOUIS, MISSOURI 63121

| | |
|---|---|
| Tel: (314) 725-3129 | Single/sb: $45 |
| Best Time to Call: Evenings | Open: All year |
| Host: Judy Nelson | Reduced Rates: 5% seniors |
| Location: 15 mi. N of St. Louis | Breakfast: Continental |
| No. of Rooms: 2 | Pets: No |
| Max. No. Sharing Bath: 4 | Children: No |
| Double/pb: $70 | Smoking: No |
| Single/pb: $60 | Social Drinking: No |
| Double/sb: $55 | |

The Dreamcatcher is a cozy bed and breakfast located in a quiet suburb of Greendale, twenty minutes from the St. Louis riverfront. This home away from home offers comfort and privacy. Guest rooms are located on the second floor of this charming brick Colonial. Common space includes a sitting room with a TV, VCR, and a variety of reading material. Guests are also invited to relax in the living room and eat in the convivial atmosphere of the dining room or, after a busy day, enjoy the private garden that provides a stress-free environment to unwind in. The Dreamcatcher is within walking distance of golfing, tennis, a park, and the University of Missouri campus. Public transportation is nearby and includes the newest rapid transit train system to downtown—the Metrolink. Judy is a lifetime resident, a nurse and teacher who loves to meet people.

## Lafayette House ☉
### 2156 LAFAYETTE AVENUE, ST. LOUIS, MISSOURI 63104

| | |
|---|---|
| Tel: (314) 772-4429 | Max. No. Sharing Bath: 4 |
| Hosts: Sarah and Jack Milligan | Double/pb: $60 |
| No. of Rooms: 5 | Double/sb: $50 |
| No. of Private Baths: 2 | Suite: $75 |

Open: **All year**
Breakfast: **Full**
Pets: **Sometimes**
Children: **Welcome (crib)**

Smoking: **Permitted**
Social Drinking: **Permitted**
Minimum Stay: **2 nights in suite**
Airport/Station Pickup: **Yes**

This 1876 Queen Anne mansion is located in the historic district overlooking Lafayette Park. The house is furnished comfortably with some antiques and traditional furniture. The suite on the third floor, accommodating six, has a private bath and kitchen. Your hosts serve a special egg dish and homemade breads each morning, and offer wine, cheese, and crackers later. They will gladly take you on tour or can direct you to the Botanical Gardens, Convention Center, and other nearby attractions.

## Preston Place ✪
**1835 LAFAYETTE AVENUE, ST. LOUIS, MISSOURI 63104**

Tel: **(314) 664-3429; fax: (314) 644-6929**
Best Time to Call: **6–10 PM**
Host: **Jenny Preston**
No. of Rooms: **2**
No. of Private Baths: **2**
Double/pb: **$70–$80**
Single/pb: **$60–$70**

Open: **All year**
Breakfast: **Full**
Credit Cards: **MC, VISA**
Pets: **No**
Children: **No**
Smoking: **No**
Social Drinking: **Permitted**
Station Pickup: **Yes**

Preston Place combines big-city convenience with historical ambiance in a beautiful Victorian town house. Located in Lafayette Square Historic District, and minutes from downtown St. Louis, this B&B provides easy access to businesses and most tourist attractions, including the Gateway Arch. Jenny restored the house, creating a calm and elegant oasis in the midst of the city. The parlors welcome you with rich Moroccan colors, while the bedrooms soothe with tranquil pastels. Heart-healthy breakfasts are the norm, but those who wish to indulge will be offered a selection of waffles, French toast, and other traditional dishes.

## Soulard Inn ✪
**1014 LAMI, ST. LOUIS, MISSOURI 63104**

Tel: **(314) 773-3002**
Host: **Ray Ellerbeck**
Suites: **$55–$85**
Open: **All year**
Reduced Rates: **Available**

Breakfast: **Full**
Pets: **Sometimes**
Children: **Welcome**
Smoking: **No**
Social Drinking: **Permitted**

One of the oldest buildings in St. Louis, this recently renovated inn is a showplace in the Soulard neighborhood, which takes its name from a French naval officer who disembarked here in 1796. Guests are only moments from the finest blues and jazz clubs, superb restaurants, and other entertainment. Your host promises to give you the highest level of service and one of the best breakfasts you've ever eaten.

## The Winter House ✪
**3522 ARSENAL STREET, ST. LOUIS, MISSOURI 63118**

Tel: **(314) 664-4399**
Hosts: **Kendall and Sarah Winter**
Location: **1 mi. S of I-44; 1 mi. W of I-55**
No. of Rooms: **3**
No. of Private Baths: **3**
Double/pb: **$65–$70**
Single/pb: **$60**
Suites: **$85 for 2**

Open: **All year**
Reduced Rates: **After 2nd night**
Breakfast: **Continental, plus**
Credit Cards: **AMEX, DC, MC, VISA**
Pets: **No**
Children: **Welcome**
Smoking: **No**
Social Drinking: **Permitted**

This ten-room Victorian, built in 1897, features a first-floor bedroom with a pressed-tin ceiling, and a second-floor suite with a balcony and decorative fireplace. Breakfast, served in the dining room on crystal and antique Wedgwood, always includes fresh-squeezed orange juice. Fruit, candy, and fresh flowers are provided in bedrooms; tea and live piano are available by reservation. Nearby attractions include the Missouri Botanical Garden, which adjoins Tower Grove Park, a Victorian walking park on the National Register of Historic Places. The Arch, Busch Baseball Stadium, the zoo, the symphony, and Union Station are all within four miles, and fine dining is in walking distance. There is a $15 surcharge for one night stays.

# Dairyland Bed and Breakfast ⊙
### ROUTE 2, BOX 2875, SEYMOUR, MISSOURI 65746

| | |
|---|---|
| Tel: **(417) 935-2320** | Breakfast: **Continental** |
| Best Time to Call: **After 8 PM** | Pets: **No** |
| Hosts: **Jo and Jeff Shrable** | Children: **Welcome** |
| Location: **50 mi. SE of Springfield** | Smoking: **No** |
| Guest cottage: **$60** | Social Drinking: **No** |
| Open: **All year** | Airport Pickup: **Yes** |
| Reduced Rates: **7th night free** | |

Dairyland Bed and Breakfast is a private farmhouse situated on a well-maintained family dairy farm in the heart of the Ozarks. Accommodations are clean, comfortable, and available to only one family or party at a time. The country decor and many "cowlectables" create a unique atmosphere. There is a modern kitchen equipped with a stove, refrigerator, dishwasher, microwave, and cooking utensils. Breakfast may be enjoyed in the sunny country kitchen or on the screened patio. Your hosts have been dairy producers for 11 years and are now raising ostriches. You are invited to help feed the calves, observe the miracle of birth during the calving season, or get acquainted with the ostriches. Local Amish communities and the home of *The Little House on the Prairie* author Laura Ingalls Wilder are nearby.

# The Schwegmann House B&B Inn ⊙
### 438 WEST FRONT STREET, WASHINGTON, MISSOURI 63090

| | |
|---|---|
| Tel: **(800) 949-2262** | Open: **All year** |
| Hosts: **Cathy and Bill Nagel** | Breakfast: **Full** |
| Location: **50 mi. W of St. Louis** | Credit Cards: **MC, VISA** |
| No. of Rooms: **8** | Pets: **No** |
| No. of Private Baths: **8** | Children: **Welcome, weekdays** |
| Double/pb: **$59.50–$75** | Smoking: **No** |
| Suite: **$99–$120** | Social Drinking: **Permitted** |

This three-story 1861 Georgian brick home—listed on the National Register of Historic Places—overlooks the Missouri River in the historic district of Washington. Guest rooms are tastefully decorated with antiques and locally handmade quilts. The Miller's suite boasts a thermo-massage tub for two, a bottle of Missouri wine, and breakfast delivered to your door. This B&B is located in the heart of Missouri River Wine Country where there is much for guests to enjoy, including 11 nearby wineries, biking, hiking, antique shops, historic sites, unique gift shops, and excellent cuisine. A bountiful breakfast of local fare is served each morning.

# Washington House B&B Inn ✪
## 3 LAFAYETTE STREET, WASHINGTON, MISSOURI 63090

Tel: **(314) 239-2417**
Hosts: **Kathy and Chuck Davis**
Location: **50 mi. W of St. Louis**
No. of Rooms: **3**
No. of Private Baths: **3**
Double/pb: **$75–$85**
Single/pb: **$65**

Open: **All year**
Breakfast: **Full**
Pets: **No**
Children: **Welcome**
Smoking: **No**
Social Drinking: **Permitted**

Facing the Missouri River, this two-story brick Federal-style building was built as an inn during the late 1830s. In the heart of the historic district, avid preservationists Kathy and Chuck have painstakingly restored it, using period antiques and decorations of the era. The rooms are air-conditioned and have canopy beds. This is wine country, and many nearby wineries offer tours and tasting.

# MONTANA

Kalispell • • Columbia Falls
Lakeside • • Somers
Polson • • Big Sandy
• Ronan

Glendive •

Stevensville • • Corvallis • Helena
Hamilton • • Billings
• Bozeman

Red Lodge •

## Bed and Breakfast Western Adventure
### P.O. BOX 4308, BOZEMAN, MONTANA 59772-4308

Tel: **(406) 585-0557**
Best Time to Call: **10 AM**
Coordinator: **Paula Deigert**
States/Regions Covered: **Idaho;
Montana; South Dakota—Black
Hills; Wyoming**

Rates (Single/Double):
Modest: **$35–$49**
Average: **$50–$64**
Luxury: **$65–$195**
Credit Cards: **MC, VISA**

These areas—famous for their national parks, fishing streams, ski resorts, and spectacular scenery—are perfect for outdoor enthusiasts. Enjoy the wonders of Glacier Park in Montana, Yellowstone Park in Wyoming, and Mt. Rushmore in South Dakota. Then explore the fascinating past of the Old West with rodeos, Native American pow-wows, and other attractions that celebrate the history and the natural resources of the four states.

## Sky View ✪
### BOX 408, BIG SANDY, MONTANA 59520

Tel: **(406) 378-2549; 386-2464**
Best Time to Call: **Anytime**
Hosts: **Ron and Gay Pearson and family**
Location: **75 mi. N of Great Falls**
No. of Rooms: **3**
Double/pb: **$50**
Single/pb: **$40**
Guest Cottage: **$40–$60**
Open: **May 1–Dec. 1**

Reduced Rates: **Families**
Breakfast: **Continental**
Other Meals: **Available**
Pets: **Sometimes**
Children: **Welcome**
Smoking: **Permitted**
Social Drinking: **Permitted**
Airport/Station Pickup: **Yes**

Sky View is a working ranch located in an area known for its wild and rugged ambience, sparse population, and spectacular scenery. It's in the heart of Lewis and Clark country, just off a major highway to Glacier National Park. The Pearson family enjoys people of all ages and looks forward to sharing its lifestyle with guests, keeping you informed of local rodeos, Indian powwows, river float trips, tours, and hunting and fishing opportunities. Children enjoy their playground, and baby-sitters are available. A public swimming pool and tennis courts are nearby.

## The Josephine Bed & Breakfast
### 514 NORTH 29TH STREET, BILLINGS, MONTANA 59101

Tel: **(406) 248-5898**
Best Time to Call: **Anytime**
Hosts: **Doug and Becky Taylor**
No. of Rooms: **5**
No. of Private Baths: **3**
Max. No. Sharing Bath: **4**
Double/pb: **$68**
Single/pb: **$58**
Double/sb: **$58**
Single/sb: **$48**

Open: **All year**
Reduced Rates: **Medical and extended stays**
Breakfast: **Full**
Credit Cards: **AMEX, MC, VISA**
Pets: **No**
Children: **Welcome, over 12**
Smoking: **No**
Social Drinking: **Permitted**
Airport Pickup: **Yes**

This lovely, historic home is comfortably elegant. The porch, with its swing and quaint seating, offers the ideal place for breakfast or relaxing. Charming picket fences, shade trees, and flowers take you back in time. Each room is individually decorated with antiques, collectibles, and old photographs. Doug, a Billings native, enjoys cooking and travel, Becky enjoys crafts and antiques, and both are knowledgeable about the area. The B&B is within walking distance of downtown's museums, galleries, theaters, and shopping. It's only minutes to the airport, horse-racing rodeos, golf courses, and historic attractions. Skiing and Little Big Horn (Custer) Battlefield are an hour away; Yellowstone National Park is a beautiful 3-hour drive via scenic Beartooth Pass.

# Kirk Hill Bed & Breakfast ✪
## 7960 SOUTH 19TH ROAD, BOZEMAN, MONTANA 59715

Tel: **(406) 586-3929; (800) 240-3929**
Best Time to Call: **6–9 PM**
Hosts: **Charlie and Pat Kirk**
Location: **6 mi. S of Bozeman**
No. of Rooms: **3**
Max. No. Sharing Bath: **4**
Double/sb: **$55–$65**
Single/sb: **$50–$60**

Open: **All year**
Breakfast: **Continental**
Credit Cards: **MC, VISA**
Pets: **No**
Children: **Welcome, over 12**
Smoking: **No**
Social Drinking: **Permitted**

Kirk Hill Bed & Breakfast is a 1905 farmhouse tucked among the mountains surrounding Gallatin Valley. Charlie and Pat raise Irish setters, horses, llamas, sheep, ducks, and cashmere goats; pictures of these animals decorate guests' bedrooms. You might see less domesticated species on the Kirk Hill Nature Trail, on forty acres adjacent to the B&B property. For more outdoor adventures, your hosts can arrange horseback tours, rafting trips, and guides for hunting and fishing. For winter sports, Bridger and Big Sky Skiing Areas are within an hour's drive. In Bozeman, one big attraction is the Museum of the Rockies, known for its dinosaur collection and planetarium. The city is also the home of Montana State University, with an enrollment of about ten thousand students.

# Millers of Montana Bed & Breakfast Inn ✪
## 1002 ZACHARIA LANE, BOZEMAN, MONTANA 59715

Tel: **(406) 763-4102**
Hosts: **Doug and Joyce Miller**
Location: **12 mi. SW of Bozeman**
No. of Rooms: **4**
No. of Private Baths: **2**
Max. No. Sharing Bath: **4**
Double/pb: **$60–$70**
Double/sb: **$50**

Single/sb: **$45**
Open: **All year**
Reduced Rates: **7th day free**
Breakfast: **Full**
Pets: **Sometimes**
Children: **Welcome**
Smoking: **No**
Social Drinking: **Permitted**

This Cape Cod–style house is on a secluded 20-acre ranch, with breathtaking views of the Spanish Peaks and the Bridger Mountains. Quiet and comfortable, the B&B is furnished with country pieces and antiques. Yellowstone National Park is one hour away, and it's only 30 minutes to the Madison, Jefferson, and Yellowstone Rivers. For blue-ribbon trout fishing, walk over to the Gallatin River. Bozeman itself, home of Montana State University and the Museum of the Rockies, is worth visiting. Doug is in construction, and ranching, softball, and fishing are his hobbies. Joyce, a full-time hostess who retired from a culinary career, is interested in cooking, sewing, and crafts.

## Torch and Toes B&B

**309 SOUTH THIRD AVENUE, BOZEMAN, MONTANA 59715**

Tel: **(406) 586-7285; (800) 446-2138**
Best Time to Call: **8 AM–noon**
Hosts: **Ronald and Judy Hess**
Location: **100 mi. SE of Helena**
No. of Rooms: **4**
No. of Private Baths: **4**
Double/pb: **$65–$70**
Single/pb: **$55**
Open: **All year**

Reduced Rates: **Government employees**
Breakfast: **Full**
Pets: **No**
Children: **Welcome**
Smoking: **No**
Social Drinking: **Permitted**
Airport/Station Pickup: **Yes**

Set back from the street, this Colonial Revival house is centrally located in the Bon Ton Historic District. Lace curtains, leaded glass windows, and period pieces remind one that this is a house with a past. Ron is a professor of architecture at nearby Montana State University; Judy is a weaver interested in historic preservation. Their home is furnished in a charming blend of nostalgic antiques, humorous collectibles, and fine furnishings. Breakfast always includes a special egg dish, fresh fruit, and muffins. Afterward, relax on the redwood deck in summer, or by a cozy fire in winter. Nearby attractions include blue-ribbon trout streams, hiking, skiing, and the Museum of the Rockies. Yellowstone National Park is one and a half hours away.

## Voss Inn ✪

**319 SOUTH WILLSON, BOZEMAN, MONTANA 59715**

Tel: **(406) 587-0982**
Best Time to Call: **9:30 AM–9:30 PM**
Hosts: **Bruce and Frankee Muller**
Location: **3 mi. from I-90**
No. of Rooms: **6**
No. of Private Baths: **6**
Double/pb: **$80–$90**
Single/pb: **$70–$80**

Open: **All year**
Breakfast: **Full**
Credit Cards: **MC, VISA**
Pets: **No**
Children: **Sometimes**
Smoking: **No**
Social Drinking: **Permitted**

This handsome 100-year-old brick mansion, flanked by Victorian gingerbread porches, is set like a gem on a tree-lined street in historic Bozeman. The bedrooms are elegantly wallpapered and furnished with brass and iron beds, ornate lighting, oriental throw rugs over polished hardwood floors—a perfect spot for a first or second honeymoon. The parlor has a good selection of books, as well as a chess set for your pleasure. It's north of Yellowstone, on the way to Glacier, with trout fishing, mountain lakes, and skiing within easy reach. Don't miss the Museum of the Rockies on the Montana State University campus ten blocks away.

# Bad Rock Country Bed & Breakfast ✪
### 480 BAD ROCK DRIVE, COLUMBIA FALLS, MONTANA 59912

| | |
|---|---|
| Tel: **(406) 892-2829; (800) 422-3666** | Open: **All year** |
| Hosts: **Jon and Sue Alper** | Breakfast: **Full** |
| Location: **15 mi. from Glacier Park** | Credit Cards: **AMEX, CB, DC, DISC,** |
| No. of Rooms: **7** | **MC, VISA** |
| No. of Private Baths: **7** | Pets: **No** |
| Double/pb: **$95–$120** | Children: **Welcome, over 10** |
| Suites: **$135** | Smoking: **No** |

Nestled on 30 acres in a gorgeous farming valley, Bad Rock Country Bed & Breakfast is located only twenty minutes from Glacier National Park. Guests can enjoy spectacular views of the nearby 7200-foot Swan Mountains and the magic of the quiet countryside. Watch wild geese flying overhead or listen to coyotes howling at night. The main house, furnished with old Western antiques, has three guest rooms. Two exquisite square-hewn log buildings offer four rooms that have gas log fireplaces and handmade lodgepole pine furniture. Breakfasts feature Belgian waffles heaped with huckleberries, Montana potato pie, and sundance eggs. Later you may want to soak in the secluded hot tub at a time reserved exclusively for you. Summertime offers white-water rafting, horseback riding, jet skiing, canoeing, swimming, and fishing. In the winter there's downhill and cross-country skiing, snowmobiling, and dog sledding. Museums, galleries, casinos, and antique stores are found in the nearby towns of Kalispell, Whitefish, Bigfork, and Columbia Falls.

# Daybreak Bed & Breakfast ✪
### 616 WILLOW CREEK ROAD, CORVALLIS, MONTANA 59828-9717

| | |
|---|---|
| Tel: **(406) 961-4530** | Breakfast: **Full** |
| Hosts: **Ann and Lynda LeFevre** | Pets: **Sometimes** |
| Location: **35 mi. N of Missoula** | Children: **No** |
| No. of Rooms: **3** | Smoking: **No** |
| No. of Private Baths: **3** | Social Drinking: **No** |
| Double/pb: **$60** | Minimum Stay: **2 nights** |
| Suites: **$70** | Airport/Station Pickup: **Yes** |
| Open: **All year** | |

Daybreak Bed & Breakfast is situated between the Sapphire and Bitterroot Mountain ranges in the Bitterroot Valley farming area. Guest rooms are furnished with antiques and are individually decorated with your comfort in mind. A hearty breakfast is served in the formal dining room; specialties may include pancakes, waffles, innovative egg casseroles, homemade muffins, breads, and fresh-ground coffee. You may take a leisurely stroll through the gardens, enjoy the sunset from the deck, or build a bonfire as the evening cools.

## The Hostetler House Bed & Breakfast ✪
**113 NORTH DOUGLAS STREET, GLENDIVE, MONTANA 59330**

Tel: **(406) 365-4505**
Best Time to Call: **Anytime**
Hosts: **Craig and Dea Hostetler**
No. of Rooms: **2**
Max. No. Sharing Bath: **4**
Double/sb: **$50**
Single/sb: **$45**
Open: **All year**

Reduced Rates: **Weekly, seniors**
Breakfast: **Full**
Credit Cards: **DISC, MC, VISA**
Pets: **No**
Children: **No**
Smoking: **No**
Social Drinking: **Permitted**
Airport/Station Pickup: **Yes**

Located one block from the Yellowstone River and two blocks from downtown shopping and restaurants, the Hostetler House is a charming 1912 historic home with two comfortable guest rooms done in casual country decor. Nearby are parks, a swimming pool, tennis courts, antique shops, churches, a golf course, a museum, Dawson Community College, fishing, hunting, and hiking. Guests may relax in the hot tub, sitting room, enclosed sunporch, or on the deck. Wake up to the smell of freshly ground gourmet coffee, tea, and homemade bread. A full breakfast is served on Grandma's china in the dining room, sun porch, or on the deck. Dea is an interior decorator who grew up on a nearby wheat farm, and Craig is a mechanical engineer, pilot, and avid outdoorsman.

## Deer Crossing ✪
**396 HAYES CREEK ROAD, HAMILTON, MONTANA 59840**

Tel: **(406) 363-2232; (800) 763-2232**
Best Time to Call: **8 AM**

Host: **Mary Lynch**
Location: **45 mi. S of Missoula**

No. of Rooms: **5**  
No. of Private Baths: **5**  
Double/pb: **$65–$75**  
Bunk House: **$100, sleeps 2–5**  
Suites: **$90**  
Open: **All year**  
Reduced Rates: **5% seniors**  
Breakfast: **Full**

Other Meals: **Available**  
Credit Cards: **MC, VISA**  
Pets: **Horses**  
Children: **Welcome**  
Smoking: **No**  
Social Drinking: **Permitted**  
Airport/Station Pickup: **Yes**

Here is your invitation to experience Western hospitality at its finest. Deer Crossing is situated along the Lewis and Clark Trail on 24 acres of tall pines and pasture overlooking the Bitterroot Valley. Sit back and relax, or get involved in the ranch's daily activities. There are historic sites to visit, while athletic types can go swimming, rafting, fishing, skiing, hiking, and hunting. Accommodations include a large guest room, a suite with a spacious tub and a window overlooking the fields, and a bunkhouse that gives guests the feel of the Old West.

## The Sanders—Helena's Bed & Breakfast ✪
### 328 NORTH EWING, HELENA, MONTANA 59601

Tel: **(406) 442-3309**  
Best Time to Call: **Day**  
Hosts: **Bobbi Uecker and Rock Ringling**  
No. of Rooms: **7**  
No. of Private Baths: **7**  
Double/pb: **$80–$98**  
Open: **All year**

Breakfast: **Full**  
Credit Cards: **DISC, MC, VISA**  
Pets: **No**  
Children: **Welcome**  
Smoking: **No**  
Social Drinking: **Permitted**

The Sanders—Helena's Bed & Breakfast was built in 1875 by Harriet and Wilbur Sanders and was restored 112 years later. The decor combines the spirit of days gone by with the comforts of today. Guest rooms are spacious and reflect turn-of-the-century styles with brass beds and high ceilings, plus TV, phone, and a view of Helena and the surrounding mountains. This B&B is located within three blocks of St. Helena's Cathedral, the original Governor's Mansion, the Holter Museum, the Myrna Loy Theatre, and the historic downtown area. Also nearby are the State Capitol, the Montana Historical Museum, Grandstreet Theatre, and many fine restaurants.

## Creston Country Willows ✪
### 70 CRESTON ROAD, KALISPELL, MONTANA 59901

Tel: **(800) 257-7517**  
Best Time to Call: **8 AM–10 PM**  
Hosts: **Tom and Marlene Brunaugh**  
Location: **11 mi. E of Kalispell**  
No. of Rooms: **4**  
No. of Private Baths: **4**  
Double/pb: **$75–$85**

Single/pb: **$60–$70**  
Open: **All year**  
Reduced Rates: **10% Oct.–May, after 7th night; 5% seniors**  
Breakfast: **Full**  
Credit Cards: **MC, VISA**  
Pets: **No**

Children: **Welcome, over 7**          Social Drinking: **Permitted**
Smoking: **No**

Tom and Marlene welcome you to Creston Country Willows, a charming two-story farmhouse built in the 1920s. Guest rooms are decorated in old country style with oak and antique furniture. Relax on the porch or under golden willow trees while enjoying the view of the majestic mountains and the smell of the climbing sweet peas. Or take a leisurely stroll on the one-acre property. Awake to the aroma of freshly brewed coffee, then tuck into a hearty breakfast featuring a fresh fruit plate and all the huckleberry pancakes you can eat. Nearby attractions include Glacier National Park, Hungry Horse Dam, Gatiss Gardens, and Flathead Lake.

## Angel Point Guest Suites ✪
**829 ANGEL POINT ROAD, BOX 768, LAKESIDE, MONTANA 59922**

Tel: **(406) 844-2204; (800) 214-2204**
Best Time to Call: **Mornings**
Hosts: **Linda and Wayne Muhlestein**
Location: **12 mi. S of Kalispell**
Suites: **$110–$120**
Open: **All year**
Breakfast: **Full**

Credit Cards: **MC, VISA**
Pets: **No**
Children: **Welcome, over 12**
Smoking: **No**
Social Drinking: **Permitted**
Minimum Stay: **2 nights**

This secluded, luxurious getaway was constructed and designed with couples in mind. Exclusively located on Angel Point peninsula on Flathead Lake, the inn has a private beach, dock, lake platforms, gazebo, firepit, and huge bench-swings nestled amidst giant fir trees. Each suite includes original artwork, a grand balcony with log railings, immense windows with panoramic views, a complete kitchen, and a sitting area with fine furniture. While the property is so spectacular most guests don't want to leave, some of the local attractions are Glacier National Park, Big Mountain winter sports, Jewel Basin Hiking Area, scenic golf courses, and white-water rafting. But first, you'll tuck in a wonderful Western breakfast.

## Hawthorne House ✪
**304 THIRD AVENUE, EAST, POLSON, MONTANA 59860**

Tel: **(406) 883-2723; (800) 290-1345**
Best Time to Call: **After 5 PM,
   weekends**
Hosts: **Gerry and Karen Lenz**
Location: **70 mi. N of Missoula**
No. of Rooms: **4**
Max. No. Sharing Bath: **4**
Double/sb: **$50**

Single/sb: **$45**
Open: **All year**
Breakfast: **Full**
Pets: **No**
Children: **Welcome, over 12**
Smoking: **No**
Social Drinking: **No**

In the small western Montana town of Polson, at the foot of Flathead Lake, you'll find Hawthorne House, an English Tudor home on a quiet shady street. In summer, cheerful window boxes welcome the weary traveler. The house is furnished with antiques from Karen's grandparents. There are plate collections, Indian artifacts, and glassware. The kitchen has some interesting collections. Breakfast is always special, with something baked fresh each morning. Nearby attractions include Glacier National Park, the National Bison Range, Kerr Dam, and great scenic beauty. Golf abounds. There are always activities on the lake and river.

## Hidden Pines Bed & Breakfast ○
### 792 LOST QUARTZ ROAD, POLSON, MONTANA 59860

Tel: **(406) 849-5612; (800) 505-5612**
Best Time to Call: **10 AM–10 PM**
Hosts: **Earl and Emy Atchley**
Location: **10 mi. NW of Polson Mt.**
No. of Rooms: **4**
Max. No. Sharing Bath: **4**
Double/pb: **$60**

Double/sb: **$45**
Open: **All year**
Breakfast: **Full**
Pets: **No**
Children: **Welcome**
Smoking: **No**
Airport/Station Pickup: **Yes**

Stress and tension melt away in the quiet surroundings of Hidden Pines Bed & Breakfast. Relax on the deck of this rustic retreat and watch squirrels and deer graze right in front of you. Bring your canoe and bathing suit for fun in Flathead Lake; pack binoculars for viewing

Wild Horse Island. Cross-country skis are useful when the snow flies, and hiking shoes will come in handy year-round. At the end of the day, unwind in the living room and tune in to your favorite TV show or screen a movie on the VCR. Depending on your appetite, Emy will serve you a full country breakfast or lighter Continental fare.

## Swan Hill ✪
### 460 KINGS POINT ROAD, POLSON, MONTANA 59860

| | |
|---|---|
| Tel:(406) 883-5292; (800) 537-9489 | Double s/b: **$75** |
| Best Time to Call: **Evenings** | Open: **All year** |
| Hosts: **Larry and Sharon Whitten** | Breakfast: **Full** |
| Location: **60 mi. N of Missoula** | Credit Cards: **MC, VISA** |
| No. of Rooms: **4** | Pets: **Sometimes** |
| No. of Private Baths: **3** | Children: **Welcome, over 12** |
| Max. No. Sharing Bath: **4** | Smoking: **No** |
| Double p/b: **$85** | Social Drinking: **Permitted** |

A spacious redwood home on ten acres, Swan Hill overlooks the majestic Mission Mountains and Flathead Lake. Year-round, guests can go swimming, whatever the weather—the 7000-square-foot home contains an indoor pool, as well as a sauna. Of scenic interest nearby are Glacier National Park and the Bison Range, while Jewel Basin has excellent hiking. Golfers have a good choice of courses and there are plenty of fishing spots. Visits to Western art galleries, antique shops, summer theater, and fine restaurants will fill your days. This B&B is wheelchair accessible.

## Willows Inn ✪
### 224 SOUTH PLATT AVENUE, RED LODGE, MONTANA 59068

| | |
|---|---|
| Tel: **(406) 446-3913** | Guest Cottages: **$70 for 2** |
| Best Time to Call: **Mornings,** | Open: **All year** |
| **afternoons** | Reduced Rates: **10% after 4th night;** |
| Hosts: **Elven, Kerry, and Carolyn** | **10% seniors** |
| **Boggio** | Breakfast: **Continental** |
| Location: **60 mi. SW of Billings** | Credit Cards: **DISC, MC, VISA** |
| No. of Rooms: **5** | Pets: **No** |
| No. of Private Baths: **3** | Children: **Welcome** |
| Max. No. Sharing Bath: **4** | Smoking: **No** |
| Double/pb: **$55–$65** | Social Drinking: **Permitted** |
| Double/sb: **$55** | Minimum Stay: **2 nights in cottage** |
| Single/sb: **$50** | |

Tucked beneath the majestic Beartooth Mountains in the northern Rockies, the historic town of Red Lodge provides an ideal setting for this charming three-story Queen Anne. Flanked by giant evergreens and colorful flower beds, the Inn is reminiscent of a bygone age, complete with white picket fence, gingerbread trim, and front porch swing. Overstuffed sofas and wicker pieces complement the warm and cheerful decor. Delicious homebaked pastries are Elven's specialty—she uses her own Finnish recipes for these mouthwatering treats. Championship rodeos, excellent cross-country and downhill skiing, opportunities to hike, golf, and fish abound in this special area, still unspoiled by commercial progress. Yellowstone National Park is only 65 miles away.

## The Timbers Bed and Breakfast
### 1184 TIMBERLANE ROAD, RONAN, MONTANA 59864

| | |
|---|---|
| Tel: **(406) 676-4373; (800) 775-4373** | Suites: **$85–$115; sleeps 2** |
| Best Time to Call: **10 AM** | Open: **Jan. 3–Dec. 18** |
| Hosts: **Doris and Leonard McCravey** | Breakfast: **Full, Continental** |
| Location: **65 mi. N of Missoula** | Credit Cards: **MC, VISA** |
| No. of Rooms: **2** | Pets: **No** |
| No. of Private Baths: **1** | Children: **Welcome, over 10** |
| Max. No. Sharing Bath: **4** | Smoking: **No** |
| Double/sb: **$70–$85** | Social Drinking: **Permitted** |

The Timbers is situated at the base of the Rocky Mountain Mission Range on 21 secluded acres, midway between Glacier National Park and Missoula, Montana. The house has a wraparound deck, and is glassed in to provide a magnificent view of the Missions. Cathedral ceilings, hand-hewn beams, a barnwood dining area, and furnishings that Doris and Leonard collected give their home a sophisticated yet warm country feel. Leonard can tell you about his 27 years on the professional rodeo circuit while you enjoy one of Doris's wonderful country breakfasts. Nearby attractions include Flathead Lake, National Bison Range, Glacier National Park, golf, and water sports, fishing, horseback riding, skiing, white-water rafting, art galleries, local rodeos, and powwows.

## Osprey Inn Bed & Breakfast
### 5557 HIGHWAY 93 SOUTH, SOMERS, MONTANA 59932

| | |
|---|---|
| Tel: **(406) 857-2042; (800) 258-2042** | Guest Cottage: **$90** |
| Best Time to Call: **9 AM–9 PM** | Open: **May 15–Oct. 1** |
| Hosts: **Sharon and Wayne Finney** | Breakfast: **Full** |
| Location: **8 mi. S of Kalispell** | Credit Cards: **AMEX, MC, VISA** |
| No. of Rooms: **5** | Pets: **No** |
| No. of Private Baths: **4** | Children: **Welcome, over 9** |
| Double/pb: **$90** | Smoking: **No** |
| Single/pb: **$85** | Social Drinking: **Permitted** |
| Suite: **$170** | |

Yes, you can see osprey—as well as geese, loons, and grebes—from the deck of this rustic lakeshore retreat. In the summer, guests are welcome to bring along a boat or canoe; in the winter, pack your skis.

Cameras and binoculars come in handy throughout the year. You'll start the day with fresh seasonal fruit, home-baked cinnamon rolls, and pancakes with homemade fruit syrups.

## Country Caboose ✪
**852 WILLOUGHBY ROAD, STEVENSVILLE, MONTANA 59870**

Tel: **(406) 777-3145**
Host: **Lisa Thompson**
Location: **35 mi. S of Missoula**
No. of Rooms: **1**
No. of Private Baths: **1**
Double/pb: **$50**
Single/pb: **$50**

Open: **May–Sept.**
Breakfast: **Full**
Pets: **No**
Children: **Welcome**
Smoking: **No**
Social Drinking: **Permitted**

If you enjoy romantic train rides, why not spend the night in an authentic caboose? This one dates back to 1923, is made of wood, and is painted red, of course. It is set on real rails in the middle of the countryside. The caboose sleeps two and offers a spectacular view of the Bitterroot Mountains, right from your pillow. In the morning, breakfast is served at a table for two. Specialties include huckleberry pancakes, quiche, and strawberries in season. Local activities include touring St. Mary's Mission, hiking the mountain trails, fishing, and hunting.

# NEBRASKA

Osmond •    • Dixon

• Omaha

Gretna •

• Chappell

Crete •

## The Cottonwood Inn ✪
**802 SECOND STREET, CHAPPELL, NEBRASKA 69129**

Tel: **(308) 874-3250**
Best Time to Call: **8 AM–9 PM**
Hosts: **Barb and Bruce Freeman**
Location: **130 mi. E of Cheyenne**
No. of Rooms: **6**
Max. No. Sharing Bath: **4**
Double/sb: **$40**
Single/sb: **$35**
Open: **All year**

Reduced Rates: **10% seniors**
Breakfast: **Full**
Other Meals: **Available**
Credit Cards: **MC, VISA**
Pets: **Sometimes**
Children: **Welcome (crib)**
Smoking: **No**
Social Drinking: **Permitted**

Built as a rooming house in 1917, the Cottonwood Inn still has its
original floors, light fixtures, and dumbwaiter. The balconies and the
large front porch are perfect places to enjoy a summer evening. In
cooler months, you can sit around the living room fireplace. Signs of
the Old West abound in Chappell—the Oregon and Mormon trails,
the Pony Express, and the first transcontinental railroad and highway

all went through this town, which boasts a restored period home and an art museum. Other amenities include the public golf course, tennis courts, and swimming pool.

## The Parson's House ✪
### 638 FOREST AVENUE, CRETE, NEBRASKA 68333

| | |
|---|---|
| Tel: **(402) 826-2634** | Open: **All year** |
| Hosts: **Harold and Sandy Richardson** | Breakfast: **Full** |
| Location: **25 mi. SW of Lincoln** | Pets: **No** |
| No. of Rooms: **2** | Children: **No** |
| Max. No. Sharing Bath: **4** | Smoking: **No** |
| Double/sb: **$35** | Social Drinking: **No** |
| Single/sb: **$30** | Airport/Station Pickup: **Yes** |

Enjoy warm hospitality in this newly refinished, turn-of-the-century home tastefully decorated with antiques. Doane College lies one block away; the beautiful campus is just the place for a leisurely afternoon stroll. It's just a short drive to Lincoln, the state's capital and home of the University of Nebraska. Harold, a Baptist minister with the local U.C.C. church, runs a remodeling business while Sandy runs the bed and breakfast. After a day's activity, they invite you to relax in their modern whirlpool tub and make their home yours for the duration of your stay.

## The Georges ✪
### ROUTE 1, BOX 50, DIXON, NEBRASKA 68732

| | |
|---|---|
| Tel: **(402) 584-2625** | Breakfast: **Full** |
| Best Time to Call: **6:30 AM–7 PM** | Other Meals: **Available** |
| Hosts: **Marie and Carolyn George** | Pets: **Sometimes** |
| Location: **35 mi. W of Sioux City, Iowa** | Children: **Welcome** |
| No. of Rooms: **4** | Smoking: **No** |
| Max. No. Sharing Bath: **4** | Social Drinking: **Permitted** |
| Double/sb: **$40** | Airport/Station Pickup: **Yes** |
| Single/sb: **$35** | Foreign Languages: **Swedish** |
| Open: **All year** | |

The Georges have a large, remodeled farmhouse with a spacious backyard. They offer the opportunity to see a farming operation firsthand, right down to the roosters crowing and the birds singing in the morning. They prepare a hearty country breakfast featuring homemade jellies and jams. The Georges are close to Wayne State College and Ponca State Park.

## Bundy's Bed and Breakfast ✪
### 16906 SOUTH 255, GRETNA, NEBRASKA 68028

Tel: (402) 332-3616
Best Time to Call: 7 AM–9 PM
Hosts: Bob and Dee Bundy
Location: 30 mi. S of Omaha
No. of Rooms: 4
Max. No. Sharing Bath: 4
Double/sb: $35

Single/sb: $20
Open: All year
Breakfast: Full
Pets: Sometimes
Children: No
Smoking: No
Social Drinking: No

The Bundys have a pretty farmhouse painted white with black trim. Here you can enjoy country living just 30 minutes from downtown Lincoln and Omaha. The rooms are decorated with antiques, attractive wallpapers, and collectibles. In the morning, wake up to farm-fresh eggs and homemade breads. The house is just a short walk from a swimming lake, and is three miles from a ski lodge.

## The Offutt House
### 140 NORTH 39TH STREET, OMAHA, NEBRASKA 68131

Tel: (402) 553-0951
Host: Jeannie K. Swoboda
Location: 1 mi. from I-80
No. of Rooms: 9
No. of Private Baths: 9
Double/pb: $65-$95
Single/pb: $55-$85
Suites: $85–$100

Open: All year
Reduced Rates: After 5th night
Breakfast: Continental
Pets: Sometimes
Children: Welcome
Smoking: Restricted
Social Drinking: Permitted

This comfortable mansion, circa 1894, is part of the city's Historic Gold Coast, a section of handsome homes built by Omaha's wealthiest residents. Offering peace and quiet, the rooms are air-conditioned, spacious, and furnished with antiques; some have fireplaces. Jeannie will direct you to nearby attractions such as the Joslyn Museum or the Old Market area, which abounds with many beautiful shops and fine restaurants. She graciously offers coffee or wine in late afternoon.

## Willow Way Bed & Breakfast ✪
### ROUTE 2, BOX A20, OSMOND, NEBRASKA 68765

Tel: (402) 748-3593
Best Time to Call: After 6 PM
Hosts: Norman and Jacquie Lorenz
Location: 130 mi. NW of Omaha
No. of Rooms: 4
No. of Private Baths: 2
Max. No. Sharing Bath: 4
Double/pb: $45
Single/pb: $35

Double/sb: $45
Single/sb: $35
Open: All year
Breakfast: Full
Pets: Yes
Children: Welcome
Smoking: No
Social Drinking: Permitted

Your hosts are retired dairy farmers who run an antique store and an interior decorating business in addition to this B&B. They make baskets using the local red willow, hence the name Willow Way. Jacquie and Norman built their guest house in 1988 out of lumber from several barns and houses in the area. Osmond is a town of about 800 midway between O'Neal, Nebraska, and Sioux City, Iowa. Ashfall Fossil Beds State Historical Park is thirty miles to the west. Whether you want to inspect fossils or just relax, your hosts promise to give you old-fashioned small-town hospitality.

---

**For key to listings, see inside front or back cover.**

✪ This star means that rates are guaranteed through December 31, 1996, to any guest making a reservation as a result of reading about the B&B in *Bed & Breakfast U.S.A.—1996* edition.

Important! To avoid misunderstandings, always ask about cancellation policies when booking.

Please enclose a self-addressed, stamped, business-size envelope when contacting reservation services.

For more details on what you can expect in a B&B, see Chapter 1.

Always mention *Bed & Breakfast U.S.A.* when making reservations!

If no B&B is listed in the area you'll be visiting, use the form on page 323 to order a copy of our "List of New B&Bs."

We want to hear from you! Use the form on page 325.

# NEVADA

• Washoe Valley　　　• East Ely

## Bed & Breakfast Southwest Reservation Service—Nevada ✪

**6916 EAST MARIPOSA, SCOTTSDALE, ARIZONA 85251**

Tel: **(602) 947-9704; (800) 762-9704**
Best Time to Call: **10 AM–8 PM**
Coordinators: **Jo and Jim Cummings**
States/Regions Covered: **Southern Nevada**
Descriptive Directory of B&Bs: **$3, SASE**

Rates (Single/Double):
Modest: **$40–$60**
Average: **$50–$65**
Luxury: **$65–$up**

Specializing in unique homestays with private suites and guest houses, this service offers exciting experiences to the traveler coming to the Southwest. Jo and Jim are residents of the area and can give firsthand information about sport activities, dining opportunities, art exhibits and can answer your questions about the great Southwest. The Cummingses will be happy to help you plan your vacation with gracious hosts throughout the region. Bed & Breakfast Southwest is always looking for unique hosts and enthusiastic guests.

## Steptoe Valley Inn ✪
**P.O. BOX 151110, 220 EAST 11TH STREET, EAST ELY, NEVADA 89315-1110**

Tel: **(702) 289-8687 June–Sept.;**
  **(702) 435-1196 (Oct.–May)**
Hosts: **Jane and Norman Lindley**
Location: **70 mi. W of Great Basin National Park**
No. of Rooms: **5**
No. of Private Baths: **5**
Double/pb: **$79**
Single/pb: **$68**

Open: **June–Sept.**
Breakfast: **Full**
Credit Cards: **AMEX, MC, VISA**
Pets: **No**
Children: **By arrangement**
Smoking: **No**
Social Drinking: **Permitted**
Foreign Languages: **Spanish**

This Inn opened in July 1991 after major reconstruction. Located near the Nevada Northern Railway Museum, it was originally Ely City Grocery of 1907. The five second-floor rooms have country decor and private balconies, and the elegant Victorian dining room and library are downstairs. The large yard has mature trees, a gazebo, and rose garden. Norman is an airline captain and ex-rancher and Jane is a retired stewardess and local tour guide. Their guests can enjoy cool nights, scenic countryside, the "Ghost Train of Old Ely," the Great Basin National Park, and Cave Lake State Park, or just relax on the veranda!

# Deer Run Ranch Bed and Breakfast ✪

**5440 EASTLAKE BOULEVARD, WASHOE VALLEY, CARSON CITY, NEVADA 89704**

Tel: **(702) 882-3643**
Best Time to Call: **6–9 AM;**
  **6–9 PM**
Hosts: **David and Muffy Vhay**
Location: **8 mi. N of Carson City**
No. of Rooms: **2**
No. of Private Baths: **2**
Double/pb: **$80–$95**
Open: **All year**

Reduced Rates: **$10 less Mon.–Thurs.**
Breakfast: **Full**
Credit Cards: **AMEX, MC, VISA**
Pets: **No**
Children: **Welcome, over 12**
Smoking: **No**
Social Drinking: **Permitted**
Minimum Stay: **2 nights, holidays and
    special events weekends**

Deer Run Ranch, a working alfalfa farm, overlooks Washoe Lake and the Sierra Nevada Mountains. Navajo rugs, old photographs, and paintings by well-known local artists grace the comfortable guest areas, lending Western ambience to this house designed and built by your host, who is an architect. Your hosts also have a pottery studio, woodshop, and large garden on the premises. Things to do in the area include skiing, biking, hiking, and hang gliding; Washoe Lake State Park is next door. For fine dining, casino hopping, and entertainment, Lake Tahoe, Reno, Virginia City, and Carson City are only minutes away.

# NEW MEXICO

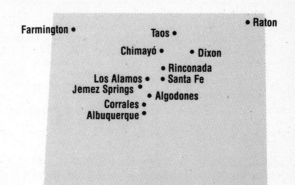

Farmington •
Taos •
• Raton
Chimayó •
• Dixon
• Rinconada
Los Alamos •
• Santa Fe
Jemez Springs •
Corrales •
• Algodones
Albuquerque •

## Bed & Breakfast Southwest Reservation Service—New Mexico ✪
**6916 EAST MARIPOSA, SCOTTSDALE, ARIZONA 85251**

Tel: **(602) 947-9704; (800) 762-9704**
Best Time to Call: **10 AM–8 PM**
Coordinators: **Jo and Jim Cummings**
States/Regions Covered: **New Mexico**

Rates (Single/Double):
  Modest: **$40–$60**
  Average: **$50–$65**
  Luxury: **$65–Up**
Descriptive Directory of B&Bs: **$3, SASE**

Specializing in unique homestays with private suites and guest houses, this service offers exciting experiences to the traveler coming to the Southwest. Jo and Jim are residents of the area and can give firsthand information about sport activities, dining opportunities, art exhibits and can answer your questions about the great Southwest. The Cummingses will be happy to help you plan your vacation with gracious hosts throughout the region. Bed & Breakfast Southwest is always looking for unique hosts and enthusiastic guests.

## Anderson's Victorian House ✪
**11600 MODESTO AVENUE NORTHEAST, ALBUQUERQUE, NEW MEXICO 87122**

| | |
|---|---|
| Tel: **(505) 856-6211** | Single/sb: **$30** |
| Best Time to Call: **7–8:30 AM;** | Open: **All year** |
| **4–9 PM** | Reduced Rates: **10% families; weekly** |
| Hosts: **Judy and Jerris Anderson** | Breakfast: **Full** |
| Location: **3.8 mi. E from Rte. I-25N** | Other Meals: **Available** |
| No. of Rooms: **3** | Pets: **Sometimes** |
| No. of Private Baths: **1** | Children: **Welcome, over 4** |
| Max. No. Sharing Bath: **4** | Smoking: **No** |
| Double/pb: **$50** | Social Drinking: **Permitted** |
| Single/pb: **$40** | Airport Pickup: **Yes** |
| Double/sb: **$35** | |

Anderson's Victorian House is a newly constructed, two-story house on a one-acre tract with spectacular views. Guest rooms are decorated with antiques and pieces your hosts collected in their world travels. Horseback riding, skiing, hiking, and golf are available nearby. Judy and Jerris will gladly direct you to the Sandia Ski Area, Albuquerque's Old Town, Sante Fe, the Indian Cultural Center, and other points of interest. Prize-winning coffee cake, muffins, and more are breakfast delights. Cheese and wine or coffee, tea, and cookies are served in the evening.

## Canyon Crest ✪
**5804 CANYON CREST NORTHEAST, ALBUQUERQUE, NEW MEXICO 87111**

| | |
|---|---|
| Tel: **(505) 821-4898** | Double/sb: **$40–$60** |
| Best Time to Call: **7 AM–10 PM** | Single/sb: **$40** |
| Hosts: **Jan and Chip Mansure** | Open: **All year** |
| Location: **7 mi. NE of Albuquerque** | Breakfast: **Continental** |
| No. of Rooms: **2** | Pets: **No** |
| Max. No. Sharing Bath: **4** | Children: **Welcome, over 10** |
| Double/pb: **$50–$65** | Smoking: **No** |
| Single/pb: **$40** | Social Drinking: **No** |

Warm hospitality awaits you upon entering this two-story contemporary home furnished in Southwestern decor. Enjoy the splash of color from the hosts' prize-winning batik pictures and floral arrangements, as well as antiques and collectibles from their teachings and travels in Africa. After a great day of skiing, hiking, ballooning, antiquing, visiting galleries and museums, exploring Indian pueblos or golfing, come home to a cup of coffee or tea and good conversation with Jan and Chip. Indulge in a quiet night's sleep and awaken to a hearty breakfast of cereal, muffins, and fresh fruit.

## The Corner House ✪

**9121 JAMES PLACE NORTHEAST, ALBUQUERQUE, NEW MEXICO 87111**

| | |
|---|---|
| Tel: **(505) 298-5800** | Open: **All year** |
| Host: **Jean Thompson** | Reduced Rates: **10% families, seniors** |
| Location: **4 mi. N of I-40** | Breakfast: **Full** |
| No. of Rooms: **3** | Other Meals: **Available** |
| No. of Private Baths: **1** | Pets: **Sometimes** |
| Max. No. Sharing Bath: **3** | Children: **Welcome (crib)** |
| Double/pb: **$50–$65** | Smoking: **No** |
| Double/sb: **$40–$50** | Social Drinking: **Permitted** |
| Single/sb: **$30–$35** | |

Jean welcomes you to her handsome Southwestern-style home, decorated in a delightful mix of antiques and collectibles. Breakfast specialties include Jean's homemade muffins. The Corner House is located in a quiet residential neighborhood within view of the magnificent Sandia Mountains. It is convenient to Old Town Albuquerque, Santa Fe, many Indian pueblos, and the launch site for the International Balloon Fiesta.

## Enchanted Vista ✪

**10700 DEL REY NORTHEAST, ALBUQUERQUE, NEW MEXICO 87122**

| | |
|---|---|
| Tel: **(505) 823-1301** | Breakfast: **Continental, plus** |
| Best Time to Call: **Before 10 PM** | Pets: **Welcome** |
| Hosts: **Tillie and Al Gonzales** | Children: **Welcome** |
| Location: **In Albuquerque** | Smoking: **No** |
| Suites: **$45–$74** | Social Drinking: **Permitted** |
| Open: **All year** | Foreign Languages: **Spanish** |
| Reduced Rates: **10% seniors** | |

Beautifully landscaped, with rock gardens and a pond, the Enchanted Vista sits on one acre overlooking the Sandia Mountains and the longest tram in the world. Guest suites are roomy and the decor is Southwest pueblo. The International Balloon Fiesta grounds are five minutes away; historic Old Town, Indian Cultural Center, and many of Albuquerque's fine museums are within twenty minutes. Sandia Shadow Winery, within walking distance, offers free tours and wine tasting daily. After a day of sightseeing, return to a quiet peaceful night and enjoy the sight of Albuquerque's city lights.

## Rio Grande House ✪

**3100 RIO GRANDE BOULEVARD NORTHWEST, ALBUQUERQUE,
NEW MEXICO 87107**

Tel: **(505) 345-0120**
Best Time to Call: **Anytime**
Hosts: **Richard Gray and James Hughes**
Location: **4 mi. N of Rte. I-40, Exit Rio
   Grande Blvd.**
No. of Rooms: **5**
No. of Private Baths: **5**
Double/pb: **$55–$85**

Single/pb: **$45–$55**
Open: **All year**
Breakfast: **Full**
Pets: **Sometimes**
Children: **Welcome**
Smoking: **Permitted**
Social Drinking: **Permitted**

This landmark white adobe residence is close to historic Old Town,
major museums, Rio Grande Nature Center, and the International
Balloon Fiesta launch site. Southwestern charm is reflected through
the beamed ceilings, brick floors, and kiva fireplaces. Museum-quality
antiques and collectibles from East Africa, Nepal, Yemen, and Pakistan
are used to decorate each room. Jim, a college professor, writer, and
actor, will be happy to relate their history.

## Hacienda Vargas ✪

**1431 EL CAMINO REAL, P.O. BOX 307, ALGODONES,
NEW MEXICO 87001**

Tel: **(505) 867-9115; (800) 261-0006**
Best Time to Call: **8:30 AM–5 PM**
Hosts: **Paul and Julie DeVargas**
Location: **2 mi. S of Santa Fe, 25 mi. N
   of Albuquerque**
No. of Rooms: **6**
No. of Private Baths: **6**
Double/pb: **$69–$89**
Suites: **$89–$129**
Open: **All year**

Reduced Rates: **Available**
Breakfast: **Full**
Credit Cards: **MC, VISA**
Pets: **No**
Children: **Welcome, over 12**
Smoking: **No**
Social Drinking: **Permitted**
Minimum Stay: **Balloon Fiesta,
   Christmas, Indian Market**
Foreign Languages: **Spanish, German**

Hacienda Vargas is a romantic hideaway in a historic old adobe hacienda, completely restored and elegantly decorated with antiques. The beautiful rooms have fireplaces and private entrances; two suites have Jacuzzi tubs. Use the hot tub and the barbecue area in the gardens and admire the majestic view of the New Mexico Mesas and Sandia Mountains. Golf, fishing, snow skiing, horseback riding, and hiking are nearby. This B&B is conveniently located south of Santa Fe and north of Albuquerque. Romance packages are available. Paul and Julie are ex-bankers who love history and have traveled extensively.

## La Posada de Chimayó ✪
### P.O. BOX 463, CHIMAYÓ, NEW MEXICO 87522

| | |
|---|---|
| Tel: (505) 351-4605 | Reduced Rates: **Weekly in winter** |
| Host: **Sue Farrington** | Breakfast: **Full** |
| Location: **30 mi. N of Santa Fe** | Credit Cards: **MC, VISA (for deposits)** |
| No. of Rooms: **4** | Pets: **Sometimes** |
| No. of Private Baths: **4** | Children: **Welcome, over 12** |
| Double/pb: **$85** | Smoking: **No** |
| Single/pb: **$75** | Social Drinking: **Permitted** |
| Open: **All year** | Foreign Languages: **Spanish** |

Chimayó is known for its historic old church and its tradition of fine Spanish weaving. This is a typical adobe home with brick floors and *viga* ceilings. The suite is composed of a small bedroom and sitting room, and is made cozy with Mexican rugs, handwoven fabrics, comfortable furnishings, and traditional corner fireplaces. Sue's breakfasts are not for the fainthearted, and often feature stuffed French toast or chiles rellenos. Wine or sun tea are graciously offered after you return from exploring Bandelier National Monument Park, the Indian pueblos, cliff dwellings, and the "high road" to Taos.

## Sagebrush Circle Bed & Breakfast
### 23 SAGEBRUSH CIRCLE, CORRALES, NEW MEXICO 87048

| | |
|---|---|
| Tel: (505) 898-5393 | Reduced Rates: **Available** |
| Best Time to Call: **8:30 AM–9 PM** | Breakfast: **Continental** |
| Hosts: **Barbara and Victor Ferkiss** | Other Meals: **Available** |
| Location: **10 mi. NW of Old Town** | Pets: **No** |
| **Albuquerque** | Children: **Welcome, 12 and older** |
| No. of Rooms: **2** | Smoking: **No** |
| No. of Private Baths: **2** | Social Drinking: **Permitted** |
| Double/pb: **$65–$80** | Minimum Stay: **2 nights** |
| Single/pb: **$58–$72** | Airport/Station Pickup: **Yes** |
| Open: **All year** | |

Sagebrush Circle is a dramatic pueblo-style home nestled in the hills of Corrales, a Spanish village settled in the sixteenth century. All rooms have magnificent views of the Sandia Mountains. During cooler mornings, freshly brewed coffee and homemade breads and muffins are served in the great room, which has a 16-foot beamed ceiling. In warmer weather, guests can eat outdoors. As you dine, you may hear the neighing of horses or see brilliantly colored balloons rise in the turquoise sky—they float over the house during Balloon Fiesta in October. Barbara and Victor are always delighted to give advice and information about the area.

## The Sandhill Crane B&B ✪
### 389 CAMINO HERMOSA, CORRALES, NEW MEXICO 87048

| | |
|---|---|
| Tel: **(800) 375-2445; (505) 898-2445** | Open: **All year** |
| Best Time to Call: **8 AM–6 PM** | Reduced Rates: **Available** |
| Hosts: **Carol Hogan and Phil Thorpe** | Breakfast: **Full** |
| Location: **10 mi. NW of Albuquerque** | Other Meals: **Available** |
| No. of Rooms: **3** | Credit Cards: **AMEX, MC, VISA** |
| No. of Private Baths: **2** | Pets: **No** |
| Max. No. Sharing Bath: **4** | Children: **Welcome, over 8** |
| Double/pb: **$85** | Smoking: **No** |
| Single/pb: **$75–$85** | Social Drinking: **Permitted** |
| Suites: **$125–$150, sleeps 4** | |

Located near Rio Grande Bosque, this romantic adobe hacienda has spectacular mountain views. Enjoy memorable breakfasts and sunrises in this warm, friendly Southwestern-style B&B. Relax behind wisteria-draped walls or walk miles of trails in nearby Rio Grande Bosque. Tours, massages, and horseback riding can be arranged. Sandhill Crane is centrally located for exploring the enchantment of New Mexico.

## La Casita Guesthouse ✪
### P.O. BOX 103, DIXON, NEW MEXICO 87527

| | |
|---|---|
| Tel: **(505) 579-4297** | Pets: **No** |
| Hosts: **Sara Pene and Celeste Miller** | Children: **Welcome** |
| Location: **25 mi. S of Taos** | Smoking: **No** |
| Guest Cottage: **$75–$115, sleeps 2–4** | Social Drinking: **Permitted** |
| Open: **All year** | Foreign Languages: **Spanish** |
| Breakfast: **Continental** | |

The rural mountain village of Dixon is home to many artists and craftspeople. La Casita is a traditional New Mexico adobe with *vigas*, *latillas*, and Mexican tile floors. Guests enjoy use of the living room, fully equipped kitchen, two bedrooms, one bath, and a lovely patio. It is a perfect spot for relaxing and is just minutes from the Rio Grande, river rafting, hiking, and cross-country skiing. Indian pueblos, ancient

Anasazi ruins, museums, art galleries, horseback-riding ranches, and alpine skiing are within an hour's drive. Sara and Celeste are weavers.

## Silver River Adobe Inn ✪
### P.O. BOX 3411, FARMINGTON, NEW MEXICO 87499

Tel: **(505) 325-8219**
Best Time to Call: **Anytime**
Hosts: **Diana Ohlson and David Beers**

Location: **180 mi. NW of Albuquerque**
No. of Rooms: **1**
No. of Private Baths: **1**

Suite: **$55–$115**
Open: **All year**
Breakfast: **Continental**
Credit Cards: **MC, VISA**
Pets: **No**

Children: **Welcome, over 12**
Smoking: **No**
Social Drinking: **Permitted**
Airport/Station Pickup: **Yes**

Silver River Adobe Inn is a newly constructed, traditional New Mexican home with massive timber beams and exposed adobe. From its cliffside perch, it overlooks the fork of the San Juan and La Plata rivers. Indian reservations, Aztec ruins, and ski slopes are all within striking distance of this B&B.

## Dancing Bear B&B ✪
**314 SAN DIEGO LOOP (MAILING ADDRESS: P.O. 128), JEMEZ SPRINGS, NEW MEXICO 87025**

Tel: **(505) 829-3336; (800) 422-3271**
Best Time to Call: **8 AM–8 PM**
Host: **Carol A. Breen**
Location: **60 mi. N of Albuquerque**
No. of Rooms: **4**
No. of Private Baths: **4**
Suites: **$60–$115**

Open: **All year**
Breakfast: **Full**
Credit Cards: **MC, VISA**
Pets: **No**
Children: **Welcome**
Smoking: **No**
Social Drinking: **Permitted**

You are sure to find serenity at this river retreat at the base of a dramatic sandstone mesa, a bit off the beaten path from Santa Fe. During your stay you will have the opportunity to visit the owner's on-site pottery studio. (Workshops and lessons can be arranged.) Local artisans' handcrafted pieces are exhibited throughout the house, and some are for sale. As you get ready for bed, you can anticipate having breakfast by candlelight or by the riverside. The resident chef is sure to whip up homemade muffins and other culinary delights; special dietary needs are never a problem.

## Jemez River B&B Inn ✪
**16445 HIGHWAY 4, JEMEZ SPRINGS, NEW MEXICO 87025**

Tel: **(505) 829-3262**
Best Time to Call: **8 AM–10 PM**
Hosts: **Larry and Roxe Ann Clutter**
Location: **40 mi. NW of Albuquerque**
No. of Rooms: **6**
No. of Private Baths: **6**
Double/pb: **$99–$109**
Open: **All year**
Reduced Rates: **10% seniors**

Breakfast: **Full**
Other Meals: **Available**
Credit Cards: **AMEX, CB, DC, DISC, MC, VISA**
Pets: **Seeing-eye dogs only**
Children: **Welcome, over 12**
Smoking: **No**
Social Drinking: **Permitted**

The Jemez River Bed & Breakfast Inn is a new, adobe-style, American Indian–decorated home built during the winter of 1993–94. It is nestled on three and a half acres in a valley directly beneath the towering Jemez Mountains Virgin Mesa and is surrounded by mighty cottonwood trees, rolling hills and arroyos. Breathtaking views of the morning, sun-drenched Mesa, its splendid colors, and the immense tent rocks overlooking the Inn can be seen from grand, picturesque windows that surround a sizable breakfast table, assuring everyone an enchanting image while enjoying a hearty breakfast. The endless murmur of the Jemez River, located in its own backyard, can be heard from your room, and its soothing song will lull you into a deep sleep. The Inn has six air-conditioned rooms, each with private bath, and most important, sound-proofing between the rooms for the privacy the guests deserve. Each room is individually named and decorated with Southwestern Indian tribes' and pueblos' authentic artifacts, pottery, rugs, paintings, arrowheads, kachina dolls, and much more. The rooms surround a large outdoor garden plaza filled with birds—hundreds of hummingbirds—and other wildlife, with an underground spring supplying an oversize, continuous-flowing bird bath that cascades into a small stream that in turn incrementally makes its way to the river just behind the Inn. Each room has individual access to and from the plaza, as well as the many stone-lined trails that follow the overflowing spring through vast cottonwood trees, large rocks and crevices that lead to several secluded and relaxing spots along the Jemez River. Come and experience for yourself the restful atmosphere of the Jemez River B&B Inn.

## Casa del Rey Bed & Breakfast
**305 ROVER, LOS ALAMOS, NEW MEXICO 87544**

| | |
|---|---|
| Tel: **(505) 672-9401** | Open: **All year** |
| Best Time to Call: **After 5 PM** | Reduced Rates: **Weekly; families** |
| Host: **Virginia L. King** | Breakfast: **Continental, plus** |
| No. of Rooms: **2** | Pets: **No** |
| Max. No. Sharing Bath: **4** | Children: **Welcome, over 5** |
| Double/sb: **$45** | Smoking: **No** |
| Single/sb: **$35** | Social Drinking: **Permitted** |

This adobe contemporary home is located in the quiet residential area of White Rock, and is situated in the Jemez Mountains with a view of Santa Fe across the valley. The surroundings are rich in Spanish and Indian history. Pueblos, museums, Bandelier National Monument, skiing, hiking trails, tennis, and golf are all within easy reach. Virginia is rightfully proud of her beautifully-kept house, with its pretty flower gardens. In summer, her breakfast of granola, home-baked rolls and muffins, along with fruits and beverages, is served on the sunporch, where you can enjoy the lovely scenery.

## The Red Violet Inn ✪
### 344 NORTH SECOND STREET, RATON, NEW MEXICO 87740

Tel: (505) 445-9778; (800) 624-9778
Best Time to Call: 9 AM–8 PM
Hosts: John and Ruth Hanrahan
Location: 1 mi. from I-25, Exit 455
No. of Rooms: 4
No. of Private Baths: 2
Max. No. Sharing Bath: 4
Double/pb: $65–$70
Double/sb: $60
Single/sb: $50

Open: Mar. 1–Jan. 30
Breakfast: Full
Credit Cards: AMEX, MC, VISA
Other Meals: Available
Pets: No
Children: Welcome, over 8
Smoking: No
Social Drinking: Permitted
Airport/Station Pickup: Yes

Follow the Santa Fe Trail and step back into the past at this appealing 1902 redbrick Victorian home three blocks from Raton's historic downtown. Guests have use of the parlor, dining room, porches, and enclosed flower-filled yard. Repeat visitors arrange to be on hand for the classical music and social hour, from 5:30 to 6:30 PM. Late arrivals are welcomed with a glass of sherry. Full breakfast is served in the formal dining room, accompanied by friendly conversation. A theater and a gallery are within a few blocks, and hiking and fishing facilities are six miles away. Other area attractions include a golf course, several antique shops and a museum; Capulin Volcano National Monument is only 30 minutes away.

## Casa Rinconada del Rio ✪
### BOX 10A, TAOS HIGHWAY 68, RINCONADA, NEW MEXICO 87531

Tel: (505) 579-4466
Host: JoAnne Gladin-de la Fuente
Location: 20 mi. S of Taos; 45 mi. N. of Santa Fe
Guest Houses: $55–$130
Open: All year

Breakfast: Continental
Pets: Sometimes
Children: Welcome
Smoking: Yes
Social Drinking: Permitted
Foreign Languages: Greek

Casa Rinconada is nestled in the canyon of Sangre de Cristo Mountains, the spectacular backdrop for this historic northern village. Thirty-foot *vigas* adorned with skulls and lights border the entry to the guest houses—two traditional tin-roofed adobes which are artfully decorated for your comfort and pleasure. The backyard is an orchard where guests are invited to enjoy seasonal fruit and stroll along the banks of the legendary Rio Grande. Indian pueblos, opera, galleries, rafting, historic churches and more are all within a short drive.

## Bed & Breakfast of New Mexico ✪
### P.O. BOX 2805, SANTA FE, NEW MEXICO 87504

Tel: (505) 982-3332
Best Time to Call: 9 AM–5 PM

Coordinator: Rob Bennett
States/Regions Covered: Statewide

Descriptive Directory: **Free**
Rates (Single/Double):
  Average: **$75 / $90**

Luxury: **$95 / $200**
Credit Cards: **AMEX, DISC, MC, VISA**

Do come and enjoy the Santa Fe Opera in summer, the vibrant colors of the aspens in autumn, or skiing in winter. Don't miss the Indian pueblos and ancient cliff dwellings, the national forest areas, art colonies, museums, and Taos.

## Alexanders Inn ✪

**529 EAST PALACE AVENUE, SANTA FE, NEW MEXICO 87501**

Tel: **(505) 986-1431**
Best Time to Call: **7:30 AM–10 PM**
Hosts: **Carolyn Lee and LeeAnne Reilly**
Location: **50 mi. N of Albuquerque**
No. of Rooms: **7**
No. of Private Baths: **5**
Max. No. Sharing Bath: **4**
Double/pb: **$85–$135**
Double/sb: **$75–$85**
Guest Cottage: **$140–$150**
Open: **All year**

Reduced Rates: **Available**
Breakfast: **Continental plus**
Credit Cards: **MC, VISA**
Pets: **Sometimes**
Children: **Welcome, over 6 in main house, any age in cottage**
Smoking: **No**
Social Drinking: **Permitted**
Minimum Stay: **2 nights weekends**
Foreign Languages: **French**

Built in 1903 as a Craftsman-style home, the Inn has been restored to include dormer windows and skylights. Large new porches overlook bountiful gardens in both the front and back of the Inn, where guests enjoy breakfast and homemade cookies and lemonade. In keeping with the turn-of-the-century style inside are hardwood floors, fireplaces, antiques, quilts, and stenciling throughout. Additional bathrooms were also added. Alexanders Inn is located five blocks from the Plaza and two blocks from a multitude of galleries on Canyon Road. An air of peace and tranquility pervades the Inn, providing an ideal place to relax for the weary traveler.

## American Artists Gallery-House ✪

**FRONTIER ROAD, P.O. BOX 584, TAOS, NEW MEXICO 87571**

Tel: **(505) 758-4446; (800) 532-2041**
Best Time to Call: **Anytime**
Hosts: **LeAn and Charles Clamurro**
Location: **3 blocks from Main St.**
No. of Rooms: **7**
No. of Private Baths: **7**
Double/pb: **$75–$105**
Guest Cottage: **$75–$105**

Open: **All year**
Breakfast: **Full**
Pets: **No**
Children: **Welcome**
Smoking: **No**
Social Drinking: **Permitted**
Airport/Station Pickup: **Yes**

This charming hacienda is filled with artwork, and has a splendid view of Taos Mountain. Your hosts will gladly advise on shops and boutiques. Their home is close to Rio Grande Gorge State Park, 900-year-old Taos Pueblo, and places to go fishing, skiing, and rafting.

Fireplaces, the outdoor hot tub, gardens, and a sculpture courtyard will delight you.

## Harrison's B&B ✪

P.O. BOX 242, TAOS, NEW MEXICO 87571

| | |
|---|---|
| Tel: **(505) 758-2630** | Open: **All year** |
| Hosts: **Jean and Bob Harrison** | Reduced Rates: **10% after 4th night** |
| Location: **1½ mi. from Rte. 64** | Breakfast: **Full** |
| No. of Rooms: **2** | Pets: **No** |
| No. of Private Baths: **2** | Children: **Welcome (crib)** |
| Double/pb: **$40–$50** | Smoking: **No** |
| Single/pb: **$30–$40** | Social Drinking: **Permitted** |

The Harrisons have lived in this large adobe just outside of Taos for 25 years. The house overlooks town from the foot of the western mesa and, framed by trees and bushes, boasts lovely mountain views. Inside, original works of art enhance the Southwestern decor. The Harrisons are just over two miles from the Taos plaza, and are conveniently located near many outdoor pursuits, including skiing, hiking, fishing, and river rafting.

## Touchstone Bed & Breakfast Inn ✪

110 MABEL DODGE LANE, P.O. BOX 2896, TAOS,
NEW MEXICO 87571-2896

| | |
|---|---|
| Tel: **(505) 758-0192; fax: (505) 758-3498** | Reduced Rates: **10% seniors, 7th night free** |
| Best Time to Call: **11 AM–2 PM** | Breakfast: **Full** |
| Host: **Bren Price** | Credit Cards: **AMEX, MC, VISA** |
| Location: **1 mi. N of Taos Plaza** | Pets: **No** |
| No. of Rooms: **6** | Children: **Welcome, over 12** |
| No. of Private Baths: **6** | Smoking: **No** |
| Double/pb: **$75–$85** | Social Drinking: **Permitted** |
| Suites: **$95–$135** | |

Situated on two acres bordering Pueblo lands, Touchstone Bed & Breakfast Inn offers a quiet ambiance. The property boasts full mountain views, towering cottonwoods, evergreens, wildflower gardens, a trout stream and an impressive apple orchard. Antiques, kiva fireplaces, *viga* ceilings, fine art, oriental rugs, down pillows and comforters, and custom designed baths—some with Jacuzzis—complete the most luxurious accommodations. A gourmet breakfast is served each morning in an atrium that has a fireplace designed by Tony Luhan and overlooks the courtyard. Guests may use the video collection and cassette library as well as an outdoor hot tub. All rooms have cable TV, VCR, and phones.

# NORTH DAKOTA

• **Stanley**

## The Triple T Ranch ✪
**RR 1, BOX 93, STANLEY, NORTH DAKOTA 58784**

Tel: **(701) 628-2418**
Best Time to Call: **Anytime**
Hosts: **Joyce and Fred Evans**
Location: **60 mi. W of Minot**
No. of Rooms: **2**
Max. No. Sharing Bath: **4**
Double/sb: **$40**
Single/sb: **$35**

Open: **All year**
Reduced Rates: **Available**
Breakfast: **Full**
Pets: **Sometimes**
Children: **Welcome (crib)**
Smoking: **No**
Social Drinking: **No**

You're warmly invited to come to Joyce and Fred's rustic ranch home, where you're welcome to take a seat in front of the stone fireplace, put your feet up, and relax. There's a lovely view of the hills and the valley, and their herd of cattle is an impressive sight. Lake Sakakawea, for seasonal recreation such as fishing and swimming, is 11 miles away. Indian powwows, area rodeos, and hunting for Indian artifacts are fun. The State Fair is held every July.

---

**For key to listings, see inside front or back cover.**

---

✪ This star means that rates are guaranteed through December 31, 1996, to any guest making a reservation as a result of reading about the B&B in *Bed & Breakfast U.S.A.*—1996 edition.

---

Important! To avoid misunderstandings, always ask about cancellation policies when booking.

---

Please enclose a self-addressed, stamped, business-size envelope when contacting reservation services.

---

For more details on what you can expect in a B&B, see Chapter 1.

---

Always mention *Bed & Breakfast U.S.A.* when making reservations!

---

If no B&B is listed in the area you'll be visiting, use the form on page 323 to order a copy of our "List of New B&Bs."

---

We want to hear from you! Use the form on page 325.

# OREGON

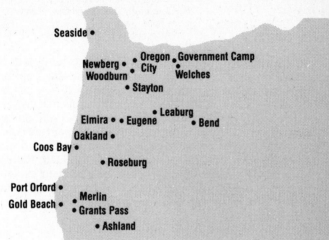

## Northwest Bed and Breakfast Travel Unlimited
### 610 SW BROADWAY, SUITE 606, PORTLAND, OREGON 97205

Tel: **(503) 243-7616**
Coordinator: **LaVonne Miller**
States/Regions Covered: **California,**
  **Oregon, Washington;**
  **Canada—British Columbia**

Rates (Single/Double):
  Modest:  **$35–$55 / $45–$65**
  Average:  **$50–$65 / $65–$85**
  Luxury:    **$65–$100 / $85–$165 +**
Credit Cards: **AMEX, MC, VISA**
Descriptive Directory: **$7.95**

Northwest Bed and Breakfast is a network established in 1979 of hundreds of host homes and inns throughout the Pacific Northwest. Send $7.95 for a directory of the lodgings, which include city, suburban, and rural sites in coastal, mountain, and desert regions. There is a $10 surcharge for one-night stays.

## Cowslip's Belle Bed & Breakfast ✪
### 159 NORTH MAIN STREET, ASHLAND, OREGON 97520

| | |
|---|---|
| Tel: **(800) 888-6819; (503) 488-2901** | Breakfast: **Full** |
| Hosts: **Jon and Carmen Reinhardt** | Credit Cards: **MC, VISA** |
| Location: **285 mi. S of Portland** | Pets: **No** |
| No. of Rooms: **4** | Children: **Welcome, over 10** |
| No. of Private Baths: **4** | Smoking: **No** |
| Double/pb: **$75–$115** | Social Drinking: **Permitted** |
| Single/pb: **$70–$110** | Minimum Stay: **2 nights weekends** |
| Open: **All year** | **June–Sept.** |
| Reduced Rates: **Available** | Airport/Station Pickup: **Yes** |

From the moment you step inside this 1913 Craftsman bungalow or its adjacent carriage house, you will receive modern-day comfort sprinkled with old-fashioned hospitality. Snuggle up to one of the resident teddy bears. Guest rooms have luxurious queen beds, caressed by soft white linens, down comforters, and air-conditioning. Indulge your sweet tooth with a melt-in-your-mouth homemade chocolate truffle, placed on your pillow when your bed is turned down each evening. Daily fare includes a scrumptious breakfast with a hearty serving of lively conversation. Whether you wish to explore Ashland by foot or by car, Jon and Carmen will be happy to help you plan your itinerary and assist you with reservations for dinner, bike rentals, and raft trips.

## Mt. Ashland Inn ✪
### 550 MT. ASHLAND ROAD, P.O. BOX 944, ASHLAND, OREGON 97520

| | |
|---|---|
| Tel: **(503) 482-8707; (800) 830-8707** | Open: **All year** |
| Best Time to Call: **11 AM–7 PM** | Breakfast: **Full** |
| Hosts: **Elaine and Jerry Shanafelt** | Other Meals: **Dinner available** |
| Location: **6 mi. from I-5, Exit 6** | **Nov.–Mar. only by arrangement** |
| No. of Rooms: **5** | Pets: **No** |
| No. of Private Baths: **5** | Children: **Welcome, over 10** |
| Double/pb: **$85–$130** | Smoking: **No** |
| Single/pb: **$80–$125** | Social Drinking: **Permitted** |

Nestled among tall evergreens, this beautifully handcrafted log structure is situated on a mountain ridge with views of the Cascade Mountains, including majestic Mt. Shasta. Inside, hand carvings, oriental rugs, homemade quilts, antiques, and finely crafted furniture provide an atmosphere of comfort and elegance. Breakfasts are hearty to satisfy the appetites of skiers and hikers who take advantage of nearby trails. For quiet relaxation, you are welcome to enjoy the sunny deck or curl up with a book by the large stone fireplace.

# Royal Carter House ✪
## 514 SISKIYOU BOULEVARD, ASHLAND, OREGON 97520

Tel: (503) 482-5623
Best Time to Call: **Mornings**
Hosts: **Alyce and Roy Levy**
No. of Rooms: **4**
No. of Private Baths: **4**
Double/pb: **$64–$84**
Suites: **$84**

Open: **All year**
Breakfast: **Full**
Pets: **No**
Children: **Welcome, over 7**
Smoking: **No**
Social Drinking: **Permitted**
Airport/Station Pickup: **Yes**

This beautiful 1909 Craftsman home is listed on the National Register of Historic Places. Located four blocks from Ashland's famous Shakespeare Theatre, it is surrounded by lovely old trees in a parklike setting. It is suitably modernized but retains the original room structure. Alyce has added decorator touches of vintage hats and old periodicals to the antique furnishings. The Levys have traveled extensively abroad and will share stories of their experiences with you. Southern Oregon State College is six blocks away.

## The Woods House Bed & Breakfast Inn ✪
### 333 NORTH MAIN STREET, ASHLAND, OREGON 97520

| | |
|---|---|
| Tel: **(503) 488-1598; (800) 435-8260** | Breakfast: **Full** |
| Best Time to Call: **10 AM–10 PM** | Credit Cards: **MC, VISA** |
| Hosts: **Françoise and Lester Roddy** | Pets: **No** |
| Location: **4 blks. N of Downtown Plaza** | Children: **Welcome, over 12** |
| No. of Rooms: **6** | Smoking: **No** |
| No. of Private Baths: **6** | Social Drinking: **Permitted** |
| Double/pb: **$65–$112** | Minimum Stay: **2 days June–Oct.;** |
| Single/pb: **$65–$107** | **weekends Nov.–May** |
| Open: **All year** | Station Pickup: **Yes** |
| Reduced Rates: **Available** | |

The Woods House is located in Ashland's historic district four blocks from the Shakespearean theater, shops, restaurants, and 100-acre Lithia Park. The Inn, a 1908 Craftsman home renovated in 1984, has six sunny and spacious guest rooms. Simple furnishings, comprising warm woods, antique furniture and linens, watercolors, oriental carpets, and leather books, combine with high-quality amenities to create a sophisticated comfortable atmosphere. The terraced English gardens provide many areas for guests to relax and socialize. Françoise previously worked in human resources and event planning and is skilled in calligraphy, cooking, and needlecrafts. Lester has spent the past 25 years in business management and consulting. Their aim is to make each guest feel like a special friend, not just a paying customer. They strive to anticipate guests' needs and cheerfully accommodate the unexpected, always maintaining the highest standards of cleanliness, cordiality, and fine food.

## Farewell Bend Bed & Breakfast
### 29 NW GREELEY, BEND, OREGON 97701

| | |
|---|---|
| Tel: **(503) 382-4374** | Reduced Rates: **10% weekly** |
| Best Time to Call: **Anytime** | Breakfast: **Full** |
| Host: **Lorene Bateman** | Credit Cards: **AMEX** |
| Location: **160 mi. SE of Portland** | Pets: **No** |
| No. of Rooms: **3** | Children: **Welcome, over 12** |
| No. of Private Baths: **3** | Smoking: **No** |
| Double/pb: **$70–$80** | Social Drinking: **Permitted** |
| Open: **All year** | Airport/Station Pickup: **Yes** |

Farewell Bend is a recently renovated 1920s Dutch Colonial just minutes from shops, restaurants, and Drake Park—where the town music festival takes place every June and hungry ducks and geese demand bread crumbs year-round. It's only 17 miles to Mt. Bachelor for skiing, and white-water rafting on the Deschutes is a special warm-weather treat. Afterward, settle in the living room with sherry or tea, read a book, or watch a movie on the VCR. All bedrooms have king-size beds, down comforters, and hand-stitched quilts, and bathrooms are supplied with terry robes. Full breakfasts are served in the sunny dining room.

## Old Tower House B&B ✪
### 476 NEWMARK AVENUE, COOS BAY, OREGON 97420

| | |
|---|---|
| Tel: (503) 888-6058; fax: (503) 888-6058 | Open: All year |
| | Breakfast: Full |
| Hosts: Don and Julia Spangler | Credit Cards: MC, VISA |
| Location: 5 mi. W of Coos Bay | Pets: No |
| No. of Rooms: 3 | Children: Welcome, over 10 by arrangement |
| Max. No. Sharing Bath: 4 | |
| Double/sb: $60–$75 | Social Drinking: No |
| Guest Cottage: $60 | Airport Pickup: Yes |
| Suites: $75 | |

Built in 1872, this Victorian home is on the National Historic Register and is furnished with antiques throughout. All three guest rooms have pedestal sinks and share two full baths with clawfoot tubs. For relaxing, a spacious parlor is offered. For seclusion you might want to enjoy the Carriage House loft suite with a queen-size bed, clawfoot tub, kitchen, and sitting room with TV, or the Ivy Cottage with a double bed and a private bath.

## McGillivray's Log Home and Bed and Breakfast ✪
### 88680 EVERS ROAD, ELMIRA, OREGON 97437

| | |
|---|---|
| Tel: (503) 935-3564 | Open: All year |
| Best Time to Call: 8 AM–8 PM | Breakfast: Full |
| Host: Evelyn McGillivray | Credit Cards: MC, VISA |
| Location: 14 mi. W of Eugene | Pets: No |
| No. of Rooms: 2 | Children: Welcome |
| No. of Private Baths: 2 | Smoking: No |
| Double/pb: $50–$70 | Social Drinking: Permitted |
| Single/pb: $40–$60 | Airport/Station Pickup: Yes |

This massive home is situated on five acres covered with pines and firs. The air-conditioned structure is designed with six types of wood, and features a split-log staircase. Guests may choose from a spacious, wheelchair-accessible bedroom, or an upstairs room that can accommodate a family. All are beautifully decorated in a classic Americana motif. Evelyn usually prepares buttermilk pancakes using an antique griddle her mother used to use. She also offers fresh-squeezed juice from farm-grown apples and grapes, fresh bread, eggs, and all the trimmings. It's just three miles to a local vineyard; country roads for bicycling and a reservoir for fishing and boating are close by.

## Getty's Emerald Garden B&B ❂
### 640 AUDEL, EUGENE, OREGON 97404

| | |
|---|---|
| Tel: (503) 688-6344 | Breakfast: **Full** |
| Best Time to Call: **Anytime** | Credit Cards: **AMEX, MC, VISA** |
| Hosts: **Bob and Jackie Getty** | Pets: **No** |
| Location: **3 mi. N of Eugene** | Children: **Welcome** |
| No. of Rooms: **1 suite** | Smoking: **No** |
| Suite: **$50–$55** | Social Drinking: **Permitted** |
| Open: **All year** | Airport/Station Pickup: **Yes** |
| Reduced Rates: **10% weekly** | |

Bob and Jackie have lived in Eugene for more than thirty years and can help you plan a wonderful vacation. Their contemporary home has vaulted ceilings, large windows, and a cozy living room with a fireplace. Full breakfasts feature specialties from your hosts' garden. Guests have use of the family room and its piano, TV, and VCR; less sedentary types will want to borrow bicycles and head out for the area's scenic trails. For more activity, visit the local park, which has a heated swimming pool, sauna, hot tubs, jogging trails, and playground. Hult Center for the Performing Arts, Lane County Fairgrounds, the University of Oregon, golf courses, Valley River Shopping Center, and City Center are all within a ten-minute drive.

## The House in the Woods ❂
### 814 LORANE HIGHWAY, EUGENE, OREGON 97405

| | |
|---|---|
| Tel: (503) 343-3234 | Reduced Rates: **Available** |
| Best Time to Call: **Mornings; evenings** | Breakfast: **Full** |
| Hosts: **Eunice and George Kjaer** | Pets: **No** |
| Location: **3 mi. from I-5** | Children: **Welcome, under 1** |
| No. of Rooms: **2** | **and over 14** |
| No. of Private Baths: **2** | Smoking: **No** |
| Max. No. Sharing Bath: **2** | Social Drinking: **Permitted** |
| Double/pb: **$75** | Airport/Station Pickup: **Yes** |
| Single/pb: **$42** | Foreign Languages: **German** |
| Open: **All year** | |

This turn-of-the-century home is situated in a wooded glen surrounded by fir trees, rhododendrons, and azaleas. Inside, you'll find oriental rugs on the original hardwood floors, antiques, and a square grand piano. Guest rooms always have fresh flowers. Breakfast is served in the formal dining room or beside the warmth of the Franklin stove. Specialties of the house include breads, fruit soups, and a variety of egg dishes. The neighborhood is full of wildlife and bicycle and jogging trails, yet is close to shops, art galleries, museums, wineries, and restaurants.

## Maryellen's Guest House ✪
### 1583 FIRCREST, EUGENE, OREGON 97403

| | |
|---|---|
| Tel: **(503) 342-7375** | Reduced Rates: **10% weekly** |
| Best Time to Call: **9 AM–9 PM** | Breakfast: **Full** |
| Hosts: **Maryellen and Bob Larson** | Other Meals: **Available** |
| Location: **1 mi. off I-5, Exit 191-192** | Credit Cards: **MC, VISA** |
| No. of Rooms: **2** | Pets: **No** |
| No. of Private Baths: **2** | Children: **Welcome, over 12** |
| Double/pb: **$76** | Smoking: **No** |
| Single/pb: **$66** | Social Drinking: **Permitted** |
| Open: **All year** | Airport/Station Pickup: **Yes** |

Maryellen's Guest House is a contemporary hillside home with casual elegance. This B&B is close to the University of Oregon, Hendrick's Park, and shopping. Each guest room is private and spacious with a sitting area, TV, and phone. A guest refrigerator, games, books, Ping-Pong, bicycles, and a pool and hot tub located on the spacious cedar decks are available for your enjoyment. A bountiful breakfast is served in the dining room, or you may request special room service.

## The Oval Door ✪
### 988 LAWRENCE STREET, EUGENE, OREGON 97401

| | |
|---|---|
| Tel: **(503) 683-3160**; fax: **(503) 485-5339** | Breakfast: **Full** |
| | Credit Cards: **AMEX, MC, VISA** |
| Hosts: **Judith McLane and Dianne Feist** | Pets: **No** |
| No. of Rooms: **4** | Children: **By arrangement** |
| No. of Private Baths: **4** | Smoking: **No** |
| Double/pb: **$65–$88** | Social Drinking: **Permitted** |
| Single/pb: **$60–$83** | Minimum Stay: **2 nights during** |
| Open: **All year** | **conventions, University functions** |

This inviting 1920s-style home was built as a B&B in 1990. From its location in the heart of downtown Eugene, it's an easy walk to fine restaurants and the Hult Performing Arts Center. The University of Oregon campus is also nearby. Scrumptious breakfasts include a seasonal fruit dish, homemade breads, and a special entree, such as zucchini filbert waffles. You'll also find extra touches like terry robes, Perrier water, Frango Mints, and the Tub Room with its whirlpool bath for two, music, candles, and bubbles.

## Pookie's Bed 'n' Breakfast on College Hill ✪
### 2013 CHARNELTON STREET, EUGENE, OREGON 97405

| | |
|---|---|
| Tel: **(503) 343-0383**; **(800) 558-0383** | No. of Rooms: **2** |
| Hosts: **Pookie and Doug Walling** | No. of Private Baths: **1** |
| Location: **110 mi. S of Portland** | Max. No. Sharing Bath: **4** |

Double/pb: **$80–$90**  
Single/pb: **$70–$80**  
Double/sb: **$65**  
Single/sb: **$55**  
Open: **All year**  
Reduced Rates: **20% families**

Breakfast: **Full**  
Pets: **No**  
Children: **Welcome, over 6**  
Smoking: **No**  
Social Drinking: **Permitted**

Although it has been remodeled on the outside, this Craftsman-style house, built in 1918, retains much of its original interior charm. One room has antique mahogany furniture and a queen-size bed; the other has oak furnishings and either a king or twin beds. Pookie's is in a quiet older neighborhood just south of downtown, where you'll find great shopping, excellent dining, and access to the Hult Performing Arts Center. The University of Oregon campus is all of a mile away. Early morning coffee is served in the small sitting room upstairs. A full breakfast, with specialties like quiche and orange custard baked French toast, follows.

## Endicott Gardens ✪

**95768 JERRY'S FLAT ROAD, GOLD BEACH, OREGON 97444**

Tel: **(503) 247-6513**  
Best Time to Call: **10 AM–Noon**  
Hosts: **Stewart and Mary Endicott**  
No. of Rooms: **4**  
No. of Private Baths: **4**  
Double/pb: **$55**  
Single/pb: **$45**

Open: **All year**  
Breakfast: **Continental, plus**  
Pets: **Sometimes**  
Children: **Welcome**  
Smoking: **Permitted**  
Social Drinking: **Permitted**  
Airport/Station Pickup: **Yes**

This classic contemporary B&B is across the road from Rogue River, famous for fishing and riverboat trips to white water. The guest rooms are located in a private wing of the house with decks overlooking the forest, mountains, and beautiful grounds. Homegrown strawberries, blueberries, apples, and plums are often featured in delicious breakfast treats served on the deck or in the dining room. In cool weather, the living room with its cozy fireplace is a favorite gathering spot. Stewart and Mary will be happy to share their collection of restaurant menus from nearby eating establishments with you.

## Falcon's Crest Inn ✪

**87287 GOVERNMENT CAMP LOOP HIGHWAY, P.O. BOX 185,  
GOVERNMENT CAMP, OREGON 97028**

Tel: **(503) 272-3403; (800) 624-7384**  
Hosts: **BJ and Melody Johnson**  
Location: **54 mi. E of Portland**  
No. of Rooms: **5**  
No. of Private Baths: **5**  
Double/pb: **$85–$99.50**

Suites: **$110–$169; sleeps 2**  
Open: **All year**  
Reduced Rates: **Nov.–Mar.; with ski package**  
Breakfast: **Full**  
Other Meals: **Available**

| | |
|---|---|
| Credit Cards: **AMEX, DISC, MC, VISA** | Smoking: **No** |
| Pets: **No** | Social Drinking: **Permitted** |
| Children: **Welcome, over 6** | Airport/Station Pickup: **Yes** |

Falcon's Crest Inn is nestled among the firs on the 4000-foot level of Mount Hood. The two-story glass front of this elegant, intimate B&B provides a spectacular view of Ski Bowl, a year-round recreational area. Duffers can head to the 27-hole championship course just 12 miles from the front door, and those who love water sports can occupy themselves with fishing, swimming, and white-water rafting. The bedrooms, which are decorated with family heirlooms and keepsakes, have forest or mountain views. In the morning, fresh muffins and a beverage are delivered to your door. Then you'll breakfast on hearty fare like buttermilk pancakes, waffles, or French toast.

## Ahlf House Bed & Breakfast ✪
### 762 N.W. 6TH STREET, GRANTS PASS, OREGON 97526

| | |
|---|---|
| Tel: **(503) 474-1374; (800) 863-1374** | Open: **All year** |
| Hosts: **Ken and Cathy Neuschafer** | Breakfast: **Full** |
| Location: **2 blocks from downtown Grants Pass** | Pets: **No** |
| | Children: **No** |
| No. of Rooms: **4** | Smoking: **No** |
| Double/pb: **$60–$75** | Social Drinking: **Permitted** |
| Single/pb: **$55–$70** | Airport/Station Pickup: **Yes** |

Ahlf House is located on a main street on a hill overlooking the surrounding mountains. The house dates back to 1902, and is listed on the National Register of Historic Places. The rooms are beautifully appointed and furnished in fine antiques. Guest rooms feature fluffy comforters, down pillows, fresh flowers, and candles. Enjoy a cup of fresh coffee first thing in the morning in the quiet of your room or on the sunny front porch. Your coffee is followed by a full gourmet breakfast including fruit, fresh-baked muffins, and homemade jams and jellies. There is much to explore in Grants Pass, which is set on the Rogue River and is surrounded by the beautiful Cascade Mountains. Your hosts can direct you to guided fishing, raft trips, and jet boats. In the evening, return to this lovely Victorian for evening dessert.

## The Washington Inn Bed & Breakfast ✪
### 1002 NORTHWEST WASHINGTON BOULEVARD, GRANTS PASS, OREGON 97526

| | |
|---|---|
| Tel: **(503) 476-1131; (503) 479-3378** | Max. No. Sharing Bath: **2** |
| Host: **Bill Thompson** | Double/pb: **$50–$65** |
| Location: **½ mi. from I-5** | Single/pb: **$40–$55** |
| No. of Rooms: **3** | Double/sb: **$40–$55** |
| No. of Private Baths: **2** | Open: **All year** |

Reduced Rates: **Available**
Breakfast: **Continental**
Pets: **No**

Children: **Welcome, over 14**
Smoking: **No**
Social Drinking: **Permitted**

The Washington Inn is a charming Victorian listed on the National Register of Historic Places. Each guest room is named for one of Bill's three children and offers individual charms. Linda's is a large suite with fireplace, queen-size bed, private bath, and balcony overlooking the mountains; Pattie's Parlor is a spacious red room with fireplace and large private bath with claw-footed tub; Sally's Sunny View overlooks the mountains, has a canopied bed, and is decorated in delicate pink. Your host offers bicycles for exploring the area, and many interesting shops and restaurants are within easy walking distance. Fishing, rafting, and jet-boat rides can be enjoyed on the Rogue River. If you prefer, spend the afternoon relaxing on the porch swing, taking in the view.

## Marjon Bed and Breakfast Inn ○
**44975 LEABURG DAM ROAD, LEABURG, OREGON 97489**

Tel: **(503) 896-3145**
Host: **Marguerite Haas**
Location: **24 mi. E of Eugene**
No. of Rooms: **2**
No. of Private Baths: **2**
Double/pb: **$95**
Suites: **$125**

Open: **All year**
Breakfast: **Full**
Pets: **No**
Children: **No**
Smoking: **Permitted**
Social Drinking: **Permitted**
Airport/Station Pickup: **Yes**

This cedar chalet is located on the banks of the McKenzie River. The suite overlooks the river and a secluded Japanese garden, and features a sunken bath. The other has a fish bowl shower and a view of a 100-year-old apple tree. Relax in the living room with its wraparound seating and massive stone fireplace. One of the walls is made entirely of glass with sliding doors that lead to a terrace that faces the river. A multicourse breakfast is served there on balmy days. Waterfalls, trout fishing, white-water rafting, and skiing are all nearby.

## Pine Meadow Inn B&B ○
**1000 CROW ROAD, MERLIN, OREGON 97532**

Tel: **(503) 471-6277; (800) 554-0806**
Hosts: **Maloy and Nancy Murdock**
Location: **10 mi. NW of Grants Pass**
No. of Rooms: **4**
No. of Private Baths: **4**
Double/pb: **$80–$110**
Open: **All year**

Reduced Rates: **10% weekly**
Breakfast: **Full**
Pets: **No**
Children: **Welcome, over 8**
Smoking: **No**
Social Drinking: **Permitted**
Minimum Stay: **No**

Secluded on nine acres of meadow and woods, Pine Meadow Inn B&B is styled after Midwestern farmhouses, and features a wraparound porch with comfortable wicker furniture. There are many exciting choices of things to do: white-water rafting, walking, biking, jogging, visiting the California redwoods, Crater Lake, the Shakespeare Festival, or historic Jacksonville. When your day is complete you might want to read a book from the library in the quiet sitting room, which has a fireplace. Or take a dip in the hot tub. All guest rooms have queen-size beds with private baths, window seat or sitting area. Awake in the morning to a healthful gourmet breakfast.

## Secluded B&B ✪

**19719 NORTHEAST WILLIAMSON ROAD, NEWBERG, OREGON 97132**

| | |
|---|---|
| Tel: **(503) 538-2635** | Single/sb: **$50** |
| Best Time to Call: **8 AM** | Open: **All year** |
| Hosts: **Del and Durell Belanger** | Breakfast: **Full** |
| Location: **27 mi. SW of Portland** | Pets: **No** |
| No. of Rooms: **2** | Children: **Welcome, under 1 and** |
| No. of Private Baths: **1** | **over 6** |
| Max. No. Sharing Bath: **4** | Smoking: **No** |
| Double/pb: **$60** | Social Drinking: **No** |
| Double/sb: **$50** | |

A rustic home with a gambrel roof and sunny decks, this B&B is secluded, but not isolated. Set on 10 wooded acres, it is near several

notable wineries. George Fox College is also in the area. Your hosts' hobbies include gardening, cooking, and carpentry; Durell made the stained-glass windows that accent the house. The mouth-watering breakfasts might include fresh shrimp omelettes, Grand Marnier French toast, or Dutch babies swathed in apple-huckleberry sauce and whipped cream, accompanied by juice, fruit, and coffee or tea.

## Beckley House B&B ✪
**338 SOUTHEAST 2ND STREET, P.O. BOX 198, OAKLAND, OREGON 97462**

Tel: **(503) 459-9320**
Hosts: **Rich and Karen Neuharth**
Location: **60 mi. S of Eugene**
No. of Rooms: **2**
No. of Private Baths: **2**
Double/pb: **$60–$85**
Open: **All year**

Reduced Rates: **15% Nov.–Mar., 10% seniors**
Breakfast: **Full**
Pets: **Sometimes**
Children: **Welcome**
Smoking: **No**
Social Drinking: **Permitted**

The Beckley House is a two-story Classic Revival Victorian home, listed on the Historic Register. Reflecting a nostalgic era, this home is comfortably furnished in period-style antiques. Oakland is a quiet peaceful town in the historic district. It was the second town settled in Oregon and organized the state's first school district. Walk three blocks to Tolly's restaurant downtown. Enjoy a carriage ride, wine tours or visit Rochester Covered Bridge and the Umpqua River. Rich is a software engineer and consultant, Karen manages the bed and breakfast and runs a catering business.

## Inn of the Oregon Trail ✪
### 416 SOUTH MCLOUGHLIN, OREGON CITY, OREGON 97045

| | |
|---|---|
| Tel: **(503) 656-2089** | Open: **All year** |
| Best Time to Call: **8 AM–9 PM** | Breakfast: **Full** |
| Hosts: **Mary and Tom DeHaven** | Credit Cards: **MC, VISA** |
| Location: **13 mi. SE of Portland** | Pets: **No** |
| No. of Rooms: **4** | Children: **Welcome, over 12** |
| No. of Private Baths: **4** | Smoking: **No** |
| Double/pb: **$55–$85** | Social Drinking: **Permitted** |
| Suites: **$75–$85** | |

A superb Gothic Revival home built in 1867 by a Willamette River captain, Inn of the Oregon Trail is listed on the National Register of Historic Places. In fact, this Oregon City neighborhood is filled with distinctive buildings and museums—ask your hosts to recommend walking and driving tours. You'll have plenty of energy for sightseeing after one of Tom's ample breakfasts of juice, coffee, eggs, pancakes, or French toast.

## Home by the Sea Bed & Breakfast
### 444 JACKSON STREET, PORT ORFORD, OREGON 97465-0606

| | |
|---|---|
| Tel: **(503) 332-2855** | Open: **All year** |
| Best Time to Call: **8 AM–8 PM** | Breakfast: **Full** |
| Hosts: **Alan and Brenda Mitchell** | Credit Cards: **MC, VISA** |
| Location: **54 mi. N of California border** | Pets: **No** |
| No. of Rooms: **2** | Children: **No** |
| No. of Private Baths: **2** | Smoking: **No** |
| Double/pb: **$75–$85** | Social Drinking: **Permitted** |
| Suite: **$85; sleeps 2** | |

Alan and Brenda built this contemporary home overlooking a stretch of the Oregon coast that will take your breath away. Both guest rooms have queen Oregon myrtlewood beds and cable TV. It's a short walk to restaurants, public beaches, historic Battle Rock Park, and the town's harbor, the home port of Oregon's only crane-launched commercial fishing fleet.

## Oak Ridge Bed & Breakfast ✪
### 3010 WEST MILITARY ROAD, ROSEBURG, OREGON 97470

| | |
|---|---|
| Tel: **(503) 672-2168; (800) 428-2428** | No. of Rooms: **2** |
| Best Time to Call: **AM** | No. of Private Baths: **2** |
| Hosts: **Bob and Nita Butcher** | Double p/b: **$55** |
| Location: **69 mi. S of Eugene** | Open: **All year** |

Breakfast: **Full**  
Pets: **No**  
Children: **No**

Smoking: **No**  
Social Drinking: **Permitted**

Tall windows, a spiral staircase, and Indian crafts highlight the living room of this cedar mansard house shaded by native oaks. Each of the airy corner bedrooms has a ceiling fan, chairs, and a comfortable, handcrafted bed. You'll awaken to coffee brought to your door. Follow it up with Continental breakfast in your room, or a heartier, full-course meal in the dining area. Even the jam is homemade, from fruit your hosts picked themselves. Wineries, rafting, fishing, and Wildlife Safari number among the local attractions. Originally a schoolteacher, Bob spent twenty-five years with the National Park Service, working from Puerto Rico to Alaska; Nita is a full-time homemaker.

## Anderson's Boarding House Bed & Breakfast ○
**208 NORTH HOLLADAY DRIVE, SEASIDE, OREGON 97138**

Tel: **(503) 738-9055; (800) 995-4013**  
Host: **Barb Edwards**  
Location: **½ mi. from Rte. 101**  
No. of Rooms: **6**  
No. of Private Baths: **6**  
Double/pb: **$70–$80**  
Single/pb: **$65–$75**  
Guest Cottage: **$110; sleeps 6, $600 weekly**

Open: **All year**  
Reduced Rates: **Available**  
Breakfast: **Full**  
Credit Cards: **MC, VISA**  
Pets: **No**  
Children: **Welcome**  
Smoking: **No**  
Social Drinking: **Permitted**  
Airport/Station Pickup: **Yes**

Located on the banks of the Necanicum River, this rustic Victorian was built as a private residence in 1898. During World War I, the house became a boarding home. After an extensive renovation, the wood walls and beamed ceilings have been restored to their original charm. Guest rooms feature brass or white iron beds, down quilts, family heirlooms, wicker, and wood. Claw-footed tubs, window seats, antiques, and a picture of grandma make you feel as if this house is your own. A fire is often burning in the fir-paneled parlor, and an old melody sounds just right on the old-fashioned Victrola. A 100-year-old guest cottage with wood paneling, country furnishings, bedroom, loft, and river view is also available. Breakfast specialties such as cheese-and-egg strata, orange French toast, and blueberry scones are served in the dining room or outside on the wraparound porch. The house is just four blocks from the ocean and two blocks from downtown.

## Horncroft ○
**42156 KINGSTON LYONS DRIVE, STAYTON, OREGON 97383**

Tel: **(503) 769-6287**  
Hosts: **Dorothea and Kenneth Horn**  
Location: **17 mi. E of Salem**

No. of Rooms: **3**  
No. of Private Baths: **1**  
Max. No. Sharing Bath: **4**

| | |
|---|---|
| Double/pb: **$45** | Breakfast: **Full** |
| Single/pb: **$40** | Pets: **No** |
| Double/sb: **$35** | Children: **Sometimes** |
| Single/sb: **$30** | Smoking: **No** |
| Open: **All year** | Social Drinking: **Permitted** |

This lovely home is situated in the foothills of the Cascade Mountains on the edge of Willamette Valley. In summer, swim in the heated pool or hike on one of the scenic nature paths. The area is dotted with farms, and the valley is abundant in fruits, berries, and vegetables. Willamette and Oregon State Universities are nearby. The Mount Jefferson Wilderness hiking area is an hour away. A guest comments, "The hospitality and breakfasts were top-notch!"

## Old Welches Inn ✪
### 26401 EAST WELCHES ROAD, WELCHES, OREGON 97067

| | |
|---|---|
| Tel: **(503) 622-3754** | Open: **All year** |
| Best Time to Call: **After 6 PM** | Breakfast: **Full** |
| Hosts: **Judith and Ted Mondun** | Credit Cards: **AMEX, MC, VISA** |
| Location: **50 mi. E of Portland** | Pets: **Dogs welcome** |
| No. of Rooms: **3** | Children: **Welcome, over 12** |
| Max. No. Sharing Bath: **3** | Smoking: **No** |
| Double/sb: **$79.50–$94.50** | Social Drinking: **Permitted** |
| Cottage: **$100–$175; sleeps 5** | Minimum Stay: **2 nights holidays** |

Built as a resort in the late 19th century, the Old Welches Inn is a large white Colonial with blue shutters. The house stands on the edge of the Mt. Hood wilderness area, crisscrossed by miles of hiking and ski trails. Fishermen may carry poles to the back of the B&B property, where they can drop lines in the Salmon River. And just across the road, golfers will find that 27 holes await. You'll be ready for action after a full, Southern-style breakfast, highlighted by home-baked muffins, biscuits, and breads.

## The Carriage House ✪
### 515 SOUTH PACIFIC HIGHWAY, WOODBURN, OREGON 97071

| | |
|---|---|
| Tel: **(503) 982-6321** | Open: **All year** |
| Best Time to Call: **Before 9 AM; after 6 PM** | Breakfast: **Full** |
| | Credit Cards: **MC, VISA** |
| Hosts: **Lawrence and Marilyn Paradis** | Pets: **Sometimes** |
| Location: **30 mi. S of Portland** | Children: **Welcome** |
| No. of Rooms: **2** | Smoking: **No** |
| Max. No. Sharing Bath: **4** | Social Drinking: **Permitted** |
| Double/sb: **$50** | Airport/Station Pickup: **Yes** |
| Single/sb: **$45** | Foreign Languages: **French** |

The Carriage House is a 1906 Victorian known for its peaceful country elegance. Completely restored, it is furnished with family treasures and heirloom quilts. Lawrence and Marilyn keep horses and an antique buggy in a carriage house next to the inn. This is an excellent location for visiting the Enchanted Forest, the Oregon State Fair, the Octoberfest in Mt. Angel, the Bach Festival, historic Champoeg, and numerous antique shops and wineries.

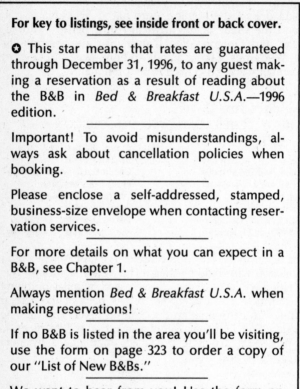

**For key to listings, see inside front or back cover.**

✪ This star means that rates are guaranteed through December 31, 1996, to any guest making a reservation as a result of reading about the B&B in *Bed & Breakfast U.S.A.*—1996 edition.

Important! To avoid misunderstandings, always ask about cancellation policies when booking.

Please enclose a self-addressed, stamped, business-size envelope when contacting reservation services.

For more details on what you can expect in a B&B, see Chapter 1.

Always mention *Bed & Breakfast U.S.A.* when making reservations!

If no B&B is listed in the area you'll be visiting, use the form on page 323 to order a copy of our "List of New B&Bs."

We want to hear from you! Use the form on page 325.

# SOUTH DAKOTA

- • Webster
- • Belle Fourche
- • Spearfish
- • Whitewood
- Lead •
- • Rapid City
- • Custer
- • Canova

## Candlelight B&B ✪
### 819 5TH AVENUE, BELLE FOURCHE, SOUTH DAKOTA 57717

Tel: (605) 892-4568
Best Time to Call: **Afternoon**
Hosts: **Delbert, Lorene, and Beth Goodwin**
Location: **60 mi. NW of Rapid City**
No. of Rooms: **4**
No. of Private Baths: **1**
Max. No. Sharing Bath: **4**
Double/pb: **$60**
Double/sb: **$60**

Single/sb: **$50**
Open: **Memorial Day weekend–Labor Day weekend; special arrangement**
Breakfast: **Full**
Credit Cards: **MC, VISA**
Pets: **No**
Children: **Welcome, over 5**
Smoking: **No**
Social Drinking: **Permitted**
Minimum Stay: **2 nights special events**

This cozy Victorian home, located at the gateway to the Black Hills, greets you with a friendly welcome. Guest rooms are tastefully decorated with personal touches, creating a homelike atmosphere. Candlelight breakfasts are full and hearty, featuring farm-fresh bacon and sausage, egg dishes, warm scones, muffins, specialty breads, custards, fresh fruits, or yogurts. Upon your arrival, refreshments are served, including fresh-brewed iced tea, cookies and bars. Devil's Tower, the Passion Play, Spearfish Canyon, and historic Deadwood are among the nearby attractions. Candlelight lies within walking distance of Belle Fourche's historic Main Street, the Round-up Grounds and softball fields, and is conveniently located on Highway 85.

## Skoglund Farm ✪
**CANOVA, SOUTH DAKOTA 57321**

| | |
|---|---|
| Tel: **(605) 247-3445** | Reduced Rates: **Under 18** |
| Best Time to Call: **Early mornings;** | Breakfast: **Full** |
| **evenings** | Other Meals: **Dinner included** |
| Hosts: **Alden and Delores Skoglund** | Pets: **Welcome** |
| Location: **12 miles from I-90** | Children: **Welcome (crib)** |
| No. of Rooms: **5** | Smoking: **Permitted** |
| Max. No. Sharing Bath: **3** | Social Drinking: **Permitted** |
| Single/sb: **$30** | Airport/Station Pickup: **Yes** |
| Open: **All year** | |

This is a working farm where the emphasis is on the simple, good life. It is a welcome escape from urban living. You may, if you wish, help with the farm chores, or just watch everyone else work; the family raises cattle, fowl, and peacocks. You are welcome to use the laundry facilities or play the piano. The coffeepot is always on.

## Custer Mansion Bed & Breakfast ✪
**35 CENTENNIAL DRIVE, CUSTER, SOUTH DAKOTA 57730**

| | |
|---|---|
| Tel: **(605) 673-3333** | Breakfast: **Full** |
| Hosts: **Millard and Carole Seaman** | Pets: **No** |
| Location: **42 mi. W of Rapid City** | Children: **Welcome** |
| No. of Rooms: **6** | Smoking: **No** |
| No. of Private Baths: **4** | Social Drinking: **No** |
| Max. No. Sharing Bath: **4** | Minimum Stay: **2 nights, holidays,** |
| Double/pb: **$60–$90** | **peak season** |
| Double/sb: **$50–$55** | Foreign Languages: **Spanish** |
| Open: **All year** | |
| Reduced Rates: **Off-season, extended** | |
| **stays** | |

Built in 1891, this Victorian Gothic home is listed on the National Register of Historic Places. The interior blends Victorian elegance, country charm, and Western hospitality. Guests enjoy clean quiet accommodations and a delicious home-cooked breakfast. Custer Mansion is centrally located to all Black Hills attractions including Mt. Rushmore, Custer State Park, Crazy Horse Memorial and much more.

# Cheyenne Crossing B&B ✪
## HC 37, BOX 1220, LEAD, SOUTH DAKOTA 57754

| | |
|---|---|
| Tel: **(605) 584-3510, 584-2636** | Reduced Rates: **Families; groups** |
| Hosts: **Jim and Bonnie LeMar** | Breakfast: **Full** |
| Location: **Junction Hwys. 85 and 14A** | Other Meals: **Available** |
| No. of Rooms: **3** | Credit Cards: **DISC, MC, VISA** |
| Max. No. Sharing Bath: **4** | Pets: **No** |
| Double /pb: **$85** | Children: **Welcome, over 6** |
| Double/sb: **$69** | Smoking: **No** |
| Single/sb: **$59** | Social Drinking: **Permitted** |
| Open: **All year** | |

This two-story frame building with its facade of rough-sawed pine is situated in the heart of Spearfish Canyon. The main floor houses a typical country general store and cafe; the guest quarters are upstairs. From 1876 to 1885 the original building was a stop for the Deadwood–Cheyenne stagecoach. After it burned down in 1960, the present building was built to replace it. Jim and Bonnie will be delighted to map out special trips tailored to your interests. Spend the day visiting Mt. Rushmore and Crazy Horse Monument, pan for gold, hike, or fish for trout on Spearfish Creek, which flows behind the store. It's also close to the Black Hills Passion Play. Sourdough pancakes are a frequent breakfast treat. A new two-bedroom creekside cabin with fireplace and whirlpool bath is now available.

# Abend Haus Cottage & Audrie's Cranbury Corner Bed & Breakfast ✪
## 23029 THUNDERHEAD FALLS ROAD, RAPID CITY, SOUTH DAKOTA 57702-8524

| | |
|---|---|
| Tel: **(605) 342-7788** | Suites: **$85** |
| Best Time to Call: **9 AM–9 PM MST** | Open: **All year** |
| Hosts: **Hank and Audrie Kuhnhauser** | Breakfast: **Full** |
| Location: **¼ mi. from Hwy. 44** | Pets: **No** |
| No. of Rooms: **6** | Children: **No** |
| No. of Private Baths: **6** | Smoking: **No** |
| Double/pb: **$85** | Social Drinking: **Permitted** |
| Guest Cottage: **$85–$125** | |

At this country home and five-acre estate in a secluded Black Hills setting just 30 miles from Mt. Rushmore and 7 miles from Rapid City, you can experience charm and old-world hospitality. There are free trout fishing, biking, and hiking on the property, which is surrounded by thousands of acres of national forest land. Each suite has a private entrance, bath, hot tub, patio, cable TV, and refrigerator. Full breakfasts are served.

# Cliff Creek Bed & Breakfast ✪
## R.R. 8, BOX 975, RAPID CITY, SOUTH DAKOTA 57702

Tel: **(605) 399-9970**
Hosts: **Dave and Judy Knecht**
Location: **10 mi. W of Rapid City**
No. of Rooms: **3**
No. of Private Baths: **3**
Double/pb: **$85**
Guest Cottage: **$85; sleeps 3**

Suite: **$85**
Open: **May 1–Labor Day**
Breakfast: **Full**
Pets: **No**
Children: **Welcome, over 10**
Smoking: **No**
Social Drinking: **Permitted**

Experience country pleasures in a spectacular setting: this B&B is located on Rapid Creek, below a slate cliff that crosses the stream. Spend the day watching as bald eagles soar overhead, deer graze in the meadow, ducks splash in the water, and wild birds dine at the feeders. Fish from your hosts' barbecue-equipped deck or practice your putting stroke on their green. From this Black Hills location, Mt. Rushmore, Deadwood, and Pactola Lake are easily accessible, and recreational options include hiking, biking, hunting, boating, golfing, skiing, and gambling. The main house offers two accommodations. The guest room has a balcony overlooking the stream, a queen-size bed, and cable TV; the suite has a king-size bed and two twin beds. There is also a separate guest cottage.

# Bed and Breakfast Domivara ○
## 2760 DOMIVARA ROAD, RAPID CITY, SOUTH DAKOTA 57702-6008

Tel: **(605) 574-4207**
Best Time to Call: **Mornings; 6–8 PM**
Host: **Betty Blount**
Location: **26 mi. SW of Rapid City**
No. of Rooms: **4**
No. of Private Baths: **4**
Double/pb: **$70–$75**
Single/pb: **$60–$65**

Open: **All year**
Breakfast: **Full**
Pets: **Sometimes**
Children: **Welcome**
Smoking: **No**
Social Drinking: **Permitted**
Minimum Stay: **2 nights**

Enjoy Western hospitality in a unique log home located in the pictur-esque Black Hills of South Dakota. The homey wood interior is decorated with comfortable antiques and accents of stained glass. A large picture window overlooks the countryside where you may see an occasional wild turkey or deer. Betty Blount offers complimentary snacks served with coffee. She prepares a variety of special breakfast dishes including sourdough pancakes, egg soufflés, fresh trout, and homemade blueberry muffins. There are good restaurants nearby. Domivara is conveniently located just 20 minutes from Mt. Rushmore and the Crazy Horse memorial.

# Eighth Street Inn ○
## 735 EIGHTH STREET, SPEARFISH, SOUTH DAKOTA 57783

Tel: **(605) 642-9812; (800) 642-9812**
Hosts: **Sandy and Brad Young**
Location: **44 mi. W of Rapid City**
No. of Rooms: **5**
No. of Private Baths: **2**
Max. No. Sharing Bath: **4**
Double/pb: **$65–$85**
Double/sb: **$55–$65**
Open: **All year**

Reduced Rates: **Available**
Breakfast: **Full**
Other Meals: **Available**
Credit Cards: **MC, VISA**
Pets: **Sometimes**
Children: **Welcome**
Smoking: **No**
Social Drinking: **Permitted**
Airport/Station Pickup: **Yes**

A Queen Anne–style home (circa 1900) listed on the National Register of Historic Places, the Inn is filled with family heirlooms that possess character as well as beauty. Each guest room has special features like bay windows, brass beds, and cozy comforters. The original fir woodwork and open staircase are rare finds. From the B&B's location three blocks from downtown, guests can enjoy shopping, fine dining, antique shops, parks, and the historic fish hatchery. Athletic types can go hiking, nordic and alpine skiing, and snowmobiling. Movie fans will want to visit nearby Spearfish Canyon, site of the winter scene in *Dances with Wolves*. As avid hikers, cyclists and skiers, Sandy and Brad are eager to help guests plan outdoor adventures. Moreover, Sandy promises to prepare a healthful and mouthwatering breakfast to suit any appetite.

## Lakeside Farm ✪
### RR 2, BOX 52, WEBSTER, SOUTH DAKOTA 57274

| | |
|---|---|
| Tel: **(605) 486-4430** | Single/sb: **$30** |
| Hosts: **Joy and Glenn Hagen** | Open: **All year** |
| Location: **60 mi. E of Aberdeen on** | Breakfast: **Full** |
| **Hwy. 12** | Pets: **No** |
| No. of Rooms: **2** | Children: **Welcome** |
| Maximum No. Sharing Bath: **4** | Smoking: **No** |
| Double/sb: **$40** | Social Drinking: **No** |

This 750-acre farm where Joy and Glenn raise oats and corn is located in the Lake Region where recreational activities abound. You are certain to be comfortable in their farmhouse, built in 1970 and furnished in a simple, informal style. You will awaken to the delicious aroma of Joy's heavenly cinnamon rolls or bread and enjoy breakfast served on the enclosed porch. Nearby attractions include Fort Sisseton and the June festival that recounts Sam Brown's historic ride. You will also enjoy the Blue Dog fish hatchery and the Game Reserve. Dakotah, Inc., manufacturers of linens and wall hangings, is located in Webster. They have an outlet shop where great buys may be found.

## Rockinghorse Bed & Breakfast ✪
### RR 1, BOX 133, WHITEWOOD, SOUTH DAKOTA 57793

| | |
|---|---|
| Tel: **(605) 269-2625** | Reduced Rates: **Available** |
| Hosts: **Sharleen and Jerry Bergum** | Breakfast: **Full** |
| Location: **30 mi. NW of Rapid City** | Credit Cards: **MC, VISA** |
| No. of Rooms: **3** | Pets: **Sometimes** |
| No. of Private Baths: **3** | Children: **Welcome** |
| Double/pb: **$45–$65** | Smoking: **No** |
| Guest Cottage: **$100–$250** | Social Drinking: **No** |
| Open: **All year** | Airport/Station Pickup: **Yes** |

A cedar clapboard–sided house, built in 1914 to accommodate local timber teams, Rockinghorse was moved from its first site by Jerry and Sharleen, who have lovingly restored the interior. Handsome wood floors, columns, and trims grace the living and dining areas, and the original stairway is still usable. Antiques, lace and country delights complement the homey atmosphere. Rockinghorse is situated at the base of the rustic Black Hills, where deer graze in nearby fields and wild turkeys strut across the valley below the house. Nature walks and panoramic views will appeal to the artist/photographer. Domestic animals abound—after a rooster's crow awakens you, you may pet a bunny in the petting zoo, visit the horses, take a buggy ride, or watch the art of wool spinning.

# UTAH

Salt Lake City •
• Sandy

Saint George •  • Springdale
• Bluff

## Bluff Bed and Breakfast ○
### BOX 158, BLUFF, UTAH 84512

Tel: **(801) 672-2220**
Host: **Rosalie Goldman**
Location: **On Rtes. 163 and 191**
No. of Rooms: **2**
No. of Private Baths: **2**
Double/pb: **$70–$75**
Single/pb: **$65–$70**
Open: **All year**

Breakfast: **Full**
Other Meals: **Available**
Pets: **No**
Children: **Welcome**
Smoking: **No**
Social Drinking: **Permitted**
Airport/Station Pickup: **Yes**
Foreign Languages: **French**

Close to the Four Corners (the junction of Colorado, New Mexico, Arizona, and Utah), this Frank Lloyd Wright–style home is nestled among huge boulders at the foot of redrock cliffs, near the San Juan River. On the main highway between Grand Canyon and Mesa Verde, it is secluded on seventeen desert acres. Across the river is the Navajo Reservation, and prehistoric ruins have been discovered nearby. Simply furnished, it is bright and tidy; large picture windows frame four different spectacular views. Rosalie prepares your breakfast of choice, from oatmeal to steak.

## Seven Wives Inn
### 217 NORTH 100 WEST, ST. GEORGE, UTAH 84770

| | |
|---|---|
| Tel: **(801) 628-3737; (800) 600-3737** | Suites: **$125** |
| Best Time to Call: **After 9 AM** | Open: **All year** |
| Hosts: **Jay and Donna Curtis, and** | Reduced Rates: **Special business rate** |
| **Alison and Jon Bowcutt** | **(single occupancy) $45** |
| Location: **125 mi. NE of Las Vegas** | Breakfast: **Full** |
| No. of Rooms: **12** | Credit Cards: **AMEX, DC, MC, VISA** |
| No. of Private Baths: **12** | Children: **By arrangement** |
| Double/pb: **$55–$80** | Smoking: **No** |
| Single/pb: **$55–$80** | Social Drinking: **Permitted** |

This delightful inn is featured on the walking tour of St. George; it is just across from the Brigham Young home and two blocks from the historic Washington County Court House. Your hosts offer traditional Western hospitality. Their home is decorated with antiques collected in America and Europe. Bedrooms are named after some of the seven wives of Donna's polygamous great-grandfather. A gourmet breakfast is served in the elegant dining room that will give you a hint of the past. St. George is located near Zion and Bryce national parks, boasts eight golf courses, and is noted for its mild winters. Dixie College is nearby. There's a swimming pool for your pleasure.

## Anton Boxrud Bed & Breakfast Inn ✪
### 57 SOUTH 600 EAST, SALT LAKE CITY, UTAH 84102

| | |
|---|---|
| Tel: **(801) 363-8035; (800) 524-5511** | Double/sb: **$55–$69** |
| Best Time to Call: **5 PM–9 PM** | Single/sb: **$45–$55** |
| Hosts: **C. Keith Lewis and Mark A.** | Suites: **$99–$119** |
| **Brown** | Open: **All year** |
| Location: **5 blocks from downtown** | Breakfast: **Full** |
| No. of Rooms: **7** | Credit Cards: **AMEX, MC, VISA** |
| No. of Private Baths: **3** | Pets: **No** |
| Max. No. Sharing Bath: **4** | Children: **Welcome** |
| Double/pb: **$79–$89** | Smoking: **No** |
| Single/pb: **$79–$89** | Social Drinking: **Permitted** |

The Anton Boxrud Bed & Breakfast is a charming, restored Victorian inn, located in a historic district of Salt Lake City, just half a block from the governor's mansion. A hearty breakfast and you're on your way to Utah's many cultural events and world-renowned outdoor activities. Within walking distance, you will find three large shopping malls, the world-famous Mormon Temple Square and Genealogical Library, museums, galleries, restaurants, and more. During the summer months, join your hosts on the veranda for evening hors d'oeuvres and great conversation.

## Alta Hills Farm ✪
**10852 SOUTH 20TH EAST SANDY, SANDY, UTAH 84092**

| | |
|---|---|
| Tel: **(801) 571-1712; (800) 571-1713** | Reduced Rates: **10% weekly, seniors** |
| Hosts: **Blaine and Diane Knight** | Breakfast: **Continental** |
| Location: **15 mi. S of Salt Lake** | Credit Cards: **DISC, MC, VISA** |
| No. of Rooms: **4** | Pets: **Yes** |
| No. of Private Baths: **2** | Children: **Welcome** |
| Max. No. Sharing Bath: **4** | Smoking: **No** |
| Double/pb: **$78** | Social Drinking: **No** |
| Double/sb: **$58** | Airport/Station Pickup: **Yes** |
| Open: **Sept. 1–May 31** | |

This B&B is nestled at the base of the Rocky Mountains fifteen minutes from the Alta and Snow Bird ski resorts. Alta Hills Farm has been an English Huntseat Equestrian Center for the past twenty years. In the summer the Knights run a riding camp for children of all ages. Their home has a warm, spacious English country style. Every evening, guests can relax with hot apple cider in a private living room with a fireplace. You are also invited to join the Knights downstairs. Blaine and Diane love kids and welcome families who come to ski or to enjoy beautiful Salt Lake.

## O'Toole's Under the Eaves
**P.O. BOX 29, 980 ZION PARK BOULEVARD, SPRINGDALE, UTAH 84767**

| | |
|---|---|
| Tel: **(801) 772-3457** | Suites: **$125** |
| Hosts: **Rick and Michelle O'Toole** | Open: **All year** |
| Location: **45 mi. E of St. George** | Reduced Rates: **Available** |
| No. of Rooms: **6** | Breakfast: **Full** |
| No. of Private Baths: **4** | Credit Cards: **MC, VISA** |
| Max. No. Sharing Bath: **4** | Pets: **No** |
| Double/pb: **$75** | Children: **By arrangement** |
| Single/pb: **$65** | Smoking: **No** |
| Double/sb: **$60** | Social Drinking: **Permitted** |
| Single/sb: **$50** | |

Under the Eaves is a historic stone-and-stucco cottage located at the gate of Zion National Park. Constructed of massive sandstone blocks from the canyon, the guest house has served as a landmark for visitors to Zion for more than 50 years. Choose from two antique-filled bedrooms or a luxurious suite. The garden cottage dates from the 1920s and has two nonconnecting private bedrooms and baths.

# WASHINGTON

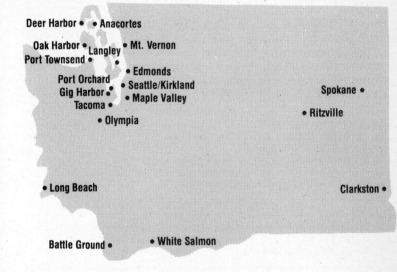

Deer Harbor • • Anacortes
Oak Harbor • Langley • Mt. Vernon
Port Townsend •
• Edmonds
Port Orchard • Seattle/Kirkland
Gig Harbor • • Maple Valley
Tacoma •
• Olympia
Spokane •
• Ritzville
• Long Beach
Clarkston •
Battle Ground • • White Salmon

## Pacific Bed & Breakfast Agency ✪
**701 NORTHWEST 60TH STREET, SEATTLE, WASHINGTON 98107**

Tel: **(206) 784-0539**; fax: **(206) 782-4036**
Best Time to Call: **9 AM–5 PM**
Coordinator: **Irmgard Castleberry**
States/Regions Covered: **Statewide; Canada—Vancouver, Victoria, British Columbia**

Descriptive Directory: **$5**
Rates (Single/Double):
  Modest:  **$45 / $45**
  Average: **$55 / $85**
  Luxury:  **$85 / $200**
Credit Cards: **AMEX, MC, VISA**
Minimum Stay: **2 nights in Seattle**

Victorians, contemporaries, island cottages, waterfront houses, and private suites with full kitchens are available. Most are close to downtown areas, near bus lines, in fine residential neighborhoods, or within walking distance of a beach. Many extras are included, such as pickup service, free use of laundry facilities, guided tours and more. The University of Washington and the University of Puget Sound are nearby. There is a $5 surcharge for one-night stays.

## A Burrow's Bay B&B
### 4911 MACBETH DRIVE, ANACORTES, WASHINGTON 98221

Tel: **(360) 293-4792**
Hosts: **Beverly and Winfred Stocker**
Location: **92 mi. N of Seattle**
Suites: **$95; sleep 2–4**
Open: **All year**
Breakfast: **Continental, plus**

Credit Cards: **MC, VISA**
Pets: **Sometimes**
Children: **Welcome**
Smoking: **No**
Social Drinking: **Permitted**
Airport/Station Pickup: **Yes**

Enjoy sweeping views of the San Juan Islands from this lovely contemporary Northwest home. The guest suite consists of a large sitting room with a view and a comfortable bedroom with a blue-and-tan motif and wall-to-wall carpeting. You are sure to enjoy the privacy and relaxation of having your own private deck, fireplace, TV, and a separate entrance. Beverly and Winfred offer Continental-plus breakfast. They are located within walking distance of Washington Park, restaurants, and ferry rides to the nearby islands. Your hosts will be glad to provide touring advice for day trips to Victoria, B.C., Deception Pass, and Port Townsend.

## The Channel House
### 2902 OAKES AVENUE, ANACORTES, WASHINGTON 98221

Tel: **(360) 293-9382; (800) 238-4353;**
   **fax: (360) 299-9208**
Hosts: **Dennis and Patricia McIntyre**

Location: **65 mi. N of Seattle; 18 mi.**
   **W of I-5, Exit 230**
No. of Rooms: **6**

| | |
|---|---|
| No. of Private Baths: **6** | Credit Cards: **AMEX, DISC, MC, VISA** |
| Double/pb: **$69–$89** | Pets: **No** |
| Cottage: **$95** | Children: **Welcome, over 12** |
| Open: **All year** | Smoking: **No** |
| Breakfast: **Full** | Social Drinking: **Permitted** |

Built in 1902 by an Italian count, this three-story Victorian house has stained-glass windows, rare antiques, gracious ambience, and is in mint condition. The guest rooms have beautiful views of Puget Sound and the San Juan Islands. It's an ideal getaway for relaxing in the "cleanest corner of the country." Your hosts serve gourmet breakfasts in front of the fireplace. The communal hot tub is a treat after salmon fishing, tennis, or golf. And it's only minutes from the ferry for visiting Victoria, British Columbia.

## Sunset Beach B&B ○
**100 SUNSET BEACH, ANACORTES, WASHINGTON 98221**

| | |
|---|---|
| Tel: **(360) 293-5428; (800) 359-3448** | Open: **All year** |
| Best Time to Call: **8 AM–10 PM** | Reduced Rates: **Available** |
| Hosts: **Joann and Hal Harker** | Breakfast: **Full** |
| Location: **80 mi. NW of Seattle** | Credit Cards: **MC, VISA** |
| No. of Rooms: **3** | Pets: **No** |
| No. of Private Baths: **1** | Children: **Welcome, over 12** |
| Max. No. Sharing Bath: **4** | Smoking: **No** |
| Double/pb: **$79** | Social Drinking: **Permitted** |
| Double/sb: **$69** | |

This B&B is located on exciting Rosario Straits. Relax and enjoy the view of seven major islands from the decks, stroll on the beach or walk in the beautiful Washington Park, adjacent to the private gardens. Guests have private entry, bathrooms, and TV. Full breakfast is served. It's only five minutes to San Juan Ferries, fine restaurants, marina, and convenience store nearby. The sunsets are outstanding.

## Teddy Bear House ○
**18404 NORTHEAST 109 AVENUE, BATTLE GROUND, WASHINGTON 98604**

| | |
|---|---|
| Tel: **(206) 687-4328** | Open: **All year** |
| Hosts: **Bertha and Bill Dasher** | Breakfast: **Full** |
| Location: **20 mi. NE of Portland,** | Pets: **Sometimes** |
|    **Oregon** | Children: **Welcome, over 12** |
| No. of Rooms: **2** | Smoking: **No** |
| Max. No. Sharing Bath: **4** | Social Drinking: **No** |
| Double/sb: **$60** | |

Located in southwest Washington, the heart of the beautiful Pacific Northwest, this home can be your hub for exploring the Columbia

Gorge National Scenic Area, Mt. St. Helens National Monument and the historic Fort Vancouver Restoration. A working grist mill is a few miles away and the Lewis and Clark Railroad excursion train station is nearby. Teddy Bear House is named for Bertha's large collection of teddy bears and teddy bear memorabilia which are used in the decor throughout the house. You will enjoy this quiet secluded country home surrounded by flowers, lawn and large fir, dogwood and maple trees.

## The Cliff House ✪
**1227 WESTLAKE DRIVE, CLARKSTON, WASHINGTON 99403**

| | |
|---|---|
| Tel: **(509) 758-1267** | Breakfast: **Full** |
| Best Time to Call: **8 AM–8 PM** | Other Meals: **Available** |
| Hosts: **Doug and Sonia Smith** | Credit Cards: **MC, VISA** |
| Location: **8 mi. W of Clarkston** | Pets: **No** |
| No. of Rooms: **2** | Children: **Welcome, over 10** |
| No. of Private Baths: **2** | Smoking: **No** |
| Double/pb: **$70–$80** | Social Drinking: **Permitted** |
| Single/pb: **$65–$75** | Minimum Stay: **2 nights on weekends** |
| Open: **All year** | **and holidays** |
| Reduced Rates: **10% seniors; weekly** | Airport/Station Pickup: **Yes** |

Breathtaking is one of the best ways to describe The Cliff House's view of the Snake River, 500 feet below. Chief Timothy State Park, named for the Nez Percé Indian leader, lies along the river. Depending on the season, you may see geese, ducks, pheasant, deer, even an occasional bald eagle in the area. White-water rafting and jet boat trips along North America's deepest gorge, Hells Canyon, can be arranged. Your hosts set out different breakfasts each day; apple pancakes, waffles, and stratas are among the typical offerings.

## Palmer's Chart House ✪
**P.O. BOX 51, ORCAS ISLAND, DEER HARBOR, WASHINGTON 98243**

| | |
|---|---|
| Tel: **(360) 376-4231** | Open: **All year** |
| Hosts: **Majean and Don Palmer** | Breakfast: **Full** |
| Location: **50 mi. N of Seattle** | Pets: **No** |
| No. of Rooms: **2** | Children: **Welcome, over 10** |
| No. of Private Baths: **2** | Smoking: **No** |
| Double/pb: **$60–$70** | Social Drinking: **Permitted** |
| Single/pb: **$45–$50** | Foreign Languages: **Spanish** |

It's just an hour's ride on the Washington State ferry from Anacortes to Orcas Island. Seasoned travelers, Majean and Don know how to make your stay special. Each guest room has a private deck from which to view the harbor scene. Blueberry pancakes are a breakfast specialty. *Amante*, the 33-foot sloop, is available for sailing with Don, the skipper.

# Aardvark House **O**
**7219 LAKE BALLINGER WAY, EDMONDS, WASHINGTON 98026**

| | |
|---|---|
| Tel: **(206) 778-7866** | Single/sb: **$45** |
| Best Time to Call: **Anytime** | Open: **All year** |
| Hosts: **Jim and Arline Fahey** | Breakfast: **Full** |
| Location: **13 mi. N of Seattle** | Pets: **No** |
| No. of Rooms: **3** | Children: **Welcome (crib, high chair)** |
| Max. No. Sharing Bath: **4** | Smoking: **No** |
| Double/sb: **$55** | Social Drinking: **Permitted** |

This lovely lakefront home is within walking distance of a four-star restaurant and a city bus. Your hosts, a well-traveled retired Air Force couple, enjoy square dancing, outdoor living, gardening, and swimming. They'll be glad to take you on a cruise around Lake Ballinger on their barge. Breakfasts are varied, with home-grown raspberries, blueberries, and plums, and entrees like coddled eggs, omelettes, and the house specialty, sourdough waffles cooked outdoors over a wood fire.

# Driftwood Lane Bed and Breakfast **O**
**724 DRIFTWOOD LANE, EDMONDS, WASHINGTON 98020**

| | |
|---|---|
| Tel: **(206) 776-2686** | Single/pb: **$45** |
| Best Time to Call: **8–10 AM; 6–9 PM** | Open: **All year** |
| Hosts: **Ed and Lois Schaeffer** | Breakfast: **Continental** |
| Location: **15 mi. N of Seattle** | Pets: **No** |
| No. of Rooms: **1** | Children: **No** |
| No. of Private Baths: **1** | Smoking: **No** |
| Double/pb: **$50** | Social Drinking: **Permitted** |

This contemporary home in the heart of Edmonds reflects the relaxed life-style of the town, where you can take in Puget Sound and the snowcapped Olympic Mountains. Listen to the cry of seagulls and watch nearby ferryboats as you walk along the beach or savor the excellent cuisine in town. Or catch a lingering sunset from the Schaeffers' deck. Their newly decorated guest room has a queen-size bed and an adjoining private bath. Continental breakfast is highlighted by fresh fruits, applesauce, and preserves from your hosts' own trees.

# The Harrison House **O**
**210 SUNSET AVENUE, EDMONDS, WASHINGTON 98020**

| | |
|---|---|
| Tel: **(206) 776-4748** | Open: **All year** |
| Hosts: **Jody and Harve Harrison** | Breakfast: **Continental** |
| Location: **15 mi. N of Seattle** | Pets: **No** |
| No. of Rooms: **2** | Children: **No** |
| No. of Private Baths: **2** | Smoking: **No** |
| Double/pb: **$55–$65** | Social Drinking: **Permitted** |
| Single/pb: **$45–$55** | |

This new, informal, waterfront home has a sweeping view of Puget Sound and the Olympic Mountains. It is a block north of the ferry dock and two blocks from the center of this historic town. Many fine restaurants are within walking distance. Your spacious room has a private deck, TV, wet bar, telephone, and king-size bed. The University of Washington is nearby.

## Hudgens Haven ✪
### 9313 190 SOUTH WEST, EDMONDS, WASHINGTON 98020

| | |
|---|---|
| Tel: (206) 776-2202 | Single/pb: $45 |
| Best Time to Call: 4–8 PM | Open: All year |
| Hosts: Lorna and Edward Hudgens | Breakfast: Continental |
| Location: 20 min. from downtown Seattle | Pets: No |
| | Children: Welcome, over 10 |
| No. of Rooms: 1 | Smoking: No |
| No. of Private Baths: 1 | Social Drinking: Permitted |
| Double/pb: $50 | |

Hudgens Haven is located in a picture postcard town on Puget Sound. Windows on the west side boast a lovely view of the waterfront. The guest room is furnished with antiques as well as a queen-size bed, rocker, and plenty of drawer space. Edmonds, located 20 minutes from downtown Seattle, is a former lumber town with interesting old houses and an abundance of small shops and excellent restaurants. Continental breakfast is included in the room rate, but for an additional $3.50 per person, Lorna will gladly prepare her hearty woodsman's breakfast.

## The Maple Tree ✪
### 18313 OLYMPIC VIEW DRIVE, EDMONDS, WASHINGTON 98020

| | |
|---|---|
| Tel: (206) 774-8420 | Open: All year |
| Hosts: Marion and Hellon Wilkerson | Breakfast: Continental |
| Location: 15 mi. N of Seattle | Pets: No |
| No. of Rooms: 1 | Children: Welcome, over 5 |
| No. of Private Baths: 1 | Smoking: No |
| Double/pb: $50 | Social Drinking: Permitted |
| Single/pb: $45 | |

The Maple Tree is a beautifully restored older home with landscaped grounds. Located across the street from Puget Sound, it commands a stunning view of the Olympic Mountains. You're welcome to watch the activity on Puget Sound through the telescope in the solarium. Lounge on the brick patio or watch the sun set over the snowcapped mountains as you sip a glass of Washington State wine. Hellon and Marion enjoy having guests and exchanging travel experiences with them. Hellon loves to cook; both like to work in their rose garden.

# Olde Glencove Hotel ✪
**9418 GLENCOVE ROAD, GIG HARBOR, WASHINGTON 98329**

| | |
|---|---|
| Tel: **(206) 884-2835** | Open: **All year** |
| Hosts: **Lawrence and Luciann Nadeau** | Breakfast: **Full** |
| No. of Rooms: **4** | Pets: **No** |
| No. of Private Baths: **2** | Children: **Welcome** |
| Max. No. Sharing Bath: **4** | Smoking: **No** |
| Double/sb: **$65** | Social Drinking: **Permitted** |
| Suites: **$85** | |

Built in 1897, this historic landmark is a perfect location for honeymoons, anniversaries or any romantic weekend. Located on the water, the Olde Glencove Hotel offers guests a lovely view and a unique peaceful atmosphere. Lawrence and Luciann have painstakingly restored their lovely home to its authentic 1890s ambiance, complete with antiques of the period, wood-burning stoves, velvet chairs, stained glass windows and lamps. They want to share their home with experienced world travelers, interesting local folks and gentle people who appreciate antiques and fine accommodations.

# Peacock Hill Guest House ✪
**9520 PEACOCK HILL AVENUE, GIG HARBOR, WASHINGTON 98332**

| | |
|---|---|
| Tel: **(206) 858-3322** | Open: **All year** |
| Best Time to Call: **4–6 PM** | Breakfast: **Full** |
| Hosts: **Steven and Suzanne Savlov** | Pets: **No** |
| Location: **50 mi. S of Seattle** | Children: **Welcome, over 16** |
| No. of Rooms: **2** | Smoking: **No** |
| No. of Private Baths: **2** | Social Drinking: **Permitted** |
| Double/pb: **$80** | Minimum Stay: **2 nights** |
| Suites: **$95** | Station Pickup: **Yes** |

As you descend toward the quaint fishing village of Gig Harbor you take in a panoramic view of majestic Mount Rainier towering over ship masts, galleries, restaurants, and a potpourri of shops. This contemporary home sits on a wooded hilltop and has large picture windows that offer a postcard view of the harbor. In the morning you'll awaken to the aroma of a gourmet breakfast; it will give you the energy you need for a picturesque walk around the marina, or a drive to the nearby museums, gardens, zoo, and aquarium. The Scandinavian village of Poulsbo is 40 minutes away. It's a little bit farther to the Bainbridge Island Ferry, which takes you to Seattle's Pike Place Market where you can sample the sights and smells of a large open market. Summit Winter Sports Area is one hour away and has excellent skiing.

## Shumway Mansion
### 11410-99 PLACE NORTH EAST, KIRKLAND, WASHINGTON 98033

| | |
|---|---|
| Tel: **(206) 823-2303; fax: 822-0421** | Suites: **$95; sleeps 4** |
| Best Time to Call: **9 AM–7 PM** | Open: **All year** |
| Hosts: **Richard and Sallie Harris, and** | Breakfast: **Full** |
| **Julie and Marshall Blakemore** | Credit Cards: **AMEX, MC, VISA** |
| Location: **5 mi. NE of Seattle** | Pets: **No** |
| No. of Rooms: **8** | Children: **Welcome, over 12** |
| No. of Private Baths: **8** | Smoking: **No** |
| Double/pb: **$65–$82** | Social Drinking: **Permitted** |

This stately 24-room mansion, built in 1909, has a regal presence overlooking Lake Washington. The eight antique-filled guest rooms, including a charming corner suite, pair today's comforts with intricately carved pieces from yesteryear. Richard and Sallie will indulge your palate with variety-filled breakfasts that always feature homemade scones and jams. Within a short distance are water and snow recreation, an athletic club, downtown Seattle, and lots of shopping. After a busy day, return "home" and relax in front of the fire with a seasonal treat.

## Log Castle Bed & Breakfast ✪
### 3273 EAST SARATOGA ROAD, LANGLEY, WASHINGTON 98260

| | |
|---|---|
| Tel: **(360) 221-5483** | Breakfast: **Full** |
| Best Time to Call: **8 AM–9 PM** | Credit Cards: **MC, VISA** |
| Hosts: **Jack and Norma Metcalf** | Pets: **No** |
| Location: **40 mi. N of Seattle** | Children: **Welcome, over 11** |
| No. of Rooms: **4** | Smoking: **No** |
| No. of Private Baths: **4** | Social Drinking: **No** |
| Double/pb: **$90–$115** | Airport/Station Pickup: **Yes** |
| Open: **All year** | |

You don't have to build your castle on the sand on Whidbey Island, because one already awaits you. The imaginative design of this log lodge includes an eight-sided tower where any modern-day princess would feel at home. Taredo wood stairways, leaded and stained-glass motifs, and comfortable furnishings create a rustic yet sophisticated atmosphere. The four guest rooms all offer beautiful views of the surrounding mountains and water. Relax beside a large stone fireplace, take a rowboat ride or a long walk on the beach. Your hosts offer breads and cinnamon rolls right from the oven as part of a hearty breakfast served on a big, round, log table. Host Jack Metcalf is a state senator and also loves to entertain when he is not working at the legislature.

# Boreas Bed and Breakfast ✪

**607 NORTH BOULEVARD, P.O. BOX 1344,
LONG BEACH, WASHINGTON 98631**

Tel: **(360) 642-8069**
Best Time to Call: **9 AM–9 PM**
Hosts: **Sally Davis and Coleman White**
Location: **100 mi. W of Portland,
  Oregon**
No. of Rooms: **4**
No. of Private Baths: **2**
Max. No. Sharing Bath: **4**
Double/pb: **$85–$95**
Single/pb: **$75**
Double/sb: **$65–$75**
Single/sb: **$55–$65**

Open: **All year**
Reduced Rates: **Available**
Breakfast: **Full**
Credit Cards: **MC, VISA**
Pets: **Sometimes**
Children: **Welcome, 6 and over**
Smoking: **No**
Social Drinking: **Permitted**
Minimum Stay: **2 nights on weekends,
  May 15–Sept 15**
Airport/Station Pickup: **Yes**

Located 20 minutes north of the Columbia River, this 1920s beach home is remodeled in an eclectic style, mixing art and antiques with comfort and casualness. The house sits on the primary dunes with only an expanse of sand and grasses between it and the Pacific. A stone fireplace dominates the two large living rooms, which face the ocean, and a lovely path winds through the dunes to the surf. From this quiet residential area, it is still only a short walk to shopping, the boardwalk, and restaurants. The twenty-eight-mile stretch of wild Pacific coast is a hiking and cycling paradise complete with bird sanctuaries, lighthouses, and panoramic vistas. Your hosts enjoy travel and outdoor activities as well as sharing ideas and experiences with their guests.

# Maple Valley Bed & Breakfast ✪

**20020 SOUTHEAST 228, MAPLE VALLEY, WASHINGTON 98038**

Tel: **(206) 432-1409**
Best Time to Call: **9 AM–9 PM**
Hosts: **Jayne and Clarke Hurlbut**
Location: **26 mi. SE of Seattle**
No. of Rooms: **2**
Max. No. Sharing Bath: **4**
Double/sb: **$50–$65**
Single/sb: **$45–$60**

Open: **All year**
Reduced Rates: **Families**
Breakfast: **Full**
Pets: **Sometimes**
Children: **Welcome**
Smoking: **No**
Social Drinking: **Permitted**
Airport Pickup: **Yes**

After a good night's sleep in either of the B&B's guest rooms—one with a four-poster log bed and the other complete with a pink rosebud tea set—you'll come down to breakfast at a table that overlooks the lawn, the Hurlbuts' resident peacocks, and a wildlife pond teeming with a variety of Northwestern birds. If the morning is cool, you'll be warmed by a stone fireplace and you won't go away hungry after orange juice, lemon-blueberry muffins, a plate-size hootenanny pancake (served with whipped cream, strawberries, slivered almonds, and syrup), ham, sausage or bacon, fresh-ground coffee, tea, or hot chocolate.

## The White Swan Guest House ✪
**1388 MOORE ROAD, MT. VERNON, WASHINGTON 98273**

Tel: (360) 445-6805
Best Time to Call: **Mornings; evenings**
Host: **Peter Goldfarb**
Location: **60 mi. N of Seattle, 6 mi. SE of La Conner**
No. of Rooms: **3**
Max. No. Sharing Bath: **3**
Double/sb: **$75**
Single/sb: **$65**

Guest Cottage: **$125–$165; sleeps 4**
Open: **All year**
Reduced Rates: **Weekly in cottage**
Breakfast: **Continental**
Credit Cards: **MC, VISA**
Pets: **No**
Children: **Welcome (in cottage)**
Smoking: **No**
Social Drinking: **Permitted**

Surrounded by farmland and country roads, this storybook Victorian farmhouse, built in 1898, is painted crayon yellow and framed by English-style gardens. There's a wood stove in the parlor, wicker chairs on the porch, books for browsing, and a unique collection of old samplers. A platter of homemade chocolate chip cookies is waiting for you on the sideboard. It's only 6 miles to LaConner, a delightful fishing village brimful of interesting art galleries, shops, waterfront restaurants, and antique stores. The San Juan ferries are a half hour away.

## North Island B&B ✪
**1589 NORTH WEST BEACH ROAD, OAK HARBOR, WASHINGTON 98277**

Tel: (360) 675-7080
Best Time to Call: **Weekdays**
Hosts: **Jim and Maryvern Loomis**

Location: **65 mi. NW of Seattle**
No. of Rooms: **2**
No. of Private Baths: **2**

Double/pb: **$90**
Single/pb: **$85**
Open: **All year**
Breakfast: **Continental**
Credit Cards: **AMEX, DISC, MC, VISA**

Pets: **No**
Children: **No**
Smoking: **No**
Social Drinking: **No**

Ships of all kinds sail by as the sound of ocean waves lulls you to sleep at night at North Island B&B. Located on the west shore of historic and picturesque Whidbey Island, this is a newly-constructed home on 175 feet of private beach. Ample parking, king-size beds, and a fireplace combine to give guests the very best in accommodations. Guests have access to the beach, yard, and living room. Breakfast, served between 8:30 and 9:30 AM, features fresh fruit in season, juice, homemade breads and muffins, cereals, and freshly ground coffee or tea.

## Puget View Guesthouse ✪
**7924 61ST NORTHEAST, OLYMPIA, WASHINGTON 98516**

Tel: **(360) 459-1676**
Best Time to Call: **Evenings**
Hosts: **Dick and Barbara Yunker**
Location: **4½ mi. from I-5, Exit 111**
No. of Rooms: **1 cottage**
No. of Private Baths: **1**
Guest Cottage: **$89–$102; sleeps 4**
Open: **All year**

Reduced Rates: **Families; weekly; off-season**
Breakfast: **Continental, plus**
Credit Cards: **MC, VISA**
Pets: **Sometimes**
Children: **Welcome**
Smoking: **No**
Social Drinking: **Permitted**

This charming waterfront guest cottage is located next to Tolmie State Park and adjacent to Dick and Barbara's log home. The panoramic Puget Sound setting makes it a popular, romantic getaway. You are apt to discover simple pleasures such as beachcombing or birdwatching and activities such as kayaking or scuba diving. Your breakfast, an elegant repast, is brought to the cottage. You are welcome to use the beachside campfire for an evening cookout or to barbecue on your deck.

## "Reflections"—A Bed and Breakfast Inn ✪
**3878 REFLECTION LANE EAST, PORT ORCHARD, WASHINGTON 98366**

Tel: **(206) 871-5582**
Best Time to Call: **Anytime**
Hosts: **Jim and Cathy Hall**
Location: **15 mi. W of Seattle**
No. of Rooms: **4**
No. of Private Baths: **2**
Max. No. Sharing Bath: **4**
Double/pb: **$65**
Single/pb: **$65**
Double/sb: **$55**

Single/sb: **$55**
Suites: **$90**
Open: **All year**
Breakfast: **Full**
Credit Cards: **MC, VISA**
Pets: **No**
Children: **Welcome, over 15**
Smoking: **No**
Social Drinking: **Permitted**

This sprawling Colonial home stands majestically on a bluff overlooking Puget Sound and Bainbridge Island. Each cheerful guest room, furnished with New England antiques, affords superb views of the water and ever-changing scenery. Port Orchard offers a variety of diversions, from small shops filled with antiques and crafts, to marinas, parks, and boat excursions around the peninsula.

## Holly Hill House ✪
### 611 POLK, PORT TOWNSEND, WASHINGTON 98368

| | |
|---|---|
| Tel: **(360) 385-5619** | Breakfast: **Full** |
| Best Time to Call: **After 11 AM** | Credit Cards: **MC, VISA** |
| Host: **Lynne Sterling** | Pets: **No** |
| Location: **60 mi. NW of Seattle** | Children: **Welcome, over 12** |
| No. of Rooms: **5** | Smoking: **No** |
| No. of Private Baths: **5** | Social Drinking: **Permitted** |
| Double/pb: **$72–$86** | Minimum Stay: **2 nights festival** |
| Suite: **$125** | **weekends** |
| Open: **All year** | |

Built in 1872, Holly Hill House is the former residence of R. C. Hill, who served variously as mayor, state representative, and the first banker of Port Townsend. Each room, lavishly furnished with Victorian antiques, is lovingly maintained down to the stippled woodwork. The grounds feature distinctive plantings, including holly trees and two unusual Camperdown elms known as upside-down trees. Nearby are marinas, golf courses, fishing sites, beaches, and many fine restaurants for your dining pleasure.

## The Portico ✪
### 502 SOUTH ADAMS STREET, RITZVILLE, WASHINGTON 99169

| | |
|---|---|
| Tel: **(509) 659-0800** | Open: **All year** |
| Best Time to Call: **Days; evenings** | Breakfast: **Full** |
| Hosts: **Mary Anne and Bill Phipps** | Other Meals: **Available** |
| Location: **60 mi. SW of Spokane** | Credit Cards: **AMEX, DISC, MC, VISA** |
| No. of Rooms: **2** | Pets: **No** |
| No. of Private Baths: **2** | Children: **Welcome** |
| Double/pb: **$59–$74** | Smoking: **No** |
| Single/pb: **$53–$68** | Social Drinking: **Permitted** |

This stately 1902 mansion, listed on the National Register of Historic Places, combines Queen Anne and Classical Revival architecture. The interior is distinguished by gleaming oak woodwork, wood-spindled screens and columns, a grand entry staircase, and antique furnishings. In season, the grounds are resplendent with flowers, wild berries, fruit trees, and a vegetable garden, making for some tasty treats. Bill, a retired Air Force officer, and his wife, Mary Anne, provide a romantic setting that lets guests experience the serenity of this rural eastern Washington community.

## Chelsea Station on the Park ✪
**4915 LINDEN AVENUE NORTH, SEATTLE, WASHINGTON 98103**

Tel: **(206) 547-6077; (800) 400-6077**
Best Time to Call: **10 AM–9 PM**
Hosts: **John Griffin and Karen Carbonneau**
Location: **Seattle's North end**
No. of Rooms: **6**
No. of Private Baths: **6**
Double/pb: **$89–$104**
Open: **All year**

Reduced Rates: **Off-season, weekly**
Breakfast: **Full**
Credit Cards: **AMEX, DC, DISC, MC, VISA**
Pets: **No**
Children: **Welcome, over 12**
Smoking: **No**
Social Drinking: **Permitted**

Chelsea Station on the Park, circa 1929, is nestled between the Freemont neighborhood and Woodland Park. Largely decorated in Mission style, the house features antiques throughout. Guest rooms have king- or queen-size beds complete with soft down comforters. Awake to the aroma of fresh coffee, followed by a hearty breakfast including delicious selections such as orange French toast or ginger pancakes. Freshly-baked cookies are always available. Take in the Seattle Rose Garden, the famous Freemont Troll, or just go for a leisurely stroll through the neighborhood. Enjoy the warm and casual mood at Chelsea Station on the Park, a place to refresh your spirit.

## Mildred's Bed & Breakfast ✪
**1202 15TH AVENUE EAST, SEATTLE, WASHINGTON 98112**

Tel: **(206) 325-6072**
Best Time to Call: **Mornings**
Hosts: **Mildred and Melodee Sarver**
Location: **3 mi. NE of City Center**
No. of Rooms: **3**
No. of Private Baths: **3**
Double/pb: **$85**
Single/pb: **$75**

Open: **All year**
Breakfast: **Full**
Credit Cards: **AMEX, DC, MC, VISA**
Pets: **No**
Children: **Welcome**
Smoking: **No**
Social Drinking: **Permitted**

Mildred's is the ultimate trip-to-grandmother's fantasy come true. A large white 1890 Victorian, it's the perfect setting for traditional, caring B&B hospitality. Guest rooms on the second floor have sitting alcoves, lace curtains, and antiques. Mildred's special touches, like coffee and juice delivered to your room one-half hour before breakfast, and tea and cookies on arrival, make her guests feel truly pampered. Across the street is historic 44-acre Volunteer Park with its art museum, flower conservatory, and tennis courts. An electric trolley stops at the

front door and there is ample street parking. It is just minutes to the city center, freeways, and all points of interest.

## Prince of Wales ✪
### 133 THIRTEENTH AVENUE EAST, SEATTLE, WASHINGTON 98102

Tel: **(206) 325-9692; (800) 327-9692**
Best Time to Call: **10 AM–9 PM**
Host: **Carol Norton**
Location: **In heart of Seattle**
No. of Rooms: **4**
No. of Private Baths: **4**
Double/sb: **$70–$90**
Suites: **$90–$110**
Open: **All year**

Reduced Rates: **10% weekly**
 **Nov.–Mar.**
Breakfast: **Full**
Credit Cards: **AMEX, DISC, MC, VISA**
Pets: **No**
Children: **Welcome**
Smoking: **No**
Social Drinking: **Permitted**
Foreign Languages: **Italian, Spanish**

From this convenient address, it's just a brief walk to the Convention Center and a short bus ride to the Space Needle, Pikes Place Market, and downtown Seattle's many other attractions. In the evening, you're sure to be tempted by the menus of neighborhood restaurants. Carol serves a delicious breakfast. All rooms have king or queen beds, private baths, and great views.

## Roberta's Bed and Breakfast
**1147 SIXTEENTH AVENUE EAST, SEATTLE, WASHINGTON 98112**

Tel: **(206) 329-3326**; fax: **(206) 324-2149**
Host: **Roberta Barry**
No. of Rooms: **5**
Single/pb: **$75–$85**
Open: **All year**

Breakfast: **Full**
Credit Cards: **MC, VISA**
Pets: **No**
Children: **Welcome, over 12**
Smoking: **No**
Social Drinking: **Permitted**

Roberta's is a 1903 frame Victorian with a large, old-fashioned front porch. The house is located in a quiet, historic neighborhood near the heart of the city. The cheerful rooms all boast queen-size beds. The Peach Room has bay windows, oak furniture, and Grandma's fancy desk; the Rosewood Room has a window seat and built-in oak bookcase; all five rooms are filled with books. In the morning you'll smell a pot of coffee right beside your door. That's just a warm-up for the large breakfast to come. The specialty of the house is Dutch Babies, a local dish, served with powdered sugar or fresh berries. For your convenience the *New York Times* and local newspapers are available every morning.

## Seattle Guest Cottage ✪
**2424 N.W. MARKET # 300, SEATTLE, WASHINGTON 98107**

Tel: **(206) 783-2169**
Host: **Inge Pokrandt**

Location: **1 mi. from I-5**
No. of Rooms: **4**

| | |
|---|---|
| No. of Private Baths: **2** | Pets: **No** |
| Suite: **$45** | Children: **Welcome (crib)** |
| Guest Cottage: **$85 for 2** | Smoking: **No** |
| Open: **All year** | Social Drinking: **Permitted** |
| Breakfast: **Continental** | Minimum Stay: **2 nights** |
| Credit Cards: **AMEX, MC, VISA** | Foreign Languages: **German** |

Built in 1925, this charming two-bedroom cottage is close to downtown, the University of Washington, fine beaches, and all sightseeing. Enjoy the privacy, the fine oak furniture, the fireplace, and all the little touches that make you feel welcome. The private suite in Inge's home has a full kitchen, and some breakfast food is provided. Fresh flowers, fruits, and candy all spell out a warm welcome. The cedar deck in the sunny backyard is most enjoyable.

## Spokane Bed & Breakfast Reservation Service
**627 EAST 25TH, SPOKANE, WASHINGTON 99203**

| | |
|---|---|
| Tel: **(509) 624-3776** | Descriptive Directory: **Free** |
| Best Time to Call: **8 AM–7 PM** | Rates (Single/Double): |
| Coordinator: **Pat Conley** | Modest: **$40 / $45** |
| States/Regions Covered: | Average: **$45 / $50** |
| **Canada—British Columbia,** | Luxury: **$62 / $92** |
| **Vancouver, Victoria; Idaho—Coeur** | Credit Cards: **AMEX, MC, VISA** |
| **d'Alene, Laclede, Sandpoint;** | Minimum Stay: **Only on 3-day** |
| **Washington—Seattle, Spokane,** | **weekends** |
| **Yakima** | |

You can't beat the attractions of the Spokane area: excellent skiing and snowmobiling, perfect lakes for waterfront sports, large family-oriented parks, museums, symphonies, opera, and theater. This service will put you in touch with all manner of guest houses, from charming riverfront contemporaries to elegant, turn-of-the-century homes.

## Marianna Stoltz House ✪
**427 EAST INDIANA, SPOKANE, WASHINGTON 99207**

| | |
|---|---|
| Tel: **(509) 483-4316; (800) 978-6587** | Breakfast: **Full** |
| Hosts: **James and Phyllis Maguire** | Credit Cards: **AMEX, DC, DISC, MC,** |
| No. of Rooms: **4** | **VISA** |
| No. of Private Baths: **2** | Pets: **No** |
| Max. No. Sharing Bath: **4** | Children: **Welcome, over 12** |
| Double/pb: **$65–75** | Smoking: **No** |
| Single/pb: **$55–$60** | Social Drinking: **Permitted** |
| Open: **All year** | Airport/Station Pickup: **Yes** |

The Marianna Stoltz House, a Spokane landmark, is a classic American Foursquare home built in 1908. Period furnishings complement the house's woodwork, tile fireplace, and leaded glass bookshelves and cupboards. The bedroom quilts are heirlooms from Phyllis's mother, the B&B's namesake. The Maguires are Spokane natives—Phyllis grew up in this very house—and can tell you about local theaters, museums, and parks. Full breakfasts consist of juice, fruit, muffins, and main dishes such as sausage-cheese strata and puffy Dutch pancakes with homemade syrup.

## A Greater Tacoma B&B Reservations Service ✪
3312 NORTH UNION AVENUE, TACOMA, WASHINGTON 98407
E-mail: tacomabnbs@aol.com

Tel: (206) 759-4088; fax: (206) 759-4025
Best Time to Call: **After 10 AM**
Coordinator: **Sharon Kaufmann**
States/Regions Covered: **Bremerton, Enumclaw, Fox Island, Gig Harbor, Mt. Rainier, Olalla, Olympia, Puyallup, Silverdale, Tacoma**

Descriptive Directory: **Free**
Rates (Single/Double):
  Modest **$50 / $65**
  Average **$75 / $85**
  Luxury **$95 / $165**
Credit Cards: **AMEX, MC, VISA**

Greater Tacoma B&B Reservations offers more than twenty inspected and licensed accommodations. Prefer full or Continental breakfast? Shared or private bath? Have your choice at homes that range from a cozy cottage to a historic waterfront mansion. Some sites have extra amenities like hot tubs and romantic Jacuzzis.

## Commencement Bay B&B ✪
3312 NORTH UNION AVENUE, TACOMA, WASHINGTON 98407
E-mail: greatviews@aol.com

Tel: (206) 752-8175; fax: (206) 759-4025
Best Time to Call: **9 AM–9 PM**
Hosts: **Bill and Sheri Kaufmann**
Location: **1 mi. N of Tacoma**
No. of Rooms: **3**
No. of Private Baths: **3**
Double/pb: **$75–$105**
Open: **All year**

Reduced Rates: **Available**
Breakfast: **Full**
Credit Cards: **AMEX, MC, VISA**
Pets: **No**
Children: **Welcome, over 12**
Smoking: **No**
Social Drinking: **Permitted**
Airport/Station Pickup: **Yes**

An elegantly decorated Colonial home overlooking scenic north end Tacoma, this B&B has dramatic bay and mountain views from both the rooms and the common areas. Guests can enjoy a quiet, relaxing fireside reading area, an outdoor hot tub in a lovely garden, a casual game room with large-screen TV, microwave, and refrigerator—even an office for business travelers (with a fax/modem available). The B&B offers guests cable TV, VCR, or telephone in select rooms, an early businessman's breakfast on weekdays, and transportation to nearby universities or downtown business areas. It is close to several waterfront parks, jogging/hiking trails, great restaurants, quaint shops (including antiques), and easy freeway access. A delicious breakfast and different gourmet coffees are served daily.

## Inge's Place ✪
### 6809 LAKE GROVE SW, TACOMA, WASHINGTON 98499

| | |
|---|---|
| Tel: **(206) 584-4514** | Suites: **$60** |
| Host: **Ingeborg Deatherage** | Open: **All year** |
| Location: **3 mi. from I-5** | Reduced Rates: **Available** |
| No. of Rooms: **3** | Breakfast: **Full** |
| No. of Private Baths: **1** | Pets: **No** |
| Max. No. Sharing Bath: **4** | Children: **Welcome** |
| Double/pb: **$50** | Smoking: **No** |
| Single/pb: **$40** | Social Drinking: **Permitted** |
| Double/sb: **$45** | Airport/Station Pickup: **Yes** |
| Single/sb: **$35** | Foreign Languages: **German** |

This spic-and-span home is in a lovely Tacoma suburb called Lakewood. Feel welcome to use the hot tub, large backyard, and patio. There are many restaurants and shopping centers within walking distance, and several nearby lakes where fishing is excellent. Tacoma is the gateway to Mount Rainier. Inge is a world traveler, teacher, and enthusiast about B&Bs.

## Keenan House ✪
### 2610 NORTH WARNER, TACOMA, WASHINGTON 98407

| | |
|---|---|
| Tel: **(206) 752-0702** | Double/sb: **$55** |
| Best Time to Call: **Evenings** | Single/sb: **$50** |
| Host: **Lenore Keenan** | Open: **All year** |
| Location: **2½ mi. from I-5** | Breakfast: **Full** |
| No. of Rooms: **4** | Pets: **No** |
| No. of Private Baths: **2** | Children: **Welcome** |
| Max. No. Sharing Bath: **4** | Smoking: **No** |
| Double/pb: **$65** | Social Drinking: **Permitted** |
| Single/pb: **$55** | |

This spacious Victorian house is located in the historic district near Puget Sound. It is furnished in antiques and period pieces. Afternoon tea is served, and ice is available for cocktails; fruit and croissants are served with breakfast. Local possibilities include Puget Sound, Vashon Island, the state park, zoo, and ferry. It's only five blocks to the University of Puget Sound.

## Llama Ranch Bed & Breakfast ✪
### 1980 HIGHWAY 141, WHITE SALMON, WASHINGTON 98672

| | |
|---|---|
| Tel: **(509) 395-2786; (800) 800-LAMA** **[5262]** | Location: **50 mi. E of Portland, Oreg.** |
| | No. of Rooms: **5** |
| Hosts: **Jerry and Rebeka Stone** | Max. No. Sharing Bath: **4** |

Double/sb: **$55**
Single/sb: **$45**
Open: **All year**
Reduced Rates: **$5 less Dec.–Mar.;**
    **15% weekly**
Breakfast: **Full**

Credit Cards: **DISC, MC, VISA**
Pets: **Sometimes**
Children: **Welcome**
Smoking: **No**
Social Drinking: **Permitted**

Jerry and Rebeka enjoy sharing their love of llamas with their guests, and it is a rare person who can resist a llama's charm. Their B&B commands stunning views of Mt. Adams and Mt. Hood. The guest rooms are unpretentious and comfortable. Llama Ranch is located on 97 acres at the base of the Mt. Adams Wilderness Area. Nearby activities include horseback riding, white-water rafting, plane trips over Mount St. Helens, water sports, and cave exploration. The less adventurous are certain to enjoy learning about the ranch's serene animals.

# WISCONSIN

Lac Du Flambeau •
Eagle River • • Phelps
• Fish Creek
Cable •
Eau Claire • • Green Bay
Stevens Point • Manitowoc •
La Farge • • Cedarburg
Baraboo • • Portage
Madison • • Milwaukee
• Eagle
Mineral Point •

## Gollmar Mansion Inn ✪
### 422 3RD STREET, BARABOO, WISCONSIN 53913

Tel: **(608) 356-9432**
Best Time to Call: **10 AM–9 PM**
Hosts: **Linda and Thomas Luck**
Location: **200 mi. NW of Chicago**
No. of Rooms: **3**
No. of Private Baths: **3**
Double/pb: **$75**
Open: **All year**

Breakfast: **Full**
Credit Cards: **MC, VISA**
Pets: **No**
Children: **Welcome, over 7**
Smoking: **No**
Social Drinking: **Permitted**
Station Pickup: **Yes**

Welcome to the Gollmar Mansion Inn, an exquisite Victorian circus home laden with charming treasures, unique features, and a wealth of history. Original hand-painted ceiling frescoes, beveled glass, chandeliers, furniture and antiques will delight antique connoisseurs. Guest rooms all have queen beds and are named after the exceptional Gollmar women who were 19th-century circus performers. Isabell's room is pristine and elegant in white and periwinkle. Leora's Country Meadow Room is soft and romantic, with hearts and flowers. Viola's Attic Room is peachy and private with French Impression prints. Guests may relax in the parlor or sit on the porch and enjoy the view. Breakfast may include apple pancakes, French toast, pastries, and fruit. The Inn is located within four blocks of downtown Baraboo. Your hosts will be happy to supply you with maps and acquaint you with the area. The summer of 1995 will bring Luxem Gallery of Gifts featuring arts, crafts, and dried floral arrangements.

## Pinehaven ✪
### E13083 STATE HIGHWAY 33, BARABOO, WISCONSIN 53913

| | |
|---|---|
| Tel: **(608) 356-3489** | Open: **All year** |
| Best Time to Call: **5 PM–10 AM** | Breakfast: **Full** |
| Hosts: **Lyle and Marge Getschman** | Credit Cards: **MC, VISA** |
| Location: **10 mi. from I-90** | Pets: **No** |
| No. of Rooms: **4** | Children: **Welcome, over 5** |
| No. of Private Baths: **4** | Smoking: **No** |
| Double/pb: **$65–$75** | Social Drinking: **Permitted** |
| Single/pb: **$60–$70** | |

Lyle and Marge's home is nestled in a pine grove with a beautiful view of the Baraboo Bluffs and a small private lake. Guest rooms have air-conditioning. The full breakfast may include fresh-baked muffins, coffee cakes, egg dishes, meat, fruit, and juice. Eat in the dining room, on the deck, or on the screened-in porch. Play the baby grand piano. Feel free to take a leisurely stroll in these inviting surroundings. A tour to see your hosts' Belgian draft horses and antique wagons and sleighs on the farm side of the highway, and wagon or sleigh rides pulled by the Belgians, may be arranged. Fine restaurants and numerous activities abound in the area.

## The Victorian Rose ✪
### 423 THIRD AVENUE, BARABOO, WISCONSIN 53913

| | |
|---|---|
| Tel: **(608) 356-7828** | Open: **All year** |
| Hosts: **Bob and Carolyn Stearns** | Breakfast: **Full** |
| Location: **40 mi. N of Madison** | Pets: **No** |
| No. of Rooms: **3** | Children: **No** |
| No. of Private Baths: **3** | Smoking: **No** |
| Double/pb: **$65–$80** | Social Drinking: **Permitted** |

The Victorian Rose is located on a large corner lot, surrounded by sugar maples and pine trees, within walking distance of Baraboo's historical sites, specialty shops, and galleries. The Stearns family welcomes you to their beautifully restored nineteenth-century "Painted Lady," furnished with roses, lace, antiques, and heirloom collectibles. Guests can enjoy a game or book in the library parlor or watch old classic movies by the fireplace with a cup of tea and sweet treats. Appropriately enough, guest rooms are decorated in Victorian decor. A full gourmet candlelight breakfast awaits guests in the morning.

## Connors Bed & Breakfast ✪
ROUTE 1, BOX 255, CABLE, WISCONSIN 54821

| | |
|---|---|
| Tel: (715) 798-3661; (800) 848-3932 | Breakfast: Full |
| Hosts: Alex and Mona Connors | Credit Cards: MC, VISA |
| Location: 1.7 mi. N of Cable | Pets: Sometimes |
| No. of Rooms: 3 | Children: Welcome |
| No. of Private Baths: 1 | Smoking: No |
| Max. No. Sharing Bath: 4 | Social Drinking: Permitted |
| Double/sb: $55 | Minimum Stay: 2 nights Berkebeiner |
| Suites: $90 | weekend |
| Open: All year | |

Once a seventy-seven-acre farm, Connors Bed & Breakfast lies approximately forty miles south of Lake Superior, surrounded by the Chequamegon National Forest. This central location gives guests easy access to the treasures of the nearby lakes, golf, downhill and cross-country skiing, casinos, and numerous day trips. There is a private cross-country ski trail on the property. Alex and Mona are both retired and live on the property full-time.

## Stagecoach Inn Bed & Breakfast ✪
W61 N520 WASHINGTON AVENUE, CEDARBURG, WISCONSIN 53012

| | |
|---|---|
| Tel: (414) 375-0208 | Open: All year |
| Hosts: Brook and Liz Brown | Breakfast: Continental |
| Location: 20 mi. N of Milwaukee | Credit Cards: AMEX, DISC, MC, VISA |
| No. of Rooms: 12 | Pets: No |
| No. of Private Baths: 12 | Children: Welcome, over 12 |
| Double/pb: $70 | Smoking: No |
| Suites: $105 | Social Drinking: Permitted |

The Inn, listed on the National Register of Historic Places, is housed in a completely restored 1853 stone building in downtown historic Cedarburg. The rooms, air-conditioned for summer comfort, combine antique charm with modern conveniences. Each bedroom is decorated with antiques and trimmed with wall stenciling. A candy shop and a pub that is a popular gathering place for guests occupy the first floor. Specialty stores, antique shops, a winery, a woolen mill, and a variety of fine restaurants are within walking distance.

## Eagle Centre House B&B ☉
### W370 S9590 HIGHWAY 67, EAGLE, WISCONSIN 53119

Tel: **(414) 363-4700**
Best Time to Call: **7 AM–10 PM**
Hosts: **Riene Wells Herriges and Dean Herriges**
Location: **30 mi. SW of Milwaukee**
No. of Rooms: **5**
No. of Private Baths: **5**
Double/pb: **$85**
Single/pb: **$85**

Suites: **$135**
Open: **All year; closed Christmas Eve**
Reduced Rates: **Available**
Breakfast: **Full**
Credit Cards: **AMEX, MC, VISA**
Pets: **No**
Children: **Welcome, over 12**
Smoking: **No**
Social Drinking: **Permitted**

Eagle Centre House is an authentic replica of an 1846 Greek Revival stagecoach inn built on 20 secluded acres. From the front parlor to the third-floor bedrooms, you will admire the splendid collection of antiques. Take a seat on the porch or in the parlor and browse through period publications. Even the breakfast specialties are inspired by the 19th century. There are hiking and cross-country ski trails in both Kettle Moraine State Forest and Old World Wisconsin, an unusual outdoor museum. Other athletic options include downhill skiing, sledding, biking, golfing, horseback riding, and waterfront sports.

## Brennan Manor, Old World Bed and Breakfast ☉
### 1079 EVERETT ROAD, EAGLE RIVER, WISCONSIN 54521

Tel: **(715) 479-7353**
Best Time to Call: **Days**
Hosts: **Connie and Bob Lawton**
Location: **3 mi. E of Eagle River**
No. of Rooms: **4**
No. of Private Baths: **4**
Double/pb: **$69–$85**
Single/pb: **$59–$79**
Guest Cottage: **$650 weekly; sleeps 6**
Open: **All year**

Reduced Rates: **10% seniors; 15% weekly**
Breakfast: **Full**
Credit Cards: **MC, VISA**
Pets: **No**
Children: **No**
Smoking: **No**
Social Drinking: **Permitted**
Airport/Station Pickup: **Yes**

Built in the 1920s, the era of the great lumber barons, this lakeside country estate combines a relaxed atmosphere and old-world charm. With its 30-foot timbered ceiling, large arched windows, massive stone fireplace, and hand-hewn woodwork, the great room may conjure up King Arthur's Camelot. For summer fun, there's boating, golfing, biking, water skiing, canoeing, fishing, and more. Winter sports enthusiasts will enjoy cross-country and downhill skiing, as well as the 500 miles of marked snowmobile trails that begin at the B&B's front door.

# The Atrium Bed & Breakfast ✪
## 5572 PRILL ROAD, EAU CLAIRE, WISCONSIN 54701

Tel: **(715) 833-9045**
Best Time to Call: **8 AM–8 PM**
Hosts: **Celia and Dick Stoltz**
Location: **90 mi. E of Minneapolis**
No. of Rooms: **3**
No. of Private Baths: **1**
Max. No. Sharing Bath: **4**
Double/pb: **$75**
Single/pb: **$70**
Double/sb: **$65**

Single/sb: **$60**
Open: **All year**
Reduced Rates: **$10 less Sun.–Thurs.**
Breakfast: **Continental**
Credit Cards: **MC, VISA**
Pets: **No**
Children: **Welcome, over 12**
Smoking: **No**
Social Drinking: **Permitted**

Named for its most unusual feature, this contemporary bed and breakfast is built around a twenty-foot by twenty-foot atrium where guests enjoy a leisurely breakfast in a natural setting. Exotic trees and plants reach toward the windowed ceiling and the sound of the fountain's trickling water brings the outdoors in to complete the ambiance. The Atrium is nestled on 15 wooded acres on Otter Creek that beckon the explorer. Follow the winding trails into the woods or watch the many varieties of wildlife right from the living room. Guests are always welcome to read by the fire, watch TV, or gather around the pump organ for a sing-along. Enjoy the best of both worlds at a woodland hideaway only minutes from shopping malls, restaurants, and the University of Wisconsin, Eau Claire.

# Thorp House Inn & Cottages
## 4135 BLUFF ROAD, P.O. BOX 490, FISH CREEK, WISCONSIN 54212

Tel: **(414) 868-2444**
Best Time to Call: **8 AM–10 PM**
Hosts: **Christine and Sverre Falck-Pedersen**
No. of Rooms: **3**
No. of Private Baths: **3**
Double/pb: **$90**
Cottages: **$75–$125**
Open: **All year**

Reduced Rates: **Weekly**
Breakfast: **Continental**
Pets: **No**
Children: **Welcome, in cottages**
Smoking: **Yes, in cottages**
Social Drinking: **Permitted**
Minimum Stay: **3 nights summer and holiday weekends**
Foreign Languages: **Norwegian**

Thorp House is a turn-of-the-century country Victorian inn perched on a wooded hill overlooking Green Bay. The beach, shops, restaurants, and Peninsula State Park are just a stroll away. Four elegant guest rooms re-create romantic periods of the past with fine antiques and accessories, documentary wall coverings, and European lace. Each room has a private bath (one with a whirlpool), central air-conditioning, and ceiling fans. Guests have their own parlor with its original granite fireplace. A delicious home-baked breakfast is included. Also available: country cottages with wood-burning fireplaces,

full kitchens and baths (some with whirlpools), decks, and views of the bay. For those of you who don't mind paying a higher rate, 1 room is available.

## The Astor House ✪
### 637 SOUTH MONROE AVENUE, GREEN BAY, WISCONSIN 54301

Tel: **(414) 432-3585**
Best Time to Call: **8 AM–4 PM**
Host: **Doug Landwehr**
Location: **In Green Bay**
No. of Rooms: **5**
No. of Private Baths: **5**
Double/pb: **$79–$109**
Suites: **$89–$129**
Open: **All year**
Reduced Rates: **$79 Thurs., multi night, multi rooms**

Breakfast: **Continental**
Credit Cards: **AMEX, MC, VISA**
Pets: **No**
Children: **Welcome**
Smoking: **No**
Social Drinking: **Permitted**
Minimum Stay: **2 nights holiday weekends**

Welcome to the 1888 Astor House, where gracious seclusion, peace, and personal attention are yours from the time you enter the Astor Historic Neighborhood, near Green Bay's City Centre. The five distinctive guest suites are incredibly decorated and equipped with queen or

king beds, private shower or whirlpool bath, telephones, cable TV, VCR, CD and tape decks, refrigerators, and air-conditioning. Breakfast includes homemade baked goods, fruit and gourmet coffee. Enjoy the public and private gardens, luxuriate in a gentle whirlpool for two, bask before a roaring fire, or sample the many shops, restaurants, theaters, events, and activities in the Green Bay area. The Astor House is designed for either the vacationer or the business visitor.

## Trillium ✪
### ROUTE 2, BOX 121, LA FARGE, WISCONSIN 54639

Tel: **(608) 625-4492**
Best Time to Call: **Mornings; evenings**
Hosts: **Joe Swanson and Rosanne Boyett**
Location: **40 mi. SE of La Crosse**
Guest Cottage: **$70 for 2**
Open: **All year**
Breakfast: **Full**

Reduced Rates: **Single guest; weekly; winter, after first night**
Pets: **No**
Children: **Welcome (crib)**
Smoking: **Permitted**
Social Drinking: **Permitted**
Airport/Station Pickup: **Yes**

This private cottage is on a working farm located in the heart of a thriving Amish community. It has a large porch and is surrounded by an orchard, garden, and a lovely tree-shaded yard. There's a path beside the stream that winds through woods and fields. The cottage is light and airy, with comfortable wicker furniture. Nearby attractions include the Elroy-Sparta Bike Trail, Mississippi River, trout streams, and cheese factories.

## Ty Bach B&B ✪
### 3104 SIMPSON LANE, LAC DU FLAMBEAU, WISCONSIN 54538

Tel: (715) 588-7851
Best Time to Call: 8 AM–10 PM
Hosts: Janet and Kermit Bekkum
Location: 70 mi. N of Wausau
No. of Rooms: 2
No. of Private Baths: 2
Double/pb: $50–$60

Single/pb: $45–$55
Open: All year
Breakfast: Full
Pets: Sometimes
Children: No
Smoking: No
Social Drinking: Permitted

In Welsh, *ty-bach* means "little house." Located on an Indian reservation in Lac du Flambeau, this modern little house overlooks a small, picturesque Northwoods lake. Sit back on the deck and enjoy the beautiful fall colors, the call of the loons, and the tranquility of this out-of-the-way spot. Choose from two comfortable rooms: one features a brass bed, the other opens onto a private deck. Your hosts offer oven-fresh coffee cakes, homemade jams, and plenty of fresh coffee along with hearty main entrees.

## Annie's Bed & Breakfast
### 2117 SHERIDAN DRIVE, MADISON, WISCONSIN 53704

Tel: (608) 244-2224
Hosts: Anne and Larry Stuart
No. of Rooms: 2 suites
No. of Private Baths: 2
Suites: $94–$109 for 2; $154–$169
  for 4
Open: All year
Reduced Rates: 4th night free
  weekdays only

Breakfast: Full
Credit Cards: AMEX, MC, VISA
Pets: No
Children: Welcome, over 12
Smoking: No
Social Drinking: Permitted
Minimum Stay: 2 nights
Airport/Station Pickup: Yes

When you want the world to go away, come to Annie's, a quiet inn with a beautiful view of meadows, water, and woods. This charming, fully air-conditioned cedar shake home has been a getaway for travelers since 1985. The house is a block from a large lake and directly adjoining Warner Park, allowing guests a broad selection of activities, including swimming, boating, tennis, hiking, and biking during summer, and cross-country skiing and skating in winter. The four antique-filled guest rooms are full of surprises and unusual amenities. There is a great-hall dining room, a pine-paneled library with a well-stocked wood stove, and a soothing double whirlpool surrounded by plants.

The unusually lovely gardens, with romantic gazebo and pond, have been selected for the annual Madison Garden Tours.

## Arbor Manor Bed and Breakfast ☉
**1304 MICHIGAN AVENUE, MANITOWOC, WISCONSIN 54220**

| | |
|---|---|
| Tel: **(414) 684-6095** | Reduced Rates: **Available** |
| Best Time to Call: **Evenings** | Breakfast: **Full, Continental** |
| Hosts: **Jay and Lou Ann Spaanem** | Credit Cards: **MC, VISA** |
| Location: **60 mi. N of Milwaukee** | Pets: **No** |
| No. of Rooms: **3** | Children: **Welcome, over 12** |
| No. of Private Baths: **3** | Smoking: **No** |
| Double/pb: **$90–$95** | Social Drinking: **Permitted** |
| Open: **All year** | Airport/Station Pickup: **Yes** |

Arbor Manor is located in an area of historic houses near Lake Michigan. This Greek Revival–style home has luxurious accommodations—antiques, air-conditioning, and king- and queen-size beds furnish the spacious rooms. Despite its small-town atmosphere, Manitowoc has museums, a theater, and golfing facilities, plus hiking trails and Lake Michigan fishing. A short trip will take you to Wisconsin's famous Door County peninsula. Your hosts Lou Ann, a former teacher, and Jay, an accountant, promise to make your stay as pleasant as possible. The Lake Michigan Car Ferry leaves here and goes to Ludington, Michigan.

## Marie's Bed & Breakfast ✪
**346 EAST WILSON STREET, MILWAUKEE, WISCONSIN 53207**

| | |
|---|---|
| Tel: **(414) 483-1512** | Breakfast: **Full** |
| Best Time to Call: **8 AM–8 PM** | Credit Cards: **MC, VISA** |
| Host: **Marie M. Mahan** | Pets: **No** |
| No. of Rooms: **4** | Children: **Welcome** |
| Max. No. Sharing Bath: **4** | Smoking: **No** |
| Double/sb: **$58–$70** | Social Drinking: **Permitted** |
| Open: **All year** | Airport/Station Pickup: **Yes** |

Your hostess has decorated this turn-of-the-century Victorian with an eclectic mixture of antiques, collectibles, and her own original artwork. Give yourself time to walk around the historic Bay View neighborhood, with its many architectural styles. Downtown Milwaukee is just six minutes away. Breakfast, served in the garden when weather permits, is highlighted by homemade breads, pastries, and a variety of locally-prepared sausages.

## The Wilson House Inn ✪
**110 DODGE STREET, MINERAL POINT, WISCONSIN 53565**

| | |
|---|---|
| Tel: **(608) 987-3600** | Hosts: **Bev and Jim Harris** |
| Best Time to Call: **Evenings** | Location: **50 mi. SW of Madison** |

| | |
|---|---|
| No. of Rooms: **4** | Open: **All year** |
| No. of Private Baths: **2** | Breakfast: **Full** |
| Max. No. Sharing Bath: **4** | Credit Cards: **MC, VISA** |
| Double/pb: **$65–$70** | Pets: **No** |
| Single/pb: **$60–$65** | Children: **Welcome (crib)** |
| Double/sb: **$50–$65** | Smoking: **No** |
| Single/sb: **$45–$60** | Social Drinking: **Permitted** |

The Wilson House Inn is located in the heart of the beautiful uplands area. This red-brick Federal mansion was built in 1853 by Alexander Wilson, who became one of the state's first attorneys general. A veranda was added later, and it is where guests are welcomed with lemonade. The rooms are airy, comfortable, and furnished in antiques. Mineral Point was a mining and political center in the 1880s, and it is filled with many historic sites. Fishing, golfing, swimming, skiing, and the House on the Rock are all nearby.

## The Limberlost Inn
**HIGHWAY 17, #2483, PHELPS, WISCONSIN 54554**

| | |
|---|---|
| Tel: **(715) 545-2685** | Reduced Rates: **10% weekly** |
| Hosts: **Bill and Phoebe McElroy** | Breakfast: **Full** |
| No. of Rooms: **2** | Pets: **No** |
| Max. No. Sharing Bath: **4** | Children: **Welcome, over 10** |
| Double/sb: **$47** | Smoking: **No** |
| Open: **All year** | Social Drinking: **Permitted** |

The Inn was designed and constructed by Bill and Phoebe McElroy. They picked a fine spot for their log home, just a minute from one of the best fishing lakes and largest national forests in the state. Each guest room is decorated with antiques, and the beds all have cozy down pillows and hand-stitched coverlets. Breakfast is served on the screened porch, by the fieldstone fireplace, in the dining room, or in your room. Stroll through the garden, rock on the porch swing, or take a picnic lunch and explore the streams and hiking trails. When you return, a Finnish sauna and a glass of wine or a mug of beer await.

## Country Aire ✪
**N4452 COUNTY U, BOX 175, PORTAGE, WISCONSIN 53901**

| | |
|---|---|
| Tel: **(608) 742-5716** | Suites: **$75** |
| Best Time to Call: **Evenings** | Open: **All year** |
| Hosts: **Bob and Rita Reif** | Breakfast: **Continental** |
| Location: **37 mi. N of Madison** | Pets: **No** |
| No. of Rooms: **3** | Children: **Welcome** |
| No. of Private Baths: **2** | Smoking: **No** |
| Double/pb: **$60** | Social Drinking: **Permitted** |
| Single/pb: **$50** | |

Forty acres of woods and meadows surround this spacious country home, built into a hillside overlooking the Wisconsin River. The house has open cathedral ceilings and a beautiful view from every room. Choose from comfortable bedrooms with queen-size or twin beds; the kids will enjoy the room with bunk beds. Guests are welcome to use the tennis court or go canoeing on the river. In the winter, skating can be enjoyed on the pond, and the area is perfect for cross-country skiing. Devil's Head and Cascade Mountain are close by for downhill skiing. Bob and Rita are minutes away from the Wisconsin Dells, Baraboo, and Devil's Lake State Park. Relax at the end of the day in the serenity of this beautiful country setting.

## Dreams of Yesteryear Bed & Breakfast ✪
**1100 BRAWLEY STREET, STEVENS POINT, WISCONSIN 54481**

| | |
|---|---|
| Tel: **(715) 341-4525** | Open: **All year** |
| Best Time to Call: **After 4 PM** | Breakfast: **Full** |
| Hosts: **Bonnie and Bill Maher** | Credit Cards: **AMEX, DISC, MC, VISA** |
| Location: **30 mi. S of Wausau** | Pets: **No** |
| No. of Rooms: **6** | Children: **Welcome, over 12** |
| No. of Private Baths: **4** | Smoking: **No** |
| Double/pb: **$55–$125** | Social Drinking: **Permitted** |
| Single/pb: **$50–$120** | Airport/Station Pickup: **Yes** |

Dreams, listed on the National Register of Historic Places and featured in *Victorian Homes* magazine, was designed by architect J. H. Jeffers, who also designed the Wisconsin Building at the St. Louis World's Fair of 1904. Lavish in Victorian detail, the home is handsomely decorated, with floral wallpapers and period furniture. One bathroom has a claw-footed tub and a pedestal sink. Bonnie, a University of Wisconsin secretary and square-dance caller, and Bill, owner of a water-conditioning business, love to talk about the house and its furnishings. Skiing, canoeing, shopping, and university theater, among other activities, are in close proximity.

# WYOMING

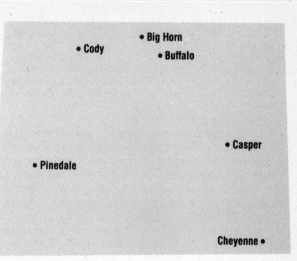

- Big Horn
- Cody
- Buffalo
- Casper
- Pinedale
- Cheyenne

## Spahn's Big Horn Mountain Bed and Breakfast
P.O. BOX 579, BIG HORN, WYOMING 82833

Tel: (307) 674-8150
Hosts: **Ron and Bobbie Spahn**
Location: **15 mi. SW of Sheridan**
No. of Rooms: **2**
No. of Private Baths: **2**
Double/pb: **$65–$95**
Open: **All year**

Cabins: **$65–$100**
Breakfast: **Full**
Pets: **No**
Children: **Welcome (baby-sitter)**
Smoking: **No**
Social Drinking: **Permitted**
Airport/Station Pickup: **Yes**

Ron and Bobbie Spahn and their two children built their home and this authentic log cabin. The house is set on 40 acres of whispering pines, and borders the Big Horn Mountain forestland, which stretches for over a million acres. The main house has two guest bedrooms with private baths, a three-story living room, and an outside deck. The cabin is secluded from the main house and features a queen-size bed, a shower bath, and an old-fashioned front porch. You are invited to sip a drink beside the wood stove, or take in the 100-mile view from an old porch rocker. Ron Spahn is a geologist and former Yellowstone Ranger. He can direct you to nearby fishing and hunting and can also tell you where to find the best walking and cross-country skiing trails.

# Cloud Peak Inn ✪
**590 NORTH BURRITT AVENUE, BUFFALO, WYOMING 82834**

Tel: **(307) 684-5794**
Best Time to Call: **Anytime**
Hosts: **Rick and Kathy Brus**
Location: **115 mi. N of Casper**
No. of Rooms: **5**
No. of Private Baths: **3**
Max. No. Sharing Bath: **4**
Double/pb: **$55–$75**
Single/pb: **$50–$65**
Double/sb: **$45–$55**
Single/sb: **$40–$50**

Open: **All year**
Reduced Rates: **Available**
Breakfast: **Full**
Other Meals: **Available**
Credit Cards: **AMEX, MC, VISA**
Pets: **No**
Children: **Welcome**
Smoking: **No**
Social Drinking: **Permitted**
Airport/Station Pickup: **Yes**

Built in 1912, this home is an expanded bungalow with a generous front porch. The grand curved staircase leads to spacious guest rooms decorated with period antiques. In the parlor and dining room, ten-foot wood-beamed ceilings enhance the feeling of luxury. Guests are encouraged to relax by the fossilized fireplace or in the Jacuzzi sun room. You'll wake up to a three-course breakfast ranging from full country entrees to gourmet delights. The Big Horn Mountains offer something for everyone, including fishing, hiking, sightseeing, horseback riding, and boating. During spring, the wildflower display is unrivaled. Come and see what the West is all about.

# Bessemer Bend Bed & Breakfast ✪
**5120 ALCOVA ROUTE, BOX 40, CASPER, WYOMING 82604**

Tel: **(307) 265-6819**
Hosts: **Opal and Stan McInroy**
Location: **10 mi. SW of Casper**
No. of Rooms: **3**
Max. No. Sharing Bath: **4**
Double/sb: **$45**
Single/sb: **$35**
Open: **All year**

Reduced Rates: **$5 less after 1st night**
Breakfast: **Full**
Credit Cards: **MC, VISA**
Pets: **Sometimes**
Children: **Welcome**
Smoking: **No**
Social Drinking: **Permitted**
Airport/Station Pickup: **Yes**

This two-level ranch house offers great views of the North Platte River and Bessemer Mountain; the McInroys' property was once part of the Goose Egg Ranch, as commemorated in Owen Wister's *The Virginian*. Western history buffs will want to visit other points of interest, such as the site of the Red Butte Pony Express Station. In Casper you'll find a wealth of museums, parks, and restaurants. The sports-minded will be challenged by local options ranging from rock climbing and hang gliding to fishing and skiing. For indoor diversions, the McInroys' recreation room is equipped with a Ping-Pong table, an exercise bike, and plenty of books and games. Breakfasts feature coffee, fresh fruit or juice, toast, sourdough pancakes, and an egg casserole.

# Adventurers' Country B&B ✪
## 3803 I-80, SOUTH SERVICE ROAD, CHEYENNE, WYOMING 82001

Tel: **(307) 632-4087**
Best Time to Call: **Early AM, after 5 PM**
Hosts: **Chuck and Fern White**
Location: **13 mi. E of Cheyenne**
No. of Rooms: **4**
No. of Private Baths: **4**
Double/pb: **$65–$75**
Suite: **$140, sleeps 4**
Open: **All year**

Reduced Rates: **10% seniors, 15% families**
Breakfast: **Full**
Other Meals: **Available**
Pets: **Permitted, in kennels**
Children: **Welcome**
Smoking: **No**
Social Drinking: **Permitted**
Airport Pickup: **Yes**

Adventurers' bed and breakfast is situated on a knoll, surrounded by 102 acres of prairies and green pastures. The expansive front lawn, tree-lined adobe courtyard with flower-filled gardens, and comfortable front porch welcome guests to the Southwestern-style ranch home. All bedrooms have either king- or queen-size beds. There's also a private living room with a fireplace, TV, VCR, books, and games for your feel-at-home comfort. Breakfasts are homemade and healthy, dinners are available with prior notice. Chuck and Fern also offer a horseback package.

# The Lockhart Inn ✪
## 109 WEST YELLOWSTONE AVENUE, CODY, WYOMING 82414

Tel: **(307) 587-6074; (800) 377-7255**
Best Time to Call: **After noon**
Host: **Cindy Baldwin**
No. of Rooms: **7**
No. of Private Baths: **7**
Double/pb: **$65–$90**
Open: **All year**
Breakfast: **Full**

Other Meals: **Available**
Credit Cards: **CB, DISC, MC, VISA**
Pets: **No**
Children: **Welcome**
Smoking: **No**
Social Drinking: **Permitted**
Airport/Station Pickup: **Yes**

Once the home of Cody's famous turn-of-the-century novelist, Caroline Lockhart, Cindy's historic frontier home has been beautifully restored while retaining the flavor of the Old West. The old-fashioned decor is combined with such modern amenities as cable TV, phones, and individually controlled heat. Breakfast is graciously served on fine china in the dining room. The house is located 50 miles from the eastern entrance to Yellowstone National Park, and there's plenty to do in addition to relaxing on the front porch. The Trail Town Museum, Buffalo Bill Historical Center, and the Cody Nightly Rodeo are just some of the attractions.

# Window on the Winds ✪
## 10151 HIGHWAY 191, P.O. BOX 135, PINEDALE, WYOMING 82941

Tel: (307) 367-2600
Hosts: **Doug and Leanne McKay**
Location: **75 mi. S of Jackson**
No. of Rooms: **4**
Max. No. Sharing Bath: **4**
Double/sb: **$60–$68**
Single/sb: **$50**
Open: **All year**

Reduced Rates: **Available**
Breakfast: **Full**
Other Meals: **Available**
Credit Cards: **MC, VISA**
Pets: **Welcome**
Children: **Welcome**
Smoking: **No**
Social Drinking: **Permitted**

Pinedale, at the base of the Wind River Mountains in western Wyoming, is on one of the major routes to Grand Teton and Yellowstone National Parks. The Winds offers world-class hiking and fishing in the summer and snowmobiling and Nordic skiing in the winter. Or, go exploring with your hosts' self-guided driving tour of historic Sublette County and Oregon Trail sites. The comfortable log home, decorated in striking Western and Plains Indians themes, is a rustic retreat—the perfect base for your Wyoming vacation. There is room for pets and kids and a large garage to store extra gear. Hosts Leanne and Doug are archaeologists who enjoy sharing their unique perspective on the cultural heritage of the area.

# 6

## *Canada*

---

## ALBERTA

---

*Note: All prices listed in this section are quoted in Canadian dollars.*

### Alberta Bed & Breakfast ✪
**P.O. BOX 15477, M.P.O., VANCOUVER, BRITISH COLUMBIA, CANADA V6B 5B2 (FORMERLY EDMONTON, ALBERTA)**

---

Tel: **(604) 944-1793**
Best Time to Call: **8 AM–2 PM**
Coordinator: **June Brown**
Provinces/Regions Covered:
  **Alberta—Banff, Calgary, Canmore, Edmonton, Jasper; British Columbia—Kamloops, Vancouver, Victoria, Whistler**

Rates (Single/Double):
  Modest:   **$30 / $40**
  Average:  **$35 / $45**
  Luxury:   **$45–$90 / $50–$95**
Credit Cards: **No**

Try a bit of Canadian western hospitality by choosing from June's variety of lovely homes in Alberta and British Columbia. Make a circle tour of Calgary, Banff, Lake Louise, the Columbia Icefields, Jasper, and Edmonton, and stay in B&Bs all the way. Send two dollars for a descriptive list of the cordial hosts on her roster, make your selections, and June will do the rest. The agency is closed on Canadian holidays and October through March. There's a $5 surcharge for each Banff, Jasper, and Victoria reservation.

### Brink Bed and Breakfast ✪
**79 SINCLAIR CRESCENT S.W., CALGARY, ALBERTA, CANADA T2W 0M1**

---

Tel: **(403) 255-4523**
Best Time to Call: **Mornings**
Host: **Helen G. Scrimgeour-Brink**
Location: **In Calgary**

No. of Rooms: **3**
No. of Private Baths: **1**
Max. No. Sharing Bath: **4**
Double/pb: **$65**

Double/sb: **$55**
Single/sb: **$45**
Suite: **$70**
Open: **All year**
Breakfast: **Full**
Other Meals: **Available**

Pets: **Sometimes**
Children: **Welcome**
Smoking: **Permitted**
Social Drinking: **Permitted**
Airport/Station Pickup: **Yes**

Helen is a native Calgarian and a retired registered nurse who decided to open a bed and breakfast. Each bedroom is tastefully decorated. The suite "Sarah's Garden" is a private retreat with a queen-size bed, TV, loveseat, and complete bath. The "Teddy Bear" room is a single room across the hall from a full bathroom. The "Bed of Roses" room, on another level, has a comfortable double bed and is adjacent to a half-bath and a family room with a TV and a wide collection of books. Breakfast, served in a sunny dining room, features specialties like homemade scones, muffins, French toast, pancakes, fruit compote, and freshly-squeezed juice. There is a large deck and well-landscaped private backyard. A traditional British afternoon tea, picnic baskets, or an evening meal are offered at an additional cost. There is a $5 surcharge for one-night stays.

## Harrison's B&B Home ✪

**6016 THORNBURN DRIVE NORTHWEST, CALGARY, ALBERTA, CANADA T2K 3P7**

Tel: **(403) 274-7281**
Best Time to Call: **7–8 AM; 4–7 PM**
Host: **Susan Harrison**
Location: **In Calgary, ¼ mi. from Hwy. 2**
No. of Rooms: **2**
Max. No. Sharing Bath: **4**
Double/sb: **$50**

Single/sb: **$30**
Open: **All year**
Breakfast: **Full**
Pets: **No**
Children: **Welcome, over 10**
Smoking: **Restricted**
Social Drinking: **Permitted**

Sound environmental practices are followed at this cozy bungalow in a well-treed, quiet residential neighborhood where birds and squirrels are regular visitors. Your host's interests are gardening to attract birds, walking Calgary's extensive pathway and park system, hiking and cross-country skiing in Kananaskis Country and Banff (in the Canadian Rockies, one-hour drive west), art exhibitions, and secondhand shopping. The B&B is within ten miles of Calgary Exhibition and Stampede, the Calgary Zoo and Prehistoric Park, and the University of Calgary. Nose Hill Park, shopping, and restaurants are in walking distance.

# BRITISH COLUMBIA

*Note: All prices listed in this section are quoted in Canadian dollars.*

## Canada-West Accommodations ✪
P.O. BOX 86607, NORTH VANCOUVER, BRITISH COLUMBIA,
CANADA V7L 4L2

Tel: **(604) 929-1424; (800) 561-3223;**
  fax: **(604) 929-6692**
Best Time to Call: **Daily to 10 PM**
Coordinator: **Ellison Massey**
Regions Covered: **Greater Vancouver,**
  **Victoria, Kelowna, Whistler**

Rates (Single/Double):
  Average: **$55–$65 / $75–$95**
Credit Cards: **AMEX, MC, VISA**

This registry has over 100 hosts with comfortable bed-and-breakfast accommodations. All serve a full breakfast, and most have a private bath for guest use. When traveling through British Columbia, visitors should note that B&Bs are available within a day's drive of one another. Canada-West features friendly host families eager to share their knowledge of cultural and scenic attractions.

## Deep Cove Bed & Breakfast ✪
2590 SHELLEY ROAD, NORTH VANCOUVER, BRITISH COLUMBIA,
CANADA V7H 1J9

Tel: **(604) 929-3932;** fax: **(604) 929-**
  **9330**
Hosts: **Diane and Wayne Moore**
Location: **8 mi. NE of Vancouver**
No. of Rooms: **2**
No. of Private Baths: **2**
Double/pb: **$85**
Single/pb: **$75**

Open: **All year**
Reduced Rates: **Available**
Breakfast: **Full**
Credit Cards: **MC, VISA**
Pets: **No**
Smoking: **No**
Social Drinking: **Permitted**

Only fifteen minutes from downtown Vancouver, Deep Cove Bed & Breakfast combines the privacy of a large secluded property with easy access to all major points of interest. The separate guest cottage is ideally suited for honeymoons and getaways. Guest rooms in the cottage have private baths, entrances, parking, and TV. Guests are invited to relax in the garden and in the outdoor cedar hot tub. Breakfast is served in the morning room or on the patio. Diane will be happy to direct you to all the special places that make Vancouver so exciting.

## Poole's Bed & Breakfast ✪
**421 WEST ST. JAMES ROAD, NORTH VANCOUVER,
BRITISH COLUMBIA, CANADA V7N 2P6**

Tel: **(604) 987-4594**
Best Time to Call: **9 AM–9 PM**
Hosts: **Doreen and Arthur Poole**
Location: **5 mi. N of Vancouver**
No. of Rooms: **2**
Max. No. Sharing Bath: **4**
Double/sb: **$55**
Single/sb: **$40**

Open: **All year**
Reduced Rates: **Available**
Breakfast: **Full**
Pets: **No**
Children: **Welcome**
Smoking: **No**
Social Drinking: **Permitted**
Station Pickup: **Yes**

On a lovely tree-lined street near the North Shore Mountains sits this quiet, Colonial home. The Pooles' residential neighborhood is close to the bus, restaurants, downtown Vancouver, Stanley Park, Capilano Suspension Bridge, Grouse Mountain Skyride, and Vancouver Island Ferry. Doreen and Arthur are retirees who are happy to assist you with information and directions. They'll serve you an abundant candlelight breakfast in the dining room.

## Haynes Point Lakeside Guest House ✪
**3619 87TH STREET, RR 1, SITE 93, COMP. 2, OSOYOOS,
BRITISH COLUMBIA, CANADA V0H 1V0**

Tel: **(604) 495-7443**
Best Time to Call: **Before 8 AM;
4–5 PM**
Hosts: **June and John Wallace**
Location: **75 mi. S of Kelowna**
No. of Rooms: **3**
No. of Private Baths: **1**
Max. No. Sharing Bath: **4**
Double/pb: **$75**
Single/pb: **$50**

Double/sb: **$60–$65**
Single/sb: **$50**
Open: **All year**
Breakfast: **Full**
Pets: **No**
Children: **No**
Smoking: **No**
Social Drinking: **Permitted**
Station Pickup: **Yes**

Haynes Point Lakeside Guest House is an attractive hillside bed and breakfast home offering comfort and pleasant surroundings. Whether it be a honeymoon, business trip, a golf or skiing holiday, or just a weekend getaway, June and John will show you unforgettable Canadian hospitality. After an exhausting day, stroll through the English garden, relax at picnic tables on a large deck, or rest in the hammock shaded by a sycamore tree. In summer, enjoy the air-conditioning; in winter nestle by the Grandpa Fisher stove to watch TV or a video. There are eight wineries within thirty miles, plus an autumn Wine Festival. It's only a five-minute walk to the Haynes Point Provincial Park and ecological reserve.

# Weston Lake Inn ✪

**813 BEAVER POINT ROAD, SALT SPRING ISLAND,
BRITISH COLUMBIA, CANADA V8K 1X9**

Tel: **(604) 653-4311**
Hosts: **Susan Evans and Ted Harrison**
Location: **30 mi. N of Victoria**
No. of Rooms: **3**
No. of Private Baths: **3**
Double/pb: **$90–$110**
Single/pb: **$80–$100**
Open: **All year**
Reduced Rates: **10% weekly
  Oct.–June; 5% July–Sept.**

Breakfast: **Full**
Credit Cards: **MC, VISA**
Pets: **Sometimes**
Children: **Welcome, over 14**
Smoking: **No**
Social Drinking: **Permitted**
Foreign Languages: **French**

Nestled on a knoll of flowering trees and shrubs overlooking Weston Lake, the Inn offers old-world charm in a comfortable new home. The house is on a 10-acre farm on Salt Spring Island, the largest of British Columbia's Gulf Islands. Each guest room overlooks the countryside and has a down comforter. The rooms all have different finishing touches. Throughout the house there are a number of original Canadian art pieces and intricate petit-point needlework crafted by your host, Ted. Breakfast is a full-course meal served to the sounds of classical music in the antique-filled dining room. Eggs Benedict, quiche, homemade muffins, and jams are specialties of the house. Fresh eggs from the chickens and produce from the organic vegetable garden. Guests can relax in the hot tub, on the garden terrace, or enjoy a book in the lounge beside a wood-burning stove. It's just a few steps to swimming, boating, and fishing. You can also follow forest trails or take to a bicycle and explore this quaint island with its country roads, pastoral beauty, and talented artisans. Ask your hosts about the sailing charters they are now offering.

# The Grahams Cedar House B&B ✪

**1825 LANDSEND ROAD, RR 3, VICTORIA-SIDNEY, BRITISH
COLUMBIA, CANADA V8L 5J2**

Tel: **(604) 655-3699; fax: (604) 655-
  1422**
Hosts: **Kay and Dennis Graham**
Location: **15 mi. N of Victoria**
Suite: **$89–$159**
Open: **All year**
Reduced Rates: **Weekly**

Breakfast: **Full**
Pets: **No**
Children: **No**
Smoking: **No**
Social Drinking: **Permitted**
Airport Pickup: **Yes**

This modern chalet rests in a woodsy setting of tall pines and green ferns, minutes from the Swartz Bay and Anacortes ferries. Parks, marinas, and the beach are all nearby. The spacious, air-conditioned four-room suite has a king-size bed, a romantic Jacuzzi, and a private deck overlooking lush natural strolling gardens.

## Beautiful Bed & Breakfast ✪

428 WEST 40 AVENUE, VANCOUVER, BRITISH COLUMBIA, CANADA V5Y 2R4

Tel: **(604) 327-1102**
Best Time to Call: **Evenings**
Hosts: **Corinne and Ian Sanderson**
Location: **In Vancouver**
No. of Rooms: **4**
No. of Private Baths: **1**
Max. No. Sharing Bath: **4**
Double/sb: **$75–$85**
Single/sb: **$60–$70**

Open: **All year**
Reduced Rates: **10% less weekly**
Breakfast: **Full, Continental**
Pets: **No**
Children: **Welcome, over 14**
Smoking: **No**
Social Drinking: **Permitted**
Foreign Languages: **French**

Relax in elegance in a gorgeous new Colonial home furnished with antiques, views, and fresh flowers. This is a great central location on a quiet residential street, just five minutes from downtown and within walking distance of Queen Elizabeth Park, Van Dusen Gardens, tennis, golf, three cinemas, wonderful restaurants, swimming, and a major shopping center. It's one block from bus to downtown, ferries, airport, and United British Columbia. Enjoy a view of the north shore mountain peaks or Vancouver Island and Mount Baker, comfortable beds, a large attractive backyard—and friendly helpful hosts who will assist you with your travel plans.

## Johnson House Bed & Breakfast ✪

2278 WEST 34TH AVENUE, VANCOUVER, BRITISH COLUMBIA, CANADA V6M 1G6

Tel: **(604) 266-4175**
Best Time to Call: **10:30 AM–9:30 PM**
Hosts: **Sandy and Ron Johnson**
Location: **1½ mi. from Rte. 99, Oak St. Exit**
No. of Rooms: **3**
No. of Private Baths: **1**
Max. No. Sharing Bath: **4**
Double/pb: **$89–$125**
Single/pb: **$80–$120**

Double/sb: **$65–$75**
Single/sb: **$60–$70**
Open: **All year**
Reduced Rates: **Long stays, winter**
Breakfast: **Full**
Pets: **No**
Children: **Welcome, over 8**
Smoking: **No**
Social Drinking: **Permitted**

Sandy and Ron invite you to their charming home on a quiet tree-lined avenue in Vancouver's lovely Kerrisdale district. Outside, a rock garden and sculpture catch the visitor's eye; inside, wooden carousel animals add to the homey decor. After a good night's rest on brass beds, you'll be treated to homemade muffins, breads, and jams. Then it's time to explore downtown Vancouver—a good selection of shops, restaurants, and city bus stops are only a few blocks away.

## Kenya Court Ocean Front Guest House ✪

**2230 CORNWALL AVENUE, VANCOUVER, BRITISH COLUMBIA, CANADA V6K 1B5**

Tel: **(604) 738-7085**
Hosts: **The Williamses**
Location: **20 mi. from the U.S. border**
Suites: **$85 up**
Open: **All year**
Breakfast: **Full**

Pets: **No**
Children: **Welcome, over 8**
Smoking: **No**
Social Drinking: **Permitted**
Foreign Languages: **French, German, Italian**

There is an unobstructed view of the park, ocean, mountains, and downtown Vancouver from this heritage building on the waterfront. Across the street are tennis courts, a large heated outdoor saltwater pool, and walking and jogging paths along the water's edge. Just minutes from downtown, it's an easy walk to Granville Market, the Planetarium, and interesting shops and restaurants. All the rooms are large and tastefully furnished. Breakfast is served in a glass solarium with a spectacular view of English Bay.

## Town & Country Bed & Breakfast Reservation Service ✪

**BOX 74542, 2803 WEST 4TH AVENUE, VANCOUVER, BRITISH COLUMBIA V6K 1K2**

Tel: **(604) 731-5942**
Coordinator: **Helen Burich**
States/Regions Covered: **Vancouver, Vancouver Island, Victoria**

Rates (Single/Double):
  Modest: **$35–$45 / $45–$55**
  Average: **$40–$50 / $55–$65**
  Luxury: **$55–$90 / $65–$160**
Minimum Stay: **2 nights**

Helen has the oldest reservation service in British Columbia. She has dozens of host homes, many of which have been accommodating guests for ten years. Ranging from modest homes to lovely heritage homes, they are a 15–20-minute drive to Stanley Park, beaches, Capilano and Lynn Canyons, Grouse Mountain Skyride, museums, and galleries; neighborhood restaurants and shopping areas are usually within walking distance. There are also a couple of cottages and self-contained suites. There is a $5 surcharge for Victoria and Vancouver Island reservations. In addition to normal business hours, Helen is often available evenings and weekends.

## Dunroamin'
**616 AVALON ROAD, VICTORIA, BRITISH COLUMBIA,
CANADA V8V 1N8**

| | |
|---|---|
| Tel: **(604) 383-4106** | Single/sb: **$50** |
| Hosts: **Theresa and Pat Devlin** | Open: **All year** |
| No. of Rooms: **3** | Reduced Rates: **Available** |
| No. of Private Baths: **1** | Breakfast: **Full** |
| Max. No. Sharing Bath: **4** | Pets: **No** |
| Double/pb: **$75** | Children: **Welcome** |
| Single/pb: **$55** | Smoking: **No** |
| Double/sb: **$70** | Social Drinking: **Permitted** |

Built in 1906, this Edwardian home sits on a quiet street, just three blocks from the Inner Harbour, the famous Empress Hotel and five blocks from downtown Victoria. Theresa and Pat have restored this B&B and furnished it with antiques, period reproductions, cross-stitching and ceramics. Enjoy a full English breakfast in the morning served with gracious hospitality.

## West Bay Bed & Breakfast ✪
**715 SUFFOLK STREET, VICTORIA, BRITISH COLUMBIA,
CANADA V9A 3J5**

| | |
|---|---|
| Tel: **(604) 386-7330** | Reduced Rates: **Available** |
| Hosts: **Yvette and Ralf Craig** | Breakfast: **Full** |
| No. of Rooms: **6** | Credit Cards: **AMEX, MC, VISA** |
| No. of Private Baths: **6** | Pets: **No** |
| Double/pb: **$60–$95** | Children: **Welcome, over 4** |
| Single/pb: **$55–$90** | Social Drinking: **Permitted** |
| Open: **All year** | Foreign Languages: **French, German** |

West Bay Bed & Breakfast is located on the west side of downtown Victoria. The house is a modern California-style home with a high-tech kitchen, 22-foot dining room, living room, sunroom, and large deck all overlooking the Strait of Juan de Fuca and the Olympic Mountains. Guest rooms are decorated in bright whimsical themes, have private entrance, bar fridge, microwave, dishes, and queen-size beds. Breakfast includes fruit salad, homemade granola muesli, yogurt, juice, coffee, tea, and a variety of egg dishes, pancakes, casseroles, and home-baked breads.

## Beachside Bed and Breakfast Registry
**4208 EVERGREEN AVENUE, WEST VANCOUVER,
BRITISH COLUMBIA, CANADA V7V 1H1**

| | |
|---|---|
| Tel: **(604) 922-7773; (800) 563-3311;** fax: **(604) 926-8073** | **Vancouver, Victoria, Whistler Mountain Area** |
| Coordinators: **Gordon and Joan Gibbs** | Rates (Single/Double): |
| Regions Covered: **Chemainus,** **Nanaimo, North Shore, Parksville,** | Average: **$65 / $80–$125** |
| | Luxury: **$80 / $100–$200** |

This newly organized B&B network emphasizes exceptional properties. Experience warm Canadian hospitality in well-maintained, tastefully decorated homes. Hosts offer everything from romantic luxury locations to quiet peaceful retreats. Gordon and Joan are world travelers who have run their own B&B for ten years; Gordon is also a certified tour guide.

## Beachside Bed and Breakfast ✪

**4208 EVERGREEN AVENUE, WEST VANCOUVER,**
**BRITISH COLUMBIA, CANADA V7V 1H1**

Tel: **(604) 922-7773; (800) 563-3311;**
   fax: **(604) 926-8073**
Hosts: **Gordon and Joan Gibbs**
Location: **4 mi. NW of Vancouver**
No. of Rooms: **3**
No. of Private Baths: **3**
Double/pb: **$110–$180**

Open: **All year**
Breakfast: **Full**
Credit Cards: **MC, VISA**
Pets: **No**
Children: **Welcome**
Smoking: **No**
Social Drinking: **Permitted**

Guests are welcomed to this beautiful waterfront home with a fruit basket and fresh flowers. The house is a Spanish-style structure, with stained-glass windows, located at the end of a quiet cul-de-sac. Its southern exposure affords a panoramic view of Vancouver. A sandy beach is just steps from the door. You can watch the waves from the patio or spend the afternoon fishing or sailing. The hearty breakfast features homemade muffins, French toast, and Canadian maple syrup. Gordon and Joan are knowledgeable about local history, and can gladly direct you to Stanley Park, hiking, skiing, and much more.

# Appendix:
# UNITED STATES AND CANADIAN TOURIST OFFICES

Listed here are the addresses and telephone numbers for the tourist offices of every U.S. state and Canadian province. When you write or call one of these offices, be sure to request a map of the state and a calendar of events. If you will be visiting a particular city or region, or if you have any special interests, be sure to specify them as well.

## State Tourist Offices

Alabama Bureau of Tourism and
  Travel
401 Adams Ave.
Montgomery, Alabama 36103
(205) 242-4169 or (800) ALABAMA
  [252-2262]

Alaska Division of Tourism
P.O. Box 110801
Juneau, Alaska 99811-0801
(907) 465-2010

Arizona Office of Tourism
1100 W. Washington Street
Phoenix, Arizona 85007
(602) 542-8687 or (800) 842-8257

Arkansas Department of Park and
  Tourism
1 Capitol Mall
Little Rock, Arkansas 72201
(501) 682-7777 or (800) 643-8383 or
  (800) 828-8974

California Office of Tourism
801 K Street, Suite 1600
Sacramento, California 95814
(800) 862-2543 or (916) 322-2881

Colorado Dept. of Tourism
1625 Broadway
Suite 1700
Denver, Colorado 80202
(303) 592-5510 or (800) 255-5550

Connecticut Department of Economic
  Development—Vacations
865 Brook Street
Rocky Hill, Connecticut 06067-3405
(203) 258-4355 or (800) CT-BOUND
  [262-6863]

Delaware Tourism Office
99 Kings Highway, P.O. Box 1401
Dover, Delaware 19903
(302) 739-4271 or (800) 441-8846

Washington, D.C. Convention and
  Visitors' Association
1212 New York Avenue N.W.
Suite 600
Washington, D.C. 20005
(202) 789-7000

Florida Division of Tourism
126 W. Van Buren Street
Tallahassee, Florida 32399-2000
(904) 487-1462

Georgia Tourist Division
Box 1776
Atlanta, Georgia 30301
(404) 656-3590 or (800) 847-4842

Hawaii Visitors Bureau
2270 Kalakaua Avenue
Suite 801
Honolulu, Hawaii 96815
(808) 923-1811

Idaho Travel Council
700 W. State Street
P.O. Box 83720
Hall of Mirrors, 2nd floor
Boise, Idaho 83720-0093
(800) 635-7820 or (208) 334-2470

Illinois Office of Tourism
310 South Michigan Avenue
Suite 108
Chicago, Illinois 60604
(312) 744-2400 or (312) 814-4732 or
    (800) 822-0292 or (800) 223-0121
    (out of state)

Indiana Tourism Development
    Division
1 North Capitol, Suite 100
Indianapolis, Indiana 46204-2288
(317) 232-8860 or (800) 759-9191

Iowa Tourism Office
200 East Grand Ave.
Des Moines, Iowa 50309
(515) 242-4705 or (800) 345-IOWA
    [4692]

Kansas Travel and Tourism Division
700 SW Harrison Street, Suite 1300
Topeka, Kansas 66603-3712
(913) 296-2009 or (800) 252-6727

Kentucky Department of Travel
    Development
Capitol Plaza Tower, 22nd floor
500 Mero Street
Frankfort, Kentucky 40601-1974
(502) 564-4930 or (800) 225-8747
    (out of state)

Louisiana Office of Tourism
P.O. Box 94291
Baton Rouge, Louisiana 70804-9291
(504) 342-8119 (within Louisiana) or
    (800) 633-6970 (out of state)

Maine Publicity Bureau
P.O. Box 2300
97 Winthrop Street
Hallwell, Maine 04347
(207) 582-9300 or (800) 533-9595

Maryland Office of Tourist
    Development
217 E. Redwood Street
Baltimore, Maryland 21202
(410) 333-6611 or (800) 719-5900

Massachusetts Office of Tourism
100 Cambridge Street—13th Floor
Boston, Massachusetts 02202
(617) 727-3201 or (800) 447-MASS
    [6277] (out of state)

Michigan Travel Bureau
Department of Commerce
P.O. Box 30226
Lansing, Michigan 48909
(517) 373-0670 or (800) 543-2YES [2937]

Minnesota Tourist Information Center
121 7th Place East
#100 Metro Square
St. Paul, Minnesota 55101-2112
(612) 296-5029 or (800) 657-3700
    (out of state)

Mississippi Division of Tourism
P.O. Box 1705
Ocean Springs, Mississippi 39566-1705
(601) 359-3297 or (800) 927-6378

Missouri Division of Tourism
P.O. Box 1055
Jefferson City, Missouri 65102
(314) 751-4133 or (800) 877-1234

Travel Montana
1424 9th Avenue
Helena, Montana 59620
(406) 444-2654 or (800) 548-3390

Nebraska Division of Travel and
    Tourism
P.O. Box 94666
Lincoln, Nebraska 68509
(402) 471-3791 or (800) 228-4307 (out of
    state) or (800) 742-7595 (within
    Nebraska)

Nevada Commission on Tourism
Capitol Complex
Carson City, Nevada 89710
(702) 687-4322 or (800) NEVADA 8
[638-2328]

New Hampshire Office of Travel and
    Tourism Development
P.O. Box 1856
Concord, New Hampshire 03302-1856
(800) FUN-IN-NH [386-4664] or (603)
    271-2666

New Jersey Division of Travel and
    Tourism
C.N. 826
Trenton, New Jersey 08625
(609) 292-2470 or (800) 537-7397

New Mexico Department of Tourism
491 Old Santa Fe Trail
Santa Fe, New Mexico 87503
(505) 827-7400, (800) 545-2040, or (800)
545-2040 (out of state), (505) 827-
7402 (FAX)

New York State Division of Tourism
1 Commerce Plaza
Albany, New York 12245
(518) 474-4116 or (800) 225-5697
(in the Northeast except Maine)

North Carolina Travel and Tourism
Division
430 North Salisbury Street
Raleigh, North Carolina 27611
(919) 733-4171 or (800) VISIT NC
[847-4862]

North Dakota Tourism Promotion
Liberty Memorial Building
604 E. Boulevard
Bismarck, North Dakota 58505
(701) 224-2525 or (800) HELLO ND
[435-5663]

Ohio Division of Travel and Tourism
77 South High Street, 29th Floor
P.O. Box 1001
Columbus, Ohio 43266
(800) 282-5393

Oklahoma Division of Tourism
P.O. Box 60,000
Oklahoma City, Oklahoma 73146
(405) 521-2406 or (800) 522-8565
(within Oklahoma)

Oregon Economic Development
Tourism Division
775 Summer Street N.E.
Salem, Oregon 97310
(503) 378-3451 or (800) 547-7842

Pennsylvania Bureau of Travel
Marketing
Department of Commerce
453 Forum Building
Harrisburg, Pennsylvania 17120
(717) 787-5453 or (800) 847-4872

Puerto Rico Tourism Company
23rd Floor
575 Fifth Avenue
New York, New York 10017
(212) 599-6262 or (800) 223-6530
or (800) 866-STAR [7827]

Rhode Island Department of
Economic Development
Tourism and Promotion Division
7 Jackson Walkway
Providence, Rhode Island 02903
(401) 277-2601 or (800) 556-2484
(East Coast from Maine to Virginia,
also West Virginia and Ohio)

South Carolina Division of Tourism
1205 Pendleton St.
Columbia, South Carolina 29201
(803) 734-0122

South Dakota Division of Tourism
Capitol Lake Plaza
711 East Wells Avenue
Pierre, South Dakota 57501
(605) 773-3301 or (800) 732-5682
(out of state) or (800) 952-2217
(within South Dakota)

Tennessee Tourist Development
P.O. Box 23170
Nashville, Tennessee 37202-3170
(615) 741-2158

Texas Dept. of Commerce
Division of Tourism
P.O. Box 12728
Austin, Texas 78711-2728
(512) 462-9191 or (800) 452-9292

Utah Travel Council
Council Hall
Capitol Hill
Salt Lake City, Utah 84114
(801) 538-1030 or (800) 200-1160

Vermont Department of Travel and
Tourism
134 State Street
Montpelier, Vermont 05602
(802) 828-3236 or (800) VERMONT
[837-6668]

Virginia Division of Tourism
901 E. Byrd St.
Richmond, Virginia 23219
(804) 786-4484 or (800) 932-5827

Washington State Tourism
Development Division
P.O. Box 42500
101 General Administration Building
Olympia, Washington 98504
(206) 586-2088 or (800) 544-1800 (out
of state)

Travel West Virginia
2101 E. Washington Street
Charleston, West Virginia 25305
(800) CALL WVA [225-5982] or (304) 558-2286

Wisconsin Division of Tourism
P.O. Box 7606
Madison, Wisconsin 53707-7606
(608) 266-2161 or (800) 372-2737 (within Wisconsin and neighboring states) or (800) 432-8747 (out of state)

Wyoming Travel Commission
I-25 and College Drive
Cheyenne, Wyoming 82002
(307) 777-7777 or (800) 225-5996 (out of state)

# Canadian Province Tourist Offices

Alberta Tourism, Parks, and Recreation
City Center Building
10155 102 Street
Edmonton, Alberta, Canada T5J 4L6
(403) 427-4321 (from Edmonton area) or 800-661-8888 (from the U.S. and Canada)

Tourism British Columbia
1117 Wharf Street
Victoria, British Columbia, Canada V8W 2Z2
(604) 663-6000 or (800) 663-6000

Travel Manitoba
Department 6020
7th Floor
155 Carlton Street
Winnipeg, Manitoba, Canada R3C 3H8
(204) 945-3777 or (800) 665-0040 (from mainland U.S. and Canada)

New Brunswick Tourism
P.O. Box 12345
Fredericton, New Brunswick, Canada E3B 5C3
(506) 453-8745 or (800) 561-0123 (from mainland U.S. and Canada)

Newfoundland/Labrador Tourism Branch
Department of Tourism & Culture
P.O. Box 8730
St. John's, Newfoundland, Canada A1B 4K2
(709) 729-2830 (from St. John's area) or (800) 563-6353 (from mainland U.S. and Canada)

Northwest Territories Tourism
(403) 873-7200
(800) 661-0788

Tourisme Quebec
C.P. 979
Montreal, Quebec H3C QW3
(800) 363-7777 (from 26 eastern states) or (514) 873-2015 (collect from all other U.S. locations)

Tourism Saskatchewan
1919 Saskatchewan Drive
Regina, Saskatchewan, Canada S4P 3V7
(306) 787-2300 or (800) 667-7191 (from Canada and mainland U.S., except Alaska)

Tourism Yukon
P.O. Box 2703
Whitehorse, Yukon, Canada Y1A 2C6
(403) 667-5340

# BED AND BREAKFAST RESERVATION REQUEST FORM

Dear _____
 Host's Name

I read about your home in *Bed & Breakfast U.S.A., West and Midwest 1996*, and would be interested in making reservations to stay with you.

My name: _____

Address: _____
 street

_____
 city                    state              zip

Telephone: _____
 area code

Business address/telephone: _____

_____

Number of adult guests: _____

Number and ages of children: _____

Desired date and time of arrival: _____

Desired length of stay: _____

Mode of transportation: _____
(car, bus, train, plane)

Additional information/special requests/allergies:

_____

_____

_____

_____

_____

_____

I look forward to hearing from you soon.

                                        Sincerely,

## APPLICATION FOR MEMBERSHIP

(Please type or print)
(Please refer to Preface, pages xxi–xxii, for our membership criteria.)

Name of Bed & Breakfast: _____

Address: _____

City: _____ State: _____ Zip: _____ Phone: ( ) _____

Best Time to Call: _____

Host(s): _____

Located: No. of miles _____ compass direction _____ of Major

City _____ Geographic region _____

No. of miles _____ from major route _____ Exit: _____

No. of guest bedrooms with private bath: _____

No. of guest bedrooms that share a bath: _____

How many people (including *your* family) must use the shared
bath? _____

How many bedrooms, if any, have a sink in them? _____

Room Rates:

$ _____ Double—private bath    $ _____ Double—shared bath
$ _____ Single—private bath    $ _____ Single—shared bath
$ _____ Suites
Separate Guest Cottage      $ _____ Sleeps _____

Are you open year-round? ☐ Yes ☐ No
If "No," specify when you are open: _____

How many rooms are wheelchair-accessible? _____

Do you require a minimum stay? _____

Do you discount rates at any time? ☐ No ☐ Yes

Do you offer a discount to senior citizens? ☐ No ☐ Yes: _____ %

Do you offer a discount for families? ☐ No ☐ Yes: _____ %

Breakfast: Type of breakfast included in rate:
☐ Full ☐ Continental

Describe breakfast specialties: _____
_____

Are any other meals provided? ☐ No   ☐ Yes
Lunch ☐ cost: $ _____   Dinner ☐ cost: $ _____

Do you accept credit cards? ☐ No   ☐ Yes:
☐ AMEX   ☐ DINERS   ☐ DISCOVER   ☐ MASTERCARD   ☐ VISA

Will you GUARANTEE your rates from January through December
1997? ☐ Yes   ☐ No

Note: This Guarantee applies only to those guests making reservations having read about you in *Bed & Breakfast U.S.A., West and
Midwest 1997.*

If you have household pets, specify how many:
☐ Dog(s)   ☐ Cat(s)   ☐ Other

Can you accommodate a guest's pet?
☐ No   ☐ Yes   ☐ Sometimes

Are children welcome? ☐ No   ☐ Yes   If "Yes," specify age
restriction _____

Do you permit smoking somewhere inside your house?
☐ No   ☐ Yes

Do you permit social drinking? ☐ No   ☐ Yes

Guests can be met at ☐ Airport _____   ☐ Train _____   ☐ Bus _____

Can you speak a foreign language fluently? ☐ No   ☐ Yes
Describe: _____

**GENERAL AREA OF YOUR B&B** (e.g., Boston historic district; 20 minutes from Chicago Loop):

**GENERAL DESCRIPTION OF YOUR B&B** (e.g., brick Colonial with white shutters; Victorian mansion with stained-glass windows):

**AMBIENCE OF YOUR B&B** (e.g., furnished with rare antiques; lots of wood and glass):

**THE QUALITIES THAT MAKE YOUR B&B SPECIAL ARE:**

**THINGS OF HISTORIC, SCENIC, CULTURAL, OR GENERAL INTEREST NEARBY** (e.g., one mile from the San Diego Zoo; walking distance to the Lincoln Memorial):

**YOUR OCCUPATION and SPECIAL INTERESTS** (e.g., a retired teacher of Latin interested in woodworking; full-time host interested in quilting):

If you do welcome children, are there any special provisions for them (e.g., crib, playpen, high-chair, play area, baby-sitter)?

Do you offer snacks (e.g., complimentary wine and cheese; pretzels and chips but BYOB)?

Can guests use your kitchen for light snacks? ☐ No   ☐ Yes

Do you offer the following amenities? ☐ Guest refrigerator
☐ Air-conditioning   ☐ TV   ☐ Piano   ☐ Washing machine
☐ Dryer   ☐ Hot tub   ☐ Pool   ☐ Tennis court
Other _____

What major college or university is within 10 miles?

_____

Please supply the name, address, and phone number of three personal references from people not related to you (please use a separate sheet).

Please enclose a copy of your brochure along with color photos including exterior, guest bedrooms, baths, and breakfast area. Bedroom photos should include view of the headboard(s), bedside lamps and night tables. Please show us a typical breakfast setting. Use a label to identify the name of your B&B *on each*. If you have a black-and-white line drawing, send it along. If you have an original breakfast recipe that you'd like to share, send it along, too. (Of course, credit will be given to your B&B.) **Nobody can describe your B&B better than you. Limit your description to 100 words and submit it typed, double-spaced, on a separate sheet of paper. We will of course reserve the right to edit.** As a member of the Tourist House Association of America, your B&B will be described in the next edition of our book, *Bed & Breakfast U.S.A.*, *West and Midwest*, published by Plume, an imprint of Dutton Signet, a division of Penguin USA, and distributed to bookstores and libraries throughout the U.S. The book is also used as a reference for B&Bs in our country by major offices of tourism throughout the world.

*Note:* The following will NOT be considered for inclusion in *Bed & Breakfast U.S.A.*, *West and Midwest:* B&Bs having more than 15 guest rooms. Rental properties or properties where the host doesn't reside on the premises. Rates over $85 for double occupancy. (This does not include reservation services, suites, cottages, apartments; or qualified B&Bs.) Rates exceeding $35 where 6 people share a bath. Rates exceeding $40 where 5 people share a bath, or rooms are without night tables or adequate bedside reading lamps. Applications that are incomplete, no photos, write-up etc. Applications received in states that are over-crowded; this is due to space limitations.

*Note:* If the publisher or authors receive negative reports from your guests regarding a deficiency in our standards of CLEANLINESS, COMFORT, and CORDIALITY, and/or failure to honor the rate guarantee, we reserve the right to cancel your membership.

This membership application has been prepared by:

_____
(Signature)

Please enclose your $45 membership dues.      Date: _____

Yes! ☐ I'm interested in Group Liability Insurance.
No ☐ I am insured by _____ .

Return to:
Tourist House Association of America
RD 1, Box 12A
Greentown, Pennsylvania 18426

To assure that your listing will be considered for the 1997 edition of *Bed & Breakfast U.S.A.*, *West and Midwest*, we MUST receive your completed application by March 31, 1996. Thereafter, listings will be considered only for the semiannual supplement. (See page 323.)

## APPLICATION FOR MEMBERSHIP FOR A
## BED & BREAKFAST RESERVATION SERVICE

NAME OF BED & BREAKFAST SERVICE: _____

ADDRESS: _____

CITY: _____ STATE: _____ ZIP: _____ PHONE:(    ) _____

COORDINATOR: _____

BEST TIME TO CALL: _____

Do you have a telephone answering ☐ machine?  ☐ service?

Names of state(s), cities, and towns where you have hosts (in alphabetical order, please, and limit to 10):


Number of hosts on your roster: _____

## THINGS OF HISTORIC, SCENIC, CULTURAL, OR GENERAL
## INTEREST IN THE AREA(S) YOU SERVE:



Range of Rates:
   Modest:     Single $ _____   Double $ _____
   Average:    Single $ _____   Double $ _____
   Luxury:     Single $ _____   Double $ _____

Will you GUARANTEE your rates through December 1997?
☐ Yes  ☐ No

How often do you reinspect listings? _____
Do you require a minimum stay? _____
Surcharges for one-night stay? _____
Do you accept credit cards? ☐ No   ☐ Yes:
☐ AMEX ☐ DINERS ☐ DISCOVER ☐ MASTERCARD
☐ VISA ,

Is the guest required to pay a fee to use your service?
☐ No   ☐ Yes—The fee is $ _____

Do you publish a directory of your B&B listings?
☐ No   ☐ Yes—The fee is $ _____

Are any of your B&Bs within 10 miles of a university? Which? ___

---

Briefly describe a sample host home in each of the previous categories: e.g., a cozy farmhouse where the host weaves rugs; a restored 1800 Victorian where the host is a retired general; a contemporary mansion with a sauna and swimming pool.

Please supply the name, address, and phone number of three personal references from people not related to you (please use a separate sheet of paper). Please enclose a copy of your brochure.

This membership application has been prepared by:

---

(Signature)

Please enclose your $45 membership dues.     Date: _____

If you have a special breakfast recipe that you'd like to share, send it along. (Of course, credit will be given to your B&B agency.) As a member of the Tourist House Association of America, your B&B agency will be described in the next edition of our book, *Bed & Breakfast U.S.A.*, *West and Midwest*, published by Plume, an imprint of Dutton Signet, a division of Penguin USA. Return to: Tourist House Association, RD 1, Box 12A, Greentown, PA 18426.

To ensure that your listing will be considered for the 1997 edition, we must receive your completed application by March 31, 1996. Thereafter, listings will be considered only for the semiannual supplement. (See next page.)

## INFORMATION ORDER FORM

We are constantly expanding our roster to include new members in the Tourist House Association of America. Their facilities will be fully described in the next edition of *Bed & Breakfast U.S.A., West and Midwest*. In the meantime, we will be happy to send you a list including the name, address, telephone number, etc.

For those of you who would like to order additional copies of the book, and perhaps send one to a friend as a gift, we will be happy to fill mail orders. If it is a gift, let us know and we'll enclose a special gift card from you.

---

## ORDER FORM

To:
Tourist House
Association—
Book Dept.
RD 1, Box 12A
Greentown, PA
18426

From: _____
(Print your name)
Address: _____

City _____ State _____ Zip _____

Date: _____

Please send:

☐ List of new B&Bs ($3.00), available July to December.

☐ ____ copies of *Bed & Breakfast U.S.A., West and Midwest* @ $15.00 each (includes 4th class mail)

Send to: _____

Address: _____

City _____ State _____ Zip _____

☐ Enclose a gift card from:

Please make check or money order payable to Tourist House Association.

## WE WANT TO HEAR FROM YOU!

The Tourist House Association of America is looking for Bed and Breakfasts completely set up to accommodate disabled guests.

A special section of wheelchair accessible B&B listings has been incorporated in *Bed & Breakfast U.S.A., West and Midwest*.

Requirements are comfort, cordiality, and cleanliness at a fair price. Ramps for wheelchairs, reach bars for bathtubs and toilets, doorways wide enough and breakfast table high enough so a wheelchair can fit comfortably. Also activities that are accessible to disabled participants.

If you or someone you know meets these requirements, please fill out the enclosed form. If you need more information as to whether you qualify, contact Tourist House Association of America at (717) 676-3222.

Name of B&B: _____

Address: _____
      Street

_____
      City                          State         Zip

Please contact the following B&Bs; I think that they would be great additions to the next edition of *Bed & Breakfast U.S.A., West and Midwest*.

Name of B&B: _____

Address: _____
      Street

_____
      City                          State         Zip

Comments:

As a member of the Tourist House Association, there is no charge for this listing.

Just tear out this page and mail it to us. It won't ruin your book!

Return to:
Tourist House Association of America
RD 1, Box 12A
Greentown, Pennsylvania 18426